Scholars, Policymakers,
and International Affairs

SCHOLARS, POLICYMAKERS, AND INTERNATIONAL AFFAIRS
Finding Common Cause

Edited by Abraham F. Lowenthal and Mariano E. Bertucci

Johns Hopkins University Press

Baltimore

© 2014 Johns Hopkins University Press
All rights reserved. Published 2014
Printed in the United States of America on acid-free paper

2 4 6 8 9 7 5 3 1

Johns Hopkins University Press
2715 North Charles Street
Baltimore, Maryland 21218-4363
www.press.jhu.edu

Library of Congress Cataloging-in-Publication Data

Scholars, policymakers, and international affairs : finding common cause /
edited by Abraham F. Lowenthal and Mariano E. Bertucci.
pages cm
Includes bibliographical references and index.
ISBN 978-1-4214-1507-9 (hardcover : alk. paper) — ISBN 978-1-4214-1508-6 (pbk. : alk. paper) —
ISBN 978-1-4214-1509-3 (electronic) — ISBN 1-4214-1507-0 (hardcover : alk. paper) —
ISBN 1-4214-1508-9 (pbk. : alk. paper) — ISBN 1-4214-1509-7 (electronic) 1. International relations—
Study and teaching. 2. International relations—Research. 3. International relations—Decision
making. 4. Communication in learning and scholarship. I. Lowenthal, Abraham F., author, editor of
compilation. II. Bertucci, Mariano E., 1975– , author, editor of compilation.
JZ1237.S36 2014
327—dc23   2014002822

A catalog record for this book is available from the British Library.

Special discounts are available for bulk purchases of this book. For more information,
please contact Special Sales at 410-516-6936 or specialsales@press.jhu.edu.

Johns Hopkins University Press uses environmentally friendly book
materials, including recycled text paper that is composed of at least 30 percent
post-consumer waste, whenever possible.

For Albert O. Hirschman, Robert A. Pastor, Carlos Rico Ferrat,
and Amaury de Souza,
four model scholar-policymakers who skillfully brought
together the worlds of thought and action with what Hirschman termed
"a bias for hope"

CONTENTS

We greatly appreciate those who prepared chapters for this volume as well as all the other participants in the workshops at the University of Southern California (USC) and Brown University, including former president Ricardo Lagos of Chile and José Miguel Insulza, secretary general of the Organization of American States. Those attending the workshops but not represented in this book are listed below; those with asterisks next to their names contributed memoranda or papers, included in the bibliography.

Cynthia Arnson,* Katrina Burgess, Maxwell Cameron,* the late Amaury de Souza,* Tom Farer,* Richard Feinberg,* Kevin Gallagher, Jorge Heine,* Emma Kiselyova, Stephen Krasner,* James McGuire, Gerardo Munck, Heraldo Muñoz,* Manuel Orozco,* Manuel Pastor, Roberto Russell,* Michael Shifter,* Kathryn Sikkink,* Barbara Stallings, Pamela Starr, Roberto Suro,* Ann Tickner, Arlene Tickner,* Juan Gabriel Valdés, Arturo Valenzuela, Joaquín Villalobos,* and Carol Wise.

We are particularly grateful to the various sponsors that made this project possible: the Center for International Studies, the School of International Relations, the Office of the Provost, and the Jesse Unruh Institute at USC; the International Development Research Centre of Canada; the United Nations Development Program; the Vidanta Foundation of Mexico; and the Watson Institute for International Studies, Brown University. We are in debt, as well, to the former director of USC's School of International Relations, John Odell; to the director of the USC Center for International Studies, Patrick James; to Richard Snyder, our host at Brown; and to the staff members of USC and Brown. We express our appreciation, as well, to Vestal McIntyre, who edited most of the chapters; to Linda Strange for her meticulous copy editing; to Michael Taber, who produced the index; and especially to Suzanne Flinchbaugh and her colleagues at Johns Hopkins University Press.

Mariano Bertucci would like to express his deep gratitude to those who support him tirelessly: his parents, Alfredo and María Elena, his amazing wife, Jennifer, his son, Tomás, and his new baby girl who, as these acknowledgments are written, is set to arrive any moment. Mariano would also like to especially thank Abe Lowenthal for conceiving, co-organizing, raising the funds for, and convening an outstanding group of international scholars and policymakers to discuss these issues and for working closely with him in preparing this volume. For Mariano as well as for others (some of them contributors to this volume), Abe has been a mentor and an example of how to effectively build bridges between the worlds of ideas and action, not only through research but through the establishment of institutions that, working at the intersection of theory and practice, will transcend many lifetimes.

Abe Lowenthal expresses his great appreciation to Mariano Bertucci, who co-organized the workshop, contributed his own chapter, and helped prepare the entire volume and its final chapter, all while writing his dissertation and devoting himself to his family.

Abe also takes this opportunity to thank all those who have made possible his professional career: parents, teachers, mentors, colleagues, and students. He also thanks those who have helped build, manage, and support the several institutions where he has found congenial space to pursue both academic and policy interests: Harvard University, Princeton University, USC, Brown University, the Brookings Institution, the Council on Foreign Relations, the Woodrow Wilson International Center for Scholars, the Inter-American Dialogue, the Pacific Council on International Policy, and the Public Policy Institute of California. He expresses special appreciation to the Ford Foundation, which gave him his first experiences in Latin America and with US policy issues there by sending him to the Dominican Republic and Peru, and thereafter backed many of his projects and institutional initiatives. The Ford Foundation's role in encouraging policy-relevant academic research in Latin America, the United States, and elsewhere deserves wider recognition.

Finally, Abe offers his most special thanks to Jane Jaquette, his wife, who has contributed so much to this project and to every aspect of his life.

Scholars, Policymakers,
and International Affairs

Building Bridges between the Worlds of Thought and Action

ABRAHAM F. LOWENTHAL

This book addresses an important but too often neglected issue: how to enhance exchange between scholars and policymakers so as to improve policies and strengthen social science research and teaching. It draws on contributions by outstanding social scientists who are keenly interested in making public and international policies more effective and by senior policymakers who want to use academic research for that same purpose. The contributors have diverse national and disciplinary backgrounds and rich experience with policy issues in the Americas, Europe, and Asia.

The literature on scholar-practitioner interaction in the field of international relations discusses a gap, even a chasm, between those who study and those who act.[1] Many policymakers think of scholars as absorbed in abstract and self-referential debates and as primarily interested in crafting theories (and impressing other scholars) rather than in illuminating, much less recommending solutions to, the pressing issues that policymakers must address. Many scholars, in turn, disdain the simplifications and lack of analytical rigor they often attribute to policymakers, whom they typically perceive as interested in processes and outcomes but not in understanding causality. Both analysts and practitioners have commented that this gap has widened as scholars become more devoted to formal modeling and quantitative techniques, while policymakers have ever less time to make decisions with limited information in a rapidly changing world.

The contributors to this book do not deny that there are serious obstacles to fruitful interaction between scholars and policymakers; many chapters knowledgeably discuss these obstacles. But we all believe that mutually beneficial exchange, mindful of differences, is a worthwhile goal that has sometimes been achieved, and many report here on their personal experience in doing so. We have worked together to become more self-conscious and explicit about what works in practice and what does not, and why and how.

The volume discusses cases of fruitful scholar-policymaker interaction on such issues as alleviating poverty, targeting financial sanctions, promoting democratic governance, improving gender equity, and managing the US-Mexico border; it also examines cases, such as counternarcotics policy and citizen security, where academic analysis has thus far mostly failed to affect policy. We explore how scholars can contribute more effectively to the articulation, development, implementation, legitimation, evaluation, and course correction of international policies. The book also considers whether and how scholarship and teaching can be enhanced by more systematic exposure to the policymaking sphere. It suggests concrete ways to better connect the worlds of thought and action, scholarship and policy, in order both to have a positive impact on confronting problems and to enrich academic analysis and instruction.

Some Personal Background

This volume derives in part from my own professional experience as an academic political scientist committed to trying to help understand and improve policy. My first academic publication was on foreign aid as a political instrument, and my doctoral dissertation and first book focused on the US military intervention in the Dominican Republic in 1965.[2] My book made two main points: first, that what a government at the highest levels most fears ("a second Cuba," in that instance) structures the information the bureaucracy collects and analyzes and thereby skews perceptions, often leading to faulty decisions; and second, that foreign policy is often made not through broad and deliberate strategic choices but rather one decision at a time, by very busy officials who do not usually question the premises under which everyone is operating.

The dissertation led me to analyze the historical pattern of US relations with the countries of the entire Caribbean Basin region. For decades, the United States had largely ignored these countries, except when Washington officials perceived that an extra-hemispheric power could challenge US regional dominance. The United States was then prepared to intervene militarily and sometimes also to become actively involved, at least for a while, in economic and social development programs. But these positive programs invariably faded as soon as the perceived threat receded. Each military intervention left a legacy of resentment that, more often than not, led to another crisis down the road.[3]

I gained access in 1968 to a classified report by an internal State Department task force that had been asked by Secretary of State Dean Rusk to define the preferred state of US-Caribbean relations 25 years into the future and to suggest US initiatives to achieve these desired conditions over that period. Task force members concluded that 25 years was too far off to say anything meaningful. Cuba and Puerto Rico, moreover, each presented difficult political issues that the task force thought could not be addressed in the time available. The resulting report was predictably unimaginative.

This experience led me to wonder whether strategic planning could be effectively done within the government and whether scholars might achieve more impact on policy from outside government than from within. I was subsequently invited to serve in the Ford, Carter, and Clinton administrations, but in each case declined. One reason was skepticism about the difference my entering government would make; in retrospect, I wish I had tried, in part because I would have learned.

Eventually, in 1974, I gave a lecture suggesting that the United States has a long-term national interest in conditions in the nearby countries and territories of the Caribbean Basin but that this interest does not derive, as traditionally conceived, solely from the possibility that extra-hemispheric powers might take advantage of regional circumstances to challenge the United States. Rather, the combined facts of high birth rates, low economic growth, gross inequities, and proximity were likely to cause a major long-term flow of migration into this country. It is in the US national self-interest, I argued, to invest in the socioeconomic and political development of these countries: to have a more stable, peaceful, and congenial neighborhood; to nurture better conditions for US investors, firms, and tourists; and, above all, to encourage growth and thereby decrease the pressures for mass immigration.

As soon as my lecture was finished, an assistant to Secretary of State Henry Kissinger told me that he agreed absolutely with my argument but that I should reframe it as a means of countering communist influence in the hemisphere. Only on that basis, he emphasized, would Congress ever appropriate the needed resources. This well-intentioned advice made me more aware that policy-oriented analysis can be undercut by what it takes to get ideas heard within a system operating under fixed or outmoded concepts.

Throughout my academic career, I have framed research projects with policy choices firmly in mind. My work has focused on such questions as these: How do multiple US government agencies and interest groups interact to produce policy outcomes on different kinds of issues, and how could this process be reformed to achieve more coherent and effective policies? What are the internal fault lines within authoritarian regimes, what points of leverage exist to expand these, and how can improved understanding of these processes be employed to facilitate transitions toward democratic governance? Under what conditions, if any, can the US government and other external government and nongovernmental actors foster and reinforce democratic governance abroad? How can Californians identify and promote their international interests in the era of globalization, within the constraints of a federal system that reserves foreign policy to the central government?[4] Much of my work has concentrated on identifying prevailing assumptions underlying policy and suggesting how reframing issues might produce better policy results. And much of my writing has aimed beyond academic specialists to the policy community and the broader public. I have published several university press books and essays in *World Politics, International Security, Latin American Research Review*, and other academic journals, but have also contributed frequently to *Foreign Affairs, Foreign Policy*, the *Journal of Democracy*, the *Washington Quarterly*, and other policy reviews, and to *Harper's*, the *Atlantic*, the *New York Times*, the *Washington Post*, and many other newspapers.

My interest in drawing on research and analysis to improve the quality of policy-making also shaped my approach to institution building: at the Latin American Program of the Woodrow Wilson International Center for Scholars, the Inter-American Dialogue, and the Pacific Council on International Policy in Los Angeles. In each effort, I worked with others to frame core policy-relevant questions and to promote exchanges of ideas about these among thought and action leaders from different national and political perspectives. We sought to improve communication and mutual comprehension between scholars and practitioners, between opinion shapers and decision makers, and between North Americans and Latin Americans. And we built bridges among the academic, business, nongovernmental, and government sectors: to connect scholars who have policy interests, business executives who have civic concerns, people from nongovernmental organizations (NGOs) who have conceptual and institution-building qualities with public officials who are open to engaging with all these. Such transectoral connections significantly increase the likelihood that studies and ideas can have a practical impact.

Given these experiences, I have often been approached by students and junior colleagues who ask my advice on whether and how it is possible to help shape foreign policy and international affairs from an academic post. They are usually of academic bent and vocation, but they also want to affect the world beyond the classroom and the learned journals. They sense that this is difficult in an academic career, where the incentives are biased toward theory, abstraction, and the discipline.

Reflecting on how to encourage those who want to combine scholarly and policy interests led me to convene an international workshop, held at the University of Southern California (USC) during my last week of teaching in the School of International Relations, to consider how to enhance the frequency, quality, and impact of scholar-practitioner interchange.

Forty-one colleagues from 11 countries in the Americas and Europe participated;

27 prepared brief written statements to generate discussion. We were pleased that Assistant Secretary of State Arturo Valenzuela and US Ambassador to Brazil Thomas Shannon could join us in the midst of their active service, and that Heraldo Muñoz, undersecretary general of the United Nations and director of the Latin American and Caribbean Division of the UN Development Program, could deliver a keynote address. We were gratified, as well, that former president Fernando Henrique Cardoso of Brazil—a preeminent scholar-statesman—sent remarks by video, commenting on our long-standing shared commitment to promoting exchange between scholars and policymakers and emphasizing how much we both owe to Professor Albert O. Hirschman, our good friend and mentor. Our deliberations gave rise to this book. To produce a manageable volume, it was necessary to select a fraction of the workshop memoranda for further development.

A Preview

Apart from this introduction, our volume includes 15 chapters, organized in 6 parts. Part I broadly discusses opportunities and challenges that face those who want to bring academic research, techniques, and findings into the policy process. Each of the authors, Chappell Lawson of the Massachusetts Institute of Technology and the late Robert A. Pastor of American University, draws on unique experiences in the US government and in nongovernmental entities focused on policy issues. Lawson served on the staff of the National Security Council during the Clinton administration, directed a study group of the Pacific Council on International Policy on "Managing the US-Mexico Border" in 2007–8, and then worked with the study group's first chairman, Alan Bersin, to improve border policy and practice from their positions in the US Customs and Border Protection Agency in the Obama administration. Lawson proposes three goals: to get more qualified and appropriate scholars into government without compromising their distinctive qualities and standards; to enhance the quality of academic and policy-focused research; and to improve the flow of useful information and concepts from scholars to policymakers. He suggests concrete steps to achieve these goals that could be taken by individual scholars, universities, funders, think tanks and other quasi-academic entities, and international policy journals, as well as by government agencies themselves.

Pastor began his Washington career as executive director of the nongovernmental Linowitz Commission on US–Latin America relations, brought that commission's recommendations to his post as Latin American director in the Carter administration's National Security Council, and later worked closely with former president Carter at the Carter Center. He discusses how academic ideas can influence policy, how the policy process reshapes those ideas, and how NGOs can help bring the worlds of government and universities into fruitful synergy. Career government officials mainly focus on solving problems one at a time, while scholars (and other political appointees) generally start with big ideas. The outcome of their interaction is largely determined by how committed the president and cabinet officers are to changing a policy and whether the political environment will permit these changes. Pastor uses the Carter Center's pioneering work on election mediation in Nicaragua to illustrate how an academically generated innovation can make an important policy difference. He also briefly discusses the "North American idea" that he and others developed in the academic world, a visionary concept with enormous potential to transform policy. Specific projects and programs that embody this concept are already supported by majorities of public opinion in the United States, Mexico, and Canada, but the overarching framework is, thus far, resisted by political leaders in all three countries. "Ideas can matter, but much else is needed," for them do so.

Part II discusses the role of scholars in setting agendas and framing issues, highlighting some conditions when this role can be successful and others when it is much less so. Jane S. Jaquette, a policy analyst in the US Agency for International Development (USAID) in 1979–80, examines how scholars helped shape US foreign policy by providing ways for USAID to respond to a congressional mandate to include "women in development" in US foreign assistance programs. She emphasizes the importance of Arvonne Fraser, a politically adept and well-connected policy entrepreneur, in attracting scholars and inserting their ideas into the policy process, and she notes the convergence of other factors to create a window of opportunity for introducing new concepts, data, and policy proposals developed in the academic world. Although considerable progress was made in designing and implementing projects to extend credit, education, and training to women, the political transformation wrought by the Reagan administration redefined "women in development" in ways consistent with its free-market agenda, with negative consequences for women and children—and thus turning many feminist scholars into harsh critics of USAID rather than partners of policymakers. Jaquette concludes that opportunities for effective scholar-policy cooperation are "ultimately a matter of political will."

Peter Andreas of Brown University addresses a topic on which scholars have been notoriously unable to affect policy: the international narcotics trade. Neither economists (who are active on many other public policy issues) nor political scientists are influential on this highly politicized question. Those few scholars who do tackle this issue aim their writing at a broad public audience rather than either to advance a disciplinary theoretical debate or to affect policymaking directly. Most academic work on the "drug war" focuses on explaining its failures and rejects the moralizing discourse that has framed the policy debate thus far. Drawing on his own varied experiences and on that of two influential think tank advocates of drug policy reforms, Andreas emphasizes that the academic world typically leads young scholars with policy interests to think they must choose sides rather than straddle the academic-policy divide. But Andreas emphasizes that scholars could potentially help reshape public policy by facilitating closed-door dialogue with policymakers on hard questions, offering detailed cost-benefit analyses of different approaches to reducing the use and trade of narcotics, studying the impact on civil-military relations of militarizing antinarcotics efforts, and comparing the effects of diverse approaches to the narcotics trade and other illicit commerce in different regions and eras. Even in this difficult terrain, there are ways to foster academic-policy interaction.

In part III, three leading Latin American scholar-practitioners call upon their high-level experience in academia, national governments, international organizations, and prominent think tanks to illustrate both that social scientists can influence public policy and why this is sometimes very difficult and to propose steps that might help overcome the gap between academic research and public policy.

Blanca Heredia draws on her stints as deputy undersecretary in the Mexican Ministry of the Interior and as provost of CIDE (Centro de Investigación y Docencia Económicas), a leading Mexican university. She observes that the scholar-policymaker gap in her country results not mainly from the reciprocal institutional insularities that characterize the United States but rather from the relative dearth of policy-relevant knowledge in Mexico's social science community. Mexican social science tends to be abstract, theoretical, and unempirical. There are few good descriptions of major institutions and actors or of policymaking processes on issues as central as justice, security, and education. Young and well-trained social scientists could produce policy-relevant research but will need clear professional incentives to do so. Heredia also identifies improved ways of disseminating research, not only to policymaking elites but also to broader segments of the public, who could push for needed policy reforms and thus help overcome strong political resistance to the introduction of new issues and policy options. In this connection, Heredia discusses the exceptional documentary *Presunto Culpable*, which vividly underlines the deficiencies of Mexico's justice system, and the effort by the Organization for Economic Cooperation and Development center in Mexico to raise public awareness of the country's severe educational deficits, as documented by the Program for International Student Assessment (PISA), which compares student achievement internationally.

Nora Lustig writes from her vantage point as senior advisor and chief of the

Poverty and Inequality Unit at the Inter-American Development Bank. She shows that the transformation of well-trained scholars interested in policy into influential practitioners in important policymaking positions played a fundamental role in designing, shaping, and protecting Mexico's Progresa/Oportunidades program. That program's emphasis on conditional cash transfers has been extremely successful in alleviating poverty in Mexico and broadly influential in shaping social policy throughout Latin America and beyond. Such scholar-practitioners as Santiago Levy promoted a new conceptual approach to poverty reduction, assured the technical quality and effectiveness of the program's design, incorporated rigorous evaluations of impact, engaged scholarly interest, both in Mexico and abroad, and persuaded politicians to implement the programs and keep them in place from administration to administration.

Kevin Casas-Zamora makes use of his experience as vice president of Costa Rica and at senior levels of the UN Development Program and the Organization of American States to analyze why scholarly research has thus far contributed so little to addressing the most pressing public policy problem in Central America: the horrific violence that plagues these societies, undermining citizen security and hollowing out the rule of law. A relative lack of interest from the academic community and the absence of reliable data combine with the intense pressure on policymakers to manage public anxiety and gain political advantage to produce a debate that is "guided by whims, pseudo-facts, and political posturing." This syndrome is reinforced by the lack of academic capacity in the region to propose evidence-based policy alternatives, given the absence of systematic data collection and evaluation of existing programs and the very few civilian experts on security in academia, civil society organizations, governments, and legislatures. Moreover, most of the region's criminological research, focused on the social determinants of criminal behavior, projects the fundamental transformation of the social order as the only solution to criminal violence—not an option policymakers can readily adopt. Despite this grim appraisal, Casas-Zamora suggests that precisely the pervasive concern about criminal violence may open the way for scholars to contribute: by asking better questions, generating more reliable data, developing relevant indicators, bringing comparative analysis to bear, and deliberately focusing some attention on policy prescriptions for the short run, even while retaining a long-term approach.

Part IV takes up diverse ways that scholars can help shape, legitimize, implement, evaluate, and revise policy. Thomas J. Biersteker reflects on his experience and that of Brown University's Watson Institute for International Studies, which he directed for 12 years, in analyzing, shaping, promoting, implementing, and evaluating measures to target financial sanctions as an international instrument aimed to influence the behavior of states that violate international norms. He highlights the importance of specialized "transnational policy networks," groups of individuals who share a common expertise and technical language as well as broadly shared normative concerns, but not necessarily agreement on specific policy alternatives. Biersteker details how scholars and policymakers brought together by the Watson Institute analyzed the comparative efficacy of different kinds of sanctions for diverse situations, designed improved mechanisms and procedures, helped gain international consensus for their adoption, and trained personnel for governments and international organizations. He discusses comparative advantages scholars have for some of the necessary tasks and shows how scholars and policymakers can gain from systematic and structured interaction with each other in specially designed formats and venues. Aware of the risks for scholarly detachment and intellectual integrity arising from an active engagement in policy, Biersteker emphasizes the usually underappreciated benefits of such engagement for scholarship, as well as various means of managing and reducing the inevitable risks.

Mitchell A. Seligson, a scholar on democratization, especially in Latin America, and principal investigator in a major long-term USAID project on democratic governance, argues that the links between scholars and policymakers have been far more dynamic and productive in US government programs to promote democracy than is usually the case. He attributes this positive synergy largely to the entry into government bureaucracy (mainly in USAID) of scholars whose academic backgrounds inclined them toward evidence-based approaches for evaluating the impact of democracy promotion projects. These bridge figures then helped establish long-term collaboration between USAID and university-based scholars to measure the level and quality of democratic governance and to foster systematic program evaluation, involving the collection of baseline data, survey research, randomized controlled experiments, and externally conducted reviews of ongoing programs. Much work remains to be done before scholars might be able to advise what kinds of projects are most likely to achieve desired results in specific settings, but they are already contributing new concepts, measures, and awareness to democracy promotion practitioners—an improvement over approaches prevalent not long ago.

Mariano E. Bertucci draws on his interviews with top Argentine officials, conducted in connection with his dissertation research, to chronicle the important roles of scholars and their work, both outside and inside government, in helping Argentina dramatically reorient its foreign policy in the 1990s. Argentina switched then from systematic confrontation with the United States in pursuit of foreign policy "autonomy" to reliable alignment with the United States as a means of advancing the country's primary objective: economic development. Again, political will was very important; the determination by President Carlos Menem to construct a positive relationship with the United States was crucial. But the ability of Argentina's foreign ministry to gain acceptance of and to implement this major reorientation owes a great deal to scholars and their relationships with policymakers. Key Argentine officials sought out academic ideas and arguments: by reading, bringing scholars into both advisory and operational roles within the foreign ministry, and sponsoring and participating in scholar-policymaker dialogues on relevant issues.

Part V features two outstanding foreign policy practitioners. Thomas A. Shannon Jr., a career ambassador and perhaps the most widely respected US diplomat in Latin America in the past generation, highlights how global transformations create the need for a new kind of "long diplomacy." This new diplomacy must focus on building a thematic global agenda on today's and tomorrow's issues; recognizing that civil societies are now often principal drivers of international relations; understanding that economic and social rights have joined political rights as key goals everywhere; concentrating on the empowerment of individuals to realize their destinies, free of exclusion or discrimination; and incorporating the insights of area studies and an appreciation of regional relationships. Shannon challenges scholars and practitioners alike to fashion new partnerships, drawing on such existing modes as diplomat-in-residence and scholar-in-residence programs, think tanks, universities, and policy dialogues, but also working together to establish new mechanisms that take advantage of innovative communications technologies and novel opportunities to explore how new forces, actors, and instruments can be harnessed to address the twenty-first century's unprecedented agenda.

Rafael Fernández de Castro, chair of the international relations department at the Instituto Tecnológico Autónomo de México (ITAM), took leave from his post for nearly three years (2009–11) to serve as chief foreign policy advisor to President Felipe Calderón. Discussing three case examples, he underlines that special circumstances—such as an upcoming presidential visit abroad or the nearly simultaneous advent of new administrations in countries with major stakes in their bilateral relationship—provide unique windows for scholarly input. Policymakers recognize in such circumstances what they can gain from nonhierarchical discussion with qualified academic experts. A well-placed "broker," already in government, makes it more likely that academic ideas will reach policymakers. The likelihood that these ideas will be accepted increases, in turn, if the scholars provide clear and detailed reasoning about the costs and benefits of their proposals in terms that policymakers can easily absorb. Reflecting on his return to the university, Fernández de Castro adds that experience in government helps scholars incorporate into their work an improved understanding of political and bureaucratic processes and greater appreciation of their importance.

Part VI offers three final overviews, informed not only by the workshop but also by the authors' broad familiarity with scholar-policymaker interactions in Asia and Europe and throughout the Americas, North and South. Paul Evans, a leading Canadian academic authority on Asia, suggests that scholars and policymakers are not so separate from each other in Asia or Latin America as they usually are in the United States, whereas Canadian scholars of international relations have become quite isolated from policymaking, particularly at the political level. He points out that political direction at the top is crucial and that scholars have been more linked to career bureaucrats, whose relative influence has declined. Evans discusses East Asian "track-two" processes to bring scholars and nongovernmental leaders into sustained dialogue with government policymakers on security issues. He argues that these efforts have produced important exchanges of information, analysis, and perspectives, valuable policy initiatives, problem-solving networks, and cadres of both senior and junior scholars exceptionally well connected with counterparts around the region.

Evans distinguishes four ways that university-based research can connect with the policy world: (1) traditional scholarship, aimed at academic readers, that can be incidentally relevant to policy; (2) policy-relevant research, conducted primarily for other scholars but constructed to be cognizant of policy choices; (3) policy-related research, conceived with policymakers in mind and, indeed, often participant, such as those discussed in the Jaquette and Lustig chapters and in the track-two dialogues Evans describes; and (4) advocacy-driven research, exemplified by the activist role of scholars on climate change and, earlier, on banning the use of antipersonnel land mines. Evans suggests that the specific ways scholars may affect policy depend on a combination of personal connections, chance, and institutional constructs that emerge from those in authority who are trying to deal with complex policy problems. In today's globalized world, he asserts, the worlds of scholars and policymakers are becoming more intertwined than ever, and they are likely to become more so. It is up to scholars and policymakers, therefore, to find the best venues and ways to connect more effectively.

Laurence Whitehead draws on his experience as an analyst of comparative politics who has immersed himself in the study of power structures, political institutions, and policy choices in Europe, the Americas, Africa, and Asia, and on his deep knowledge of comparative political philosophy, going back many centuries. Adopting a "wide-angle" approach, Whitehead contextualizes the volume's chapters. He points out that they focus primarily on relations between scholars working in highly institutionalized universities and bridge institutions (such as think tanks), on the one hand, and professional public servants in established bureaucracies, on the other, and that they also reflect a period of US intellectual ascendance and the prevalence of liberal assumptions. These conditions may generally apply in contemporary North America and in Europe, Australia, New Zealand, and much of Latin America, but they are not equally relevant in other settings, or even universally in these regions or at all times.

Most of the chapters, Whitehead notes, are framed in terms of "narrowing the gap" between scholars and policymakers; they provide valuable testimony and practical suggestions about doing so. He suggests, however, that a better approach might be to concentrate on ways of more consistently achieving constructive interaction that is mutually fruitful. In some situations, this might require keeping the spheres separate, to protect academic freedoms and integrity and/or to ensure that policy choices are not skewed by academic advocacy. There has always been a tension between knowledge and power, between the aspirations to understand and to change the world, as Whitehead points out with numerous specific references. Sometimes synergy is possible, but sometimes separation is required.

The heart of the matter, Whitehead suggests, is to consider carefully what kind of relationship between academic research and policymaking is most appropriate in specific circumstances. Different kinds of scholarship can be drawn on at various stages of the policy process. But constructive scholar-policymaker engagement can become difficult or impossible in the context of polarized, mega-money-driven or repressive politics.

In the final chapter, Mariano Bertucci and I discuss the nature of and reasons for the widely noted gap between scholars and policymakers. We argue, however, that the difficulties of bridging this gap are often exaggerated and that this volume shows there are good reasons to try. We consider how to increase the likelihood that scholars wishing to engage policy issues will have good opportunities to do so and that their scholarship will not only be enriched but be positively recognized for this within their academic ranks. We discuss how to help ensure that more high-quality academic work is undertaken on high-priority policy issues for which systematic research is likely to produce policy-relevant insights, as well as how to help scholars use their policy experience to broaden and strengthen their research and teaching. We conclude by discussing how to make it easier for scholars' policy-relevant work to gain the attention of policymakers and how to encourage policymakers to avail themselves of relevant academic work. We offer concrete suggestions for consideration by scholars and students, universities, think tanks, NGOs, funding institutions, government officials and agencies, and international organizations.

This volume aims to provide valuable perspectives and practical advice on issues that are both timely and timeless and that are important not only in the United States but also in many other nations. It is intended to be useful to all those who want research and ideas to make a positive difference in the world beyond academia, as well as those who want academic work to be better informed by exposure to the realities and dilemmas of the policy arena. If, after consulting this book, scholars and policymakers on international affairs are reinforced in their resolve to engage each other more actively and creatively, and are better prepared to do so, our effort will have been well worthwhile.

NOTES

1. Among the main publications on the relations between scholars and practitioners in political science, and especially in international relations and comparative politics, are Alexander L. George, *Bridging the Gap: Theory and Practice in Foreign Policy* (Washington, DC: United States Institute of Peace Press, 1993); Christopher Hill and Pamela Beshoff, eds., *Two Worlds of International Relations: Academics, Practitioners, and the Trade in Ideas* (London: Routledge, 1994); Joseph Lepgold and Miroslav Nincic, eds., *Being Useful: Policy Relevance and International Relations Theory* (Ann Arbor: University of Michigan Press, 2000); Joseph Lepgold and Miroslav Nincic, *Beyond the Ivory Tower: International Relations Theory and the Issue of Policy Relevance* (New York: Columbia University Press, 2001); Lisa Anderson, *Pursuing Truth, Exercising Power: Social Science and Public Policy in the Twenty-first Century* (New York: Columbia University Press, 2003); two edited forums, J. Ann Tickner and Andrei Tsygankov, eds., "Risks and Opportunities of Crossing the Academy/Policy Divide," *International Studies Review* 10 (2008): 155–77, and Thomas G. Weiss and Anoular Kittikhoun, eds., "Theory vs. Practice: A Symposium," *International Studies Review* 13 (2011): 1–23; a symposium, "The Relevance of Comparative Politics for Public Life," *APSA-CP* 14, no. 2 (Summer 2003); and a cluster of autobiographical reflections by leading political scientists on bridging the policy-academy divide published in the *Cambridge Review of International Affairs* 22 (2009): 111–28. The chapters in this volume refer to these books and salient articles, but they go beyond the existing literature by presenting original research, informed reflections, and actionable proposals, drawing on personal experience.

2. Abraham F. Lowenthal, "Foreign Aid as a Political Instrument: The Case of the Dominican Republic," *Public Policy* 14 (1965): 141–60, and *The Dominican Intervention* (Cambridge, MA: Harvard University Press, 1972; republished by Johns Hopkins University Press, 1994).

3. Abraham F. Lowenthal, *Partners in Conflict: The United States and Latin America* (Baltimore: Johns Hopkins University Press, 1987), especially the chapter "The United States and the Caribbean Basin: The Politics of National Insecurity" (137–70).

4. See Abraham F. Lowenthal et al., *The Conduct of Routine Relations: The United States and Latin America*, appendix 1, "Report of the Commission on the Organization of the Government for the Conduct of Foreign Policy" (Washington, DC: US Government Printing Office, 1975); Abraham F. Lowenthal, " 'Liberal,' 'Radical,' and 'Bureaucratic' Perspectives on US–Latin American Policy: The Alliance for Progress in Retrospect," in *Latin America and the United States: The Changing Political Realities*, ed. Julio Cotler and Richard Fagen (Stanford, CA: Stanford University Press, 1974); Abraham F. Lowenthal, ed., *Exporting Democracy: The United States and Latin America* (Baltimore: Johns Hopkins University Press, 1993); and Abraham F. Lowenthal, *Global California: Rising to the Cosmopolitan Challenge* (Stanford, CA: Stanford University Press, 2009).

My interest in understanding the conditions that might facilitate transitions from authoritarian rule toward democratic governance contributed to designing and carrying out the project of the Woodrow Wilson International Center for Scholars that produced the classic volume edited by Guillermo O'Donnell, Philippe Schmitter, and Laurence Whitehead, *Transitions from Authoritarian Rule: Prospects for Democracy* (Baltimore: Johns Hopkins University Press, 1986), to which I contributed the foreword. It has also animated my current project, with Sergio Bitar, "Transitions toward Democracy: Learning from Political Leaders," sponsored by International IDEA and forthcoming as a book.

PART ONE

RECOGNIZING OPPORTUNITIES

CHAPTER ONE

What Do Scholars Bring to Government and Take Back Again?

CHAPPELL LAWSON

For at least two decades, observers have raised concerns about a growing gulf between academia and the world of government.[1] Even a passing acquaintance with Washington would seem to confirm these concerns. In few other locales is the adjective "academic" so reliably used as a synonym for "irrelevant," and few ad hominem attacks are as debilitating inside the beltway as those in which someone is described as a "professor." Meanwhile, many scholars view day-to-day debates over policy as alien to their work, expressing disdain for policymakers who appear to disregard the corpus of scholarly work on a subject when making decisions, as well as for scholars who spend time in government when they could be doing actual research.

One challenge for those who care about both scholarship and policy, then, is to assess the degree to which this gulf undermines either academia or government. An even trickier question is whether, to the extent that the gulf is undesirable, anything can be done about it.

In this chapter, I argue that the gap between scholars and policymakers is much less problematic when it comes to the flows of people than the exchange of information. The relatively limited number of scholars in policymaking posts is a natural consequence of increasing specialization within academia and the corresponding emergence of a large "quasi-academic" community inside the beltway, populated by policy analysts who spend their free time leafing through the *Plum Book* in search of potential jobs in the federal government. The second gap—inadequate communication—is more troubling because scholars and other researchers sometimes do generate knowledge that could helpfully inform policy debates, and because they could benefit from greater familiarity with the policy world in doing their research.

The goal, then, should not necessarily be to encourage more professors to serve in government (or for government officials to become professors). Rather, in a shameless misappropriation of Peter Evans's model of industrial policy, I recommend an "embedded autonomy" approach to political science research.[2] Academia should remain a separate sphere in which research is governed by norms of empirical verification and peer review ("autonomy"). At the same time, it should be in greater dialogue with the "quasi-academic" and governmental spheres, focusing scholarly research on questions of direct relevance to policymakers ("embeddedness"). This approach would both enhance policy debate and enrich political science.

Throughout this chapter, I make reference to my own experiences in government on the National Security Council staff during the Clinton administration and at US Customs and Border Protection (part of the Department of Homeland Security) during the Obama administration. In the tradition of some inside-the-beltway writing, my examples are shamelessly cherry-picked to support my claims, as well as to convey the impression that I held positions important enough to know what I am talking about. (To be balanced about it, my selection of examples from academia is equally unsystematic.)

Separate Spheres

The primary source of the gap between policy and academia lies in the way political scientists have construed their role. The core business of political scientists is teaching and research, with the emphasis at top departments being on the latter. Although, in theory, such research could be relevant to policy, several factors conspire to make that outcome unlikely.

Scientific research involves articulating testable propositions about politics, verifying or disconfirming them empirically, and extrapolating from these findings to develop "law-like" statements about political life.[3] In other words, it involves extrapolating from a class of events to offer explanations that can be used to understand putatively similar classes of events. As a result, political scientists focus on claims about general tendencies rather than on "point estimations"—that is, more on broad classes of phenomena than on the intricacies of particular cases. Such general predictions are of less interest to policymakers as they wrestle with specific decisions about specific events at a specific point. For instance, policymakers care less about lofty debates over whether sanctions "work" than they do about how a particular set of penalties would affect a particular foreign government at a particular time.[4]

Conversely, many phenomena that interest practitioners are not interesting to political scientists because they do not lend themselves to general statements about politics. One example that frequently comes up in informal conversations between practitioners and scholars is the role of leaders or—when it comes to effecting change within the US government—"policy entrepreneurs."[5] From a practitioner's perspective, replacing one individual with another can often make an enormous difference; proposals without champions inside the bureaucracy tend to languish. For scholars, however, the fact that some individuals appear to exercise an effect on events in some cases does not necessarily lead to broader inferences about politics, because outcomes that can be explained only with reference to particular personalities cannot be used to make predictions about other cases. This fact leads political scientists to downplay the impact of individual leaders and dismiss the role of leadership.[6]

The criteria used to judge scholars' work drives the wedge between academic research and policymaking even further. Central to research in political science, as in other academic disciplines, is the notion of peer review: people's work is best judged by others in the same discipline who employ shared evaluative criteria such as accuracy, generality, parsimony, and predictive power.[7] How well a scholar's work rates on these criteria generally determines his success in securing grants, getting hired at a top department, publishing articles, being cited by other scholars, making tenure, and obtaining outside offers from other institutions.

One important consequence of peer review is that the perceived importance of a scholar's work will be largely a function of its importance to the discipline, even if it has no potential application to policy. Work that provides a convincing alternative conceptual framework for a paradigm that currently dominates the discipline is considered the pinnacle of academic achievement. This sort of work typically involves the reinterpretation of already understood facts, in order to allow scientists to then proceed with their research from a better vantage point.[8] Unfortunately, such work is several steps removed from the quotidian concerns of policymakers.

In the study of politics, one of the biggest challenges is properly identifying cause and effect—that X indeed causes Y, rather than Y causing X or some third factor causing both (to say nothing of more complex causal pathways). Rarely are these challenges easy to resolve. Because work is judged according to its academic merit, "bullet-proof" research designs that deal with less policy-relevant questions tend to fare at least as well as those that deal with pressing, real-world questions that are less amenable to empirical testing. Therefore, a policy-relevant question for which the issue of causality cannot be nailed down and alternative interpretations cannot be ruled out to academic standards of rigor is—from the perspective of an academic seeking professional advancement—better left to others.

One final aspect of the professionalization of political science that leads to great distancing from the policy world is the nature of the skills investments that make for a successful academic career. Increasing demand for rigorous empirical testing and theory building has generated the need for specific methodological skills—formal modeling, advanced statistics (well beyond ordinary least squares regression), the use of randomized controlled experiments, and so forth. Although many political scientists still highly prize language training, fieldwork, country-specific knowledge, and subject-matter expertise, even these scholars also prize methodological sophistication. This fact leads graduate students to invest less time in the sorts of skills and knowledge that are most valued by the policy world—even as it makes them better scholars.

Few if any political science departments have mission statements that articulate their goals and priorities. However, the "Message from the Chair" posted on the website of America's top-ranked political science department summarizes the orientation of academic research:

> Harvard's Government Department is one of the leading political science communities in the United States. It represents a broad and changing spectrum of interests, backgrounds, and approaches. We have strength in teaching and research not only in the four main fields of political science—American politics, political theory, comparative politics, and international relations—but also in quantitative methods and formal theory as well as in thematic areas such as political economy. The Department's graduate program trains students for careers in university teaching and advanced research in political science.

Political science may produce policy-relevant research, but it does so only incidentally.[9]

It is tempting to distinguish between policy schools (the Kennedy School of Government at Harvard, the Johns Hopkins School of Advanced International Studies [SAIS], Princeton's Woodrow Wilson School of International Affairs, Tuft's Fletcher School of International Law and Diplomacy, the Georgetown School of Foreign Service, etc.) and classic political science departments.[10] In theory, policy schools—like think tanks—stand between political science and government, and in some respects they do so in practice. Review committees at policy schools may be somewhat more amenable to research that is less theoretically oriented—such as clever cost-benefit analysis of programs—than their counterparts at political science departments. Nevertheless, full-time faculty members at policy schools tend to be either former officials *or* professors; they are rarely practitioner-scholars. And where faculty members are on a tenure track, that track is similar to the track in political science or related disciplines; it depends on peer review. As a result, their research is far more theoretical than the sort of policy-relevant research conducted at think tanks.

Of course, many scholars (including all of the contributors to this volume) care deeply about public policy. They like to think that their work is of interest to people outside academia; they hope that their graduate students write dissertations that are relevant to real-world debates; and they take into account policy relevance when judging their colleagues' work. But the pressures of academic professionalization are powerful. As a result, political science research tends to be quite far removed from the decisions with which policymakers must grapple.

The Sphere in Between

A second factor contributing to the gap between policymakers and scholars is the growth of what I will call the "quasi-academic" or "policy wonk" sphere[11]—the world of think tanks, nonpartisan task forces, research centers associated with a university but not staffed by tenured faculty, and the like. As elemental forces of professionalization have altered the discipline of political science from the inside, this sphere has blossomed. Today, institutions within a five-block radius of Dupont Circle in Washington, DC, house more full-time researchers on international affairs, US foreign policy, and American politics than can be found at the top 10 political science departments combined.

Think tanks have existed in America since the early twentieth century; however, their growth really dates from the 1970s and 1980s. Most of Washington's leading think tanks are of recent vintage: the congressionally chartered Woodrow Wilson International Center for Scholars (1968), the Heritage Foundation (1973), the Cato Institute (1977), the Peterson Institute for International Economics (1981), the Open Society Institute (1984 at its earliest inception), the federally funded United States Institute for Peace (1984), the Center for Global Development (2001), the Center for American Progress (2003), and so forth. Moreover, the older institutions have expanded significantly in the past 30 years. For instance, the Carnegie Endowment for International Peace was created in 1910 but only really took off in the 1970s, when it began to publish *Foreign Policy*; it did not build a permanent home for itself on Massachusetts Avenue—a stone's throw from the Brookings Institution, SAIS, and the Peterson Institute for International Economics—until the 1990s. The American Enterprise Institute moved to Washington in 1943, but it did not have its first resident scholar until 1972. The 70-strong full-time staff now in the Council on Foreign Relations' (CFR; founded in 1921) Washington Office barely existed two decades ago. And so forth.

Many scholars are in some way affiliated with think tanks as visiting fellows or adjuncts (meaning that they often do not get paid for their work). But visitors are often engaged in purely academic projects, and the adjunct fellows often do something different at a think tank than they do in their "real jobs." The separation of political science and policy-oriented research thus remains, even within the same individual. One event that encapsulated this trend was Georgetown University's decision to divorce the Center for Strategic and International Studies in 1987. That split signaled the emergence of a large, self-sustaining sphere of policy researchers who were sufficiently expert that policymakers turned to them for advice but who were insufficiently academic to be considered as such by scholars.

Whereas scholarly research is designed to speak to other scholars, work done at think tanks is designed to speak to policymakers. Consider, for instance, the stated objectives of the Brookings Institution:

> Our mission is to conduct high-quality, independent research and, based on that research, to provide innovative, practical recommendations that advance three broad goals:
>
> · Strengthen American democracy;
> · Foster the economic and social welfare, security and opportunity of all Americans;
> · Secure a more open, safe, prosperous and cooperative international system.[12]

Quasi-academic work—from research in think tanks to task force reports—is also designed to speak to policymakers in another sense: it is explicitly *normative*. That is, it seeks to make policy recommendations. Where the analysis is done by a well-respected institution like Brookings, Carnegie, or CFR, it will present well-reasoned recommendations, with clearly articulated pros and cons of each. But it will still effectively advocate for specific policy positions that have both proponents and opponents. Practitioners like this sort of material because it provides analytical support for changes they seek to make and helps them think through the key issues surrounding a particular proposal. Academic research, by contrast, lacks this character. By the time scholars become tenured, the impulse to draw normative conclusions from their work has often been beaten out of them. At best, scholars are encouraged to articulate the policy "implications" of their work—an important step short of actual "recommendations."

In addition to being normative, quasi-academic work is *practical*. Sane participants in task forces and policy roundtables realize that their analysis and recommendations must be tempered by reality if they are to be taken seriously. For instance, a Brookings panel on reforming the American governmental system would be unlikely to recommend that the United States abolish the Senate, adopt a parliamentary form of government, prohibit all private campaign contributions, or any of the other things that political scientists might recommend. Aiming lower is typically more useful for policymakers, who in practice do not have the sort of magic wand that scholars would like to wave.

Equally important, at least some of the work that goes on in the quasi-academic world is not simply normative but *partisan*. Over the past two decades, Washington has seen the proliferation of "do tanks"—advocacy-oriented institutions that back up their advocacy with policy analysis. For instance, the Center for American Progress promises actual research, but research that serves a "progressive" agenda. Its staff consists primarily of those waiting in the wings for positions in the next Democratic administration; in the year before a presidential election, its offices sometimes feel downright ghostly. At the other end of the ideological and partisan spectrum, the American Enterprise Institute defines itself as:

> a community of scholars and supporters committed to expanding liberty, increasing individual opportunity and strengthening free enterprise. AEI pursues these unchanging ideals through independent thinking, open debate, reasoned argument, facts and the highest standards of research and exposition.[13]

AEI's staff was so thoroughly pillaged by the Reagan administration that the institution itself went through a decade-long period of crisis.

The normative slant of most quasi-academic research is often appealing to policymakers who seek analysis that supports goals they have already chosen, rather than "neutral" research on a topic. Although university scholars can provide such opinionated advice—and many do, with or without charging a fee—they are far less prepared to do so. With luck, they lack the willingness to churn out quick-and-dirty analysis in the service of a parochial agenda.

Finally, think tanks do not dedicate themselves exclusively to research. They converse informally with journalists and policymakers; they organize training events for officials; they deliver briefings and give testimony on Capitol Hill; and so forth. For instance, CFR's Program on the Congress and US Foreign Policy—just one of a number of programs run by CFR's Washington office—organizes Friday roundtable discussions with senior foreign policy staff, monthly briefings for both House and Senate chiefs of staff, and breakfast briefings for new members of Congress on "important topics."[14] Multiply that program by a factor of 10 and one gets a sense of what CFR's Washington office does; multiply it by 100 or 1,000, and one gets a sense of the sum of think tank–related activity.

For all these reasons, the quasi-academic sphere has much more to offer practitioners than the academy. Not surprisingly, when it comes to providing policymakers with advice, the expansion of the think tank world has led to a replacement of university-based scholars by think tank quasi-academics. Why should a government official fly in an expert on China from Cambridge, Massachusetts (let alone Palo Alto), when he knows of three other experts on the subject just a Metro stop away—one of whom he recently bumped into on the Hill and another of whom has a daughter at the same school as his son? True, the university scholar may have a better educational pedigree, but she is less in touch with the current debates of Washington. She does not live in his world. Most inside-the-beltway policy types, by contrast, spend hours each week interacting with officials, Hill staff, media, and each other. They have an instinct for what is relevant, what is achievable, and what is likely to fall on sympathetic ears—how policy advice can be framed, refined, and (if necessary) toned down to be effective. The whole Washington community is a ferment of colloquy and contention that scholars residing in another city, responding to rancorous peer reviews on their latest journal submission, can scarcely fathom—let alone participate in.

Just as there is variation among scholars in the extent to which they care about the policy implications of their research, so there is tremendous heterogeneity among policy wonks in the work they do. Some individuals dedicate themselves primarily to in-depth, policy-oriented research. Others spend most of their time conspiring with co-partisans and wooing the media. What unites them is that they aspire to speak to government.

Different Skill Sets

One manifestation of the rise of the quasi-academic sphere and the professionalization of political science is the replacement within government ranks of professors by quasi-academics. As an indicator of the extent to which academics participate directly in the policymaking process as government officials, I looked at the top 100 politically appointed officials in the State Department (through the level of deputy assistant secretary), the National Security Staff (through the level of senior director), and the Department of Defense (through the level of deputy assistant secretary). Although this sample is not a perfect representation of the jobs that political scientists (and scholars in related academic fields) might occupy, it is a reasonable approximation.

Not surprisingly, given that these individuals are accomplished and talented by any measure, many have varied CVs—that is, they have rarely confined their professional activities to one career path. Most, however, can fit neatly into one of eight categories: career executive branch (35), career Capitol Hill (12), electoral politics (7), business (16), nongovernmental or not-for-profit organizations (5), law (9), academia (7), and "quasi-academic" (18).[15] This last group includes individuals who meet three criteria:

1. They have received an advanced degree related to government or public policy, often a PhD but sometimes a terminal master's degree from SAIS, the Kennedy School of Government, the Fletcher School of International Law and Diplomacy, the Georgetown School of Foreign Service, or a similar institution.

2. They work at a "think tank"—typically, the Brookings Institution, the Carnegie Endowment for International Peace, the Center for Strategic and International Studies, the Center for American Progress, or CFR—or at a center affiliated with a university.[16] However, if they do work at a center, they do not have a full-time appointment in an academic department, have never held a tenure-track position, and do not publish in peer-reviewed journals.

3. Although they may have briefly served in government at some point, they did so for less than five years and did not hold a civil service position. (Otherwise, they are counted as "career government.")

As the numbers above suggest, individuals meeting these criteria have now supplanted lawyers and professors within the pool of those who, with a new administration, come into government.

In part, the relatively smaller number of university professors in government reflects who gets a job. Researchers at think tanks, after all, have been known to host dinner parties where people whom they do not particularly like but seem politically connected constitute more than half of the guests. But the replacement of scholars with quasi-academics in the halls of government also represents a specialization of tasks that would make Adam Smith proud. The reality is that academia is not necessarily good training for government service—at least relative to a career in the think tank world. Scholars do sometimes possess unique subject-matter expertise that could be useful in crafting sound public policies. But it is remarkable—especially on the foreign policy side—how little material advantage the sort of detail a scholar holds in his head actually confers. Knowledge of a foreign country is helpful, but the relevant portion of the detail that scholars laboriously collect over years can often be summarized in a two-page memo. Furthermore, experts already inside the government can furnish such information and insight, including those who have lived in the country and worked on issues related to it for years. So the sort of subject-matter expertise that scholars acquire is often useful in government, but it is rarely essential.

During my own time in government, my understanding of Mexico was occasionally helpful to me. Among other things, I was better able to gauge the likely sources and extent of resistance that US proposals would encounter south of the border. (For instance, it was clear to me that a US proposal for Mexico to actively deter undocumented northward migration would go absolutely nowhere, and I was better able to intuit that a particular US law enforcement operation—if it had been continued and eventually been exposed—would provoke a huge public backlash in Mexico.) But such instances were rare, and they affected my performance in government only marginally. For the most part, the relevant portion of the information I had so laboriously collected in a decade as a scholar could be summarized in a line or two of a memo. Moreover, both at the National Security Council and at US Customs and Border Protection, I ended up working on Mexico only a small part of each day; I spent a vanishingly small portion of my time on the specific issue of democratization in Mexico, which had been the subject of my academic research. The bulk of my work had to do with other countries and other issues, with which I was initially unfamiliar. Broader, shallower knowledge of the type acquired in the quasi-academic world is often more useful than the sort of expertise academia encourages; the further up the federal food chain one moves, the truer that becomes.

One key skill for political appointees who want to make a difference is familiarity with how things work inside the executive branch—not merely managerial competence in a general sense, of the type that might be acquired in the private sector or as a dean, but a firm grasp of the peculiarities of the public sphere. The US government is a byzantine place: an environment in which actors do not share the same goals; small mistakes can be severely punished; missteps with the media or on the Hill can be devastating; career officials have very different incentives from the political appointees to whom they theoretically report; one can inadvertently run afoul of federal ethics laws without actually doing anything unethical; and the best way to rid oneself of incompetent or treacherous subordinates is to promote them. The only way one can really learn to navigate this bureaucracy is to live in it or to have lots of friends who do. Professors rarely have either of these experiences, meaning that they may prove poor champions within government of even well-conceived proposals. Quasi-academics at least have the friends.

Equally important for officials who seek to get anything done is an understanding of the institutional processes and culture of the specific bureaucracy in which they will work. Where are the minefields, pitfalls, no-nos, and redlines? What initiatives similar to the one the official wishes to advance have already been tried, and why did they fail? What goes into a memo (marked "draft" to exclude it from being subject to the Freedom of Informational Act), and what should never be left in a written record? Who must be kept in the loop—except when they must absolutely *not* be kept in the loop? Exactly how is the fine art of bureaucratic sabotage played in that organization? (Because it is probably being played somewhere in the agency, whether or not the official is aware of that fact.)

One episode that may serve to illustrate the point concerns an effort I made to shepherd a proposal on enhanced border cooperation through the US and Mexican bureaucracies. (The proposal ultimately became the basis for a joint presidential declaration by President Obama and President Calderón.) I knew several of the key people on the US side, both from my earlier stint in government and from occasional forays into the quasi-academic realm (not from academia). These personal connections were immensely valuable in ensuring that the proposal was properly shopped around the American government before a presidential bilateral meeting— a time when both administrations were receptive to new initiatives. I also knew several key people on the Mexican side from my academic career and from task forces; at one bilateral meeting I realized that I had coauthored work with two of the eight Mexican officials sitting across the table.

Because Mexico has no functional interagency process, and the Ministry of Foreign Affairs handles communications between the two governments in ways that are sometimes more appropriate for the nineteenth century than the twenty-first, securing agreement from different bureaucracies within Mexico is exceedingly challenging. So, with the tacit connivance of the ambassador (whom I had known from an earlier stint in government), a friend on the White House National Security Staff (whom I had met 10 years before at a policy conference), and a friend in the Mexican government, I flew to Mexico City and literally carried the four-page proposal from one office to another—translating it for those few officials who were not fluent in English. Only after I had secured approval from the federal police, the principal intelligence agency, and the president's principal foreign policy advisor for the United States (whom I knew from several quasi-academic task forces) did I submit the proposal to the US State Department for interagency clearance in the United States and transmittal to the Mexican Ministry of Foreign Affairs.

This was, of course, freelance foreign policy of the most unforgivable sort, and it earned the ire of several officials in the State Department and the Mexican Foreign Ministry. But I had covered my bases just enough that I received a yellow card instead of a red one (thus surviving to commit a range of other process fouls). Most importantly from my perspective, the policy agenda moved forward at least six months faster than it would have. Given that the next presidential bilateral meeting was a year away, that I was planning to leave government in 11 months, and that my replacement was unlikely to care much about binational collaboration, the timing mattered.

It bears mentioning that many of the items in the proposal had originally been developed through a task force (for which I had been the director and my boss in government had been the chair) sponsored by the Pacific Council on International Policy and COMEXI (Mexican Council on Foreign Relations).[17] Unusually among such task forces, it both generated substantive recommendations (drawing in part on the expertise of the three academics who participated in it) and had a measurable impact on policy. But none of the laboriously researched and debated recommendations of that task force have appeared in a peer-reviewed publication, and they never will. They were devised and incubated mainly by people outside academia, presented to policy wonk audiences in the United States and Mexico, and ultimately carried into government in both countries primarily by people who had not come from academia.

Pathologies of the Quasi-academic Sphere

The discussion so far may have inadvertently conveyed the impression that the quasi-academic sphere is actually providing what government most needs. Alas, such is hardly the case.

Perhaps the most obvious problem is that advancement within think tanks does not necessarily depend on the development of sound policy proposals. The performance of policy wonks is often judged by media hits, which privileges snappy commentary and clever turns of phrase over substantive content. This metric also encourages quasi-academics to abandon policy-oriented work on an issue the moment it becomes less "hot" than some other issue and to spend much of their day responding to (or soliciting) media inquiries. Therefore, although scholars may be too "deep," quasi-academics whose agenda is driven by media coverage tend to become too shallow.

Second, the line between work that has a normative focus and work that is basically tendentious is not always clear. In some of the work produced by some think tanks and task forces, "strong argumentation" has come to trump facts. As one observer put it:

> Over the past half century, think tanks have come to play a central role in policy development—and even in the surrounding political combat. Over that period, however, the balance between those two functions—policy development and political combat—has been steadily shifting . . . At a moment when we have too much noise in politics and too few constructive ideas, these institutions may simply become part of the intellectual echo chamber of our politics, rather than providing alternative sources of policy analysis and intellectual innovation.[18]

Skill in adroitly manipulating evidence may well be better training for public life than rigorous hypothesis testing from the perspective of any one office seeker, but it is not necessarily good for the country.

It might be argued that "truth will out" in the quasi-academic sphere, as rival centers or think tanks develop different policy proposals. Unfortunately, in a world where participants are looking for their next job, losing a debate on the merits does not always lead debaters to concede defeat. In addition, funding for quasi-academic research is hardly indifferent to the nature of the conclusions reached. As a result, neither quasi-academics themselves nor the quasi-academic sphere as a whole necessarily focus on the development of sound policies.

What to Do?

Before plunging into a discussion of reform, it is worth articulating more explicitly what we want from the academic and quasi-academic worlds. Of many potentially worthy goals, I will concentrate on three: getting the right sort of people from universities and think tanks into government, enhancing the quality of academic and policy-focused research, and improving the flow of high-quality information to policymakers.

With regard to flows of people, we presumably aspire to send to Washington individuals from universities and think tanks who possess subject-matter expertise and can be effective once in government. As I suggest above, quasi-academics are more likely than university scholars to possess this mix of competencies. Therefore, there is little to lament in the displacement of scholars by quasi-academics in the corridors of power.

Regarding the quality of scholarly research, the challenge is to make research better on its own terms—that is, by improving academic research *in the eyes of academics* and quasi-academic research in the eyes of quasi-academics. To the extent that such research is also more appealing for officials, so much the better; however, I assume that there is intrinsic value in enhancing the quality of academic and quasi-academic output—whether that value comes in educating students (including future officials), increasing the general store of knowledge, or developing theories that at some point in the future may serve to inform policy debates.

Regarding the transmission of such output to officials, we presumably want academia and think tanks to provide practitioners with logically coherent, empirically well-supported argumentation that can be used in making policy decisions (including the conceptual and empirical foundations upon which analysts who wish to provide policy recommendations can build) for moments when policymakers are inclined to utilize such input. In the case of scholarly research, the challenge is to make it more relevant to policy without compromising academic rigor. In the case of studies done by think tanks or task forces, the challenge will be to make it as accurate and high-quality as possible.

Reforming the Academy

The conscious separation of academia from government allows the former to retain its autonomy. People who have served in government cannot normally jump into tenured positions when they leave office, as they lack the requisite publication record, scientific orientation, and technical skills; likewise, people whose primary professional goal is to occupy a position in government would be unlikely to prosper in the realm of peer review. The autonomy of the academic sphere ensures, in turn, that high-quality, relatively unbiased research on political life continues.

Nevertheless, it is possible to achieve "embedded autonomy"—that is, greater transmission of information from the policy world to academia and back again without compromising shared scholarly standards for evaluating research. Such a shift in the discipline toward more policy-oriented research will truly come about only if faculty advisors give this sort of direction to their doctoral students. But one place to start the process is with funders of political science research (the National Science Foundation, the Russell Sage Foundation, the United States Institute for Peace, etc.).

At present, proposals for the National Science Foundation are evaluated on two fundamental criteria: academic merit and "broader impact." The first criterion is obviously fundamental, and the correlation between different reviewers is generally quite high. The second criterion, however, is much less clearly defined, and reviewers are allowed to interpret it as something very closely related to the first—that is, impact within the community of scholars beyond the applicant's own subfield. That criterion could instead be defined explicitly to mean direct relevance to policy debates. It could even be given coequal weight with academic merit. To assist academic reviewers, funders might even include quasi-academics on the selection panel.

Would such a shift lead to a decline in scholarship or an excessive focus on certain types of projects? In reality, scholars have a number of worthy projects on which they can work at any one moment. If they are informed that one is much more in demand, they are likely to work on it first. The criteria of academic merit would remain, ensuring that such projects were researched to a high standard of rigor.

A second way to improve political science is to give scholars a better understanding of the policy world itself. Especially in the subfield of American politics, younger scholars often lack direct exposure to the way government actually operates. Such an understanding would help them to identify more policy-relevant research questions, as well as potential policy implications of their research. Crucially for the quality of research, it would also help them develop better priors (i.e., empirically better grounded hypotheses) for the questions they did choose to investigate. One experiment would be for a leading political science department to incorporate a practical component into its standard doctoral course of study. For instance, graduate students might intern at a government agency or other organization whose work was directly related to their research. Other departments could then determine whether this approach added value.

A third way to enhance scholarly research is to encourage those professors who have played a role in public life to draw on their government experience in their own research. Political scientists (and those in related fields) who return from government service are often uncertain about how to incorporate what they have learned into their published academic work, given the gap between political science research and the work they have done in government. There are few mechanisms to reintegrate scholars and few incentives for them to do anything other than return to their earlier research agenda. One ameliorative measure might be to encourage scholarly reflection on nonscholarly activities (perhaps in the form of teaching relief). In terms of improving flows of information for policymakers, one opportunity for scholars is predictive analysis. Policymakers are often hungry for prediction—what a dictator will do in response to economic sanctions, what the effect of the discovery of new oil reserves will be on a country, and so on—because it is relevant for their daily work. But few provide it. The US intelligence community generally resists offering predictions, limiting itself instead to providing otherwise unobtainable information on events as they are unfolding. For their part, scholars generally specialize in ex post explanations or make predictions that are not relevant to policy.[19] The quasi-academic sphere, meanwhile, generally offers policymakers relatively little in the way of empirically based predictions (as opposed to ideologically driven predictions or ex post explanations for events). In short, there is a demand that remains unmet. Scholars are potentially well-situated to offer predictive analysis because predictive analysis about complex events may require extensive modeling that requires an academic skill set.

Moreover, if political scientists' work is any good, it should have predictive power. Forcing scholars to take prediction seriously as an evaluative criterion would improve the quality of their arguments by forcing them to think more carefully about when their models do and do not apply in the real world. Ensuring this sort of behavior is primarily the job of peer reviewers and dissertation advisors, but one way to encourage policy-relevant predictions might be for funders to offer grants for scholars who have already published a particular claim to develop a few policy-relevant predictions that would flow from it.

Reforming the Quasi-academic Sphere

As with political science, it would be a mistake to aim for wholesale overhaul of the think tank world, and many idealistic proposals would prove impractical or expensive. For instance, it is difficult to discern how ideological bias in the think tank world could be prevented,[20] given that Washington is deeply polarized and that many policymakers seek politically congenial counsel over fact-based advice. Instead, I offer two modest measures aimed at ensuring that the output of the think tank world is of as high a quality as possible, even if some of it remains shallow or slanted.

First, promotion and retention reviews of quasi-academics could be supplemented by other metrics aimed at ensuring that so-called experts know what they are talking about and remain apprised of scholarly research related to their areas of expertise. One option might be for think tanks to ask outside scholars to evaluate the work of quasi-academics as part of the latter's normal performance reviews.

A second, related step would be to introduce a mild form of peer review into leading policy-oriented publications—in particular, *Foreign Affairs*. This model has been put into practice by the *Journal of Democracy*, which often requests outside reviews even though much of the content is solicited and editors exercise broad discretion about what to publish. Such journals might also experiment with publishing digests of academic publications, just as the *New York Times*'s Tuesday *Science Times* section scans the pages of *Science*, *Nature*, and other journals for findings of potential popular interest. In theory, such steps would make the "transmission belt" of ideas run more smoothly.

The Customer as a Producer

This chapter would be incomplete without touching on the government sphere itself. The government is the primary customer for quasi-academic work and (ideally) an ultimate customer for academic work. In this regard, the academic and quasi-academic spheres should change to better respond to government's needs, rather than the other way around. However, the government is also an enormous *generator* of both information and analysis, and access to this material could be extremely useful in enhancing the caliber of research done at think tanks and universities.

As a first step, the government should do a better job of making information on its operations available to researchers. As John McGinnis argues, "Congress and the president should . . . move to require the publication of all government data that do not undermine national security or personal privacy."[21] This would include information to which taxpayers have a right, even if the data in question do not make the agency providing them look particularly good. Automatically making such information available would make it much easier for researchers to conduct high-quality analysis of public policy. Perhaps the best thing that could come from having scholars in public life would be for them to open up government archives for policy-minded researchers.

Second, government agencies should be encouraged to adopt scientific methods when evaluating the programs they administer. Over the past three decades, social scientists have become increasingly methodologically expert and clever; the government should be drawing on this technical expertise and approach in evaluating its own operations. To cite McGinnis again:

> As a general matter, governments at all levels have made appallingly little use of social science, even as the potential of such research has vastly increased. And policymakers have been especially hesitant to use this research to analyze the effectiveness of existing government programs. Last year, David Muhlhausen of the Heritage Foundation surveyed more than five decades of government social programs;[22] in his examination, Muhlhausen found that, even though these hundreds of programs had spent trillions of dollars, the government had conducted only 13 rigorous empirical studies of their effectiveness.[23]

The Department of Education now effectively restricts its funding to studies based on randomized controlled experiments, unless the specific problem to be studied makes it impossible to use this method.[24] Such an approach, however, has not yet reached most other agencies. My own impression is that there are some crucial questions for which experimental and non-experimental data could readily be collected that would shed light on the efficacy of law enforcement efforts—from the effect of increases in personnel along the southwest border on illegal immigration to the potential security benefits of abolishing primary inspection at airports.

Conclusion

The simple fact that scholars serve in government is not necessarily good for the country or for academia. It is good for the country only if those scholars who serve are better qualified than others who might fill their posts. It is good for academia only if such service leads professors to produce better scholarly work.

Because scholars as a group are not particularly qualified for government service (nor are government officials well-trained for academic research), greater movement of people between the two spheres is not the answer. Instead, we should search for better mechanisms to ensure that information flows well between academia, the quasi-academic world, and government. Such improvements are, in turn, a matter of making each sphere better at what it does.

ACKNOWLEDGMENTS

I am grateful to the editors of this volume for valuable comments on an earlier version of this chapter. The chapter could not have been written—indeed, I would not have served in one of the government positions that helped shape my thinking on the issues I address here—without the inspiration and counsel of Abe Lowenthal, who uniquely combines the roles of scholar and practitioner.

NOTES

1. Alexander L. George, *Bridging the Gap: Theory and Practice in Foreign Policy* (Washington, DC: United States Institute of Peace Press, 1993); David Newsom, "Foreign Policy and Academia," *Foreign Policy* 101 (Winter 1995–96): 52–67; Miroslav Nincic and Joseph Lepgold, eds., *Being Useful: Policy Relevance and International Relations Theory* (Ann Arbor: University of Michigan Press, 2000); Robert D. Putnam, "APSA Presidential Address: The Public Role of Political Science," *Perspectives on Politics* 1 (June 2003): 249–55; Ernest J. Wilson III, "Is There Really a Scholar-Practitioner Gap? An Institutional Analysis," *PS: Political Science and Politics* 40 (Jan. 2007): 147–51.

2. Peter Evans, *Embedded Autonomy: States and Industrial Transformation* (Princeton, NJ: Princeton University Press, 1995).

3. Adam Przeworski and Henry Teune, *The Logic of Comparative Social Inquiry* (New York: Wiley-Interscience, 1970).

4. For a more systematic discussion of the relationship between scholars and practitioners on the issue of international sanctions, see Thomas Biersteker, chap. 8, this volume.

5. John Kingdon, *Agendas, Alternatives, and Public Policy*, 2nd ed. (Boston: Addison-Wesley Educational Publishers, 1995).

6. Daniel Byman and Kenneth M. Pollack, "Let Us Now Praise Great Men: Bringing the Statesman Back In," *International Security* 25 (Spring 2001): 107–46.

7. Przeworski and Teune, *Logic of Comparative Social Inquiry*.

8. Thomas Kuhn, *The Structure of Scientific Revolutions* (Chicago: University of Chicago Press, 1962); Imre Lakatos, *The Methodology of Scientific Research Programmes* (Cambridge: Cambridge University Press, 1978).

9. My own department has recently developed a mission statement that sounds somewhat more policy-oriented: "Societies in all regions of the world face unprecedented chal-

lenges. Globalization and economic uncertainty, immigration, asymmetric security threats, energy dependence and the environment, health care, poverty, and polarization of electorates are among the issues testing our understanding of how human communities function. In the MIT Department of Political Science, we see in these challenges the opportunity to conduct innovative, high-impact research. We believe that the strongest theoretical models emerge through observations in the field" (http://web.mit.edu/polisci/about/index.shtml, accessed Jan. 4, 2012). Nevertheless, this mission statement remains a far cry from that of Brookings.

10. See Wilson, "Is There Really a Scholar-Practitioner Gap?"

11. The term *quasi-* is employed here in its literal sense—quasi-academic work shares some but not all of the features of academic research—and does not indicate that work done in think tanks is a somehow diminished subtype of academic research. Its method of inquiry (empirical verification and conceptual extrapolation) is ostensibly similar, but its goals and prospective audience are different.

12. Brookings Institution, www.brookings.edu/about.aspx (accessed Jan. 9, 2012).

13. American Enterprise Institute, www.aei.org/about (accessed Jan. 4, 2012).

14. Council on Foreign Relations, www.cfr.org/content/about/Washington_Program _Brochure.pdf (accessed Jan. 4, 2012).

15. Where it was impossible to place them clearly in one category or another, I counted them as half a person in the top two categories into which they might fit.

16. A Republican administration, of course, would include fewer people from Brookings or the Center for American Progress and more from the American Enterprise Institute, the Heritage Foundation, the Cato Institute, the Nixon Center, and so on.

17. Pacific Council on International Policy and COMEXI, *Managing the United States–Mexico Border: Cooperative Solutions to Common Challenges*, Report of the Binational Task Force on the United States-Mexico Border, www.pacificcouncil.org/document.doc?id=30 (accessed Jan. 4, 2012).

18. Tevi Troy, "Devaluing the Think Tank," *National Affairs* 10 (Winter 2012), 75–76.

19. For an exception to the general trend, see Bruce Bueno de Mesquita's TED talk at www.ted.com/talks/bruce_bueno_de_mesquita_predicts_iran_s_future.html.

20. See Troy, "Devaluing the Think Tank."

21. John O. McGinnis, "A Politics of Knowledge," *National Affairs* 10 (Winter 2012): 63.

22. See David B. Muhlhausen, *Evaluating Federal Social Programs: Finding out What Works and What Does Not*, Heritage Foundation, Backgrounder No. 2578, July 18, 2011, http://thf_media.s3.amazonaws.com/2011/pdf/bg2578.pdf (accessed Jan. 12, 2012).

23. McGinnis, "Politics of Knowledge."

24. See Lynn Olson and Debra Viadero, "Law Mandates Scientific Base for Research," *Education Week* 21, no. 20 (Jan. 30, 2002): 1, 14, 15, www.edweek.org/ew/ew_printstory .cfm?slug=20whatworks.h21 (accessed Jan. 12, 2012); and Lesley Dahlkemper, "What Does Scientifically Based Research Mean for Schools," *SEDL Letter* 15, no. 1 (Dec. 2003), www.sedl .org/pubs/sedl-letter/v15n01/2.html (accessed Jan. 12, 2012).

CHAPTER TWO

Connecting the "Idea" World with the "Real" One
Reflections on Academe and Policy

ROBERT A. PASTOR

Recently, I posed a simple question about the reported gap between scholars and practitioners to two academics in senior positions in the Obama administration: How have ideas influenced Obama's foreign policy? Both were experts on democracy who were involved in recent debates on US policy on the Middle East. One described how she had offered the idea to her colleagues that the Middle East is a "fourth wave" of democracy, and she was surprised that no one seemed to know there had already been three waves. The second mentioned a similarly profound insight when the White House was feeling besieged by those who argued that the Egyptian revolution might turn out like the Iranian revolution. His contribution was to note that there were other, more felicitous transitions, such as those in Chile and the Philippines, and that calmed the waters.

John Maynard Keynes's comment on how practitioners are unconscious implementers of the scribbles of older scholars is often cited by academics, who would like to think that their ideas are not just relevant but potent. In that light, these two examples are sobering.

My career has tried to connect the two worlds of ideas and actions from three distinct vantage points: as academic, as policymaker, and as director of programs at an active and creative nongovernmental organization (NGO). With these three perspectives, I offer here some reflections on how ideas influence policy, how policy reshapes ideas, and how NGOs, which inhabit the world between policy and academe, can sometimes synthesize the "real" world of government and the "idea" world of universities.

In a career spanning more than 35 years I have taught at five universities, yet I never anticipated an academic career. And while I have appreciated the intellectual environment, I always looked at it as a place to conceive and challenge ideas to improve policy and the world.

Two Commissions and an Administration

The beginning of a new administration is often a superb opportunity to insert new and powerful ideas into government, particularly if there is a change in party, and commissions sometimes play a critical brokering role. Jordan Tama's book on national security commissions argues persuasively that some commissions have had a large impact on foreign policy.[1]

In the two years preceding the Carter administration, two commissions were established that approached the issue of US policy toward Latin America from two very different directions. The Commission on the Organization of the Government for the Conduct of Foreign Policy, a government commission chaired by former US ambassador Robert Murphy, concentrated on how the government should be reorganized to make better policy. One of its projects was on "The Conduct of Routine Relations" and focused on US–Latin American relations other than national security crises. The Commission on US–Latin American Relations, a blue-ribbon, private group chaired by Sol M. Linowitz, former ambassador to the Organization of American States (OAS), wrote two reports with very specific and substantive recommendations on ways to improve US policy to the region. I was involved in both projects, and the knowledge that I acquired proved exceptionally helpful during the four years that I served as the director of Latin American and Caribbean Affairs on the National Security Council (NSC), from January 20, 1977, to January 20, 1981. I wasn't sure how each package of ideas would help me do my job, but I soon learned, and what I learned might be of use to others.

The Murphy Commission was seeking an intellectual rationale to cover its real purpose, which was to end Henry Kissinger's monopoly on foreign policy by getting him to give up one of his two positions, national security advisor or secretary of state. Senator J. William Fulbright, chairman of the Senate Foreign Relations Committee, proposed the commission as a way to send a signal to President Ford. The president got the message, but by that time the Murphy Commission was already funded and organized. The commission found its intellectual rationale in a seminal book, *The Essence of Decision*, written by Graham Allison, a young professor at Harvard University's Kennedy School of Government, where I began my graduate work. Like all great books, it starts with a simple idea—that foreign policy is not always a rational decision. (This was a bigger surprise in academe than in government.) Policy, Allison argued, should be seen as the product of complex organizations or of bargaining between actors or bureaucracies.

Abraham F. Lowenthal was asked to direct the Murphy Commission's project on policymaking on Latin America, and he recruited me to do two studies. I interviewed more than 200 individuals in the executive branch, Congress, and various interest groups on a range of case studies. Like much original research, those interviews proved as influential as any theories I had learned in graduate school in shaping my ideas on how the government makes foreign policy.

The reports that I wrote on Congress and the US sugar program are less consequential than the people I met and the questions I posed.[2] I took Allison's questions about the bureaucracy as a point of departure to learn how each bureau or agency viewed Cuba, sugar policy, human rights, the Panama Canal, trade, and almost every issue on the agenda. Bill Richardson, who would later be elected to Congress and as governor of New Mexico and would serve in President Clinton's cabinet, was then working in the Congressional Relations Office of the State Department, and he explained the special importance of Congress and the consequences of the department's failure to understand or accept Congress's role and perspective. Bill inadvertently led me toward my thesis, which posited that the most crucial debate on foreign policy within the US government was not between bureaucracies but between the executive and legislative branches.

On completion of the Murphy Commission's project, Lowenthal recommended me to Sol Linowitz to become executive director of the Commission on US–Latin American Relations, which had just issued its first report identifying with clarity the issues on the agenda for the United States and recommending policies. My tasks were to work with members of Congress to convert the major features of the report into a concurrent resolution, to promote hearings on the issues, and to prepare a second report to be issued on the eve of the new administration.[3] Soon after the report was issued, Zbigniew Brzezinski, who had just been appointed national security advisor by Jimmy Carter, interviewed and hired me to head the NSC office on Latin American Affairs.

Just prior to Carter's inauguration, I drafted a letter from Sol Linowitz to Jimmy Carter and secretary of state–designate Cyrus Vance, summarizing the report and requesting that the new president give it the highest consideration. As it turned out, that letter arrived on my desk at the NSC on the day that I arrived and Carter was inaugurated—January 20, 1977. I immediately drafted a response for President Carter, expressing his gratitude for such a first-class report and promising to try to implement each and every recommendation in the report. I thought to myself: "Wouldn't it be nice if US policy could be made as easy as this!"

The Linowitz report became the guidebook for Carter's policy, but to implement that policy, the experience I acquired on the mechanism of the policy process while working on the Murphy Commission proved equally valuable. Knowing where people sat (to use the metaphor of the day) helped me to know where they would stand and to organize the chairs so that the people opposed to the new initiatives would be left standing when the music stopped.

Before joining the NSC, I wrote an article, published in the *Foreign Service Journal*, that criticized Henry Kissinger for failing to realize that his greatest foreign policy challenge was not in the Middle East or Southeast Asia but at the other end of Pennsylvania Avenue.[4] I used the Panama Canal treaties as an example. At the beginning of each session of Congress, Strom Thurmond and Jesse Helms, two conservative Southern senators, introduced a resolution warning the president not to negotiate new canal treaties. Kissinger and Ambassador Ellsworth Bunker, the canal negotiator, believed that the executive branch should negotiate the treaties first, and when these were finished, Kissinger and Bunker would testify before Congress—so the two ignored the Thurmond-Helms resolution. Kissinger seemed not to realize that the two senators were able to recruit more than 32 of their colleagues, making it impossible for the president to secure a two-thirds vote for the treaty.

I argued in the article and in my dissertation that the executive branch was acting on an obsolete constitutional concept. Richard Neustadt and Arthur Maass, Harvard professors and my mentors, argued that the US government was not based on "a separation of powers," as we had learned in grade school, but was composed of "separate institutions sharing powers"—both made laws and could veto policies. I incorporated that concept into my thesis and my approach to government.

Congress, I argued, actually made foreign policy by using a variety of instruments, including amendments to laws on foreign aid, defense, intelligence, and trade agreements. These amendments sent signals of support or concern to the executive branch about its policies. If the executive ignored those signals, Congress would tighten the laws, reducing the executive's discretion until it had no room to negotiate or execute. The executive branch, in brief, did not just execute, and Congress did not just legislate. Both branches shaped policy by an interactive process.

As the agenda and papers on the Panama Canal issues arrived for the Carter administration's first NSC meeting a few days after the inauguration, I noticed that there were 10 items on the agenda. The last was "Congress and the Public, if time permits." With a different concept in my mind as to the nature of the interaction between the president and Congress, I recommended to Dr. Zbigniew Brzezinski, the national security advisor, that he reverse the order of the agenda and put Congress first. He was convinced. He called Secretary of State Cyrus Vance and asked if he would start the meeting with the tenth item on the agenda. Vance agreed.

The NSC made three decisions: (1) conclusion of the Panama Canal treaties would be a high priority; (2) Vance would tell the Panamanian foreign minister that the United States wanted to conclude the treaties by the summer to give the

Senate time to debate and ratify them before the 1978 congressional elections made it impossible to take such a controversial decision; and (3) Linowitz, who had been appointed co-negotiator, and Bunker would immediately brief key senators and try to preempt the Thurmond-Helms resolution. Bunker and Linowitz went promptly to Capitol Hill and persuaded enough senators to reject the resolution that Thurmond and Helms decided not even to introduce it.

The old idea—that Congress and the president were two institutions defined by "a separation of powers"—had led the executive branch to complete negotiations before briefing Congress, though this so narrowed the political space for negotiations that it became impossible to secure a treaty. The new idea—that Congress makes foreign policy—derived from an alternative theory: that separate branches share powers. The implication of this new approach is that the executive should seek to influence Congress before, during, and after negotiating the treaty. Translating the idea into policy, Bunker and Linowitz persuaded Congress to allow them to negotiate the treaties.[5]

Arnold Nachmanoff, the first director of the Linowitz Commission, and Abe Lowenthal recruited a distinguished group of academics, and from their assembled work, the Linowitz Commission distilled some basic principles to guide a new policy toward Latin America. With the help of senior policymakers on the commission, they converted the broader principles into specific recommendations for policy. The two reports began by identifying the transformation of the region over the previous decade and the failure of US policy to adapt to those changes. The reports proposed an approach that "should be free of the paternalism conveyed by the rhetoric of 'special relationship' while remaining sensitive to the unique qualities of inter-American relations." The United States should work closely with Latin America to develop global approaches to economic issues rather than define a specific Latin American policy. The second report had 28 specific recommendations. Beginning with the urgent need for new Panama Canal treaties, the commission recommended 7 specific steps to forge a credible human rights policy and 11 on economic policy. It recommended normalizing relations with Cuba in a gradual and reciprocal manner, reducing arms sales, and promoting nonproliferation.[6]

It was a sweeping agenda, and one that the Carter administration embraced. To understand how ideas are transformed into policy and the similarities and differences between academic discussions and NSC meetings, it is instructive to compare the Linowitz reports with the first meeting of the Policy Review Committee (PRC)—the principal NSC committee—on Latin America on March 24, 1977. (For a declassified summary of the discussion, see the appendix to this chapter.) While the administration had already begun to develop its policies on Panama, Cuba, and

Mexico, the purpose of the PRC meeting was to organize an overall approach that could then be articulated in a major address by the president.

In Vance's absence, Deputy Secretary Warren Christopher opened the meeting by suggesting that "the best overall policy may be a non-policy . . . The U.S. should treat Latin America in a global context, rather than think about a regional policy." The group then began a discussion about whether the United States had or should have "a special relationship with Latin America." The State and Treasury Departments suggested that we drop the rhetoric about a special relationship and deal with each issue at the level that made sense. The Defense Department, the Joint Chiefs, and the CIA worried about ending the special relationship, feeling that it might encourage Latin America to form blocs against the United States. General George Brown warned that "we are going to miss them [the special relationships] when they are gone." Some would later miss the Cold War for similar reasons.

Brzezinski criticized "the notion of a special policy" as "lock[ing] us into a cycle of creating unrealistic expectations and then having to live with the subsequent disappointments. The Monroe Doctrine, which underlines this approach, is no longer valid. It represents an imperialistic legacy which has embittered our relationships." Nobody blinked, and Christopher agreed. When the Defense Department representative asked how we should react to the Soviets in the hemisphere, Brzezinski said, "We should not react reflexively . . . Individual governments have a good sense of their own independence and therefore our reactions should be contingent on the way the other Latin Americans respond."

Christopher insisted on remaining committed to human rights and reserving our warmest relationships with democracies. No one disagreed with that, although the Pentagon had caveats. There was a meandering discussion on the OAS and predictable disagreements on reducing arms sales. The decisions of the NSC—as well as a few others that were not discussed in the PRC but were in the Linowitz report, such as signing Protocol I of the hemisphere's nonproliferation treaty and the American Convention on Human Rights—were incorporated into President Carter's Pan American Day speech, on April 14, 1977.

In brief, the NSC, State, and Treasury followed the line of the Linowitz reports and were prepared to move forward. Defense, the military chiefs, and the CIA preferred the status quo. This would not be a big surprise to students of bureaucratic politics. The president's speech looked even more like the Linowitz reports than the PRC discussion, in part because I worked with the speech writers on it. By the end of the administration, all 28 recommendations had been implemented.

The Process

The transmission of the Linowitz ideas into US foreign policy was hardly as smooth as the above narrative suggests. The process, however, sheds light on the relationship between ideas and policy, between academics and practitioners, and between political appointees and the career foreign service.

Prior to World War II, the entire national security bureaucracy—the State Department, the War Department, the Army and Navy—worked in the Old Executive Office Building, adjoining the White House. When the president had a foreign policy question, he would ask the secretary of state to walk across the street to the White House. After the war, the Defense Department moved into the Pentagon, and the State Department moved into a large new building in Foggy Bottom, and before too long, both buildings were filled. The secretary of state soon found that much of the job was to manage the bureaucracy and the new embassies that opened all over the world.

As the management job overtook the task of making policy, and as cables proliferated, fewer in the government had time for reading books, and theories seemed less and less relevant. Today, some try to keep up with the foreign policy debates, but the debate that matters most is often between the political appointees and the career foreign service. If the "outsiders" do not know the bureaucratic landscape, they will get lost in the corridors of power. They rarely have any effect and are relieved when they finally find their way out.

Those working in the career foreign service are trained to be pragmatists and tend to want to solve one problem with one country at a time. The academic outsiders / political appointees prefer to start with big ideas and try to reshape policy to conform to those ideas. The outcome of their debate is determined by the degree to which the president and secretary of state are committed to changing the policy and whether the political environment allows those changes. During the Carter administration's internal debate on Latin American policy, there were few differences on Panama within the administration after the president and secretary of defense made clear the new direction. There was considerable debate on the human rights policy, with the bureaucracy initially quite resistant to downgrading relations with friendly dictatorships; but, over time, that changed.

The debates on Central America in the Carter administration were less about goals than about tactics—such as how to secure a democratic transition in Nicaragua and El Salvador—and on that, the major fissure was based as much on personality as on position. The policy on Nicaragua failed to achieve its goal of finding a democratic transition between Somoza and the Sandinistas. On El Salvador, US policymakers spent more than one year trying to keep the civilian-military regime that emerged from a coup in October 1979 from collapsing or undertaking wholesale repression. That might have been the most that could be achieved at the time and under the circumstances, but it hardly qualified as satisfactory.

By 1980, policymakers were exhausted—not just physically but intellectually. There were no new ideas on how to promote a democratic transition in a revolutionary context. The academic/political appointees believed the issue was whether it was proper for the United States to change these governments and, even if it was, whether it could be achieved. The practitioners saw the issue in terms of using various means of coercion—including the threat to overthrow a government—to change the regime. In retrospect, both debates missed the mark.[7] New ideas were needed, and they would be developed in NGOs.

The influence of the Linowitz Commission on the Carter administration's policies on Latin America was acknowledged in an unusual way when several conservatives joined together to draft the "Santa Fe Report" in anticipation of a Republican administration in 1981. One of the authors, Roger Fontaine, replaced me as national security advisor for Latin America. The "Santa Fe Report" recommended a "new"— but actually old—approach to Latin America that would replace the Carter administration's emphasis on human rights with a Cold War alliance with military regimes against the communist menace in Cuba, Nicaragua, El Salvador, and Grenada. In some ways, the tension between the incoming Reagan appointees and the career service paralleled what had happened with the Carter appointees, and the policy reflected a compromise.

Nongovernmental Organizations and Big Ideas

On leaving government, Jimmy Carter decided to establish a center to promote many of the goals he had pursued as president. In 1985, I joined the Carter Center as the first director of Latin American and Caribbean Affairs, and I eventually also set up the Democracy and Election-Monitoring Programs and the Chinese Village Elections Project.

Nongovernmental organizations tended to be either academic think tanks, like the Brookings Institution or the Carnegie Endowment for International Peace, or more activist groups such as Greenpeace or the International Rescue Committee. Carter preferred the latter, although he recruited academics and attached the Carter Center to Emory University. The health programs, directed initially by Dr. William Foege, formerly director of the Centers for Disease Control and Prevention, tended to replicate the work of the CDC, although in new areas and with more agility. The peace program began by holding conferences on arms control, the Middle East, human rights, and other contemporary issues.

In the case of the Latin America program, we decided to establish a group of former presidents and prime ministers of the Americas—called, originally, the Council of Freely-Elected Heads of Government—to find ways to promote democracy, freer trade, and greater cooperation in the region. The group stumbled upon a new and powerful technique of conflict resolution—"election mediation"—that addressed more effectively than governments the problem of facilitating democratic transitions.[8] Indeed, in the case of Nicaragua, Carter as US president and Pastor as his NSC advisor in 1978–80 had failed to achieve the democratic transition that we helped accomplish a decade later working for an NGO.[9]

There were many reasons for the different outcomes, but the main one stemmed from a different way to conceive the problem. In a sensitive third world political environment, a national government would try to keep foreign governments from interfering in its political process, particularly if the foreign government was viewed as hostile—as Anastasio Somoza viewed the Carter administration or as the Sandinista government viewed the Reagan administration. Moreover, the international community had long defined any such pressure on a political process as illegitimate. The political dynamic was different when a nongovernmental group composed of internationally respected and fair individuals sought the opportunity to observe the electoral process.

In July 1989, I was invited to attend the tenth anniversary of the Sandinista Revolution, and while there, I asked Violeta de Chamorro, the leader of the opposition UNO coalition, and the Nicaraguan president Daniel Ortega and his vice president Sergio Ramirez whether they would be interested in having the Council of Freely-Elected Heads of Government of the Carter Center observe the electoral process. In addition, I posed the same question to Francisco Fiallos, the head of the Nicaraguan Election Commission. Chamorro was thrilled, Ortega and Ramirez were open to the idea, and Fiallos said he would follow the line taken by the government. I asked each of them if they would send a letter to Carter, inviting the council and assuring unrestricted access to all stages of the electoral process. Within a month, Carter received the three invitations. That gave the group leverage that no one understood at the time, because these officials, having invited Carter, could not easily denounce him, provided he played a fair and impartial role.

We set up an office in Nicaragua, and Carter and various Latin American presidents visited Nicaragua at least once a month and listened to the opposition's complaints about the electoral process, brought the more legitimate of these complaints to the attention of Ortega, and then, in effect, mediated the terms of a free and fair election. After each trip, Carter and his colleagues would hold a press conference and describe the existing problems and the solutions, and over time, the Nicaraguan public gained confidence in them, in the elections, and in the process. By election night, the council and other observers had observed the election throughout the country and, working with the OAS and the United Nations, had orchestrated a "quick count"—a random sample of the results—that permitted the major observer groups to know the outcome even before the political parties or the Election Commission knew it. By this time, even if the Nicaraguan government had wanted to manipulate the vote count, it could not have done so without the full knowledge of the observers. Carter helped Ortega to understand that, and since he was trusted by all sides, Carter was able to negotiate the transition of power from a revolutionary government to its opposition—the first time anything like that had ever occurred.

Absent that mediation, the probability of a free or fair election in Nicaragua in February 1990 was remote, and it was even more unlikely that the two sides would have accepted the outcome. While the international political environment and the domestic political balance were important determinants in shaping the context within which the key actors made their decisions, the eventual success of a fair election accepted by belligerent parties was due to a new way of conceptualizing the challenge of a political transition. In the old way, a powerful foreign government condemned a weaker government for manipulating the electoral process, and the weaker government condemned the stronger one for interference and went about its business. In the new model, an NGO—with no power but its moral authority—observed and mediated differences in a manner that permitted both the government and the opposition to modify their approaches and accept fair terms. Policy was transformed from "intervention" to "invited mediation," permitting the most sensitive outcome—a change in government. In his massive volume on Nicaragua, Robert Kagan, who had served in Ronald Reagan's State Department, admitted that "President Reagan's policies, if continued unchanged, would probably not have led to fair elections in February 1990 . . . [and] would probably have meant many years of inconclusive struggle in Nicaragua."[10] A new idea—election mediation—made a free election possible. Ideas matter.

There is yet another long-term idea that awaits a moment when it can influence government policy in a profound way. The idea is "North America," and if grasped by the leaders and the people in the United States, Canada, and Mexico, it could reshape the three governments' relationship, competitiveness, security, and international standing. Although public opinion in all three countries favors more integrated and cooperative relations, there are groups in all three countries that feel so threatened by integration that they have resisted any and all initiatives.[11]

The idea of "election mediation" emerged from a practical, on-the-ground effort to observe an election and prevent it from failing. The idea of "North America" emerged from a "second discovery" of North America in the course of negotiating the North American Free Trade Agreement, but NAFTA was not enough, and the leaders of the three countries were insufficiently committed to use that new platform to create a more formidable entity. For this idea to take root, something will need to change. Either a crisis will compel the leaders to think of a continental way to stimulate the economies or reduce threats, or new leaders will find it politically beneficial to make the case for the continent, or, finally, grassroots groups, perhaps on the border, will persuade the governments to pay attention. Ideas can matter, but much else is needed.

Tentative Lessons

What lessons can we draw from this meandering journey? Ideas matter—sometimes in large ways, as when the Carter administration grasped the significance for inter-American relations of new Panama Canal treaties; sometimes in small ways, as when a different conception of Congress's role in foreign policy permitted a more effective strategy to secure the treaties' ratification. Sometimes the idea comes up from practical experience, such as election mediation, and sometimes it is conceptualized in the academy, such as "North America," where it might take decades before the idea takes shape on the ground. Sometimes an idea like human rights is so compelling that it takes hold and influences public policy in a short time, and sometimes an idea, such as the "special relationship," proves so subtle and abstract as to be lost to all but the most ideological.

We can ponder the gap between practitioners and academics, but the truth is that they deal with ideas from different perspectives, and the most constructive policy is usually one where the practical and the theoretical merge. Government is not the only vehicle for making policy, and academe is not the only place to formulate concepts; NGOs may be better positioned than governments to develop and implement certain ideas and policies—such as mediating elections.

Ideas that cannot find nourishment are unlikely to take root, and policies that are not grounded in ideas are unlikely to spread. The seeds and the soil need each other, and both need sunlight.

SECRET

~~UNCLASSIFIED~~ ~~SECRET~~

POLICY REVIEW COMMITTEE MEETING

Wednesday, March 24, 1977

Time and Place: 3;30 - 5:00 p.m., White House Situation Room

Subject: Latin America

Participants:

State	Treasury
Warren Christopher	Anthony Solomon
Terence Todman	Edward Bittner
William Luers	
	Arms Control and Disarmament Agency
Defense	Leon Sloss
Charles Duncan	
Major Gen. Richard E. Cavazos	Commerce
	Frank Weil
Joint Chiefs of Staff	
General George S. Brown	NSC
Lt. General William Smith	Dr. Zbigniew Brzezinski
	David Aaron
CIA	Thomas Thornton
Deputy Director Enno Knoche	Robert A. Pastor

(b)(3) ▮▮▮▮▮▮▮▮▮▮

Overall Approach: Should the U.S. Move Away From the Special Relationship?

Deputy Secretary Christopher opened the meeting by saying that the new Administration had been dealing with many specific Latin American problems -- for example, Panama, Cuba, and Mexico -- but we had not had an opportunity to develop an overall approach, particularly with respect to those economic issues which were of greatest concern to the Latin Americans.

SECRET

Declassify n: OADR SECRET ~~UNCLASSIFIED~~

(27)

He suggested that the best overall policy may be a non-policy. To follow
the remarks in the President's United Nations speech, the U.S. should
treat Latin America in a global context, rather than think about a regional
policy. The President's Pan American Day speech on April 14 provides
the natural culmination of this process and the opportunity to suggest
this approach.

He then initiated a discussion of whether the U.S. had a special relationship
with Latin America or not.

Assistant Secretary Todman suggested that we drop the rhetoric about a
special relationship and deal with Latin America on bilateral, regional,
or global levels depending on the issues. In the major economic areas,
it is necessary to deal on a global basis and develop a single policy, and
this is also the case on nuclear proliferation and immigration. But because
of the geographical proximity, Latin America impinges on us more directly
than other areas. For example, we share a border with Mexico and that
requires special policies. We have certain regional institutions, and they
require special policies.

Under Secretary Anthony Solomon agreed that we had special problems
with respect to Mexico and Brazil, but the question of the special relationship relates to the region rather than to individual countries. He suggested
that we would need special policies to these two countries. He said that
the arguments against an overall special relationship to the region are
very powerful.

Enno Knoche said that the possible consequences of ending the special
relationship would be that it would tend to encourage Latin America
to form blocs against the U.S., but he added that since this would not be
in Latin America's long-term interest, he felt such blocs would not endure.

Deputy Secretary Charles Duncan said the U.S. has had a special relationship with Latin America, and it still does. General Brown agreed, but he
said that our special military relationships are eroding, and that we are
going to miss them when they are gone. He said that this relationship --
for examp' ., the training assistance program for foreign air force
personnel -- provides an opportunity for us to influence these governments on human rights and other matters.

-3-

Intervention

Todman said that this issue aroused the greatest interest and controversy in Latin America where the U.S. has had a long history of intervention -- most recently in the Dominican Republic and Chile. Now, we are being accused of intervention on behalf of human rights. The question is: to what extent do we need to intervene?

Duncan said that we first needed to define our interests in the hemisphere, and said such a definition would be necessary to decide on the need for a "special relationship." Then, he prefers the option of "limited intervention."

Brzezinski returned to the question of whether we should have a special policy to Latin America. He said that the notion of a special policy is ahistorical. In the past, it has done nothing more than lock us into a cycle of creating unrealistic expectations and then having to live with the subsequent disappointments. The Monroe Doctrine which underlines this approach is no longer valid. It represents an imperialistic legacy which has embittered our relationships.

He recommended that if our relationships are to become healthier, then we ned to put them on a more normal footing. He said that we can do this by stressing our bilateral relations and in seeing the region's problems in a global context, as the President said in his UN speech. And we should use this as a point of departure in the Pan American Day speech. What was needed was a normalization of our relations with Latin America. We did not want another Alliance for Progress.

Christopher said that he agreed with Brzezinski's assessment.

General Brown agreed and said that we should put the statement in the context that we have recognized that Latin America had reached adulthood. Brzezinski warned, however, that such an approach was also patronizing. Instead, he said that we should encourage Latin America to diversify its relationships with other countries and regions, and that we, in turn, should differentiate our approach to different governments.

Duncan agreed that a bilateral approach makes sense, but he said the relevant question on intervention is how should we react to the Soviets in this hemisphere.

SECRET

Brzezinski said that we should not react reflexively; rather we should judge our response in terms of the likely consequences if the U.S. did not intervene ████████████████████████████████ He said that individual governments have a good sense of their own independence and therefore our reactions should be contingent on the way the other Latin Americans respond. But we cannot accept a blanket policy for all cases. Later, he said, and Solomon agreed, that a statement on nonintervention might be misinterpreted.

Leon Sloss of ACDA said that he agreed with Brzezinski's emphasis on a global and a bilateral approach, but he said that we should not discourage some regional institutions which have potential to contribute to the solution of certain problems -- for example in arms control areas.

Brzezinski agreed that we should not discourage regional institutions, but he suggested that the healthiest approach would be a hands-off one, where the Latin Americans would approach us -- instead of we, them -- to pay attention to the regional institutions.

Solomon and Brzezinski agreed that the President should redefine our relationship rather than renounce it. Solomon said that the only viable regional economic institution was the Inter-American Development Bank, and a sign of its relative importance is the fact that Secretary Blumenthal will attend its annual ministerial meeting whereas he would not attend the one at the Asian Development Bank. Even the IDB has diversified its relationships -- bringing on donors from Europe and Japan -- although we are still the biggest contributor. But in trade or aid, it is hard to see a special relationship.

David Aaron pressed the issue of the special relationship a couple of steps further. One implication of a change in strategy would involve a shift in the distribution of U.S. resources abroad. Secondly, he noted that there was, in fact, a collective consciousness in Latin America. ██ Con-structive relations demand greater specificity.

--   In ideology, we want to show an affinity for democratic states.

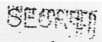

--   Economically, we need a more diversified strategy.

However, Brzezinski said we should not try to package these clusters of interests into a single policy.

Weil from Commerce agreed.

Relationships With Military Regimes

Christopher applied the approach suggested by Brzezinski to this next issue. He suggested that we adjust our relations so as to differentiate according to the kind of regime: warm relations with civilian and democratic governments, normal relations with nonrepressive military regimes, and cool but correct relations with repressive governments.

Brzezinski agreed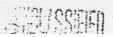Duncan and General Brown also agreed with Christopher and repeated the need to distinguish between kinds of military governments.

David Aaron suggested joining the two agreed approaches -- the movement toward globalism and establishing a closer affinity with democracies -- by a Presidential trip to selected democracies, say in Latin America as well as in Africa or Asia.

Aaron also said that if we are going to be sincere about moving toward a global approach, we must make clear that our policies with respect to democracies or repressive regimes must be the same in Latin America as in Africa or Asia. Given the special constituencies in the U.S., that would not be easy. We will have to go out of our way to do that.

Human Rights

Christopher said that it was very important for us to stay committed on our policy on human rights, but at the same time, we must explore affirmative ways to express our policy.

SECRET

SECRET   -6-

Solomon said that we should work with Congress to make clear why they
should not be thinking about a Latin American policy on human rights.
He and Christopher agreed on the need to obtain more discretionary
authority and make more relevant distinctions in the application of our
policy. If we define gross violations as torture or degrading treatment,
instead of denial of due process, then we only single out seven-ten
countries rather than 60 - 80. Then, we can have some impact.

Todman said that we should look at aid as a way to improve human rights
conditions in very poor countries.

Arms Transfers

Christopher asked whether the United States, as a declining source of
arms to Latin America, is justified in adopting a special policy on arms
transfers to Latin America.

General Brown reminded everyone that in the early Kennedy years we
tried to get Latin American governments to shift defense expenditures to
nation-building, but as sovereign states, they just turned to other sources
to buy arms.

Sloss from ACDA said that we must approach this problem globally at
both ends. Discuss it with the Soviets and with other suppliers, and at
the same time urge restraint by purchasers. If this does not work, he is
inclined to agree with George Brown.

Organization of American States

Christopher asked whether the OAS was part of the special relationship.

Todman thought the OAS was useful, but that it wasted a lot of time
because it is not well-focused. He said he would like to see it strengthened.

Christopher suggested that we alter our relationship to the OAS to the
way we relate to other regional organizations, like CENTO or ASEAN.

SECRET

Solomon asked Todman how he would strengthen the OAS, and Todman
answered that he would eliminate the Permanent Council and reduce the
U.S. contribution, but we should do so after consulting with the Latin
Americans.

Solomon said that in his experience in State and in ARA, every Administration
had tried to strengthen the OAS and tried to make it more efficient, by cutting
personnel and reorganization. The trouble is that the Latin Americans are
very sensitive to their "perks," and they perceived every effort to strengthen
the OAS as an attempt to weaken it. He concluded that the OAS was useless,
and there was nothing that could be done.

David Aaron said that if we want to follow the global approach to its
logical conclusion, then our involvement in the OAS, which once played
the role of a mini-UN, should be phased out. We really do not need it
any longer. We should say we want to deal with Latin America like
other regions.

Solomon acknowledged that that would indeed be perceived as the end
to the special relationship, but noted that before doing that, we should
look at the political ramifications and the domestic reaction, which he
predicted would be negative. In converations he has had with Latin
American leaders, they all acknowledged privately that it was a worthless
organization, but at the same time, they were horrified at the prospect
of its being abolished. But he did not see anything we could do.

In fact, Latin Americans use the global North-South forum more and even
take the SELA more seriously than they do the OAS.

Christopher said that the OAS was one of those institutions which would
not die a natural death. Whenever it looks like it will, somebody turns
the oxygen back on, and it has another life.

Aaron said that rather than try to leave it, abolish it, or resuscitate it
with new ideas, the U.S. should just ask the OAS to justify itself.

William Luers from State said that we should be careful in formulating
our policy to the OAS and more generally to the hemisphere, least our
new policy be perceived as a massive rejection of Latin America.

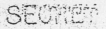

Cultural and Educational Exchanges

Todman said that the value of individual contacts is very important to increase mutual understanding.

Christopher asked whether we should return to a more enlightened and generous policy with respect to cultural and educational exchanges with Latin America. Todman nodded yes.

Technical Assistance

Christopher asked whether we should put more money into technical assistance to Latin America.

Weil from Commerce said that question brought the discussion back to the beginning: What are our interests? If they are not special, then we should not give special assistance.

Summary and Miscellaneous

Christopher noted that Todman will be meeting with the Cubans in New York, that the Canal Treaty negotiations will be continuing, and that we should be increasingly sensitive to Brazil. Any overall statement needs to take into account our concern for special problems. He noted that the discussion was a little more philosophical than usual, but that we were probing for a relationship which adapted to the new realities.

The next step is the speech at the Organization of American States.

SUGGESTED OUTLINE OF PRESIDENT'S PAN AMERICAN DAY SPEECH

1. Principles underlying the OAS -- Reaffirmation of:

   A. Nonintervention

   B. Human Rights and Social Justice

2. Today's challenge -- not reaffirmation, but:

   A. Analyze important changes in the hemisphere and international politics and economics

   B. Adapt policies and institutions in the light of these changes.

3. Need for candor -- state differences as well as commonalities

4. Important changes since 1948:

   A. The OAS -- 1948 to present

   B. The U.S. -- from the Marshall Plan to Vietnam -- detente

   C. Latin America -- the last decade -- economic development -- birth of North-South

   D. The Developing World and the International System

   E. The relevance of the Inter-American System

5. Need for a new approach not a new policy

   A. Global -- seek cooperation and to the extent desired consultation in advance of negotiations at global fora -- economic, nuclear proliferation --

   B. Encourage diversification of relationships

   C. More normal differentiated bilateralism -- human rights criteria

   D. The Inter-American System:

      OAS -- (a) human rights; (b) peace-keeping

      IDB, ECLA

5. Conclusion -- The New Challenge

ACKNOWLEDGMENTS

I would like to acknowledge the special role that Abraham Lowenthal has played in connecting the worlds of academe and policy and in providing me with my first and, in many ways, most important opportunities to play a comparable role. In the summer of 1974, Lowenthal recruited me to do research for a project he was directing for the Murphy Commission and, subsequently, he recommended me for the Linowitz Commission. Both jobs shaped my career, as did his advice and model.

NOTES

1. Jordan Tama, *Commissions and National Security Reform: How Commissions Can Drive Change during Crises* (New York: Cambridge University Press, 2011).

2. Robert A. Pastor, "Congress' Impact on Latin America: Is There a Madness in the Method?" and "U.S. Sugar Politics and Latin America: Asymmetries in Input and Impact," both in *The Conduct of Routine Economic Relations: U.S. Foreign Policy-Making to Latin America*, vol. 3, pt. 1, ed. Abraham F. Lowenthal, Commission on the Organization of the Government for the Conduct of Foreign Policy (Washington, DC: US Government Printing Office, 1975).

3. See Robert A. Pastor, "On the Congressional Effort to Influence U.S. Relations with Latin America: Congressional Foreign Policy at Its Best," *Inter-American Economic Affairs* 29, no. 3 (1975): 85–94.

4. Robert A. Pastor, "Coping with Congress' Foreign Policy," *Foreign Service Journal* 52 (Dec. 1975): 83–104.

5. For a case study of the Panama and Central American cases, using Robert Putnam's concept of "two-level games," see Robert A. Pastor, "The United States and Central America: Interlocking Debates," in *Double-Edged Diplomacy: International Bargaining and Domestic Politics*, ed. Peter Evans, Harold K. Jacobson, and Robert D. Putnam (Berkeley: University of California Press, 1993).

6. Commission on US–Latin American Relations, *The Americas in a Changing World* (Oct. 1974) and *The United States and Latin America: Next Steps* (Dec. 20, 1976), both published by the Center for Inter-American Relations (now The Americas Society) in New York.

7. For a good description of the two "debates," and particularly of the traditional way in which the State Department handled the issue, see Anthony Lake, *Somoza Falling: The Nicaraguan Dilemma* (Boston: Houghton Mifflin, 1989).

8. Robert A. Pastor, "Mediating Elections," *Journal of Democracy* 9 (Jan. 1998): 154–63.

9. For a detailed case study of the government and nongovernmental mediation in 1978–80 and 1989–90, see Robert A. Pastor, *Not Condemned to Repetition: The United States and Nicaragua*, 2nd and rev. ed. (Boulder, CO: Westview Press, 2002).

10. Robert A. Kagan, *A Twilight Struggle: American Power and Nicaragua, 1977–1990* (New York: Free Press, 1996), 722–23.

11. See Robert A. Pastor, *The North American Idea: A Vision of a Continental Future* (New York: Oxford University Press, 2011).

PART TWO

SETTING AGENDAS AND FRAMING ISSUES

CHAPTER THREE

Scholars, Policymakers, and Agenda Creation
Women in Development

JANE S. JAQUETTE

Scholars have contributed significantly to shaping US foreign policy over the past 35 years by identifying the failure of foreign assistance agencies to focus on the global roles of women in economic development, by suggesting ways that women's roles in development could be understood and enhanced, and by helping to design and implement programs with that aim.

Close cooperation between scholars and policymakers within the US Agency for International Development (USAID) in the late 1970s resulted from an unusual combination of factors: new legislation that mandated the Women in Development (WID) Office within USAID as a result of active pressure from feminist groups in Washington; President Carter's appointment of a gifted, politically visible policy entrepreneur to head the WID Office; and the lack of prior research on the subject, which created opportunities for scholars and researchers based in nongovernmental organizations (NGOs). The United Nations (UN) had declared 1975–85 the Decade for Women, providing an opportunity for USAID to take the lead on an international issue.

Those favorable factors changed, some dramatically, during the 1980s. As the United States pushed for a series of economic reforms widely termed the Washington Consensus, a widening gap emerged between the government and feminist academics. USAID/WID was unable to maintain its international role as a policy innovator. Various UN agencies, the World Bank, and other bilateral foreign assistance agencies moved into that space, providing new ideas and the impetus for "gender and development" (GAD) programs from the mid-1980s onward. The goals loosely included under women/gender and development expanded to include human rights, trafficking in women, political participation in the growing number of democratic governments worldwide, and women's roles in postconflict societies. Scholarship on women and development issues grew rapidly, but much of the academic research on women and development shifted to the United Kingdom, Canada, the Nordic countries, and the Netherlands. The George W. Bush administration's use of women's human rights as one of its reasons for invading Afghanistan and Iraq after 9/11 seemed cynical to many US feminist scholars, further deepening the divide between them and the US government. Close cooperation between scholars and policymakers outside the United States continues, however, and suggests that the gap is due to the political context, which determines both "supply" and "demand." US scholars and USAID now play relatively marginal roles in international debates on women and development.

The WID Office and Academic Research: 1977–81

The Women in Development Office at USAID (AID/WID) was established by an amendment to the Foreign Assistance Act of 1973, proposed by Senator Charles Percy (R-IL) in response to lobbying by women's groups.[1] For the WID Office to succeed, it needed to overcome its "political" origins (having been imposed on the agency rather than arising from within) and to make addressing women a legitimate goal in an organization (USAID) largely dominated by male economists, agricultural experts, and engineers, many of whom did not think that women had anything to do with development. When the WID Office was launched, there was very little research on women's economic roles and virtually none on how increasing their access to development resources could improve development outcomes. Given the lack of analysis and little practical experience in reaching women beyond population and health programs, the WID Office needed to generate research to support its mandate: to develop a clear, overarching rationale for including women in development programming and projects and to suggest specific ways to do so.[2]

In USAID, the initial reaction to establishment of the WID Office was mixed. Equity Policy Center researcher Patricia Blair wrote in 1983 that the idea of "women in development" was met with "some enthusiasm at the top, in the intellectually oriented" Program and Policy Coordination Bureau, but that "many resented the imposition of a 'feminist' perspective into an agency dominated by middle-aged, middle-class white males; a 'social' issue into a field dominated by economists; and an 'equity' issue into an institution that thinks of itself as apolitical and technocratic."[3] Further, many in the bureaucracy felt they were being asked to impose American feminism on third world countries largely hostile to "women's lib," and they objected (often to WID staff) that promoting equity for women was not an appropriate goal for a development agency.

In 1977, the WID Office was boosted by President Carter's appointment of Arvonne Fraser, head of Carter's Midwest campaign and wife of Congressman Don Fraser (D-MN), to direct the office. When I joined the WID Office as a policy analyst in 1979, there were already two professors in a staff of five: Fraser's deputy, Elsa Chaney, a Latin Americanist who had studied women legislators in Peru and Chile, and Kathleen Staudt, who had written her dissertation on agricultural policy in Kenya. Fraser and Chaney both viewed academic research as essential to defining the WID Office's mission and to providing the empirical work that would give the office the necessary expertise to weigh in on development policymaking within the agency.

The establishment of the WID Office created a "policy window," and Fraser proved to be an adept policy entrepreneur.[4] Her strategy was to triangulate three sources of pressure to give the office greater clout: the women's groups that had pushed for passage of the Percy Amendment (to keep up congressional pressure); a few crucial allies within USAID at both the staff and policy levels who were sympathetic to doing something about women; and academics on staff who could argue effectively for integrating women into development programs and projects.[5] Our job was to articulate the case for attention to women in ways that could be adopted by USAID policymakers and practitioners and to present credible evidence of progress on the issue to those in Congress and in the women's movement who were following this initiative. Fraser's influence in USAID was increased by her international visibility as head of the WID committee of the Development Assistance Committee of the Organization for Economic Cooperation and Development. Under her leadership, the WID Office took an active role in preparations for the UN's Mid-Decade Conference on Women in Copenhagen (1980) and in crafting the UN Convention on the Elimination of All Forms of Discrimination against Women (CEDAW), which was signed by President Carter in Copenhagen in 1979 and has now been ratified by 187 out of 194 countries.[6]

The main focus of USAID in the mid to late 1970s was agriculture and food production, responding in part to domestic fears of a global population explosion and Carter's personal concern about "limits to growth." USAID contracted with US agricultural universities to do research and improve extension services. The largely male experts in agriculture saw men as farmers and women as housewives and resisted efforts to include women in development planning. Female scholars involved in agricultural extension were dismissed as "home economists," and their knowledge about what women contributed to food production and household decision making was largely ignored.[7]

The WID Office had no money to fund projects in the field,[8] but Fraser leveraged its miniscule resources to fund studies, including a series of "status of women" reports, many done by local scholars, in more than 30 countries. She also contracted with the US Census Bureau to do a project comparing women and men on a range of demographic, economic, educational, and social indicators.[9] The WID Office reached out to women researchers in US land grant universities, which were already closely tied to USAID through regional consortia. One, Michigan State, began soliciting and disseminating papers in a series on women and development issues.[10] Research (in part funded by the WID Office) soon showed that women in Africa, Latin America, and Asia were in fact working in the fields and participating in family decisions about what crops to plant and what farm animals to raise for market, although these activities had remained largely invisible to the experts charged with disseminating new technologies, training, and credits.[11] As academic policy analysts, we were expected to advocate for women's inclusion in country assessments and project reviews; to push for sex-disaggregated data in pre- and post-project surveys (not standard procedure even today); and to respond to requests from inside and outside the agency for information and ideas about what kinds of initiatives could be effective in reaching women across a broad range of fields, including intermediate technologies (such as cookstoves and water pumps) and forestry.

In our efforts to persuade decision makers, project managers, and others in the USAID bureaucracy that focusing on women would be both appropriate and effective, we relied heavily on pioneering research by a Danish scholar, economist Ester Boserup, whose 1970 book *Woman's Role in Economic Development* provided a convincing argument that women were and always had been productive farmers.[12] In Africa, Boserup argued, food production had traditionally relied on "female farming systems" based on complementary roles for women and men. When colonial administrations introduced new technologies to increase the production of cash crops, they provided training, credit, and other inputs to men, leaving women in the subsistence sector, where they were still responsible for family food production and certain household expenses but were largely denied access to the resources needed to increase their productivity.

Boserup's broad conclusion was that agricultural modernization had been "bad for women." This carried potential pitfalls for us. Those who promoted market efficiency could argue that if women could not adapt to new technologies and markets, development agencies should ignore them. Those critical of markets could argue that if capitalist modernization marginalized women, USAID should not be promoting it. Our position was that if women had lost ground as a result of the mistakes made by colonial bureaucracies, a development strategy committed to getting resources to women could reverse the trend, empowering women and increasing their production and incomes at the same time. Within USAID, Boserup's concept of "female farming systems" gained some traction and created a greater willingness to include women in agricultural development projects.

Food production and population control, issues of intense public concern after Paul Ehrlich published *The Population Bomb* in 1968, had led to a shift in development thinking in the 1970s, away from infrastructure investment and toward basic human needs. In the 1970s, the growing awareness of the feminization of poverty also increased understanding of the need for WID programs and allowed the WID Office to expand its agenda to include urban as well as rural women. The office funded a study by the International Center for Research on Women (ICRW), then a new feminist development think tank, on women-headed households.[13] The report claimed that a third of households worldwide were headed by women and noted that women and children in those households were among the poorest of the poor.[14] The policy prescription was that income generation for women should be a high priority, while the absence of husbands from these women-headed households got around the objections of those in USAID who feared that increasing women's earnings risked creating conflict between husbands and wives. Once the idea caught on, income-generation projects were made available to women across the board, with the potential to empower women and improve family welfare.

By the last year of the Carter administration (which coincided with the UN's 1980 Mid-Decade Conference on Women), a clear sense of WID's core mission had emerged from interaction between scholars and policymakers.[15] WID's primary goal, as we saw it, was for women to gain access to resources—credit, education, training—that would empower them economically and in their households while addressing USAID's overall goals of poverty reduction and agricultural development. Women-specific projects emerged as the most effective way to start. These tended to be small projects, because of the limited funds available, and were directed specifically to women because, in many cultures, women—if they were allowed to leave the home at all—could not attend meetings at which men were also present. We strongly urged that all USAID projects collect sex-disaggregated data to assess their impact on women, but this was rarely carried out. We took the position that increasing women's economic clout through income generation and improved agricultural productivity and marketing was what distinguished WID from USAID's maternal and child health and population programs. We supported these, of course, but saw them as more top-down and welfarist, and we continued to push for economic empowerment.[16]

At this time, Congress passed legislation mandating that USAID spend at least $10 million annually on women and development—like the Percy Amendment itself, a result of pressure from women's groups. This was a mere drop in the bucket, given USAID's budget at that time of over $3 billion, but it meant that country missions had to report on their WID projects and on the overall impact of their programs on women. It also meant that each country mission had to have a person designated as a "WID officer" to monitor projects and collect the relevant data, and generally meant that the mission had to pay some attention to the impact of its projects on women, which had not previously been part of the agency's standard operating procedure.

The increasing focus on women in development, in USAID and internationally, created ripple effects in various fields, including a new understanding of the household as an arena of conflict as well as cooperation;[17] studies of women's work (including the many hours women spent getting potable water and collecting firewood); a case for intermediate technologies to reduce the time women spent in backbreaking and low-productivity labor; and a recognition of the value to families of educating girls.[18] New studies showed that increasing women's earnings had a more positive impact on family welfare than increasing men's incomes, because women spent more of what they earned on nutrition and schooling (and much less on alcohol, gambling, and prostitutes).[19]

The 1980s: Reagan, Structural Adjustment, and a Paradigm Shift from WID to GAD

In retrospect, the late 1970s was a period of unusually close and fruitful cooperation between scholars and a policy unit within USAID, although the scholars were few and the policy unit marginalized. The Reagan administration radically changed the political context in which USAID operated, with significant implications for the WID Office. The idea that underdevelopment was a consequence of structural factors or colonial exploitation had been fundamental to the North-South Dialogue and the UN General Assembly's call for a New International Economic Order. With strong support from British Prime Minister Margaret Thatcher, the Reagan administration flatly rejected this view, arguing instead that "statism" had choked off development and that progress would require adopting market reforms and opening up developing economies to foreign investment and trade.[20]

When Reagan took office in January 1981, there was talk that his administration would abolish the WID Office. Feminism was in retreat; the Equal Rights Amendment, passed by Congress in 1972, had not been ratified; and opposition to the amendment had been a major theme of Reagan's campaign. In the end, the Reagan administration did not abolish the WID Office, but it did significantly change the agency's policy direction in line with its pressure on aid recipients to adopt a series of pro-market reforms (the Washington Consensus). The administration reduced the size of the agency and encouraged it to contract out its services to NGOs in the United States and abroad. Now under the leadership of a career foreign service officer, the WID Office turned its attention inward, to training rather than research and policy innovation; downplayed its feminist advocacy; and focused on improving USAID's technical capacity to carry out WID projects and planning. It was able to work with the growing number of national and transnational women's NGOs that had sprung up, in part as a result of the UN's Decade for Women.[21]

The shift in USAID toward markets as the preferred means to address poverty was influenced by the work of Peruvian economist Hernando de Soto, whose book *The Other Path* emphasized the potential of small-scale entrepreneurs.[22] Revolving credit programs such as the Grameen Bank in Bangladesh and Self-Employed Women's Association in India had shown that poor women were more likely than men to pay back uncollateralized loans. Microcredit programs became an attractive new direction for USAID and the WID Office.[23] However, the antifeminist rhetoric of the Reagan campaign and the administration's efforts to limit women's reproductive rights, including cutting off funding for the UN Population Fund, distanced US feminist groups from the White House and lessened their influence on the Hill. The WID Office had been criticized by feminist scholars on the left, even when Carter was in office, but many scholars who had earlier been involved in WID-related research were now strongly opposed to the new administration. The split between "women and development" and women's studies grew wider, as women's studies were increasingly influenced by "critical studies," postmodernism, and postcolonialism, all hostile to capitalism, globalization, and US dominance.

The gap between USAID and WID academics widened as a result of US insistence on the austerity policies of the Washington Consensus. Research showed that the costs of structural adjustment programs fell disproportionately on women through the effects of male unemployment, rising informality of work, and cutbacks in government health, education, and welfare programs.[24] The original WID goal of improving women's economic opportunities gave way to efforts to establish compensatory programs to help women and children hurt by structural adjustment programs. Feminist scholars doing fieldwork abroad returned with accounts of women's hardships and marginalization, and many became activists in anti-globalization movements; feminist economists challenged the biases of a field based on a "male model" of competitive individualism;[25] and feminist political scientists challenged the Reagan administration's insistence that there was a strong positive correlation between economic and political liberalization.

Meanwhile, various UN agencies, from the International Labour Organization to the UN Statistical Office and the UN Fund for Women (UNIFEM), as well as Canadian, European, and Nordic bilateral donors, began to contest elements of the WID approach and drew on scholarly analysis to call for a paradigm shift. In 1987, British academic Caroline Moser circulated an influential essay arguing that the WID model was flawed because it focused too narrowly on small, women-only projects, which ghettoized women and reinforced the traditional sexual division of labor. Her suggested alternative approach, "gender and development," would focus not on women but on gender power relations and would go beyond women's projects to "mainstream" gender into all aspects of foreign assistance. Using Maxine Molyneux's distinction between "practical" and "strategic" gender interests (that is, women's practical needs for housing, health care, and schools for their children as opposed to the strategic advocacy of women's rights),[26] Moser argued that GAD would leave the decision about whether to address women's strategic gender needs to the recipients themselves, consistent with the goal of increasing local participation in project design. GAD would make gender an agency-wide priority, and male bureaucrats could be brought back in without having to fear that they would be criticized for failing to push hard enough against male privilege.[27]

The GAD approach was rapidly adopted, at least rhetorically, by UN agencies and many bilateral foreign assistance programs and NGOs; it was a shot in the arm for bureaucracies suffering from "WID fatigue" and male resistance. Although the GAD model was designed in part to improve bureaucratic buy-in, its impact depended on active support from policymakers, project managers, and those working in the field. Subsequent research suggests that this has been difficult to achieve. At the same time, the widespread adoption of the GAD approach signaled a further shift away from a US role in policy innovation and coincided with the increasing marginalization of US scholars in the WID policy arena.

The 1990s and Beyond

Over the past 20 years, a wide range of new issues has arisen for which a "gender lens" is deemed appropriate, including democratization, human rights (including violence against women and trafficking in women), and "postconflict" situations.[28] The bulk of the research and interchange between scholars and policymakers on these issues is taking place outside the United States. Of the English-language publications since the Fourth UN Conference on Women held in Beijing in 1995, US scholars edited or wrote only a small handful.[29] Irene Tinker, who led the international conference on WID in 1975, continues to have international influence,[30] and the George W. Bush administration's programs to address HIV/AIDs, particularly in Africa, represented a new American initiative.[31] But these examples are exceptions, not the rule. By contrast, British and Commonwealth scholars have written and edited several books on women and development,[32] while the World Bank and the UN Development Program / UNIFEM have published global assessments of women's demographic, economic, educational, and political status; the World Bank's *World Development Report 2012*, for example, is entirely dedicated to gender issues.[33]

The relative lack of scholarly work on women and development in the United States is matched by the lack of academic infrastructure. Only one US university—the University of Illinois—offers a graduate degree in women in development, as a minor field. The Institute of Development Studies (IDS) at the University of Sussex (England) offers a master's program in gender and development (as do Birzeit University, West Bank, Palestine, and the University of Heidelberg, Germany), and a core group at the University of London is working in this area. IDS has taken a leading role in connecting scholars, policymakers, and practitioners through its Bridge program and website.

In the United States, there are two important policy-oriented women and development think tanks active today. ICRW still works on poverty and women's economic empowerment and has turned to child marriage and HIV/AIDS. Gender Action, founded in 2002, monitors programs of the World Bank and other international financial institutions, has a program in Haiti, and is looking at the impact of climate change on women. But neither is as well connected to academia as is IDS or Oxfam, which edits *Gender and Development*, the only academic journal in the field. The Association for Women in Development (AWID) was founded in 1982 by Arvonne Fraser as a US-based organization to link scholars, policymakers, and "practitioners" (those who carry out development projects in the field). AWID has become a lively global forum, but its governance is international, it usually meets outside the United States, and it draws primarily policymakers and practitioners and non-US academics.[34]

US Scholars and USAID/WID Policymakers: What Conclusions Can We Draw?

The unusually close collaboration between the WID Office and scholars between 1977 and 1981 was the product of several factors. USAID was faced with a congressional mandate but had little or no expertise on the issue. The administration appointed as director a skilled and politically resourceful policy entrepreneur who actively solicited academic input, encouraged work by nascent, policy-oriented "think tanks," such as ICRW and the Equity Policy Center, and hired professors to work on her staff, thus bringing to bear a range of academic perspectives at precisely the point when the WID Office was setting its goals and establishing its turf against other bureaucratic players. Arvonne Fraser's contacts with women's groups and her international visibility gave the WID Office the political clout to set priorities and pursue approaches that combined feminist concerns with equity and USAID's focus on efficiency. There was growing academic interest in the field.[35]

This close collaboration slowed and then halted under the Reagan administration. This was partly a result of timing; WID was no longer new, and the agency developed in-house expertise as it gained experience with WID projects and programming. But it was also the product of an ideological shift. The Reagan administration put equality for women low on its agenda and dramatically changed the US approach to development and therefore USAID's role. The turn away from basic human needs to the Washington Consensus coincided with pressure to move away from feminist advocacy toward a more technical, market-oriented approach to poverty reduction. The policy response to the effect of structural adjustment policies on women was "safety nets" rather than empowerment. Many feminist scholars, appalled by the Reagan administration's antifeminism and directly exposed through their research to the negative effects of the administration's policies on poor women in the global South, became harsh critics of rather than contributors to USAID and the WID Office.

In the absence of demand for academic expertise on women in development in USAID, the initiative shifted to the Canadian and European bilaterals and to the international financial institutions. These programs did maintain ties with academic researchers and developed a solid literature on the impact of "gender and development" programming, from how-to manuals to discussions of gender mainstreaming and gender justice. The dynamic interaction between academics and policymakers in the United Kingdom, other British Commonwealth states, and the Nordic countries helped shape the practices and policies of UN agencies, the World Bank, and the regional development banks. This fact suggests that the difference between these agencies and USAID is how motivated policymakers are to seek academic input. In the United States, the political context worked against maintaining connections between scholars and policymakers.

The gap between the WID Office and academics proved difficult to reverse, even when the political context changed with Bill Clinton's election in 1992.[36] The old networks were largely gone, and the ties between land grant universities and USAID that had provided an important institutional framework in the past had now weakened. Lack of demand also meant a decline in academic interest, and the antifeminist "culture wars" of the 1980s took their toll. Today, every US college and university offers courses in international economics and foreign policy, but only a few offer courses in women in development. Students who seek careers in the field expect to work for NGOs, not for the US government, and scholars tend to be critical of USAID's role.

Perhaps WID was also a victim of its success. The radical notion that women should have greater economic power and be citizens in the fullest sense has now become conventional wisdom. Nobel prize–winning economist Amartya Sen makes gender a significant theme in his writing, and women figure importantly in the UN's Millennium Development Goals. But ongoing research suggests that the area of women and development has still not been successfully integrated into development thinking or practice. Gender mainstreaming has proven difficult to achieve and hard to evaluate.[37] Sen's work may offer important critiques of conventional economics, but he does not challenge the assumptions about "economic man" at the core of his discipline. The UN Millennium Development Goals of "environment and equity" include issues of women's health, education, and participation but do not address head-on the "strategic" issues of gender and power.

Just as researching how women are faring under the "new" democracies provides insights into the quality of those democracies, so looking at women and development can suggest ways to assess how well the global economic system is working and what needs to be done to shape it to more closely fit human needs—not just women's, but men's as well.[38] This perspective informs the World Bank's *World Development Report 2012*, which shows that real progress has been made on gender issues, but also that much more needs to be done. The arguments for women's empowerment and for addressing the barriers to women's access to resources are now widely recognized, but there is little sense of urgency. The WID Office has changed its name to the Office of Gender Equality and Women's Empowerment, and under the Obama administration, USAID has incorporated an academic as senior gender advisor.[39] But budget cuts, polarization, and the overall decline in US international influence suggest that the gap between US scholars and policymakers in the area of women and development will remain, because scholar-policymaker cooperation is ultimately a matter of political will.

ACKNOWLEDGMENTS

I thank Irene Tinker, Kathleen Staudt, Katrina Burgess, and Abraham Lowenthal for their comments on earlier drafts of this chapter and appreciate the thoughtful editorial advice of Vestal McIntyre. Any errors that remain are mine.

NOTES

1. See Irene Tinker, "Challenging Wisdom, Changing Policies: The Women in Development Movement," in *Developing Power: How Women Transformed International Development*, ed. Arvonne S. Fraser and Irene Tinker (New York: Feminist Press, 2004), 65–77.

2. Besides the WID Office, the only other notable example of a gender unit at the federal level is the Women's Bureau of the US Department of Labor. Kathleen Staudt, "Gender Politics in Bureaucracy: Theoretical Issues in Comparative Perspective," in *Women, International Development, and Politics: The Bureaucratic Mire*, 2nd ed., ed. Kathleen Staudt (Philadelphia: Temple University Press, 1997), 3–36.

3. Patricia Blair, *Women's Issues in U.S. AID Administration: Implementation of the Percy Amendment* (Washington, DC: Equity Policy Center, 1983), 3.

4. Stephen P. Krasner, "Conclusion: Garbage Cans and Policy Streams: How Academic Research Might Affect Foreign Policy," in *Power, the State, and Sovereignty: Essays on International Relations* (London: Routledge, 2009), 254–74.

5. For a detailed critical analysis of the WID Office, see Kathleen Staudt, *Women, Foreign Assistance, and Advocacy Administration* (New York: Praeger, 1985). On women and development in the United Nations, see Devaki Jain, *Women, Development, and the UN: A Sixty-Year Quest for Equality and Justice* (Bloomington: Indiana University Press, 2005), and several chapters in Fraser and Tinker, *Developing Power*. On the tension between efficiency and equity, see Jane S. Jaquette, "Gender and Justice in Economic Development," in *Persistent Inequalities*, ed. Irene Tinker (New York: Oxford University Press, 1990), 54–70.

6. But it has not been ratified by the United States. See Arvonne Fraser, "Seizing Opportunities: USAID, WID and CEDAW," in Fraser and Tinker, *Developing Power*, 164–75. On the UN Decade for Women, see Anne Winslow, ed., *Women, Politics, and the United Nations* (New York: Praeger, 1995).

7. See Kathleen Cloud, "Hard Minds and Soft Hearts: A University Memoir," and Jane Knowles "Notes from the Middle Border: WID on Campus," in Fraser and Tinker, *Developing Power*, 288–300, 301–11.

8. The WID Office budget was set at $330,000 in 1976 but grew to $1.4 million by 1979–80. Blair, "Women's Issues," 29.

9. This project resulted in the series *Women in the World*, published by the US Bureau of the Census.

10. See Michigan State University, Center for Gender in Global Context, *Gender, Development, and Globalization*, http://gencen.isp.msu.edu/gdg.

11. See, for example, Carolyn Sachs, *The Invisible Farmers: Women in Agricultural Production* (Lanham, MD: Rowman and Littlefield, 1983).

12. Ester Boserup, *Woman's Role in Economic Development* (London: Allen and Unwin, 1970).

13. ICRW was founded by Irene Tinker with Mayra Buvinic and Coralie Turbitt. Tinker, who taught at Howard University, American University, and Berkeley, was also a founder of the Equity Policy Center; her career bridges the gap between scholars and policymakers.

14. Mayra Buvinic and Nadia Youssef, "Women Headed Households: The Ignored Factor in Development Planning," discussed in Fraser, "Seizing Opportunities," 169. For a critique,

see Sylvia Chant, "Dangerous Equations: How Female-Headed Households Became the Poorest of the Poor—Causes, Consequences, and Cautions," in *Feminisms in Development: Contradictions, Contestations, and Challenges*, ed. Andrea Cornwall, Elizabeth Harrison, and Ann Whitehead (London: Zed Books, 2007), 35–48.

15. There was little feedback on WID projects. The exception was scholar Rae Lesser Blumberg, who was hired by USAID's Evaluation Office; the results of her research are reflected in her monograph *Gender, Family, and Economy: The Triple Overlap* (Thousand Oaks, CA: Sage, 1990).

16. For a feminist critique of USAID's population programs, see Jane S. Jaquette and Kathleen Staudt, "Women as 'At-Risk Reproducers': Women and US Population Policy," in *Women, Biology, and Public Policy*, ed. Virginia Sapiro (Beverly Hills, CA: Sage, 1985), 225–68.

17. Amartya Sen, "Gender and Cooperative Conflicts," in Tinker, *Persistent Inequalities*, 123–49.

18. See the study by T. Paul Schultz of Yale University showing that an additional year of a girl's education increased family incomes more than an additional year for boys, contrary to the widespread view that it was more economically advantageous to educate boys. For a review, see T. Paul Schultz, *Why Governments Should Invest More to Educate Girls*, Yale University, September 12, 2001, www.econ.yale.edu/~pschultz/cdp836.pdf.

19. See Naila Kabeer, *Reversed Realities: Hierarchies in Development Thought* (London: Verso, 1994); Kathleen Staudt, *Policy, Politics, and Gender: Women Gaining Ground* (West Hartford, CT: Kumarian Press, 1998); Jane S. Jaquette, "The Family as a Development Issue," in *Women at the Center: Development Issues and Practices for the 1990s*, ed. Gay Young, Vidyamali Samarasinghe, and Ken Kusterer (West Hartford, CT: Kumarian Press, 1993), 45–62.

20. In 1975, Daniel Patrick Moynihan, then US ambassador to the United Nations, wrote an influential essay arguing that postcolonial governments were overly influenced by British Fabian socialism. Daniel Patrick Moynihan, "The United States in Opposition," *Commentary* 59 (1975), www.commentarymagazine.com/article/the-united-states-in-opposition.

21. For a critique of "NGO-ization," see Sonia Alvarez, "Advocating Feminism: The Latin American Feminist NGO 'Boom,'" *International Feminist Journal of Politics* 1 (1999): 181–209. On the role of women's movements in general, see Amrita Basu, *Women's Movements in a Global Era* (Boulder, CO: Westview Press, 2010), and Mary E. Hawkesworth, *Political Worlds of Women: Activism, Advocacy, and Governance in the Twenty-First Century* (Boulder, CO: Westview Press, 2012).

22. Hernando de Soto's *El Otro Sendero: La Revolución Informal* was published in Spanish by his Instituto Democrácia y Libertad (Lima, Peru) in 1986 and 1987; the English version was not published until 2002. Hernando de Soto was an advisor to USAID during the 1980s.

23. But see Milford Bateman, *Confronting Microfinance: Undermining Sustainable Development* (West Hartford, CT: Kumarian Press, 2011).

24. See, for example, Pamela Sparr, *Mortgaging Women's Lives: Feminist Critiques of Structural Adjustment* (London: Zed Press, 1994), and Isabella Bakker, ed., *The Strategic Silence: Gender and Economic Policy* (London: Zed Books, 1994).

25. Diane Elson, "The Male Bias in Macro-economics: The Case of Structural Adjustment," in *The Male Bias in the Development Process*, ed. Diane Elson (Manchester: Manchester University Press, 1995), 164–90.

26. Maxine Molyneux, "Mobilization without Emancipation? Women's Issues, the State, and Revolution in Nicaragua," *Feminist Studies* 11 (1985): 127–54.

27. Caroline Moser, "Gender Planning in the Third World," first circulated in manuscript form then published in a revised form in *World Development* 17 (1989): 1799–1825. On the WID-GAD debate, see Jane S. Jaquette and Kathleen Staudt, "Women, Gender and Development," in *Women and Gender Equity in Development Theory and Practice*, ed. Jane S. Jaquette and Gale Summerfield (Durham, NC: Duke University Press, 2006), 17–63.

28. See, for example, Carol Cohn, *Women and Wars* (London: Polity Press, 2012).

29. This list would include Kathleen Staudt's edited collection *Women, International Development, and Politics: The Bureaucratic Mire* (Philadelphia: Temple University Press, 1998), and her *Policy, Politics, and Gender: Women Gaining Ground* (West Hartford, CT: Kumarian Press, 1998); Martha Nussbaum's *Women and Human Development: The Capabilities Approach* (Cambridge: Cambridge University Press, 2000), based on her work with Amartya Sen; Lourdes Beneria, *Gender, Development, and Globalization: Economics as if People Mattered* (New York: Routledge, 2003); Fraser and Tinker, *Developing Power*; Janet Henshall Momsen, *Gender and Development* (London: Routledge, 2004); and Jaquette and Summerfield, *Women and Gender Equity*.

30. Irene Tinker, *Street Foods: Urban Food and Employment in Developing Countries* (New York: Oxford University Press, 1997); Irene Tinker and Gale Summerfield, eds., *Women's Rights to House and Land: China, Laos, Vietnam* (Boulder, CO: Lynne Rienner, 1999). See also Carmen Diana Deere and Magdalena León, *Empowering Women: Land and Property Rights in Latin America* (Pittsburgh: University of Pittsburgh Press, 2001).

31. See, for example, Carole H. Browner and Carolyn F. Sargent, eds., *Reproduction, Globalization, and the State* (Durham, NC: Duke University Press, 2011).

32. A list would include, but not be limited to, Kabeer, *Reversed Realities*; Anne Marie Goetz, ed., *Getting Institutions Right for Women in Development* (London: Zed Books, 1997); Marilyn Porter and Ellen Judd, eds., *Feminists Doing Development: A Practical Critique* (London: Zed Press, 1999); Oxfam, *Development with Women* (London: Oxfam, 1999); Maxine Molyneux and Shahra Rahzavi, eds., *Gender, Justice, Development, and Rights* (Oxford: Oxford University Press, 2003); Nalini Visvanathan et al., eds., *The Women, Gender, and Development Reader* (London: Zed Books, 2007; rev. ed. 2011); Cornwall, Harrison, and Whitehead, *Feminisms in Development* ; Georgina Waylen, *Engendering Transitions: Women's Mobilization, Institutions, and Gender Outcomes* (Oxford: Oxford University Press, 2007); and Shirin Rai, *The Gender Politics of Development: Essays in Hope and Despair* (London: Zed Books, 2008).

33. World Bank, *World Development Report 2012: Gender Equity and Development* (Washington, DC: World Bank, 2011). The UN Research Institute for Social Development, where Shahra Razavi is research coordinator, published Shahra Razavi and Carol Miller, eds., *Missionaries and Mandarins: Feminist Engagement with Development Institutions*, in 1998.

34. My personal experience exemplifies the trend. I was elected president of AWID in 1991, but I am no longer an active member.

35. See, for example, the 1976 Wellesley Conference on Women and Development, led by scholar Carolyn Elliott, who then developed the Ford Foundation's Women's Studies program in India. Papers from and commentary on the conference are in Wellesley Editorial Committee, *Women and National Development* (Chicago: University of Chicago Press, 1977).

36. The first Clinton administration invited me to head the WID Office, but I was unable to do so for personal reasons. Scholars are recruited to be part of project evaluation teams and often write about their experiences. See, for example, David Hirschmann, "From 'Home Economics' to 'Microfinance': Gender Rhetoric and Bureaucratic Resistance," in Jaquette and Summerfield, *Women and Gender Equity*, 53–70.

37. Rebecca Tiessen, *Everywhere/Nowhere: Gender Mainstreaming in Development Agencies* (Bloomfield, CT: Kumarian Press, 2011).

38. Jane S. Jaquette and Sharon L. Wolchik, "Introduction," in *Women and Democracy in Latin America and Central and Eastern Europe*, ed. Jane S. Jaquette and Sharon L. Wolchik (Baltimore: Johns Hopkins University Press, 1998), 1–24.

39. Caren Grown, economist in residence at American University and recognized scholar in the field, is now a senior gender advisor at USAID. The Gender Equality and Women's Empowerment Office lists its goals as increasing women's access to resources, reducing gender-based violence, and empowering women to claim their rights and control over their own lives. Its website features programs in women in agriculture, gender equality, trafficking, and peace and security (www.usaid.gov/our_work/cross-cutting_programs/wid). It also supports women's leadership, an issue that Hillary Clinton emphasized as secretary of state. This list represents a broader but also less coherent agenda than the economic empowerment goals advanced by the WID Office during the period discussed in this chapter.

CHAPTER FOUR

Dialogue of the Deaf
Scholars, Policymakers, and the Drug War in US Foreign Relations

PETER ANDREAS

The oft-lamented divide between academia and the policy world is nowhere more starkly evident than in the US-led international "war on drugs." Indeed, it is difficult to find an issue in US foreign relations where there is a greater disconnect between scholarship and policy practice.

Why is this? Is there something inherent in the drug issue itself that makes it so impervious to the influence of scholarship and scholars? At least part of the answer is that few other issue areas in US foreign relations in general—and US–Latin American relations in particular—are as highly politicized and subjected to such moralizing discourse. Getting "tough on drugs" and going to "the source" in supply and transit countries in Latin America and elsewhere tends to be more about "sending a signal" and "showing resolve" than about dispassionate analysis of policy effectiveness and efficiency. Symbolic politics tends to trump empirical evidence and research. Indeed, evidence of failure often simply tends to generate calls for further escalation rather than a reevaluation of policy.

In this chapter, I offer some Washington-focused reflections on the scholarly-policy divide in the drug war debate, drawing from more than two decades of observing and occasionally participating in what often seems to be a dialogue of the deaf—or perhaps the problem is not lack of hearing but not liking what one hears.[1] Academics, as I argue below, have little discernible influence on the Washington policy debate on international drug control, except at the margins (in technical aspects of crop substitution schemes, and so on). To the extent that scholars are involved in the foreign policy debate on the drug war—and there are plenty of disciplinary factors inhibiting this—it is primarily as outside critics rather than as trusted advisors. So, to the extent that scholars have a receptive audience, it is more in the broader public sphere than in the halls of Congress or in the drug war bureaucracy. Their policy influence is therefore more indirect and more difficult to measure, though this does not mean it is necessarily unimportant.

Even the Economists Are Marginalized

Even economists, arguably the scholars with the greatest influence in policy circles (as noted in other chapters in this volume), remain on the sidelines in the drug war debate. Most famously, this includes the late Nobel laureate Milton Friedman, whose call for drug legalization was ignored. Indeed, the whole supply-side approach to the "war on drugs"—reducing domestic consumer demand by suppressing supply—flies in the face of the conventional economic wisdom taught in the academy. Moreover, drug enforcement in the Americas generates many of the perverse consequences of overregulation that economists have long warned against, such as rent seeking, corruption, and market distortions. Nevertheless, the US-led international drug control campaign has been strikingly immune to the barrage of anti-statist and free-market arguments by economists in recent decades that have helped propel the rolling back of government regulation, lowering of trade barriers, and loosening of controls on other cross-border market exchange.

In fact, precisely the opposite has happened: drug enforcement budgets and bureaucracies have mushroomed, trade barriers have risen, and market controls have tightened. In short, efforts to suppress the international drug trade may be the most dramatic exception to the triumph of neoliberal economic ideas in recent decades. And nowhere is this more apparent than in Washington and its relations with foreign drug-producing and transit countries. Here, instead of the famed "Washington Consensus" regarding the virtues of economic liberalization, we have an enduring "Washington Consensus" on market criminalization. Not everyone is a "true believer," but policymakers risk political suicide by openly defecting from the drug war. Everyone recognizes that the war on drugs is not going well, but it is politically taboo to advocate a radical change of course—and those that do so tend to wait until they have left government, such as former US secretary of state George Shultz and three former presidents of Latin American countries.[2]

Why are economists so missing from the drug policy debate? Part of the answer is found in how the issue is defined. The international drug trade is largely defined in the policy world as a security and law enforcement issue rather than an economic issue. So, while the International Monetary Fund, World Bank, US Commerce Department, and finance and trade ministries of drug-exporting countries in Latin America and elsewhere are staffed by armies of economists (often trained in the economics departments of US universities), the same is certainly not true of the White House Office of National Drug Control Policy, the State Department's Bureau of International Narcotics and Law Enforcement Affairs, the Department of Homeland Security, the Drug Enforcement Administration (DEA), and the interior ministries of drug-producing nations. A partial exception may be those tasked with fighting money laundering, such as within the US Treasury Department and the financial intelligence units of foreign governments—but even here, accountants and financial investigators are more common than economists. Colombian economist Francisco Thoumi, perhaps the best-known economist working on the Latin American drug trade, was hired as a consultant by the United Nations Office on Drugs and Crime to help produce the *World Drug Report*, but he was so appalled by the research standards and the level of politicization in estimating the size of the global drug trade that he later wrote a damning article about the experience.[3]

Meanwhile, university-based economists, including trade economists and development economists, rarely include illegal drug markets or illegal markets in general as a major area of study—no doubt partly because the data are so inherently bad and unreliable. Prominent exceptions to this disciplinary neglect—most notably Peter Reuter at the University of Maryland, probably the world's leading economist in work focusing on illegal drugs—are often based in public policy schools rather than economics departments. Reuter and others have long emphasized the flawed methods and questionable numbers used in official estimates regarding the size and magnitude of the drug trade, yet the demand for such numbers in the policy world has overridden concerns about their reliability.[4]

It is difficult to find an economist who is a fan of the war on drugs, but it is also difficult to find many economists who actually engage in the drug war debate. So, while one might expect economists to be the harshest critics of the war on drugs, they are the harshest silent critics. Many economists no doubt privately agree with Adam Smith that "a smuggler is a person who, although no doubt blamable for violating the laws of the country, is frequently incapable of violating those of natural justice, and would have been, in every respect, an excellent citizen had not the laws of his country made that a crime which Nature never meant to be so." Interestingly, in Adam Smith's day, smugglers were called "free traders." This is not to suggest that economists are necessarily fans of the Pablo Escobars of the world, but rather that many economists would no doubt view the rise of Pablo Escobar as a particularly perverse and unintended consequence of government intervention in the market.

The Role and Limits of Political Scientists

The lack of drug policy engagement by economists is much less true of political scientists. Yet even here, the international drug war debate is a marginalized issue—as made immediately evident by simply looking through the program of the annual conference of the American Political Science Association, major textbooks in the field, course syllabi, and mainstream disciplinary journals. International and comparative political economy scholars, like their counterparts in economics, focus almost exclusively on the licit rather than the illicit side of the global economy.[5] Most political scientists tend to view drug trafficking and drug enforcement as policing issues and therefore more the domain of criminology. Criminologists, however, mostly focus on domestic crime and crime control issues rather than their international dimensions.

The relatively small number of political scientists doing work in this area tend to aim their writings at a broader interdisciplinary and public audience rather than to advance a particular disciplinary theoretical debate. With few exceptions, they also tend to come from the subfield of comparative politics rather than international relations. Not surprisingly, many of them are Latin America specialists with region- and country-specific expertise, such as on the Andean region or Mexico. Over the years, there have also been useful collaborations between US and Latin American political scientists on drug-related issues published in various edited volumes and on frequent panels at conferences such as meetings of the Latin American Studies Association.[6] In recent years, the Transborder Institute at the University of San Diego and the Mexico Institute at the Woodrow Wilson International Center for Scholars in Washington, DC, have been important vehicles for scholars to add their voice to public discussions about the escalating drug-related violence in Mexico.

These scholars tend to engage the public debate not through regular, direct interaction with policymakers and practitioners in the drug policy world—though many of them do have such connections—but more indirectly, such as through policy articles and reports and in op-eds and other media commentary. Congressional hearings and government briefings on international drug trafficking–related issues at times include academics, but this is fairly infrequent. Outside experts are more often drawn from think tanks, such as the Brookings Institution and RAND Corporation, rather than universities, and occasionally from other Washington-based groups such as the Washington Office on Latin America. This is part of a broader trend in which Washington think tanks have increasingly filled the gap between the academic world and the policy world.

US policymakers and their counterparts in drug-exporting countries are not exactly rushing to university-based scholars for advice on how to run the drug war, and certainly not for advice on rethinking the drug war. Perhaps telling is that it is hard to identify many American political scientists who have taken a leave of absence from their university to work in government on international drug control–related issues (the Massachusetts Institute of Technology's Chappell Lawson, who worked with the US Department of Homeland Security and is a contributor to this volume, is a recent exception). In contrast, it is not difficult to point to many political scientists who have taken time out from their academic careers to work in more traditional "high politics" spheres of US foreign policy. Some prominent recent examples include Stephen Krasner and Condoleezza Rice from Stanford University.

The Council on Foreign Relations has a long-established program of placing junior scholars in policy settings for a year as International Affairs Fellows. But tellingly, these appointments are typically in the National Security Council, in policy planning at the State Department, at the Pentagon, and at Treasury. In contrast, I have not heard of a single International Affairs Fellow placed in the much less prominent and less prestigious area of international drug control or international criminal law enforcement more broadly. And if there are some cases, these are certainly rare exceptions.[7] More International Affairs Fellows are from the political science subfield of international relations than from comparative politics, yet comparative politics scholars with regional expertise are the ones most interested in international drug control–related issues in Latin America and elsewhere.

There is, of course, a fair amount of US government funding for drug-related academic research, such as through the National Institute on Drug Abuse (part of the National Institutes of Health), the National Institute of Justice (the research wing of the Department of Justice), and the Department of Homeland Security. Almost all of this funding is on domestic programs—as is funding in the field of criminology, which receives considerable funds from the US criminal justice system but is not discussed here, given the lack of significant international drug policy focus and presence. Nevertheless, some agencies, such as the US Agency for International Development (USAID), have funded research on crop substitution and alternative development in drug-exporting countries. Also, the Inter-American Foundation, which is funded by the US government but operates quasi-independently, has sponsored important alternative development projects in rural drug-producing areas of countries such as Bolivia.

For the most part, it is fair to say that this government-funded work is preoccupied with the nuts and bolts of policy implementation "on the ground," such as convincing Andean farmers to grow hazelnuts instead of coca, rather than influencing and shaping the broader drug policy debate and determining policy priorities. The latter could include, for example, the balance of spending between supply reduction and demand reduction or deciding whether or not to use the military for antidrug missions—something on which political scientists with expertise on civil-military relations might have something useful to contribute but don't seem to be consulted.

The engagement of scholars with the policy world can take more subtle forms than direct, face-to-face interaction with policy practitioners. This includes the bread-and-butter activity of most scholars: writing books and articles. The library at DEA headquarters, for instance, is full of academic books and other scholarly publications, many of which are critical of US drug policy—though who knows how much of this actually gets read. When I visited this library years ago for my own research, I noticed the book collection includes, for example, Ethan Nadelmann's pioneering study *Cops across Borders*, on the internationalization of US criminal law enforcement—a book that, as one DEA agent told me, impressed him so much that he tried to invite the author to give a talk at headquarters, until his superiors informed him that Nadelmann was persona non grata because he opposed drug prohibition.[8]

Leading international affairs journals with a policy audience, such as *Foreign Affairs* and *Foreign Policy*, also frequently publish articles by publicly engaged scholars, and these at times include articles on the war on drugs. A recent example of an article that has the potential to be highly influential is a *Foreign Affairs* piece by Mark Kleiman on how to stem Mexico's mounting drug violence.[9] Kleiman, a well-known public policy scholar at the University of California, Los Angeles, pragmatically proposes that the United States and Mexico should strategically target the most violent drug-trafficking organizations rather than drug trafficking in general. Given the timing (more than 45,000 drug-related deaths in Mexico between 2006 and 2012 and a Mexican presidential election on the horizon), the prominent venue (*Foreign Affairs*), and concrete policy prescriptions that avoid going anywhere near the "L word" (legalization), it is not difficult to imagine this article resonating and even causing a stir in at least some policy circles—in Mexico City if not in Washington. The tough, hard-nosed policy advice—aggressive "strategic strikes" against the most violent traffickers—masks the radical implications of actually following this strategy, which involves de facto decriminalization of the drug trade for traffickers who avoid violence in business disputes and interactions with government authorities.

Kleiman's article is also distinct from the writings of most academics in that it is entirely prescriptively focused—precisely what policymakers are looking for. For the most part, it is fair to say that political scientists and other academics are better at explanation than at prescription. Explanation can have important prescriptive implications, but the prescriptions are typically not placed front and center in the analysis, let alone framed in terms of a 10-point action plan.

This is certainly the case for academic work on the war on drugs. There is a great deal of scholarship on why the drug war is failing, but very little on how to win it. And, in fact, many scholars argue that it is unwinnable—something policymakers do not want to hear, even if they may agree that it's true. Abandoning the war on drugs and developing a radically different policy approach is a political nonstarter in

Washington. For most scholars, phrases such as "winning the war on drugs," "zero tolerance," and creating a "drug-free America" are not realistic objectives but rather political slogans that they shy away from. Academics offer powerful critiques of the war on drugs, but most tend not to go much beyond the standard mantra that we need to do more to reduce consumer demand—which pretty much all politicians pay lip service to, but this never seems to translate into a major change in budget allocation priorities.

The privileging of prescription over explanation in the policy world is illustrated by my own recent experience. In 2010, the Council on Foreign Relations invited me to write a report about the Mexican drug war and the US-Mexico border. The first step was to put together a one-page proposal outlining my main "argument." I did so, emphasizing how the perverse and unintended consequences of past policy choices had created a "perfect storm" on the border and outlining lessons learned for the future. However, I had completely misunderstood what they meant by "argument"—it was supposed to be an argument about how to fix the problem, not an argument about what created the problem in the first place. That would be merely background. I opted not to pursue this. I did not mind writing a report that concluded with policy recommendations that logically flowed from a detailed diagnosis of the problem, but was I less enthused and confident about writing a report presuming to know how to solve the problem. So in this particular case, I came down squarely on the academic side of the scholarly-policy divide.

Disciplinary Inhibitions

Even if the policy world were more receptive to academic input in the drug war debate, scholars face major disciplinary obstacles that inhibit greater engagement. This is, of course, true of other policy issue areas, not just drug policy.[10] In subtle and not-so-subtle ways, the professional incentives in traditional disciplines (at least outside public policy schools) have a deterrent effect. At best, engaging a broader policy audience is tolerated; at worst, it may count against you, especially if it is perceived as coming at the expense of producing theoretically focused peer-reviewed publications.

This is particularly true for junior scholars trying to build up a tenure-worthy record through peer-reviewed university press books and disciplinary journal articles. Publishing in the *American Political Science Review* or *International Organization* is the ticket to tenure in political science; publishing in *Foreign Affairs* and *Foreign Policy* is not. Publishing in the latter is acceptable if it is not perceived as coming at the expense of publishing in the former. In other words, the policy stuff is "extra" and doesn't "count." Publishing a book in the prestigious comparative politics se-ries of Cambridge University Press—selling perhaps 500 copies mostly to libraries, priced at $80 per book, and receiving favorable reviews in disciplinary journals that no one outside the field has ever heard of—gets you tenure. But publishing a book with a commercial press such as Public Affairs—selling tens of thousands of copies heavily discounted on Amazon as a "trade book" and reviewed in popular outlets such as the *New York Times*—does not.

The rules of the academic game for younger scholars are clear: spend six years keeping your head down and focused on cranking out peer-reviewed academic ar-ticles and books that advance the central theoretical debates in the field. Then, by the time you finally receive tenure, you may be so socialized in the norms of the discipline, including in writing style, and have so internalized and self-identified with the academic rewards system that any initial ambition and passion to reach a broader public audience may have been extinguished or at least greatly deflated.

Moreover, the academic rewards system continues to have a disciplining effect beyond tenure by shaping promotions and professional advancement based on scholarly productivity of a particular sort. In an academic world where mobility after tenure is highly constrained, a tenured professor's ability to get an attractive outside job offer is largely driven by his or her scholarly reputation and publishing record—and the more publications in the "right" journals and with top-tier uni-versity presses the better. These professional trajectory patterns and constraints are not universally true, of course, and there are exceptions one can point to (including many of the contributors to this volume). But they are exceptions that tend to prove the rule. And as discussed below, in some cases young scholars never even make it through the tenure hoops, opting instead to leave academia and enter the policy world full-time.

A Tale of Two Scholars Turned Drug Policy Wonks

Take the cases of Ethan Nadelmann, founder and director of the New York–based Drug Policy Alliance, with offices across the country, and Vanda Felbab-Brown, a Fellow at the Brookings Institution in Washington, DC. Nadelmann operates outside the beltway; Felbab-Brown inside. Nadelmann advocates abandoning the war on drugs and a fundamental rethinking of drug prohibition; Felbab-Brown advocates for much more modest drug policy reforms. Nadelmann is more of an activist pushing for radical policy change from the outside; Felbab-Brown is more of a Washington insider, where the range of "acceptable" policy options is far more constrained. But what the two have in common is that they bailed out early from academia because it simply proved too confining. They powerfully illustrate the difficulty of trying to bridge the academic-policy divide on the drug issue.

Nadelmann took a tenure-track assistant professor position at Princeton University's Woodrow Wilson School of Public and International Affairs in 1987, after receiving his PhD in government at Harvard University (and also earning a JD from Harvard Law School). His PhD thesis was on how US law enforcement agencies, especially the DEA, were increasingly extending their reach across borders. It was the first study of its kind, involving extensive fieldwork in Latin America and elsewhere. The book that came out of the dissertation, *Cops across Borders* (mentioned earlier), remains the most comprehensive and authoritative account ever written. Nadelmann also published a widely cited article on "international prohibition regimes" in the journal *International Organization*, the top international relations journal in the field.[11] Nadelmann, it seemed, had a very bright academic future ahead of him.

But the late 1980s also happened to be a time when the US war on drugs was heating up at home and abroad and generating intense public debate. Nadelmann joined the debate with a big splash, writing a well-timed and highly provocative article in *Foreign Policy*, "U.S. Drug Policy: A Bad Export," boldly calling for an end to the "war on drugs."[12] The buzz around the article generated a cascade of media appearances, including on *Nightline*.[13] Nadelmann emerged as the most visible, articulate, and energetic critic of prohibitionist US drug policies.

The so-called legalization debate gained so much media attention that politicians could no longer simply ignore it and hope it would go away. Congressional leaders even called for hearings on the issue, with Charles Rangel and other House leaders hoping this would discredit any talk of legalization once and for all. Nadelmann was invited to testify, giving Rangel the opportunity to publicly disparage the "Princeton assistant professor." But other than serving as symbolic theater for politicians eager to show they were committed drug warriors, the hearings did little to put an end to discussing drug war alternatives—though many advocates, including Nadelmann, increasingly talked about "harm reduction," "decriminalization," and "drug policy reform" rather than the more sweeping and controversial term "legalization" in the case of hard drugs such as cocaine and heroin.

Meanwhile, Nadelmann's tenure clock at Princeton was ticking, and no doubt some of his senior colleagues were scratching their heads and raising their eyebrows. Nadelmann ended up jumping ship at the eleventh hour before his tenure review process was completed. In 1994, billionaire philanthropist George Soros stepped in and made Nadelmann an offer he could not refuse: generous funding to set up his own drug policy research and advocacy organization. Nadelmann jumped at the opportunity and never looked back (leaving behind a half-written rough draft of a second book manuscript that gathered dust for more than a decade and a half until another assistant professor of political science updated, expanded, and finished it).[14] The organization later became the Drug Policy Alliance, considered the leading US organization promoting alternatives to the war on drugs. *Rolling Stone* even dubbed Nadelmann the "point man" for the nation's drug policy reform efforts.

The case of Felbab-Brown is more recent and less dramatic. She received her PhD in political science from MIT in 2007 and secured a tenure-track job at Georgetown University's School of Foreign Service. Felbab-Brown's dissertation focused on the relationship between counterinsurgency and counternarcotics missions in Colombia, Peru, and Afghanistan. From these detailed case studies she concluded that fighting drugs and fighting insurgents at the same time were incompatible and counterproductive—a conclusion that was not particularly new to drug policy critics but was new to the scholarly literature on conflict commodities and internal wars. The dissertation won an award and generated interest from Cornell University Press, a top-tier academic publisher.

But once in Washington, Felbab-Brown apparently had little patience or interest in engaging theoretical academic debates and playing the tenure-track game. She soon left Georgetown and moved across town to Dupont Circle to become a full-time Fellow at the Brookings Institution, where she immediately thrived by creating her own policy niche. Brookings had not had anyone permanent working on international drug trafficking issues since Paul Stares left in the mid-1990s.

Rather than being a struggling tenure-seeking assistant professor going through the grind of the long peer-review process for scholarly articles and books, Felbab-Brown was now publishing frequent policy reports on timely and important topics such as the escalating drug violence in Mexico, regularly being called on to testify before Congress on issues such as the Merida Initiative, participating in government briefings, hobnobbing in Washington policy circles, and writing op-eds and making media appearances. She was even given a publicity assistant to send out regular emails drawing attention to her latest op-ed, policy report, or testimony. No longer worried about the tenure implications, Felbab-Brown published her book in-house, with Brookings Press—and far sooner and with greater visibility in the policy world than would have been the case with Cornell University Press.[15]

I am certainly not suggesting that Nadelmann and Felbab-Brown are typical cases. Far from it—and most stories don't end nearly so well. But they each powerfully illustrate the formidable challenge of bridging the academic-policy divide in this policy realm. And, indeed, in both cases they ended up giving up on the bridge-building project altogether and formally left academia, though they maintain connections to the academic world.

Final Thoughts

I conclude by recounting a few of my own experiences dealing with the political theater that often characterizes the drug war debate in Washington, where the players are keenly aware of their audience and rarely deviate in public from carefully prepared scripts. Some time ago I spent a year at the Brookings Institution, and while there I was invited to present congressional testimony before a House Judiciary Committee panel on drug trafficking and global organized crime. The chairman of the committee began the hearings with a somber opening statement about the alarming spread of transnational criminal organizations, with their long tentacles reaching deep into America and poisoning the nation's youth with drugs. The chairman's aide, sitting nearby, interrupted him after the first few sentences, telling him that he didn't have to read the whole statement out loud because no cameras from the media were present. Everyone in the room heard this comment and burst out laughing, panelists and committee members alike. We all understood that it was a show, that we were all part of a performance, playing our designated roles. CNN had not shown up that day, but the show went on as scheduled, even if with a bit less fanfare.

My point in recounting this story is to underscore the ever-present role of symbolic politics and the theatrical characteristics of the drug war debate. It is extremely difficult to have a reasonable and sensible dialogue in such circumstances, with politicians always making sure to sound sufficiently tough on drugs and not to say anything that may come across as too lenient. This lends itself to hyperbolic declarations rather than rational conversations. Having said that, I should also note that I have also been at a number of closed-door and off-the-record meetings in Washington, typically with midlevel policy practitioners, where the participants do not always behave as if they are on stage, performing for an audience. And this opens up the possibility for real discussion, real dialogue, and real debate, because they don't worry about losing their jobs or the next election. And some of them seem to genuinely value having outside academics come in and say things that they may at least partly agree with but are reluctant to openly say themselves. In the end, though, the drug war is ultimately driven much more by the onstage theatrics than by any frank discussions and evaluations that may take place backstage.

So it is worth returning to the main question asked of me by the volume's editors: To what extent have academics overcome the scholarly-practitioner divide in the realm of the US-led international war on drugs? The answer, it seems, is strikingly little. To the extent that it has happened, it is subtle, indirect, and extremely difficult to measure. And there appears to be little prospect that this will greatly change any time soon. More realistically, university-based scholars who are inclined to engage the policy world in this particular issue area—overcoming or ignoring disciplinary inhibitions—are more likely to influence the broader public debate than specific policy decisions. This role should not be discounted or overlooked, but its policy impact is also more indirect and difficult to trace and evaluate.

It may nevertheless be worth contemplating, even if briefly, what the policy contribution of scholars *could be* if the international drug war debate in Washington were to somehow become much more open and less politically constrained. For instance, economists and public policy scholars could greatly inform policy decisions through a detailed and sophisticated cost-benefit analysis—a type of analysis that is otherwise popular in policy circles—of all aspects of the war on drugs. Some of this work, in fact, has already been done. Peter Reuter, for example, has shown that due to the pricing structure of the international drug market, it is far less cost-effective to attack supply at the point of production abroad than at the point of consumption at home. Similarly, game theorists would have much to offer in analyzing the strategic interaction between drug enforcement and drug-trafficking organizations—and would have surely predicted that President Calderón's drug war offensive in Mexico would spark much greater competition and violence between traffickers rather than reduce and tame Mexican drug trafficking.

Political scientists with decades of experience studying civil-military relations in Latin America and elsewhere would no doubt have some useful insights for the policy community regarding the implications and longer-term consequences of turning soldiers into cops through the militarization of the drug war—which is most advanced in the case of Mexico. Scholars working in comparative politics and comparative public policy could more systematically compare different policy approaches to drug control across different times and places—most obviously, drawing policy lessons from the European experience for the United States. Again, a great deal of work has already been done, though it can be updated and further developed.[16]

Historians also potentially have much to offer the policy world here, though they tend to understate the policy relevance and implications of their work. Most obviously, more attention to America's failed experiment in alcohol prohibition in the 1920s might offer powerful lessons and insights for today's war on drugs. In a policy environment chronically afflicted by historical amnesia, more historical perspective on drugs and drug control is desperately needed.[17] Last but not least, ethnographic research can make an enormously valuable contribution by helping policymakers make better sense of the on-the-ground microdynamics of communities enmeshed in various stages of the international drug trade, from peasant villages in Bolivia to favelas in Rio, Mexican border towns, and street-level dealing in America.[18] This, in turn, has the potential to generate more nuanced and customized policy interventions at the community level.

ACKNOWLEDGMENTS

I thank James McGuire, Abraham Lowenthal, and Mariano Bertucci for their comments on an earlier version of this chapter.

NOTES

1. Before going to graduate school in the early 1990s and starting an academic career, I worked for several years in Washington, DC, on international drug policy–related issues, including coauthoring a congressional report, presenting congressional testimony, writing articles for policy journals and magazines, and collaborating on a book, *Drug War Politics: The Price of Denial.* My PhD dissertation was on the politics of border control (later published as the book *Border Games: Policing the U.S.-Mexico Divide*). During my dissertation research I also spent a year in Washington as a research fellow at the Brookings Institution, and I have continued to travel to Washington for policy discussions related to transnational crime, border security, and international crime control.

2. Former presidents Fernando Henrique Cardoso of Brazil, Ernesto Zedillo of Mexico, and César Gaviria of Colombia signed the July 2010 "Vienna Declaration" calling for the decriminalization of drug use and science-based policy reforms.

3. Francisco E. Thoumi, "The Numbers Game: Let's All Guess the Size of the Illegal Drug Industry!" *Journal of Drug Issues* 1 (2005): 185–200.

4. See Peter Reuter, "The Mismeasurement of Illegal Drug Markets: The Implications of Its Irrelevance," in *Exploring the Underground Economy*, ed. Susan Pozo (Kalamazoo, MI: Upjohn Institute, 1996). For a more general discussion, see Peter Andreas and Kelly M. Greenhill, *Sex, Drugs, and Body Counts: The Politics of Numbers in Global Crime and Conflict* (Ithaca, NY: Cornell University Press, 2010).

5. There are exceptions. See, for example, H. Richard Friman, ed., *Crime and the Global Political Economy* (Boulder, CO: Lynne Rienner, 2009).

6. See, for example, Peter H. Smith, ed., *Drug Policy in the Americas* (Boulder, CO: Westview Press, 1992); Bruce Bagley and William O. Walker, eds., *Drug Trafficking in the Americas* (Miami: University of Miami North-South Center, 1994); John Bailey and Jorge Chabat, eds., *Transnational Crime and Public Security: Challenges to Mexico and the United States* (La Jolla, CA: Center for U.S.-Mexican Studies, 2002).

7. I would have been one of the exceptions but very reluctantly ended up declining the fellowship offer (after several years' delay) because I was on a short tenure clock and was worried about getting derailed. Based on my own experience, my advice to the fellowship program would be to consider also offering such opportunities to newly tenured faculty who may feel they now have more freedom and flexibility to devote a full year to immersion in the policy practitioner world.

8. Ethan A. Nadelmann, *Cops across Borders: The Internationalization of U.S. Criminal Law Enforcement* (University Park, Penn State University Press, 1993).

9. Mark Kleiman, "Surgical Strikes in the Drug Wars," *Foreign Affairs* 90 (Sept.–Oct. 2011): 89–101.

10. See especially Lawrence M. Mead, "Scholasticism in Political Science," *Perspectives on Politics* 8 (June 2010): 453–64, and Stephen M. Walt, "The Relationship between Theory and Policy in International Relations," *Annual Review of Political Science* 8 (June 2005): 27. Both Mead and Walt lament what they see as a growing disconnect between academia and the policy world.

11. Ethan A. Nadelmann, "Global Prohibition Regimes: The Evolution of Norms in International Society," *International Organization* 44 (Autumn 1990): 479–526.

12. Ethan Nadelmann, "U.S. Drug Policy: A Bad Export," *Foreign Policy*, Spring 1988, 83–108.

13. I was an editorial assistant at *Foreign Policy* at the time and was therefore keenly aware of how much attention the article was getting.

14. Peter Andreas and Ethan Nadelmann, *Policing the Globe: Criminalization and Crime Control in International Relations* (Oxford: Oxford University Press, 2006).

15. Vanda Felbab-Brown, *Shooting Up: Counterinsurgency and the War on Drugs* (Washington, DC: Brookings Institution Press, 2010).

16. See, for instance, Robert McCoun and Peter Reuter, *Drug War Heresies: Learning from Other Vices, Times, and Places* (Cambridge: Cambridge University Press, 2001). This may be the single best book on the subject, but a new and updated edition is very much needed.

17. For a particularly useful and accessible historical introduction, see David T. Courtwright, *Forces of Habit: Drugs and the Making of the Modern World* (Cambridge, MA: Harvard University Press, 2001).

18. See, for instance, Enrique Desmond Arias, *Drugs and Democracy in Rio de Janeiro: Trafficking, Social Networks, and Public Security* (Chapel Hill: University of North Carolina Press, 2006), and Patricia A. Adler, *Wheeling and Dealing: An Ethnography of an Upper-Level Drug Dealing and Smuggling Community* (New York: Columbia University Press, 1987).

PART THREE

DEVELOPING POLICY OPTIONS

CHAPTER FIVE

"Speaking Truth to Power" in Mexico
Gaps, Bridges, and Trampolines

BLANCA HEREDIA

Most contemporary work on the relationship between the social sciences and public policy focuses on the experience of the United States and therefore tends to be strongly shaped by the kinds of issues encountered in the US context. The much discussed "gap" between scholarly research and policymaking, for example, has a lot to do with the high level of institutional autonomy of academia vis-à-vis policy and politics in the United States. In Mexico, where such autonomy is weaker and where, partly as a result, the academic development of the social sciences is less advanced, the problems posed by the relationship between academia and policy are similar to those of the United States in some respects but very different in others. As in the United States, in Mexico there are many obstacles impeding mutually fruitful communication between social science scholars and practitioners. In the United States, however, much of the disconnect arises from the reciprocal institutional insularity of scholars and practitioners, while in Mexico it arises from the relative dearth of conceptual, analytical, and empirical knowledge available to policymakers in the design of policy options and from the numerous political obstacles that scholars face in seeking to shape policy.

In this chapter, based on my personal experience as an academic at two Mexican higher education institutions ITAM and CIDE (described below), as a senior manager at CIDE and the Organization for Economic Cooperation and Development (OECD), and as deputy undersecretary for political development in Mexico's Ministry of Interior, I address some of the problems in the relationship between academia and policy in the social sciences—and political science in particular—in the Mexican context. I have two main aims: to highlight the importance of the availability of relevant and useful knowledge in strengthening the ability of academic research to aid in designing policy, and to emphasize the utility of innovative forms of research dissemination that act as trampolines, helping scholars to overcome political obstacles and contribute to policies promoting more effective democracy, as well as greater prosperity and justice.

Academia and Policy: Gaps and Bridges

Stephen Krasner and others provide useful frameworks to think about the relationship between academia and the policy world in Mexico.[1] Especially relevant is Krasner's use of John Kingdon's notion of problems, policy alternatives, and politics as separate streams that only rarely coalesce thanks to the opening up of windows of opportunity.[2] Based in part on his experience as a senior academic and a senior policymaker in the US State Department and National Security Council, Krasner argues that what determines the ability of academic scholarship to influence policy lies essentially beyond the control of scholars and academic institutions, and thus it makes little sense to try to change anything in how academic research is performed in an attempt to strengthen its ability to influence policy.

My experience of scholar-practitioner relations in Mexico supports Krasner's contention that the policy impact of scholarship is mostly determined, not by what scholars do, but by the preferences and capabilities of policymakers and politicians, by opportunity, and by chance. But based on my experience, as well as on available work on the subject,[3] I believe that the potential and actual impact of social science research on policy in Mexico is also conditioned by two aspects of academic work: the specific type of scholarly research available and the manner in which it is disseminated.

Scholarship Type Matters

The importance of the type of knowledge produced by academic researchers in accounting for the variable ability of scholarship to influence policy has received considerable attention in the literature on scholar-practitioner relations, in political science in particular and in the social sciences more generally. Many authors have argued that some of the main forces limiting the ability of scholars to shape policy are the increasing focus in political science on theory and methods, especially formal modeling; the lack of incentives for policy-relevant work; and the emphasis on large statistical studies at the expense of the detailed and in-depth case studies most policymakers find more useful.[4]

While a small portion of social science research in Mexico exhibits these features of academic self-insulation, the larger problem is the dearth of what Alexander George calls "usable knowledge": description, analysis, and middle-range theorizing "that [are] closer to the types and forms of knowledge needed in policymaking."[5] In Mexico, this kind of knowledge tends to be especially scarce in research areas that are potentially relevant to policy.

Until the mid-1990s, the prevalent scholarly work in Mexican social sciences—with the exception of research on elections and in some areas of economics—tended to be highly theoretical, largely speculative, and, for the most part, lacking in a solid empirical base.[6] This type of work was neither particularly relevant nor especially useful for improving the quality of public policy. At the time, social science work in Mexican academia was underdeveloped largely due to the authoritarian regime of the Institutional Revolutionary Party, or PRI,[7] under which, for more than 60 years, relations between academia and government had little to do with the academic quality of scholarly research. Only during the 1980s and 1990s did the country begin to develop standards and incentives for the promotion of more rigorous academic work, and reliable empirical data available for research are still extremely scarce.[8]

The amount of rigorous scholarly work potentially useful for policy purposes is now much larger, thanks to the growing availability of hard data for a number of policy-relevant issues and the considerable volume and high quality of empirically based research performed at academic institutions such as Instituto Tecnológico Autónomo de México (ITAM) and Centro de Investigación y Docencia Económicas (CIDE). Despite this significant progress, the volume, quality, and accessibility of "usable knowledge" remains slim in many areas. Particularly noteworthy is the dearth of good descriptions of major institutions and actors and of policymaking processes on issues as central as justice, security, and education.

Research Dissemination: The Missing Link?

Despite the obvious importance of research dissemination in strengthening the ability of scholars to influence policy, the process of communicating results to policymakers has received less attention than one would expect in the literature on scholar-practitioner relations in political science. Available work tends to concentrate on lists of practical suggestions for scholars to increase their ability to influence policy, including the following: producing shorter and clearer versions of their research (one-pagers); making more intensive use of public relations departments in their universities; networking with policymakers; publishing op-eds and doing interviews on television or radio; and remembering that in influencing policy, timing and timeliness are crucial.[9] While, everywhere, practical tips of this sort are crucial for bolstering scholars' capacity to shape policy, they are insufficient in countries such as Mexico, where the basic communication and dissemination infrastructures between scholars and practitioners are either lacking or little developed. (These would include university web pages with complete and up-to-date information on faculty's publications, not to mention online information from the dense network of think tanks and professional journalism.)

Significantly, this approach to research dissemination disregards the need for proactive, broad, and creative strategies as avenues to circumvent strong political resistance to the introduction of certain issues and options to the policy agenda. In Mexico—but certainly not Mexico alone—key problems, as well as potentially useful instruments to address them, fail to enter the policy agenda due to major political obstacles, such as the capture of the policymaking process by concentrated pro–status quo interests and institutional arrangements that allow high levels of impunity among politicians and government officials. In this context, new forms of research dissemination that can reach a broader segment of the public may provide the most effective route to foster needed policy reform and action.

"Usable Knowledge" (or Lack Thereof) in Action

To illustrate the importance of "usable knowledge" in determining scholarship's ability to influence policy once an opportunity opens up, I describe three episodes in which the availability of such knowledge was important as part of the conditions for formulating policy options and ultimately bringing about results.

Civil Society Organizations

In 2009, a small window of opportunity opened up at the Ministry of Interior (Gobernación) for advancing charitable and advocacy Civil Society Organizations (CSOs) when Minister Gómez Mont agreed to include the strengthening of these organizations as part of the ministry's proposals for President Calderón's strategic plan for 2010. Though the CSO component had a very low priority on the president's agenda, this opening seemed worth pursuing.

The most important obstacles for the development of a clear set of policy actions aimed at strengthening CSOs were political. First, the president showed an almost complete lack of interest in the issue—in my judgment, at least partly due to his misgivings about CSOs in general and their role in the highly contested 2006 presidential elections in particular. Second, the federal government had not formulated a consistent policy on CSOs, due to a dispersion of authority and lack of effective coordination mechanisms. And third, there was a decades-long legacy of corporatist and clientelistic relations between CSOs and government.

Also, there was minimal consensus around what the main problems in the CSO field were and no robust knowledge base to help identify these problems and inform policy options for strengthening the sector. This was due to two main factors. First, the field was relatively new as an academic endeavor in Mexico—even more so than in developed countries—and there were fierce personal and institutional rivalries among the few scholars, experts, and advocacy groups working in the area. Second, basic data on the third sector in Mexico were extremely scarce: no reliable data on the total number of CSOs or on the sector's evolution over time; no consistent information on government funding; little in the way of commonly accepted classifications for different types of CSOs; and few minimally comprehensive descriptions—let alone analyses—of the multiple laws and regulations governing their operation. Thanks to the heroic efforts of a small number of scholars in recent years—mostly at ITAM, CEMEFI (Centro Mexicano para la Filantropía), Universidad Veracruzana, and El Colegio Mexiquense—we now have some useful data on employment in the third sector, on voluntary giving, and on private funding. These data are valuable but far from sufficient to develop the kind of "usable knowledge" that could give public visibility to the sector's huge challenges or aid in formulating policy options and instruments to promote its development. So, while the opportunity was missed in 2009, the experience spurred important research that might enable scholars to affect policy the next time such an opportunity arises.

Political Reform

After the intermediate federal elections of 2009, which entailed heavy losses for his party, the PAN, President Calderón—urged by Minister Gómez Mont, among others—announced 10 key reform priorities for the second part of his term. The Gobernación team completed the political reform initiative in a few months of intense technical work and political negotiations, and the president presented it to Congress in December 2009.

As the most comprehensive initiative since the mid-1990s, it got a lot of media attention, spurred much political and academic debate, elicited equally broad political reform legislative initiatives from the two major opposition parties, the PRI and PRD, but ultimately did not receive congressional approval. The most important reason for this was internal divisions within the PRI on political reform, which led the party to present two basically incompatible initiatives, one in the Senate and one in the Chamber of Deputies. This made it impossible for the government and the PAN to negotiate the reform with that party. The PRI's initiative in the Senate was led by Senator Beltrones and sought to strengthen Congress relative to the executive. The initiative in the Chamber of Deputies was backed by Governor Peña Nieto, and its overall aim was to reconcentrate power in the executive branch. Initial government negotiations with the main opposition party involved only PRI senators. Given that their proposal overlapped to some extent with the president's initiative, agreement, though difficult, appeared possible during the early stages of the negotiation. When the PRI deputies presented their own completely different initiative for political reform in the lower chamber, however, negotiations with the government stalled and ultimately broke down.

The importance awarded to political reform was the result of political factors beyond the influence of scholars: the president's strong and long-standing commitment to political reform and Minister Gómez Mont's willingness to make reform his ministry's top priority during the last months of 2009 and the beginning of 2010. This generated an important opening for initiating political reform. To take maximum advantage of it, the depth and breadth of the scholarly knowledge and data resources available to us was critical. That knowledge base—in particular, its most technical aspects having to do with constitutional engineering issues and specific electoral formulas and designs—was absolutely necessary for framing the issues, formulating novel alternatives, and using empirical evidence to assess the costs and benefits of different options in order to persuade potential allies, respond to critics, and negotiate with counterparts.

The stock of "usable knowledge"—historical, theoretical, and empirical—upon which we academics could draw to formulate, communicate, and negotiate the constitutional initiative on political reform was much larger than that available for the attempt to get government to act in favor of the strengthening of CSOs. This stock included the formidable amount of international scholarly work on political institutional design; a strong local supply of data and detailed empirical research on the evolution, structure, and operation of Mexican political institutions; and a significant community of scholars and analysts with solid professional training in political science and other relevant disciplines.

Some professional political scientists with ample academic and policy experience took part in the team in charge of political reform and were instrumental in making that research a central input of the policy process. Of particular importance in this regard was Alejandro Poiré, whose extensive technical knowledge of the issues, based on his academic work as well as his experience at the Federal Electoral Institute and his position as part of the president's inner circle, made him a pivot of the whole political reform process.

Administrative Reform: The Case of Public Personnel Systems

During the 1990s and the early twenty-first century, a strong push for so-called second-generation reforms in general and for New Public Management (NPM) came from international financial institutions and many highly influential academics in the United States, Canada, and Europe (the United Kingdom in particular). This propelled the topic of public sector modernization to the forefront of the policy agenda in several developing nations, including Mexico.

In Mexico as in other countries, NPM guided reform efforts in budgeting and also opened up space and informed experimentation in procurement and public investment. In the case of government personnel, however, the influence of NPM was less intense, given the lack of a professional civil service and the fact that most experts on public and policy administration in Mexico were not particularly receptive to the ideas of NPM. These two factors also help explain why Mexico opted for a more classical solution: the introduction of a professional civil service in the central bureaucracy of the federal government.

The first effort to create a civil service system in the federal bureaucracy occurred during the second half of the Zedillo administration (1994–2000) but proved unsuccessful. In 2000, the PRI lost the presidential election for the first time in its history, and Vicente Fox became the first PAN president. In 2003, the law creating the Professional Civil Service was passed in Congress. The system introduced by that law included a few elements drawn from NPM—performance evaluations and external contestants for filling all civil service posts—but otherwise drew mainly from traditional and well-established "Weberian" merit-based civil service models.

The Office for Government Innovation within the presidency designed the Professional Civil Service that was ultimately approved and implemented. The design process included direct input from a small group of academics and was also shaped by the need to reconcile three different legislative initiatives, one from each of the three major parties. At various points, the public officials in charge of the project sought feedback from a broader group of scholars. José Luis Méndez, a professor from El Colegio de Mexico who worked in government at that time, was the academic most closely involved in the creation of the Professional Civil Service and provided the main link for other academics to engage in the process. The recent creation of a civil service at the Federal Electoral Institute (initiated by Mauricio Merino, a scholar who was then a member of the institute's board) served as an important inspiration to Méndez and other experts who participated in establishing the new system.

The Secretaría de la Función Pública carried out the implementation of the Professional Civil Service. According to a recent paper by Méndez, the many deficiencies of implementation explain the numerous problems in the operation of the new system and its limited success as an instrument for the effective professionalization of government personnel.[10]

Informal conversations with government officials and my own experience at Gobernación suggest that the Professional Civil Service introduced during the Fox administration had serious problems. The normal rigidities such a system imposes have not been accompanied by the gains that a well-functioning civil service produces—that is, depoliticization of the bureaucracy, higher levels of professionalization, and greater policy stability. As a result, the system has produced mostly increased costs, both budgetary and administrative.

The disappointing results of the introduction of the merit-based Professional Civil Service so far are largely due to two main factors. The first is the deeply entrenched dynamics associated with pervasive patronage within the Mexican bureaucracy. The second is the coincidence among the introduction of the new civil service system, the unraveling of the old *camarilla* system, which before the 2000 change in government used to ensure discipline within the bureaucracy, and the introduction of new layers of regulations aimed at increasing transparency and accountability—whose combined impact has, so far at least, produced very high levels of fragmentation and disruption within the Mexican bureaucracy.[11]

The significant problems Mexico has experienced in the area of civil service reform are hardly unique. According to both the available literature and evaluations performed within international financial institutions, public sector reform has proved to be extraordinarily difficult in many developed as well as developing countries.[12] The difficulties experienced by civil service reform are largely political and institutional, but some appear to be rooted in the nature of the knowledge guiding the reform, especially "one size fits all" approaches and the scant use of good diagnostics based on solid empirical work. The Independent Evaluation Group's evaluation of the World Bank's work in this area, for instance, concludes that "the frequent failures of CSA—civil service administration—reform, despite continued acknowledgment of its importance, seem to reflect the lack of a coherent strategy (with isolated exceptions) and of clear diagnostic tools to address CSA issues."[13]

Research Dissemination and Political Resistance

Until very recently, the standard practices, instruments, and infrastructure for disseminating research that exist in developed countries were practically nonexistent in Mexico. Despite important progress since the late 1990s, most universities, including the largest public ones, still lack web pages with easily accessible, up-to-date information about the research conducted by their faculty. The bulk of the academic publications produced in Mexico continue to be available only in print. The number of think tanks, though larger than in the recent past, remains small, nongovernmental organizations (NGOs) with research capacities are extremely few, and investigative journalism is still in its infancy.

The Power of Dissemination: CIDE's Experience

During the 1990s, the situation in terms of research dissemination was worse still. At the time, I was provost at CIDE and, with the rest of the senior management, decided to design and launch an ambitious communication and dissemination strategy. This was both an effort to influence the country's public and policy agenda in response to the poor research situation and a signal of CIDE's renaissance after the deep institutional crisis it had experienced in the mid to late 1980s. The strategy we pursued was, at the time, quite innovative among academic institutions; it included systematic efforts to draw media attention to the work being done by CIDE and to build bridges with relevant actors in the political and policy arenas.

The combination of high-quality, unusually creative, policy-relevant academic research and an ambitious dissemination strategy allowed CIDE to draw public attention to several issues with policy import and, in so doing, helped move them from "conditions" to recognized policy problems. Particularly relevant examples of research that accomplished this movement include the original work of John Scott on the strongly regressive nature of social spending;[14] Juan Pablo Guerrero's equally original research on the budget, and particularly on the salaries of high-ranking government officials;[15] and the pathbreaking data-generation initiatives in the field of legal studies conducted by Ana Laura Magaloni and Marcelo Bergman.[16]

Legal studies at CIDE especially exemplify the value of combining rigorous and highly innovative policy-relevant scholarship with a proactive dissemination strategy. The core mission of the Department of Legal Studies from its foundation in 2001 has been to produce solid empirical research on the workings of Mexico's legal institutions. At a time when virtually no work of that kind was being produced, the department's small and mostly young faculty carried out two initial projects—one on Juicio Ejecutivo Mercantil and another on prison inmates—which generated the first sets of empirical data on the operation of the legal system ever produced in the country. The quality of the data, the severity of the problems they revealed in the operation of the judicial system, and a series of dissemination efforts in the media combined to draw the country's attention to this area.

Over time, the research carried out by CIDE's law faculty helped place Mexico's rule-of-law problems on the public agenda and aided in mobilizing support from NGOs, public intellectuals, politicians, public officials, and policy entrepreneurs. The law faculty also provided valuable research inputs for a variety of initiatives, including reform of the bankruptcy and recuperation-of-assets procedures and constitutional reform for the shift to an oral system.

An interesting episode, and the most recent spinoff of this story, was the decision of Roberto Hernandez and Layda Negrete—members of the original legal studies team at CIDE and currently PhD students at Berkeley—to produce two films: *El Túnel* and, most recently, the exceptional documentary *Presunto Culpable*.[17] Their decision to use a camera to publicize the huge deficiencies of Mexico's criminal justice system was originally motivated by frustration. What the data generated by research at legal studies revealed was appalling, terrible, almost incredible, and yet despite CIDE's best dissemination efforts, the research was not having the kind of impact we all desired and expected. So Hernandez and Negrete decided to learn a new trade—filmmaking—and present what they had learned about the workings of our judicial system in ways that could reach, touch, and move a much broader public and thereby generate societal demand for change.

Presunto Culpable has drawn extraordinary media attention and large audiences, demonstrating the exceptional quality of the film. And it suggests that novel forms of research dissemination may provide a powerful means through which to place especially novel and/or thorny policy issues on the public agenda and mobilize broad societal support capable of breaking resistance to effective policy change.[18]

This example suggests that in addition to strategies aimed at power holders, academics interested in strengthening the ability of research to promote policy and institutional change should pay greater attention to novel dissemination strategies and media vehicles oriented specifically toward citizens. This emphasis might prove especially valuable in countries like Mexico, where many of the most urgent reforms are trapped within institutional and policy spaces where resistance to change is especially strong.

PISA and Education Quality in Mexico: Hard Data and Dissemination

The Program for International Student Assessment (PISA), developed by the OECD and applied since 2000, is the most robust instrument to measure student achievement in comparative international terms. Mexico's results in early editions of the text were pretty abysmal and contributed to the adoption of a few important policy reforms, including establishment of the national test, ENLACE, and changes in curriculum for middle schools.

Policy reform proved slow and student improvements virtually nonexistent, and by 2007 it became clear that more awareness and greater mobilization of key constituencies were needed if PISA was to correct Mexico's severe deficits in education quality. A broader and more proactive dissemination and awareness-raising strategy around PISA was necessary to make it worthwhile for politicians, government officials, activists, and experts to invest time and energy in addressing the country's education problems.

The OECD's center in Mexico designed and implemented a broad media and public relations campaign aimed at both preparing the ground and maximizing the impact of the publication of the 2006 PISA results in December 2007. Backed by the robustness of PISA, along with the prestige and influence of the OECD, the campaign managed to involve the main television networks, key academic institutions (TEC de Monterrey in particular), business organizations, several NGOs, and one new think tank, Mexicanos Primero, in significantly raising public awareness about Mexico's very serious education problems. In addition, the campaign contributed to President Calderón's decision to establish a PISA target for Mexico for 2012.

In making these achievements possible, the exceptional quality of the research on which PISA was based and the institutional weight of the OECD were both crucial. Without a proactive dissemination strategy, however, the policy impact of PISA would have percolated to the policy world at a slower pace and remained mostly within the small circle of policymakers and experts involved in education. Investments in an aggressive communication strategy multiplied the study's impact.

Conclusions

Krasner argues that the links between scholarly work and policymaking are haphazard and that variables beyond the control of academia, such as policymakers' and politicians' preferences and capabilities, are central in determining the timing and extent of the policy impact of academic work. His argument fits the Mexican case quite well. However, for research to be able to influence policy once an opportunity opens up, or for scholarship itself to help turn a policy condition into a policy problem, the research in question must have been produced and must somehow be accessible to its potential policy users. The point is obvious but worth mentioning because, in the case of Mexico, windows of opportunity can often be missed precisely because the required research does not exist or is so well guarded that it is, for all intents and purposes, inaccessible.

The availability of "usable knowledge" and how it is disseminated are crucial in determining the capacity of scholarly work to influence policy in Mexico. This is due to, first, the relative scarcity of both hard data and creative and technically rigorous research in many areas of the social sciences and, second, the deeply entrenched resistance to policy change in many crucial areas of public policy. These conditions clearly impose major limitations on the ability of academic work to aid in the design and implementation of better policy. These same conditions, however—perhaps somewhat paradoxically—offer unique opportunities for reconciling rigor, relevance, and impact and thus bolstering the quality of research and policy.

One particularly noteworthy example of the potentially huge synergies between rigor and relevance can be found in Progresa/Oportunidades. As analyzed by Nora Lustig in chapter 6 of this volume, Progresa/Oportunidades is the first cash transfer program for fighting poverty and the most effective to date in reducing need in Mexico, as well as in many other developing countries. Santiago Levy's work in developing Progresa/Oportunidades is exemplary in the collection and systematization of hard data on income and wealth distribution in Mexico and in the melding of conceptual and analytical elements drawn from a variety of disciplinary sources and subfields of economics. This synthesis made the design of the program possible and proved crucial in important advances in the academic study of poverty and inequality.

At times, the peculiarly difficult conditions keeping research from shaping policy can lead scholars to break new ground. An example of this is the highly original dissemination work and strategies deployed by researchers in CIDE's legal studies department to publicize their research findings. By appealing directly to a broader public, this work has proved pivotal in raising awareness about the severity of the Mexican justice system's problems and, in so doing, has greatly aided in placing the rule of law firmly on the policy agenda—despite the formidable resistance that the issue elicits among some of the most powerful actors in Mexican politics.

To stimulate the production of "usable knowledge" that is both rigorous and relevant, academic institutions need to find ways to reconcile their many goals. This involves changes in the internal rules through which academics are evaluated, compensated, and promoted, but also requires efforts to influence the broader policy regime (i.e., Sistema Nacional de Investigadores, public funding for research, and sabbaticals) so as to make attainment of the highest scholarly standards compatible with the promotion of more applied and empirically based work.

In addition to promoting rigorous and relevant academic research, Mexican scholars and institutions should devote more resources and systematic attention to the development of broader and more effective communication and dissemination strategies. Key tasks range from the most basic, such as making sure their web pages present the research done by their faculties, to more ambitious initiatives: the electronic dissemination of publications, systematic efforts to publicize important research in the media, and the use of novel vehicles to disseminate scholarly production to the wider public beyond policy elites. This can be done in-house, but it is best pursued in association with professional partners outside academia.

Knowledge is a resource fundamental to consolidating Mexico's democracy and allowing the country to realize its economic and social potential. Mexico simply cannot afford to choose between rigor and relevance; it must learn how to harness rigorous scholarship to improve public policies.

NOTES

1. Stephen Krasner, "Conclusion: Garbage Cans and Policy Streams: How Academic Research Might Affect Foreign Policy," in *Power, the State, and Sovereignty: Essays on International Relations*, ed. Stephen Krasner (New York: Routledge, 2009), 254–74.

2. John Kingdon, *Agendas, Alternatives, and Public Policies* (New York: Longman, 1995).

3. On the importance of the availability of research that is usable for policy purposes in helping explain why and when scholarship has proved successful in shaping policy in the Mexican context, see Nora Lustig, chap. 6, and Sarah Babb, *Managing Mexico: Economists from Nationalism to Neoliberalism* (Princeton, NJ: Princeton University Press, 2004).

4. See, for example, Joseph Lepgold, "Policy Relevance and Theoretical Development in International Relations: What Have We Learned?" in *Being Useful: Policy Relevance and International Relations Theory*, ed. Miroslav Nincic and Joseph Lepgold (Ann Arbor: University of Michigan Press, 2000), 363–380; Bruce W. Jentleson, "The Need for Praxis: Bringing Policy Relevance Back In," *International Security* 26 (Spring 2002): 169–83; and Stephen Walt, "The Relationship between Theory and Policy in International Relations," *Annual Review of Political Science* 8 (June 2005): 23–48.

5. Alexander L. George and Andrew Bennet, *Case Studies and Theory Development in the Social Sciences* (Cambridge, MA: MIT Press, 2005), 266.

6. Mauricio Tenorio, "Orígenes del Centro de Investigación y Docencia Económicas," in *35 años del CIDE* (Mexico: CIDE, 2009), 5–34.

7. The three major political parties in Mexico are the PRI, Partido Revolucionario Institucional (Institutional Revolutionary Party); the PAN, Partido Acción Nacional (National Action Party); and the PRD, Partido de la Revolución Democrática (Party of the Democratic Revolution).

8. For the historical evolution of social science research in Mexico, see, among others, Mauricio Tenorio, "Stereophonic Scientific Modernism: Social Science between Mexico and the United States," *Journal of American History* 85 (1999): 1156–87; Lorenzo Meyer and Manuel Camacho, "La ciencia política en México," in *Ciencias Sociales en México, Desarrollo y Perspectivas* (Mexico City: El Colegio de México, 1979), 1–45; and Giovanna Valenti, "Tendencias de la institucionalización y la profesionalización de las ciencias sociales en México,"

in *Desarrollo y organización de las ciencias sociales en México*, ed. Francisco Javier Paoli (Mexico City: Porrúa, 1990), 431–63. For the evolution of economics research and its impact on economic policy, see Blanca Heredia, "Contested State: The Politics of Trade Liberalization in Mexico" (PhD diss., Political Science Department, Columbia University, 1996), and Babb, *Managing Mexico*.

9. R. Farmer, "How to Influence Government with Your Research: Tips from Practicing Political Scientists in Government," *PS: Political Science and Politics* 43 (Oct. 2010): 717–19; Kenneth Lieberthal, "Initiatives to Bridge the Gap," *Asia Policy* 1 (Jan. 2006): 7–15.

10. José Luis Méndez, "Implementing Developed Countries Administrative Reforms in Developing Countries: The Case of Mexico," in *Comparative Administrative Change and Reform: Lessons Learned*, ed. Jon Pierre and Patricia Ingraham (Montreal: McGill-Queen's University Press, 2010), 159–81.

11. For a full description and analysis of the administrative reforms of the Zedillo and Fox administrations, see Maria del Carmen Pardo, "La propuesta de modernización administrativa en México: Entre la tradición y el cambio," *Foro Internacional* 200 (2010): 393–421.

12. Independent Evaluation Group, World Bank, *Public Sector Reform: What Works and Why? An IEG Evaluation of World Bank Support* (Washington, DC: World Bank, 2008); Paul G. Roness and Sætren Harald, eds., *Change and Continuity in Public Sector Organizations: Essays in Honour of Per Lægreid* (Bergen, Norway: Fagbokforlaget, 2009); Alexander Kotchegura, *Civil Service Reform in Post-Communist Countries* (Leiden, Netherlands: Leiden University Press, 2008).

13. Independent Evaluation Group, *Public Sector Reform*. See Méndez, "Implementing Developed Countries Administrative Reforms."

14. See John Scott's *Who Benefits from Social Spending in Mexico?* Documento de Trabajo 208, Programa de Presupuesto y Gasto Público, CIDE-FORD (Mexico City: CIDE, 2010), and *La Otra Cara de la Reforma Fiscal: La Equidad del Gasto Público*, Folleto, Programa de Presupuesto y Gasto Público, CIDE-FORD (Mexico City: CIDE, 2001).

15. Laura Carrillo and Juan Pablo Guerrero, *Los Salarios de los Altos Funcionarios en México desde una Perspectiva Comparativa*, Documento de Trabajo 124, Programa de Presupuesto y Gasto Público, CIDE-FORD (Mexico City: CIDE, 2003).

16. Ana Laura Magaloni and Marcelo Bergman, *Encuesta de la población en reclusion*, ed. Programa de Estudios de Seguridad Pública y Estado de Derecho, División de Estudios Jurídicos, CIDE (Mexico City: CIDE, 2002); Ana Laura Magaloni and Layda Negrete, *El Poder Judicial y su política de decidir sin resolver*, DEJ Working Paper 1, División de Estudios Jurídicos (Mexico City: CIDE, 2001); Ana Laura Magaloni, *The Juicio Ejecutivo Mercantil in the Federal District Courts of Mexico: A Study of Uses and Users and Their Implications for Judicial Reform*, World Bank Report 22635 (Washington, DC: World Bank, 2002).

17. For information on the film *Presunto Culpable*, including a trailer, see www.presunto culpable.org. The film has received numerous national and international awards, including best documentary, Festival de Cine de Morelia 2009; best documentary, East End Film Fest, London, 2010; and an Emmy for best investigative journalism, September 2011.

18. As of September 26, 2011, the CNN portal www.cnn.mex.com reported that the film had been watched by almost two million people, the largest audience ever for a documentary in Mexico.

CHAPTER SIX

Scholars Who Became Practitioners
The Influence of Research on the Design, Evaluation, and Political Survival of Mexico's Antipoverty Program

NORA LUSTIG

The largest antipoverty program in Mexico's history, Oportunidades, is a conditional cash transfer program (CCT) that targets rural and urban households living in extreme poverty.[1] Launched in 1997 as Progresa, the program had its name changed to Oportunidades in early 2002, shortly after President Vicente Fox took office. Designed to complement traditional supply-side government spending in education and health (e.g., on schools, teachers, hospitals, doctors), the demand-side subsidies (e.g., the cash transfers) in Oportunidades are meant to promote school attendance and health care checkups for poor children. The cash transfers help reduce poverty in the present, while the conditions that households must meet to receive the transfers help build the future human capital of poor children. Thus, the program concurrently addresses short-term poverty and its intergenerational transmission.

From its inception, the design of Progresa/Oportunidades was influenced by academic research, and the program has been subject to numerous scholarly impact evaluation studies. These studies have helped improve the program's operational design and performance. More importantly, perhaps, evidence of its success was one of the key factors that protected Progresa from being abolished with the change in government in 2000. In December of that year, Vicente Fox became the first president elected from an opposition party—the PAN—in more than 70 years of PRI-dominated politics.[2] At the time, there were strong rumors that his newly appointed minister of social development, Josefina Vázquez Mota, would replace Progresa with a different, charity-based poverty alleviation program. This was not surprising. Traditionally, Mexico's antipoverty initiatives tended to disappear with each *sexenio*, even when the incumbent and the incoming presidents came from the same party and much of the same technocracy remained in place.[3] This had happened, for example, with COPLAMAR during the transition from José López-Portillo to Miguel de la Madrid in 1982 and with PRONASOL when Ernesto Zedillo succeeded Carlos

Salinas de Gortari at the end of 1994.[4] In the end, however, Progresa survived. It lost only its name. In fact, rather than discard the program, Fox's administration increased coverage from 2.3 to 4.2 million households and added semi-urban and urban localities. And the program survived not only the transition from Zedillo to Fox but also that from Fox to Felipe Calderón in 2006. Clearly, Oportunidades has proven to be much better shielded from politics than antipoverty programs in the past. With time, Progresa/Oportunidades has become one of the most-renowned CCTs around the world. Celebrated by academics,[5] multilateral organizations, policymakers, and the media alike, it is constantly used as a model of a successful antipoverty program.

What accounts for the success of Progresa/Oportunidades? What are the factors that explain its fame and prestige? Why was the program not scrapped in 2002? This chapter argues that the transformation of well-trained scholars into influential practitioners played a fundamental role in promoting a new conceptual approach to poverty reduction, ensuring the technical soundness and effectiveness of the program design, incorporating rigorous impact evaluations as part and parcel of the program design, persuading politicians to implement and keep the program in place, and engaging in an ongoing communication with the scholarly community both in Mexico and abroad. This conclusion is based, to a large extent, on my personal experience when senior advisor and chief of the Poverty and Inequality Unit at the Inter-American Development Bank (IDB) (1997–2001). In this capacity, I witnessed first-hand the evolution of the program and was instrumental in facilitating the first round of impact evaluation of Progresa and in promoting CCTs more broadly.

A New Approach to Poverty Reduction and the Design of Progresa/Oportunidades: The Role of Research, Scholars, and Scholar-Practitioners

Aimed at reducing current and future poverty, Oportunidades transfers cash to eligible poor families as long as certain conditions—known as "co-responsibilities"—are fulfilled. Oportunidades has three main components: education, nutrition, and health. The education component grants cash transfers based on school attendance; in-kind transfers of school supplies, which are sometimes given as an additional cash transfer; and scholarships for each year of high school that students complete, which can be retrieved from their interest-bearing account only if the student graduates by the age of 22. The nutrition and health components offer cash and in-kind transfers (nutritional supplements, vaccinations, preventive treatments, and so forth), based on regular visits to a health clinic and mothers' and teenagers' attendance at health talks. In 2007, a fourth component was added to provide beneficiaries with a subsidy for their electricity bills.[6]

Beneficiaries are selected on the basis of a multistage targeting process that depends on, among other things, a composite deprivation index known as the Sistema Unico de Puntajes (SUP). The formula of the SUP is kept confidential, but it essentially takes into account dwelling characteristics as well as the age and gender composition of the household (in particular, the presence of children and elderly members).[7] The average monthly transfer in 2005 was about $35,[8] equivalent to approximately 25% of eligible rural households' average monthly income. The program's size is significant in terms of beneficiaries yet inexpensive in terms of cost. By 2008, Oportunidades granted benefits to 4.3 million families (over 20% of the Mexican population), but its budget accounted for only 0.35% of gross domestic product (GDP) and 1.5% of public expenditures.[9] The program had come a long way since it was piloted in 1997, when it had a budget of 0.02% of GDP to serve around 300,000 families.

Along with the smaller-scale program Bolsa Escola in Brazil, Progresa/Oportunidades pioneered an innovative "technology" in antipoverty policy. It demonstrated that transferring cash to millions of households even in geographically remote areas was feasible and that cash transfers could be effectively combined with improvements in the health, education, and nutrition of children in poor households.[10] What gave rise to this innovation? What was the role of research?

Jere R. Behrman concludes that "the initial formulation of the program was motivation to basically make transfers to poor households more effective (with less leakage) and better targeted by shifting from effectively inframarginal in-kind food transfers to cash transfers conditional on behaviors affecting all household members (through the conditionalities on health and nutrition related checkups), with the schooling conditionalities added late in the pre-program development phase (Levy 2006)."[11] Research had established that price subsidies such as those for tortillas and other foods in Mexico were not really helping the poorest of the poor.[12] In addition, there was not even a clear sense of whether these subsidies contributed to better nutrition outcomes among the poor. Even though the targeted tortilla subsidy (Tortibono) and milk subsidy (Liconsa) were progressive in relative terms (i.e., the value of the subsidy *in proportion to* household income varied inversely with the latter), they were costly to operate and regressive in absolute terms (the per capita value of the subsidy varied directly with household income), primarily because the beneficiaries were urban households. The latter meant that the nonpoor received a higher share of the subsidy than the poor: the poorest population quintile received just 8.5% and 17.3% of the milk and tortilla subsidies, respectively.

Spearheaded by Santiago Levy (President Zedillo's undersecretary of budget in the Secretaria de Hacienda y Crédito Publico), the country's antipoverty spending after December 1994 became increasingly targeted to the poor.[13] The generalized (urban) consumer subsidy was gradually replaced by the targeted tortilla and milk subsidies (Tortibono and Liconsa). Even though the share of the benefits accruing to the poorest quintile rose, these two programs were costly to operate and mainly urban, and even within urban areas they were not really targeted to the poorest households. The general tortilla subsidy was scrapped in 1998, and resources previously used for food subsidies were reallocated to rural areas through Progresa. This shift transformed the broadly neutral distribution of government spending on food subsidies into a highly progressive one: the share of government resources accruing to the poorest decile increased from 8% in 1994 to 33% in 2000 (fig. 6.1).

Research had also established that paying attention to targeting mechanisms to avoid leakages and negative incentives was crucial. Finally, research had been instrumental in showing the importance of intrahousehold dynamics and why it was better to grant resources to women/mothers than to men/fathers for the transfers to be more effective in building poor children's human capital. According to Behrman, Santiago Levy suggested that research had influenced the design of Progresa regarding:

> (a) the ineffectiveness of previous food aid strategies (e.g., not well targeted, inframarginal income effects, high transaction and bureaucratic costs of in-kind programs; limitations of supply-side interventions), (b) the importance of intrahousehold allocations and therefore the need to make programs be conditional on benefits received by all household members, (c) related gender concerns, and (d) that food problems are not the same as nutritional problems . . . [T]he most important explicit studies that affected his thinking were Besley and Kanbur (1988, 1990) on food subsidy programs, Haddad and Kanbur (1989, 1990) on the extent of intrahousehold inequalities in the distribution of nutrients, Behrman and Deolalikar (1987, 1988) on low nutrient elasticities with respect to income, Schultz on schooling, Castañeda on targeting using the SISBEN in Colombia, and Streeten (1989a, b) on the poverty and on the relations between health and nutrition.[14]

Indeed, Levy's World Bank paper *Poverty Alleviation in Mexico*, which included many of the ideas that underlay the development of Progresa, includes 71 references with named authors.[15]

Another key figure in bringing scholarly work into the design of Progresa/Oportunidades was the late José "Pepe" Gómez de León, the program's first director.[16] I recollect his keen concern in developing a targeting method that would minimize perverse incentives such as making beneficiary households work less so that they

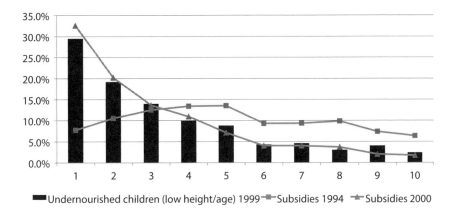

Figure 6.1 Distribution of food subsidies (percentage of total), 1994 and 2000, and un-dernourished children (low height/age), 1999, by per capita income decile. *Source:* Scott, "Eficiencia redistributiva de los programas contra la pobreza en México," graph 17; based on Encuesta Nacional de Nutrición 1988 and 1999.

would not exceed the income threshold that assured them of benefits. This gave rise to the SUP, the confidential formula used by Progresa/Oportunidades to select beneficiaries. A quantitative demographer/sociologist by training, Gómez de León directly contributed to the formalization (i.e., the mathematical formulation) of the targeting mechanism. He knew about the research by such scholars as Behrman, Gertler, and Schultz, as well as other outstanding work at the International Food Policy Research Institute (IFPRI) and the World Bank, both in Washington, DC. He was keen on making the program efficient, cost-effective, and as apolitical as possible.[17]

For close to four years, Gómez de León dedicated himself wholeheartedly to this aim. He combined visits to the field in dire circumstances, coordination of disparate government agencies, shielding of the program from clientelistic politics, and promotion of high-quality research on the program's effects (including his own research).

Very early on, Gómez de León recognized that the program's ability to survive political attacks would depend on demonstrating its success in achieving its goals, through rigorous external evaluations undertaken by internationally recognized scholars. As a result,

> *PROGRESA* incorporated data collection and systematic evaluation as an integral component from the start, with an initial experimental design in rural areas with random assignment for the first 18 months of treatment among 506 rural com-

munities (320 with treatment starting in 1998, 186 initial controls with treatment starting in 2000) with over 24,000 households and over 120,000 individuals in the evaluation sample over the 1997–2000 period and with subsequent control samples selected through propensity score matching (PSM) in both rural and urban areas. Indeed one major reason that *PROGRESA* is so well known has been the centrality of efforts at serious evaluation from the start—in contrast to other . . . anti-poverty and human resource investment programs (particularly in Brazil) on which information has not been collected to permit systematic evaluation.[18]

I recall a conversation with Gómez de León in 1997, at about the time I became senior advisor on poverty and chief of the Poverty and Inequality Unit of the IDB in September of that year. During this conversation, we agreed that it was essential to put in place an independent, high-quality evaluation of the program to help improve its performance and political resiliency. This gave rise to the organization of a workshop, convened by my unit at the IDB and held on December 10, 1997. This meeting set the stage for the subsequent comprehensive evaluation of Progresa by IFPRI.[19]

Impact Evaluation and Its Influence on Progresa's Political Survival and International Standing

The International Food Policy Research Institute was contracted by the Mexican government to undertake the initial evaluation of Progresa in 1998–2000; this was followed by a series of contracts for subsequent evaluations by the Mexican Instituto de Nutrición y Salud Pública. In addition, the government has been willing to share the rich database of Progresa/Oportunidades surveys with scholars, including students working on their theses and dissertations. As a result, Progresa/Oportunidades is probably one of the most studied programs in the developing world. It is important to note that a substantial portion of the research on the program is published in top-tier peer-reviewed journals and thus has been consistent with combining practical relevance with succeeding in academia.[20]

Many of the impact evaluation studies found that the program has had significant (in the statistical sense) positive impacts on education and health.[21] Comparing postprimary enrollment before the program (1996–97) and after the program (2002–3), one study reported an average increase of 24% in rural areas.[22] Of note was enrollment in secondary education in rural areas, which rose by 11% for girls and 7.5% for boys two years after the program was launched.[23] Another study found that demand for health services among Progresa/Oportunidades beneficiaries was

67% higher than demand in communities not participating in the program.[24] Infant mortality was found to fall at an 11% higher rate among beneficiaries than among nonbeneficiaries.[25] Another study estimated an 11% reduction in maternal mortality and a 2% reduction in infant mortality in rural communities compared with those not in the program.[26] Improved access to education and these health gains may help explain recent changes in the relative earnings of low-income workers. Better access to health services may have improved the productivity of low-skilled workers: for example, improved access to health services may translate into fewer days of work missed due to illness. Better access to health services also may have improved the cognitive development of children in poor households, thereby improving their educational achievement and productivity.[27]

In December 2000, when Vicente Fox took office, Progresa faced a serious risk of being scrapped. I had an opportunity to meet with Fox's minister of social development, Josefina Vázquez Mota, very early in the administration (in December 2000). Vázquez Mota was skeptical of Progresa. A good number of social policy analysts wrote columns and commented in the electronic media on the importance of keeping Progresa, citing the impact evaluation results as evidence of the program's success in reducing poverty and improving school attendance and health outcomes among the extremely poor. In the end, Vazquez Mota—an intelligent policymaker and shrewd politician—was persuaded, and the program survived with a vengeance. Scrapping the program would have been utterly unpopular, something that parties would want to avoid in the more democratic and competitive post–2000 election Mexico. Under Fox's administration, Progresa—renamed Oportunidades—was expanded to semi-urban and urban areas, and the number of beneficiaries increased from 2.3 to 4.2 million households. Miguel Székely, a former researcher at the IDB, was appointed undersecretary in the Ministry of Social Development, and the new director of Oportunidades was a member of the late Gómez de León's team.

In addition, Progresa/Oportunidades soon became among the leading examples for other countries to emulate. Programs similar to Progresa (some large-scale, some small) now exist in most of Latin America and beyond. While in 1997 there were only 3 programs that would qualify as CCTs, by 2008 the number had grown to 28 (fig. 6.2).[28] The World Bank, the IDB, IFPRI, and the Massachusetts Institute of Technology's Abdul Latif Jameel Poverty Action Lab,[29] as well as the governments themselves, among others, have been instrumental in collecting and disseminating the knowledge on CCTs acquired through both research and practical experience.

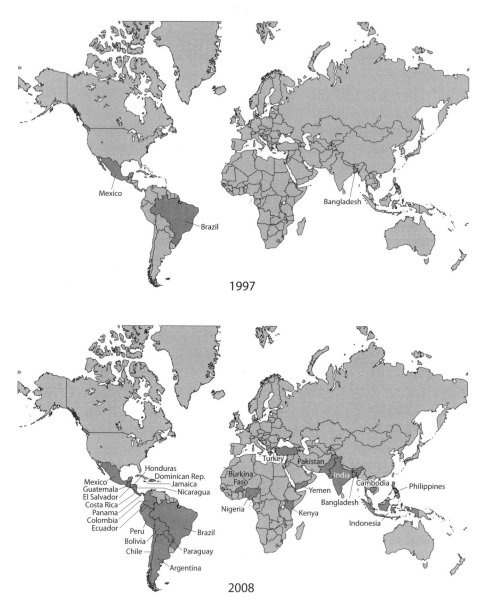

Figure 6.2 Countries with conditional cash transfer programs, 1997 and 2008. *Source:* Fiszbein et al., *Conditional Cash Transfers*, fig. 1, p. 4.

Lessons from Progresa/Oportunidades

Scholars and scholarly research have been part of Progresa/Oportunidades since its inception. A key factor was that the practitioners who played a key role in the design, implementation, and evaluation of the program had been scholars themselves at some point in their professional careers. President Zedillo had been a researcher at the Bank of Mexico on completing his PhD in economics at Yale University. Zedillo had great respect for sound and relevant economic theory and empirical analysis. He was very critical of Mexico's existing consumer and producer subsidy schemes and was quickly persuaded by the arguments put forward by Santiago Levy and others regarding the implementation of such an antipoverty program as Progresa. From previous experience, Zedillo knew that the program's ability to survive beyond his *sexenio* would depend on not making it his "personal" initiative (as had happened with PRONASOL under Salinas). In addition, Zedillo must have thought that keeping the program independent from multilateral organizations would also increase its chances to survive politically.

Santiago Levy, the program's intellectual architect in its pilot phase, has a PhD from Boston University and for many years was an academic at the Instituto Tecnológico Autónomo de Mexico and, later, at Boston University. José Gómez de León, the program's intellectual architect and its first director, had a doctorate in demography from Harvard University and worked as a scholar at El Colegio de México for several years.[30] Miguel Székely has a PhD from Oxford University and worked in the research department at the IDB. I received my PhD in economics from the University of California, Berkeley, and was a scholar at El Colegio de México before joining the Brookings Institution in 1989; I then joined the IDB in 1997. Zedillo first met Levy and Gómez de León when he was in the research department at the Bank of Mexico in the late 1970s (and perhaps even earlier). Zedillo, Gómez de León, Levy, Székely, and I met at El Colegio de México in the 1970s and 1980s. The group had in common sharing a solid academic background, a high regard for scholarly work, and a genuine concern for making antipoverty programs effective. All of us were scholars or researchers who became practitioners and, to some extent, practitioners who continued to do scholarly work (and some of us have become primarily scholars again).

The presence of scholars who became practitioners is probably a fundamental reason that research played an important role in identifying the limitations of existing programs, promoting a new approach to poverty reduction, and determining the design and adaptation of Progresa/Oportunidades over time. The existing research—impact evaluation studies in particular—had a significant effect on the program's political survival. Whether the presence of scholars who become practitioners is a necessary or sufficient condition in other settings for knowledge and research to influence policy in a positive direction is a question for further research. There are some reasons to believe that the presence of scholar-practitioners can increase the chances of success of a policy intervention (including the decision to scrap it if research shows it doesn't work). Incorporating scholars with organizational and political skills into leadership positions, particularly with control over spending decisions, can increase the probability of successful outcomes and their dissemination. Scholar-practitioners are more likely to emphasize data gathering and evaluation exercises and build them into the initial design of an intervention so as to be able to demonstrate success (or failure) and make changes to improve the policy's impact. In addition, scholar-practitioners are more likely to share data and results from evaluation exercises widely, through both mass and technical media, a process that is essential to build political/intellectual constituencies. Finally, scholar-practitioners can play a major role in spreading knowledge about successful interventions in multilateral institutions and public policy programs.[31]

ACKNOWLEDGMENTS

Earlier versions of this chapter were presented at the international workshop "Scholars and Practitioners," organized at the Center for International Studies, University of Southern California, in Los Angeles, April 26–27, 2011, and at the conference "Scholars and Practitioners" at Brown University in Providence, Rhode Island, October 3–4, 2011; an earlier version was published as a working paper of the Center for Global Development (www.cgdev.org/content/publications/detail/1425364/). I am very grateful to Nancy Lee, Abraham Lowenthal, James W. McGuire, and Mariano Bertucci, as well as the participants of both conferences, for their invaluable comments on earlier drafts. I am also very grateful to Santiago Levy for crucial and timely clarifications. Samantha Greenspun provided excellent research assistance. All errors and omissions are my responsibility.

NOTES

1. Nora Lustig, "Investing in Health for Economic Development: The Case of Mexico," in *Advancing Development—Core Themes in Global Economics*, ed. George Mavrotas and Anthony Shorrocks (New York: Palgrave Macmillan, in association with the United Nations University–World Institute for Development Economics Research, 2007).

2. PAN is Partido Acción Nacional (National Action Party); PRI is Partido Revolucionario Institucional (Institutional Revolutionary Party).

3. The *sexenio* refers to the six-year term limit on the Mexican presidency.

4. COPLAMAR, Coordinación General del Plan Nacional de Zonas Deprimidas y Grupos Marginados (Mexican Institute of Social Security—General Coordination of the National Plan for Depressed Areas and Marginalized Groups), was created in 1977 and eliminated in 1983. For more information, visit the website of the Mexican Institute of Social Security (www.imss.gob.mx/programas/oportunidades/historia.htm). PRONASOL is Programa Nacional de Solidaridad (National Solidarity Program).

5. See, for example, articles by such internationally renowned scholars as Nobel laureate Gary Becker in *Business Week*, Princeton University economist Alan Krueger in the *New York Times*, and Francis Fukuyama in the *Wall Street Journal*; all are referenced in Jere R. Behrman, *Policy-Oriented Research Impact Assessment (Poria) Case Study on the International Food Policy Research Institute (IFPRI) and the Mexican Progresa Anti-Poverty and Human Resource Investment Conditional Cash Transfer Program*, Impact Assessment Discussion Paper No. 27 (Washington, DC: IFPRI, 2007). Another indicator of the visibility of Progresa/Oportunidades is provided by the number of hits on a Google search: about 1,420,000 on Google and about 12,100 on Google Scholar. See Behrman, *Policy-Oriented Research Impact Assessment (Poria) Case Study*.

6. For details, see Samantha Greenspun, "Assessing Mexico's Anti-poverty Program 'Oportunidades': Combining and Comparing *Objective* and *Interview-based Indicators*" (MA thesis, Tulane University, New Orleans, 2011), table 4.

7. For details, see Santiago Levy, *Progress against Poverty: Sustaining Mexico's Progresa-Oportunidades Program* (Washington, DC: Brookings Institution Press, 2006).

8. In US dollars; this figure can increase in families with school-age children. In 2005, Progresa/Oportunidades granted monetary benefits and in-kind benefits equivalent to direct monetary monthly assistance of $44.30 per family. See Levy, *Progress against Poverty*.

9. Greenspun, "Assessing Mexico's Anti-poverty Program 'Oportunidades.'"

10. PRONASOL had a component called "Niños en Solidaridad" (Children in Solidarity), a cash scholarship for children attending school. In that sense it was a precursor of Progresa. However, the coverage of the program was very limited.

11. Behrman, *Policy-Oriented Research Impact Assessment (Poria) Case Study*.

12. Nora Lustig, "Solidarity as a Strategy of Poverty Alleviation," in *Transforming State Society Relations in Mexico: The National Solidarity Strategy*, ed. Wayne Cornelius, Ann L. Craig, and Jonathan Fox (San Diego: Center for US-Mexican Studies, University of San Diego, 1994), 79–96; Timothy J. Kehoe and Jaime Serra-Puche, "A General Equilibrium Analysis of Price Controls and Subsidies on Food in Mexico," *Journal of Development Economics* 21 (Apr. 1986): 65–87.

13. The concept of targeted spending as an explicit category reported separately was introduced in official public sector accounts in the mid 1990s.

14. Behrman, *Policy-Oriented Research Impact Assessment (Poria) Case Study*.

15. Santiago Levy, *Poverty Alleviation in Mexico*, Policy Research and External Affairs Working Paper 679 (Washington, DC: World Bank, 1991); Santiago Levy, "La pobreza en Mexico," in *Causas y políticas para combatirla*, ed. F. Vélez (Mexico City: ITAM and FCE, 1994), 15–112; Santiago Levy, "Interview Related to IFPRI Evaluation of the PROGRESA/Oportunidades Program," interviewed by Jere Behrman, in Behrman, *Policy-Oriented Research Impact Assessment (Poria) Case Study*, appendix; Timothy Besley and Ravi Kanbur, "Food Subsidies and Poverty Alleviation," *Economic Journal* 98, no. 392 (1998): 701–19; Lawrence

Haddad and Ravi Kanbur, *How Serious is the Neglect of Intrahousehold Inequality?*, Working Paper 296 (Washington, DC: World Bank, 1998); Lawrence Haddad and Ravi Kanbur, *Are Better-off Households More Unequal or Less Unequal?*, Working Paper Series 373 (Washington, DC: World Bank, 1990); Jere R. Behrman and Anil B. Deolalikar, "Will Developing Country Nutrition Improve with Income? A Case Study for Rural South India," *Journal of Political Economy* 95 (June 1987): 108–38; Paul Streeten, *Poverty: Concepts and Measurement*, Discussion Paper 6 (Boston: Boston University, Institute for Economic Development, 1989); Paul Streeten, *Hunger*, Discussion Paper 4 (Boston: Boston University, Institute for Economic Development, 1989). The relatively large number of citations spanning a period of 10 to 15 years suggests that the field of antipoverty analysis had built a "critical mass" of knowledge ready to be applied in practice.

16. Gómez de León was director of Progresa from 1997 to 2000, when he died of cancer (melanoma) at the age of 53.

17. Jere R. Behrman concludes that although he had "not found any citations by Gómez de León in his studies before *PROGRESA* was initiated to research by the IFPRI evaluation team members or IFPRI more broadly, . . . two of his 1999 studies with Parker (Gómez de León and Parker 1999a, b), however, do cite seven studies by IFPRI staff or by the evaluation team members that were written before the initiation of *PROGRESA* (in addition to studies that came out of the evaluation): Haddad, Hoddinott, and Alderman (1997), Haddad and Reardon (1993), Quisumbing (1994), and Schultz (1990) on gender and intrahousehold allocations; Heckman, Ichimura, and Todd (1997) and Heckman and Todd (1996) on propensity score matching estimators and evaluation; and Newman, Rawlings, and Gertler (1994) on using randomization for evaluation of social policies in developing countries. This suggests that, although Gómez de León did not cite these studies before 1997, Gómez de León and Parker in 1999 at least thought that these studies captured important dimensions of the evolving conventional wisdom on these topics at the time that Gómez de León was engaged in developing *PROGRESA*." Behrman, *Policy-Oriented Research Impact Assessment (Poria) Case Study*, 18.

18. Behrman, *Policy-Oriented Research Impact Assessment (Poria) Case Study*, 3.

19. Behrman's account of how this came about may be illustrative: "Apparently Nora Lustig, a member of the IFPRI Board of Trustees in 1994–97 and Senior Advisor on Poverty and Chief of the Inequality Unit of the Inter-American Development Bank (IDB) in 1997–2001, played a major role in facilitating the conversation between IFPRI and PROGRESA about IFPRI undertaking the evaluation (Coady 2007, Haddad 2007, Lustig 1995, 1997a, b, 2007, Parker 2007, Schultz 2007). The first documentation that I can find of that contact is an e-mail of 21 June 1995 of Lustig (1995) to Lawrence Haddad at IFPRI apparently responding to an inquiry by Haddad about a staff member working with Santiago Levy who had contacted Haddad about evaluating a Mexican pilot food stamp program (a pilot program for PROGRESA) in which Lustig says that she had mentioned Haddad's name to Levy's Chief of Staff several months earlier . . . On November 11, 1997, Lustig (1997a) sent an e-mail to Haddad, Gary Burtless at the Brookings Institute [*sic*] and 13 staff members of the World Bank (mostly empirical micro economists and policy analysts) inviting them to a workshop on December 10, 1997 to be held at the Inter-American Development Bank under the sponsorship of the Poverty and Inequality Advisory Unit (of which Lustig was the chief) 'to discuss

evaluation schemes of the recently launched target program in Mexico called PROGRESA' (she also noted that 'The workshop will start with a presentation by Dr. Jose Gomez de Leon, the Director of PROGRESA' and provided a brief summary of the program) . . . On December 3, 1997, Lustig (1997b) sent an e-mail addressed to Lawrence Haddad, Jere Behrman, Paul Gertler, Paul Schultz, and James Heckman . . . enclosing the program for the meeting on December 10, 1997, and further information and asking for references regarding these individuals' expertise. Haddad, Ruel, and Quisumbing from IFPRI (Haddad 1998), Behrman, Gertler, and Schultz all attended the meeting (Heckman did not but asked Petra Todd to attend in his place, which she did) and subsequently became increasingly involved (under Haddad's leadership and with substantial input from other IFPRI staff) in the development of the IFPRI proposal for undertaking the evaluation on which agreement was reached in the late summer of 1998." Behrman, *Policy-Oriented Research Impact Assessment (Poria) Case Study*, 19. It should be noted that under the executive vice presidency of Nancy Birdsall, the IDB became very involved in sponsoring rigorous impact evaluation of social programs.

20. See, for example, Jere R. Behrman and John Hoddinott, "Program Evaluation with Unobserved Heterogeneity and Selective Implementation: The Mexican *Progresa* Impact on Child Nutrition," *Oxford Bulletin of Economics and Statistics* 67 (2005): 547–69; Jere R. Behrman, Piyali Sengupta, and Petra Todd, "Progressing through PROGRESA: An Impact Assessment of a School Subsidy Experiment in Mexico," *Economic Development and Cultural Change* 54 (2000): 237–76; Jere R. Behrman and Emmanuel Skoufias, "Mitigating Myths about Policy Effectiveness: Evaluation of Mexico's Antipoverty Program," *Annals of the American Academy of Political and Social Science* 606 (2006): 244–75; Natalia Caldés, David Coady, and John A. Maluccio, "The Cost of Poverty Alleviation Transfer Programs: A Comparative Analysis of Three Programs in Latin America," *World Development* 34 (2006): 818–37; David Coady, "The Welfare Returns to Finer Targeting: The Case of Progresa in Mexico," *International Tax and Public Finance* 13 (2006): 217–39; David Coady and Rebecca Harris, "Evaluating Transfer Payments within a General Equilibrium Framework," *Economic Journal* 114 (2004): 778–99; Juan José Díaz and Sudhanshu Handa, "An Assessment of Propensity Score Matching as a Nonexperimental Impact Estimator," *Journal of Human Resources* 41 (2006): 319–45; Paul Gertler, "Do Conditional Cash Transfers Improve Child Health? Evidence from PROGRESA's Control Randomized Experiment," *American Economic Review: Papers and Proceedings* 94 (2004): 336–41; Susan W. Parker, Luis Rubalcalva, and Graciela Teruel, "Evaluating Conditional Schooling-Health Transfer Programs," in *Handbook of Development Economics*, vol. 4, ed. T. Paul Schultz and John Strauss (Amsterdam: North-Holland/Elsevier, 2007); and J. A. Rivera, D. Sotres-Alvarez, J. P. Habicht, T. Shamah, and S. Villalpando, "Impact of the Mexican Program for Education, Health, and Nutrition (Progresa) on Rates of Growth and Anemia in Infants and Young Children," *JAMA* 291 (2004): 2563–70.

21. See, for example, Susan Parker, "Evaluación del Impacto de Oportunidades sobre la Inscripción, Reprobación, y Abandono Escolar," in *Evaluación Externa del Impacto del Programa Oportunidades 2004*, ed. Bernardo Hernández Prado and Mauricio Hernández Ávila (Cuernavaca, Mexico: Instituto Nacional de Salud Pública, 2005); and T. P. Schultz, *The Impact of Progresa on School Enrollments: Final Report* (Washington, DC: IFPRI, 2000). See also references cited in Gerardo Esquivel, Nora Lustig, and John Scott, "Mexico: A Decade of Falling Inequality: Market Forces of State Action?" in *Declining Inequality in Latin America: A Decade*

of Change?, ed. Luis F. López-Calva and Nora Lustig (Washington, DC: Brookings Institution Press; New York: United Nations Development Programme, 2010), 175–217; in Michelle Adato and John Hoddinott, *Conditional Cash Transfers in Latin America* (Washington, DC: IFPRI, 2010); and in Greenspun, "Assessing Mexico's Anti-poverty Program 'Oportunidades.'"

22. Parker, "Evaluación del Impacto de Oportunidades sobre la Inscripción, Reprobación, y Abandono Escolar."

23. Schultz, "Impact of Progresa on School Enrollments."

24. Sergio Bautista et al., "Impacto de Oportunidades en la Morbilidad y el Estado de Salud de la Población Beneficiaria y en la Utilización de Servicios de Salud: Resultados de Corto Plazo en Zonas Urbanas y de Mediano Plazo en Zonas Rurales," in *Evaluación externa de impacto del programa Oportunidades 2004*, vol. 2, *Salud*, ed. Bernardo Hernández and Mauricio Hernández (Cuernavaca, Mexico: Instituto Nacional de Salud Pública, 2004).

25. Tania Barham, "Providing a Healthier Start to Life: The Impact of Conditional Cash Transfers on Infant Mortality" (PhD diss. / working paper, Department of Agriculture and Resource Economics, University of California, Berkeley, 2005).

26. Bernardo Hernández et al., "Evaluación del Impacto de Oportunidades en la Mortalidad Materna e Infantil," in *Evaluación externa del impacto del programa Oportunidades 2003*, vol. 2, ed. Bernardo Hernández Prado and Mauricio Hernández Ávila (Cuernacava, Mexico: Instituto Nacional de Salud Pública, 2003).

27. See, for example, Nora Lustig, "Interview Related to IFPRI Evaluation of the PROGRESA/*Oportunidades* program," interviewed by Jere R. Behrman, in Behrman, *Policy-Oriented Research Impact Assessment (Poria) Case Study*, appendix, and Lustig, "Investing in Health for Economic Development."

28. See Ariel Fiszbein and Norbert Schady, with Francisco H. G. Ferreira, Margaret Grosh, Nial Kelleher, Pedro Olinto, and Emmanuel Skoufias, *Conditional Cash Transfers: Reducing Present and Future Poverty*, World Bank Policy Research Report (Washington, DC: World Bank, 2009).

29. Abdul Lateef Jamil Poverty Action Lab, *Evaluations*, www.povertyactionlab.org /search/apachesolr_search/conditional%20cash%20transfer%20?filters=type:evaluation.

30. After José "Pepe" Gómez de León died in 2000, this is what the International Union for the Scientific Study of Population wrote on its website: "One of the most important aspects of Gómez de León's professional career was the fruitful combination of academic, policy-making and administrative pursuits . . . As a matter of fact, many of us were always amazed that he could manage to make high-quality and pertinent academic contributions at the same time as being an outstanding public servant" (www.iussp.org/Announcements/90obit_leon.php).

31. One caveat is in order. In the case of macroeconomic policy, it is quite common to see relatively close exchange between scholarly work, scholars, and practitioners. Central banks and ministers of finance the world over have former academics among their staff. This has greatly improved macroeconomic policy and, especially, crisis prevention and crisis management a great deal over the decades. However, the outcomes of such "intimacy" between research and policy are not always felicitous. Given some of their sharply negative consequences, supply-side economics and, especially, financial liberalization, are good examples where it would have been better for the advice of scholars to fall onto into politicians' deaf ears.

CHAPTER SEVEN

Missing Scholars and Hard-Nosed Cops
The Weak Research behind Citizen Security Policies

KEVIN CASAS-ZAMORA

The Latin American and Caribbean region (LAC) is, by almost all accounts and indicators, the most violent region in the world. In the course of the past decade, approximately 1.4 million people in the region lost their lives as a result of violent crime.[1] Almost 30% of the world's murders occur in LAC, although the region is home to less than 9% of the global population. Homicides are, of course, merely the most visible manifestation of a far more entrenched problem. Each year, 200 million people—one-third of the region's population—experience a violent crime, either directly or in their household.[2] Rigorous estimates place the direct and indirect costs of violence in LAC at 12% of the region's gross domestic product (GDP), a number greater than the economic output of Argentina and Chile combined.[3] Unsurprisingly, the issue of crime has become the region's dominant preoccupation. According to figures from the *2010 Report* by Latinobarómetro, a regional opinion poll, 27% of Latin Americans rank crime as their countries' most pressing concern, a three-fold increase since 2001 and a much larger figure than for any other collective challenge.[4] Although the degree of crime and concern about it vary from country to country, there is no doubt that crime and fear of crime have become defining traits of Latin American reality.

Has scientifically rigorous research contributed to public policies being implemented to confront this regional phenomenon? If the use of scholarly research—of both the purely academic and the policy-oriented kind—to inform public policies is desirable in most domains, it is vital when it comes to public security. Unlike the mistakes of the proverbial bad architect, those made by policymakers in the security realm cannot be covered with vines. Rather, those decisions are measured out in the loss of human life, in destroyed community ties, in weakened civil liberties, and in the hollowing out of the rule of law. They entail staggering individual and social costs, which in many cases linger across generations. In the light of this prospect and of the exceptional complexity of the phenomenon of crime, one would think that expert voices, endowed with scientific knowledge, would have a disproportionate influence on public security debates. Yet that's not what we see in most of LAC.

In this chapter I examine the weak connections between scientific knowledge and public security policies in the region, with a special focus on the case of Central America. This disconnect originates primarily in the severe politicization of the issue and in the lack of policy-relevant knowledge for decision makers to rely on. Citizen security policies in LAC are shaped, on the one hand, by an uncommonly strong temptation on the part of policymakers to use the issue for political profit and to act upon it guided by short-term political pressures and, on the other, by the dearth of factual information, the relative lack of interest of the academic community, and the limited practical relevance of the available criminological research. All these factors combine to generate a debased policy debate that is, more often than not, guided by whims, pseudo-facts, and political posturing. I offer a few tentative recommendations about how to increase the reliance of public security policies on scholarly knowledge, a process in which international organizations and cooperation agencies can play a key role.

This discussion mostly relies on my past experience as both policymaker and provider of policy-relevant information to government officials in Costa Rica. For nearly five years, between 2003 and 2007, I was general coordinator of the United Nations Development Program's (UNDP) *National Human Development Report* and then Costa Rica's second vice president and minister of national planning, both very useful experiences to gauge the scholar-policymaker gap discussed in this volume. I focus here on the problems found in the executive and legislative branches rather than the judiciary, where technical expertise is generally more available and international cooperation with the region has long been active. And I focus almost exclusively on the experience of Central American countries, where crime problems are truly rampant, even by LAC's dismal standards. The northern half of Central America is, arguably, the world's most violent place outside of active war zones.[5] The challenges described here and their implications are, thus, peculiarly acute in Central America.

The State of the Links

The gap between scholarly knowledge and the policymaking process has been scarcely explored in LAC, and even less so when it comes to citizen security. In the US context, however, concern about the growing distance between academics and policymakers has given rise to a thriving literature that both decries and tries to explain the phenomenon.[6] The purported roots of the problem are many and concern both the "supply" of policy-relevant knowledge and the "demand" for it from policymakers. They include very deeply entrenched incentives and cultural mores within the academic profession, which tends to prize theoretical sophistication, elaborate arguments, and long written outputs—traits that undercut the perceived relevance of academic work in debates in the policy world.

But even more attention has been paid to the nature of the policymaking process, which seldom holds true to the image of a rational exercise in which optimal alternatives are weighed and adopted in a timely fashion by actors solely preoccupied with the public interest. Policy is made by a much more haphazard process—likened to a "garbage can"[7]—in which policy outputs result from the convergence of problems, solutions, actors, and opportunities; in which the range of feasible alternatives constantly changes; and in which the odds for the adoption of a given policy proposal have less to do with its scientific merits than with its ability to address a problem perceived as urgent, the capability and influence of its advocates, and the room for solutions allowed by the political process. All of this makes the translation of expert knowledge into policy outputs far from inevitable. Yet, the literature is also clear that such translation is possible under many circumstances. "Policy windows" do open that allow for the successful convergence of a recognized problem, an expert-generated policy option, and a political process willing to give new ideas a chance.[8] This volume provides some useful examples of this convergence, notably the generation of the Progresa/Oportunidades antipoverty program in Mexico and the use of targeted financial sanctions.[9]

Even descriptions of the policymaking process that emphasize its relatively haphazard quality presuppose two conditions: first, that political incentives are not inherently stacked against the use of expert knowledge on a given issue; and second, that policy solutions are available and ready to be thrown into the "garbage can." Both assumptions may be problematic in certain contexts, a point not sufficiently emphasized in the literature. The policy debate on citizen security in Central America offers a good example to illustrate this point.

In Central America, the amount of scholarly research or even simple empirical content that supports adopting public security policies is remarkably limited. Why is this so? Because of the politicization of the issue and the dearth of knowledge about it.

A Politicized Issue

Central America's citizen security crisis creates very strong political incentives that run counter to the use of expert knowledge when adopting policies to deal with the issue. This results from two different forces. First, there is an opportunity for politicians to use the issue for political gain. The mass media's fixation on crime has exacerbated the region's anxieties and turned crime into a readily exploitable political mine, where the temptation for policymakers to *use* the issue for immediate political gain frequently trumps the desire to *solve* it through the best available policies.[10] Crime-busting politicians see their media exposure grow dramatically, especially when their hawkishness is coupled with a prowess for stirring the social prejudices against minorities that the issue frequently ignites. This is not the only way in which the issue can be exploited politically. Security policies also confer easy access to an invaluable power resource—the police. This resource may be put to legitimate uses, such as protecting the population, but also to questionable ones, as a source of patronage or even political intimidation. These incentives are negatively compounded by the perception, held by many in the Central American isthmus, that while crime is a politically sensitive issue it is not a technically demanding one, in the mold of, say, public finances or public health. As a result, the issue is normally placed in the hands of either political operators or police and military officers seldom endowed with technical training on criminology or other directly relevant academic disciplines. When it comes to citizen security, the prevalence of hardened politicians rather than technocrats among cabinet-level positions in Central America is hardly accidental.

The second force at play is society's short-term bias. When heightened levels of social anxiety surround a given issue, the short-term bias inherent in contemporary democracies—where electoral rhythms frequently determine policy outcomes—can be very powerful. Central American policymakers simply cannot afford to be seen by the public as dithering or engaging in long-winded academic debates on crime. This is, moreover, an issue where popular perceptions are strongly shaped by the mass media, which also play a visible and often unfortunate role in propagating pseudo-facts and codified explanations. Policymakers in this realm are thus forced to operate in an environment characterized by both urgency and hardened perceptions, which are very difficult to change. This creates a bias against the use of complex and sophisticated analyses, particularly if the prescriptions derived from them emphasize long-term processes to prevent violence. If policymakers are generally afforded very limited time to engage in refined policy debates and to deliver results, their time constraints and political pressures can be truly overwhelming in a security situation as deteriorated as that of Central America. To be sure, even in these circumstances it is possible to imagine uses of knowledge to, in the words of Christina Boswell, *legitimize* or *substantiate* policy decisions ultimately made for political reasons.[11] "Broken windows" criminological approaches are, after all, occasionally invoked as one of the intellectual underpinnings of "zero tolerance" and even "iron fisted" strategies against crime in Central America.[12] But this use of academic knowledge happens by exception and as a byproduct of predetermined decisions, rather than being one of the driving factors behind them. Existing political incentives leave very limited room for experts and technocrats to be influential, for evidence-based policies to trump political expediency, or for a broad discussion of alternative approaches to citizen security to take place. Action, as conspicuous as possible, not policy debate, is the name of the game.

The Dearth of Useful Knowledge

Equally complex is the second problem keeping scholarly research from affecting public security policy. Central American policymakers generally exhibit little interest in criminological information on the roots of crime or on the major policy options available to them. With very few exceptions, their approach to citizen security is infused with a police-centric view of the problem and its solutions. Thus, the technical knowledge that makes its way into the policy process tends to be of the "operational" variety and is mainly geared to improving the training, equipment, deployment, and coordination of police forces. More often than not, such knowledge is proffered by elements within the police and military institutions, which are endowed with years of practical experience and which tend to perpetuate the standard operating procedures of law enforcement institutions, even when these procedures are systemically flawed.

On occasion, however, policymakers in the region seek advice from foreign police experts, either private consultants or technical advisors provided by foreign governments, international agencies, and multilateral banks. The role of the Spanish, Canadian, and, to a lesser extent, Chilean governments in providing technical assistance for police reform in Central America is well known. So is the role of the Colombian government in training police forces, investigators, and prosecutors in matters relating to organized crime.

Having technical advice on police reform is by no means equivalent to benefiting from scholarly advice on a comprehensive criminal policy. The question, then, is why the latter is nearly always absent from policy discussions. The short answer is that, generally speaking, the region's experts and academics show a markedly limited capacity to feed the "garbage can" with fact-based policy alternatives. Four reasons go a long way toward explaining this unfortunate limitation.

The lack of reliable crime statistics. Crime-related debates in LAC, and particularly in Central America, are frequently underpinned by notoriously fragmentary and flimsy statistics. The hidden nature of the region's "black figure" results in official crime figures of questionable accuracy and low usefulness. For instance, less than one in four crimes are reported to the authorities in Costa Rica (23%) and Mexico (22%).[13] The comparable figure detected by the International Crime Victimization Survey for 33 mostly developed countries is 47%.[14] Moreover, unlike in all developed countries, regular victimization surveys are a rarity in most Latin American countries and are usually the work of private entities or international organizations. A recent Costa Rican experience illuminates this point well. Remarkably, the Ministry of Public Security failed to carry out a single victimization survey of its own until 2004, and it did so only because the UNDP and the Spanish Cooperation Agency covered the entire cost of the exercise.[15] A second, similar survey conducted in 2006 was met with extreme caution by the ministry's authorities, who ultimately refused to disseminate the results. This is hardly unusual in the region. Venezuela's authorities ceased to publish official data on homicides and other crimes in 2004 and only recently resumed releasing these data, thereby forcing security debates to be informed by figures and data collected by academic centers and not-for-profit organizations in the meantime. In all cases where authorities were reluctant to generate reliable information, one motive was clear: with the availability of rigorous public information on crime comes accountability.

The dire state of crime statistics in Central America undermines the ability to make informed policy decisions but also, even more basically, to engage in empirical research on the subject. Despite recent efforts by some international agencies (as discussed below), there is relatively little scholarly research on crime in Central America simply because most of the data are nonexistent and can be collected only at a great cost to researchers. While empirically oriented policymakers may certainly make use of a wealth of international research on crime to support their decisions, their chances of tapping into local context-relevant research are low.

The failure to evaluate public policy impact. Policy evaluation is an exotic discipline for Central American governments, one restricted, in the best of cases, to investigations into the efficiency and probity in public resource spending. Analyses of the impact of public policies are extraordinarily rare, even in Costa Rica, where the general comptroller has expressed interest in engaging in this exercise. Besides damaging the general quality of public policies in the isthmus, this lack of systematic evaluation also constitutes an obstacle to generating policy-relevant knowledge in the security realm. With the exception of occasional evaluations by this or that international donor seeking to know more about its own projects' outcomes, rigorous studies on the impact of security policies are virtually nonexistent in Central America. As a result, there is little empirical information to use in formulating effective security policies and even less to use in correcting them once they've proven unsuccessful.

The issue's ownership by specific institutional actors and the aloofness of the region's social scientists. In Central America, public security has long been seen as the province of the police, when not the armed forces. These are two institutions in which low academic training (particularly university-level training) is the clear norm, making them particularly inhospitable to scientific knowledge or active endeavors to look for it. The long-term dominance over security issues by police and military cadres has been reinforced by the dearth of civilian experts on security in governments and legislatures, as much as in academic institutions and civil society organizations. To put it bluntly, Central America's top policymakers on security are either former military/police officers or civilian politicians bereft of any formal training on the subject matter. More often than not, the latter end up relying on advice from the former.

Police and military officers' perceived mandate over the issue has bred a long history of repressive policies and human rights abuses in nearly every Central American country and nurtured severe prejudices against security-related issues among the region's social scientists. As a research area, public security has been tainted by its authoritarian connections. This has made the region's universities reluctant to forcefully engage in public security debates. This is particularly true of public universities, which are in most cases defined by their adversarial relationships with governments and military institutions. Hence, very few, if any, academic programs on security studies may be found at Central American universities or at the region's handful of independent think tanks. This limits considerably the production of rigorous local research on citizen security and at the same time perpetuates police and military officers' control over policy discussions.

The perceived lack of policy relevance of much criminological work generated in the region. Some of the best criminological research in LAC is underpinned by principles framed by the critical criminology school, which places a heavy emphasis on the social determinants of criminal behavior, the rehabilitation of offenders, social prevention policies, and, to some extent, the transformation of the prevailing social order as the only sustainable solution to criminal violence.[16] Policymakers and operators within the police forces (but not so much those in the judiciary or prison system) generally view this line of research as an intellectual justification for "soft" policies on crime and an indictment of traditional methods of dealing with criminal behavior. As a result, they view it with great suspicion, discount it as politically dangerous, and frequently denounce it as an obstacle to effective law enforcement.

To be fair, while the attention of this line of research to human rights and social risk factors cannot be overstated, much of the work it generates seems to be entirely oblivious to the short-term pressures that beset politicians or the intense anxieties about crime that pervade Latin American societies today. Moreover, it tends to have relatively little to say about organized crime, the single most important security threat in much of the region and the one that appears least amenable to long-term social prevention remedies. In the rare circumstance that a policymaker accepts the theoretical assumptions of the available criminological research, the fixation of this research with structural, long-term remedies for insecurity limits its political usefulness.

The absence of policy-relevant research has been only partially compensated for by the work of the United Nations Office on Drugs and Crime (UNODC), the Inter-American Development Bank (IDB), and, more recently, the UNDP, whose research on crime in Latin America explicitly aims to inform the policymaking process. Through a series of robust policy reports, the UNDP in particular is trying to reframe the security discussion in Central America by advocating a framework predicated on human development while remaining cognizant of the need to modernize coercive instruments in the state.[17] Although its reports thus far have helped to spark a more nuanced public discussion on citizen security in Central America, they have failed to move much beyond academic circles or shed the "soft-on-crime" tag that has marred the political influence of UN agencies on crime issues (with the notable exception of UNODC, which espouses a hardline position on narcotics issues).

Costa Rica's recent experience is, once again, telling. In 2010, President Laura Chinchilla—a security expert and former UNDP consultant herself—called on the UNDP to help design a strategic security policy for the country. Months later, when the strategic review became public, it was widely chastised by the Costa Rican press as a vague and "appeasing" document, short on the specific short-term (and mostly harsh) prescriptions demanded by a fretful public.[18] This example offers a reminder of the obstacles—reputational as much as substantive—faced by UN agencies seeking to have an effective impact in policy debates on crime in Central America.

In the end, the troubling mixture of the intense politicization of citizen security and a visible lack of policy-relevant knowledge leaves Central America—and, arguably, most of LAC—with a policy debate of questionable quality and plagued by the false dichotomy of long-term social prevention processes and short-term initiatives to control crime. As a result, it leaves the policy process disturbingly dominated by "snake oil peddlers" who are keen to resolve security problems with "iron-fisted" policies and a cavalier attitude toward the rule of law. This is as unfortunate as it is dangerous, for "iron-fisted" policies have a poor record of controlling crime in a lasting way and a stellar one of undermining human rights. Because most criminological research in Central America is so politically unaware, the suspicion displayed by policymakers toward such research leaves the issue dangerously exposed to rhetoric spewed by populists and demagogues alike.[19] Under those conditions, the policies adopted to confront this challenge are, at best, unsophisticated and ineffective and, at worst, a clear and present risk for key democratic principles. Given the calamitous state of public security in Central America, the flaws of these policy discussions are laid out for all to see.

What Is to Be Done?

There are no silver bullets for citizen insecurity, particularly in a situation as deteriorated as that in Central America. This discussion necessitates heavy doses of humility: even in the best of cases, not an awful lot is known by scholars or policymakers about what makes crime rates go up or down. However, while well short of being a recipe for magical solutions, adding scientific knowledge may lead to better policy debates and outcomes than those associated with the current sorry state of citizen security in the isthmus. This is not inevitable, of course. But operating on something more than the policymakers' whims and naked political interests would no doubt be an improvement on the status quo.

While the incentives and prejudices that block more substantive policy discussions are, as seen above, entrenched, the direness of the current situation offers an opportunity to change them. The one thing grimmer than Central America's crime rates is the pervasive sense of perplexity among the region's policymakers. Nearly all of them are at a loss as to how to deal with the crime problem effectively. Moreover, they know that the majority of the Central American population perceives this.[20] Some politicians may try to hide basic information from the public or milk the issue politically, but the odds that they will reap political benefits from the same old ways of dealing with the problem are low and falling fast. In the end, this may offer an antidote of sorts to the pervasive political posturing and, conversely, an incentive for policymakers to engage in a more rigorous quest for evidence and advice.

To enhance communication channels between scholars and policymakers and, more generally, improve the quality of citizen security debates in Central America, it is necessary to transform the discussion's empirical content, to ask better questions, to enlarge the available pool of experts and the venues of the policy debate, and, finally, to pay attention to the format of the advice being provided to policymakers.

More and Better Facts

Policymakers in Central America must start by acknowledging that making security policies without rigorous fact-based knowledge is deleterious to their societies and increasingly risky from a political standpoint. In the absence of rigorous knowledge, other kinds of knowledge, riddled with prejudices and falsehoods, will infect the debate. The empirical content of the security discussion in Central America must be radically enriched in several ways.

Governments in the region must invest in modern, reliable statistical systems and technological tools to process crime-related information. Lean crime-reporting procedures and regular victimization surveys are the minimal prerequisites if leaders and scholars are to have a meaningful discussion on crime issues.[21]

It is urgent to revamp the policy evaluation capacities of Central American governments, moving toward randomized trials to measure policy effectiveness. The simple exercise of defining relevant indicators, identifying baselines, and measuring progress regularly (through periodic victimization surveys, for instance) would be a significant improvement.[22]

Also, it is important to bring comparative information to bear on policy debates. Rigorous information about ideas and practices that have proved useful in other countries and regions could instill in Central American policymakers the notion that there is a way out of the current morass, that violence levels can indeed be countered by effective policies. As suggested above, the UNDP policy reports have proved useful in this regard, as would more meta-studies in the mold of the seminal 1998 report by Sherman et al. in the United States describing what "works, what doesn't, [and] what's promising" in crime prevention.[23]

Finally, the generation of local criminological research at universities and research institutions must be further stimulated. However, local crime scholars and criminologists must decide whether they want their work to be policy-relevant or, alternatively, a stern denunciation of the status quo, geared toward academic debates. Both courses are entirely legitimate and not entirely incompatible. Policy relevance often demands questioning the status quo. In fact, in the case of Central America's citizen security policies, it almost certainly does. The point here is that policy relevance demands scholars' awareness of the immense time and political pressures that constrain the choices of policymakers. In concrete terms: if criminological research is to be politically relevant, it has to provide policy prescriptions *in the short run*, even if the bulk of its recommendations remain focused on long-term prescriptions to mitigate the social ills that underlie most forms of criminal violence. If scholars fail to recognize this, they will condemn themselves to remaining on the sidelines of this policy debate. They will paint themselves into a corner from which they will contemplate misguided security policies being adopted, snipe at them, and denounce them as proof of a rotten status quo. Intellectually comforting though this option may be, it is also largely useless. Unfortunately, this has often been the fate of criminological research, not just in Central America, but, indeed, in LAC as a whole.

Experts who aspire to craft viable citizen security prescriptions can no more afford to be fixated with the short term than to be oblivious to it. If they fall into the former trap, they will reproduce the failings so painfully visible in Central America today, where short-term political pressures have routinely led to an undue emphasis on coercive methods to confront crime. Yet, if they fall into the latter trap, they will not catch the eye of most policymakers in these democracies, who are at least as concerned about tomorrow's headlines as about society's long-term well-being. When it comes to citizen security in Central America, the only policy-relevant knowledge is the knowledge that recognizes that long-term solutions must start, and be seen to start, tomorrow.

Better Questions

It is essential to recast the discussions about citizen security in Central America. The issue requires a comprehensive approach that avoids false dichotomies between long-term social prevention and short-term control of crime. At a minimum, a useful and policy-relevant research agenda ought to be able to generate rigorous and systematic analyses on the following issues, among others:

- The geography and dynamics of criminal behavior down to the local level
- The factors—individual as well as collective, socioeconomic as much as political—that seem to be associated with high levels of different types of crime in the region, and the complex interactions between them
- The links between state capacity and crime levels
- The factors associated with the extremely high and worsening perceptions of crime throughout the region, which very often are only weakly correlated with actual levels of crime[24]
- The links between large-scale drug trafficking, small-scale narcotics trade, and domestic drug consumption levels, on the one hand, and between all of these and crime rates, on the other
- The underlying causes of high impunity levels throughout the region and the best practices available to reduce them

- Options to enhance the levels of trust between law enforcement agencies and citizens, particularly those that may lead to citizens' greater willingness to report crime
- Best practices in the coordination of security policies and social policies at large
- The proper limits within a well-functioning democratic system for the participation—if any—of the armed forces in the fight against organized crime
- Options to improve the performance of prison systems and reduce recidivism, including the potential use of alternative methods to sanction offenders
- The most fruitful ways in which international cooperation can improve the ability of Central American societies to reduce violence levels

Most important of all, perhaps, would be the effort to systematize both successful and failed policy interventions to reduce violence in Latin America, as well as the surrounding political conditions that enable success and precipitate failure. This may go a long way toward liberating the current debate from the twin yokes of ideology and demagoguery.

More Experts

The enhancement of citizen security policies in Central America requires more than fostering better policy-relevant criminological knowledge; it also requires enlarging the pool of experts who can provide such expertise. The governments of the isthmus need to systematically train a much larger cadre of serious scholars with an interest in crime-related issues. This is essential if the police and military's stranglehold over the policy discussion—which almost inevitably allows the reproduction of the current set of policies—is to be broken. The pool of scholarly expertise available to policymakers may also widen with further cooperation from the international community, which in some areas (mainly relating to police reform) has already, for a long time, provided assistance to the region's governments. Notably, the "resident scholar" programs funded by some cooperation agencies, such as Germany's GIZ, have proven to be some of the most interesting models of scholarly and policymaker interaction. These and similar schemes allow cooperating agencies to finance and install foreign scholars in government ministries and other state institutions for prolonged periods of time. Such scholars are tasked with the double responsibility of providing policymakers with expert advice and enhancing the capabilities of their host institutions. Seldom used in the realm of security—perhaps due to the sensitive nature of the information handled by those institutions—these schemes offer a valuable mechanism for Central American policymakers to obtain prime technical and comparative knowledge in the fight against crime.

More Forums

The forums within which policy discussions take place and are framed must be broadened as well. The role of Central American legislatures in enabling a national debate on citizen security, informed by scholarly knowledge and with definite policy implications, should be encouraged. In almost all developed countries, the government periodically issues white papers that articulate the key points of, say, a national defense policy. Such documents are submitted to the legislative branch and opened up for broad scrutiny, analysis, and debate, in which scholars and civil society members freely participate. This discussion both informs and improves the mechanisms whereby a truly national defense strategy can be formulated. It also helps to substantiate the budgetary debate that would stem from such a strategy. Gradually, this practice has proliferated in analogous ways throughout LAC as well. Nothing prevents governments from engaging in a similar process relating to citizen security, especially now that nearly every Central American legislature has a Committee on Public Security. White papers would simply be another avenue for introducing scholarly knowledge into the policy process. Much more importantly, it would be a way of democratizing the process through which citizen security policies are formulated.

Friendlier Formats

Last but not least, I make a well-known general point that extends beyond the realm of public security: scholars ought to be mindful of how they format their advice. For policymakers in Central America and elsewhere, time is the most precious of commodities. Overlapping agendas, mushrooming commitments, and perpetual news cycles conspire to create a political dynamic in which there is very little time to digest substantive information before making decisions. Even in the rare cases when individual policymakers are driven by academic passion, time pressures force them to seek succinct solutions to complex problems. Hence, in most cases, scholars' practical relevance depends on their ability to make their analyses, findings, and recommendations digestible. Lengthy texts, the mainstay of academic livelihoods, have an exceedingly small chance of attracting a policymaker's eye, much less a journalist's. Short policy memos, PowerPoint presentations, and videos—in all cases containing straightforward recommendations—are the instruments of choice of real-life policy debates, particularly when dealing with quickly changing issues. This may seem frightening to someone used to the texture and nuance of academic debate, but such are the tough rules of the policy game. And scholars must remember to pay attention to the short term.

Adopting these suggestions—especially those geared toward improving the empirical content of citizen security debates—will not solve Central America's terrible security plight, of course. But their adoption can help to establish more fluid communication between policymakers and scholars, which could in turn contribute to improving the quality of policy discussions on public security in the isthmus. That may not seem like much, but it could shed a ray of light onto a dark and forbidding landscape.

ACKNOWLEDGMENTS

I thank Abraham Lowenthal, Mariano Bertucci, and Kevin Gallagher for their very useful comments on a previous version of this chapter. They are, of course, innocent of the final result.

NOTES

1. Estimation based on a 2002 World Health Organization report: Etienne G. Krug, Linda L. Dahlberg, James A. Mercy, Anthony B. Zwi, and Rafael Lozano, *World Report on Violence and Health* (New York: World Health Organization, October 3, 2002), www.who .int/violence_injury_prevention/violence/world_report/en.

2. Estimation based on data from Latinobarómetro Corporation, *2010 Report* (Santiago, Chile: Latinobarómetro, 2010), www.asep-sa.org/latinobarometro/LATBD_Latinobarometro _Report_2010.pdf.

3. Estimation from Juan Luis Londoño, Alejandro Gaviria, and Rodrigo Guerrero, eds., *Asalto al Desarrollo: Violencia en América Latina* (Washington, DC: Inter-American Development Bank, 2000). Regional GDP figures are from the World Bank, *World Development Indicators 1980–2011*, http://data.worldbank.org/indicator/NY.GNP.PCAP.CD.

4. Latinobarómetro, *2010 Report*.

5. On this topic, see Kevin Casas-Zamora, *The Travails of Development and Democratic Governance in Central America*, Foreign Policy Paper No. 28 (Washington, DC: Brookings Institution Press, June 2011).

6. Good summaries of the arguments—particularly in the field of international relations—are to be found, for example, in Joseph S. Nye, "International Relations: The Relevance of Theory to Practice," in *The Oxford Handbook of International Relations*, ed. Christian Reus-Smit and Duncan Snidal (Oxford: Oxford University Press, 2008), 648–60; Stephen D. Krasner, "Conclusion: Garbage Cans and Policy Streams: How Academic Research Might

Affect Foreign Policy," in *Power, the State, and Sovereignty: Essays on International Relations,* ed. Stephen D. Krasner (New York: Routledge, 2009), 254–74.

7. Michael D. Cohen, James G. March, and Johan P. Olsen, "A Garbage Can Model of Organizational Choice," *Administrative Science Quarterly* 17 (1972): 1–25.

8. John W. Kingdon, *Agendas, Alternatives, and Public Policies* (New York: HarperCollins, 1995).

9. See Nora Lustig, chap. 6, and Thomas Biersteker, chap 8.

10. Kevin Casas-Zamora, *The Besieged Polis: Citizen Insecurity and Democracy in Latin America* (Washington, DC: Brookings Institution–Organization of American States, 2013).

11. Christina Boswell, *The Political Uses of Expert Knowledge: Immigration Policy and Social Research* (New York: Cambridge University Press, 2009).

12. "Broken windows" refers to a widely debated criminological theory that posits that monitoring urban environments and preventing low-level vandalism have an effect in the prevention of serious crime. Its classical formulation can be found in George L. Kelling and Catherine M. Coles, *Fixing Broken Windows: Restoring Order and Reducing Crime in Our Communities* (New York: Free Press, 1998). Both its assumptions and its practical effects have been severely disputed. See, for instance, David Thacher, "Order Maintenance Reconsidered: Moving beyond Strong Causal Reasoning," *Journal of Criminal Law and Criminology* 94 (2004): 381–414.

13. Instituto Nacional de Estadística y Censos de Costa Rica (INEC) and Programa de Naciones Unidas para el Desarrollo (PNUD), *Resultados módulo sobre victimización: Encuesta de Hogares de Propósitos Múltiples* (San José, Costa Rica: INEC-PNUD, 2008), www.pnud .or.cr/images/stories/Mdulo_Victimizacin_PNUD_INEC.pdf; Instituto Ciudadano de Estudios sobre la Inseguridad (ICESI), *Séptima Encuesta Nacional sobre Inseguridad* (Mexico City: ICESI, 2010), www.icesi.org.mx/estadisticas/estadisticas_encuestasNacionales_ensi7.asp.

14. Jan Van Dijk, Robert Manchin, Van Kesteren, John van Kesteren, Sami Nevala, and Gergely Hideg, *The Burden of Crime in the EU*, Research Report: A Comparative Analysis of the European Survey of Crime and Safety (EU ICS) 2005 (Brussels: UNICRI, Gallup Europe, Max Planck Institute, CEPS, Geox, 2005).

15. Costa Rica's 2004 Citizen Security National Survey was one of the crucial inputs to PNUD, *Venciendo el Temor: (In)seguridad Ciudadana y Desarrollo Humano en Costa Rica—Informe Nacional de Desarrollo Humano 2005* (San José, Costa Rica: PNUD-Costa Rica, 2006), a policy report on the issue, which I coordinated.

16. This is particularly true of the impressive body of research generated by the UN-sponsored Latin American Institute for the Prevention of Crime and the Treatment of Offenders (ILANUD).

17. See, for instance, PNUD, *Venciendo el Temor.*

18. For the reaction of the country's two most influential media outlets, see "Limitado aporte de POLSEPAZ," *La Nación* (San José, Costa Rica), February 16, 2011, www.nacion .com/2011-02-17/Opinion/Editorial/Opinion2686566.aspx; and Pilar Cisneros, "Bla, bla, bla y Nada de Seguridad Ciudadana," *Telenoticias,* February 21, 2011, www.teletica.com/blogs -teletica/blogs_detalle.php?id=253&dept=1.

19. The 2011 presidential campaign in Guatemala—in which both main candidates, Manuel Baldizón and Otto Pérez-Molina, tried to outbid each other in terms of their tough

approach toward crime—offered a particularly disturbing example of this. Baldizón ran on a platform whose main course of action consisted of applying the death penalty across the board (broadcasting executions live, for good measure) and denouncing international human rights treaties. The symbol of the campaign by Pérez-Molina, a retired general and the eventual winner, was a clenched fist. Kevin Casas-Zamora, *Guatemala: Between a Rock and a Hard Place* (Washington, DC: Brookings Institution Press, Sept. 16, 2011).

20. In 2008, 59% of those interviewed by Latinobarómetro in the six Central American countries believed that their country was growing more unsafe every day; only 13% thought that their country was becoming safer. Latinobarómetro Corporation, *2008 Report* (Santiago, Chile: Latinobarómetro, 2008), www.asep-sa.org/latinobarometro/LATBD_Latinobaro metro_Report_2008.pdf.

21. This is an area in which international cooperation agencies and multilateral banks can play a very significant role, by facilitating the acquisition and adoption of modern information systems as a bedrock for crafting good security policies.

22. The key to policy evaluation in a democracy lies with legislatures understanding that the power of the purse entails the responsibility of good stewardship of public resources. Broadening the scope of the budgeting process to enable the state's comptrollers and auditors (such as the US General Accounting Office or Germany's Federal Accounts Tribunal) to provide timely advice to legislators on the effectiveness of different public programs is one of the most important measures to reproduce policy success and prevent failure. This point, of course, is not restricted to the field of citizen security.

23. Laurence W. Sherman, Denise C. Gottfrenson, Doris L. MacKenzie, John Eck, Peter Reuter, and Shawn D. Bushway, *Preventing Crime: What Works, What Doesn't, What's Promising* (Washington, DC: US Department of Justice, 1998).

24. On these factors, see Casas-Zamora, *Besieged Polis*.

PART FOUR

SHAPING, IMPLEMENTING, EVALUATING, AND REVISING POLICY

CHAPTER EIGHT

Scholarly Participation in Transnational Policy Networks
The Case of Targeted Sanctions

THOMAS J. BIERSTEKER

Over the past 15 years, I have collaborated closely with a former US policy official, Sue Eckert, an assistant secretary of commerce in the Clinton administration, on the analysis and reform of United Nations (UN) targeted sanctions procedures. Strategic partnerships are essential in influencing public policy, and although our record of influence has been uneven during our years of work together (as I will illustrate), the contributions of our collaborative work have been acknowledged by policy practitioners in both Europe and the United States. One of our publications was even mentioned in a WikiLeaks document released in 2011, surely some indication of policy impact.[1] The experience has given me some insights into how scholars can and do participate in policy processes.

My method of analysis at the outset is deliberately self-reflective. It draws on my participation in processes and activities intended to influence the design of targeted financial sanctions and the institutional practices associated with their implementation, with a particular, but not exclusive, focus on the UN. Where relevant, I also discuss specific attempts to influence the foreign policy of individual UN member states, including, but not restricted to, the United States. Narrative as a form allows me to illustrate in empirical detail the many and varied ways in which scholars participate in what I term "transnational policy networks."

This is not the only way to influence policy. Scholars have multiple venues for engagement in the policy process, if they are willing and able to resist the many institutional barriers to doing so. These barriers include both colleagues who do not recognize policy work as "scholarly" and tenure and promotion committees that reinforce institutionalized disincentives for effective participation in policy discourse and practice (at least until after tenure). Most scholars who are inclined to participate in policy use the authority of either their scholarly rank or institutional position to participate as public intellectuals in public discourse on contemporary policy matters. The writing of op-ed pieces for prominent newspapers, appearances on television or radio news media panels, and occasional participation in specially convened study groups on topics of current policy concern are common ways for scholars to take part in the policy process. Increasingly, some public intellectuals participate through extensive web postings or personal blogs.[2] Another means of participation in the policy process is more direct, through a periodic transition into various government policy positions interspersed throughout one's career with returns to the academy.[3]

The literature on the policy engagement of scholars has grown considerably in recent years, in part due to the conference themes of two recent past presidents of the North American International Studies Association, Ann Tickner and Thomas Weiss. The literature generally describes four different mechanisms through which scholars become engaged in and influence public policy.[4] The first is the "trickle-down" model, suggested by Stephen Walt, which argues that new ideas emerge from academic "ivory towers" before gradually filtering down into the world of applied policy analysis and popular discourse.[5] The second, mentioned above, is the model of scholars periodically moving in and out of policy positions, using their time out of office to replenish what Joseph Nye terms their "embedded intellectual capital," which they draw on extensively during their time in the policy world.[6] A third model is suggested by Ernest Wilson, who describes policy think tanks as important vehicles for transmitting focused, policy-relevant knowledge to policy practitioners.[7] A fourth model is both more laissez-faire and less immediate and suggests that it is through the classroom teaching of concepts and theories that scholars participate in the policy world, in effect planting seeds in the minds of those students who eventually go on to play a major role in policy within a generation or two.

This chapter focuses on a different type of policy engagement: the involvement of scholars in what I call specialized *transnational policy networks*. Transnational policy networks (TPNs), broadly analogous to Pierre Bourdieu's concept of a specialized "field" of expertise,[8] are constituted by a group of individuals who share a common expertise, a common technical language to communicate that expertise, broadly shared normative concerns, but not necessarily agreement on specific policy alternatives. They include transgovernmental networks,[9] but transcend them to include actors other than state officials—actors from the private sector, from international organizations, from international legal practice, and sometimes from academia. Many of the individuals participating in a TPN have experience in more than one institutional setting. Indeed, it is not unusual for US Treasury officials to end up as compliance officers in the banks they once oversaw. As I illustrate in more detail below, the different individuals in TPNs tend to play different functional roles.

Accidental Beginnings, 1998

My involvement with the issue of targeted financial sanctions had accidental, or certainly unintentional, origins. I was director of Brown University's Watson Institute for International Studies, and at one of our Board of Overseers meetings in New York, I co-presided over a session in which one of our research projects presented its results to the board. The project focused on the humanitarian consequences of comprehensive UN sanctions against Iraq.[10] I introduced the session with some general remarks about what we know about sanctions, drawing on Hufbauer, Schott, and Elliott's work at the Peterson Institute for International Economics,[11] and emphasized that financial measures generally tend to be more effective than trade measures.

At the conclusion of the session, the chair of the board, noting the large number of representatives of financial institutions at the meeting, commented that given that comprehensive measures have such negative impacts and financial measures tend to be more effective, why not target financial sanctions? He suggested the institute initiate some research on the subject, and I subsequently asked Sue Eckert, who had recently joined the institute, to develop a project jointly with me. We linked up with the Council on Foreign Relations, with which we cosponsored several meetings in New York that were attended by representatives from the UN, member states, and the private sector. Our goal was both to bring ourselves up to speed on the issues and to generate ideas for a research project. It was at one of the Council on Foreign Relations sessions that the Swiss ambassador to the UN mentioned Switzerland's sponsorship of the Interlaken Process, a series of meetings in which officials from member states, UN Secretariat staff, representatives of the private sector (from both law and finance), and a few scholars were invited to work on ways to strengthen the instrument of multilateral targeted financial sanctions.

The Influence of a UN Policy Entrepreneur, 1999–2001

After the conclusion of the second (and final) Interlaken meeting in March 1999, I was approached by a senior UN official who inquired about my reaction to the process and asked me to put my thoughts in a short memo to him. I wrote that although the process was extremely useful for the small number of individuals (approximately 100) fortunate to have attended, it would be good to try to find a way to consolidate the findings in more than a single conference report. The findings could then be disseminated to the larger community responsible for targeted financial sanctions, not only at the UN in New York, but also in the capitals of member states responsible for implementation and at the large number of financial institutions globally that actually freeze funds of targeted (designated) individuals and firms. Unbeknownst to me, the UN official shared my memo with the Swiss ambassador and proposed that the government of Switzerland subcontract to the Watson Institute the responsibility to draft a manual from the proceedings. We hired a team of highly talented Brown University student research assistants, and our team not only summarized the Interlaken proceedings in the form of draft text that could be used in future UN Security Council resolutions for different types of targeted financial sanctions but also conducted original survey research on implementation practices in a sample of member states.

The Interlaken manual is still available on the Swiss Economic Affairs Ministry's website,[12] is routinely found on the shelves of UN Permanent Mission staff responsible for sanctions issues, and is widely known in UN circles, but it is unlikely that it is regularly consulted directly in the drafting of UN Security Council Resolutions (UNSCRs). Most UNSCRs have an iterated quality to them and are the product of cutting and pasting from the most recent, similar resolution. This is not surprising, and given the turnover in UN staff (even among the Permanent Five Members of the Security Council—the P5), Sue Eckert and I find we are constantly introducing ourselves to new practitioners (in New York) responsible for sanctions. We have a historical perspective that many current practitioners lack, and we can and do point out inconsistencies or moments of institutional forgetting, as well as moments of institutional progress or learning, that are not fully appreciated by practitioners who have held the brief for UN sanctions for only a short time. It is important to note, however, that although we are occasionally consulted by practitioners on how we would formulate a particular argument or on the origins of historical precedents, we are never consulted on the drafting of UNSCRs themselves. This drafting is a highly politicized process, which explains why many resolutions are less than optimally designed. Indeed, had we been consulted, the 2011 Libyan sanctions resolution UNSCR (1970) would have looked rather different, particularly with regard to the imposition of a general arms embargo on Libya and the immediate referral to the International Criminal Court.

The Interlaken manual did, apparently, have one concrete policy outcome. I was told by a former European Commission official responsible for sanctions implementation that financial institutions in Europe were annoyed that the EC had adopted our recommendation that financial institutions increase the length of time they retain financial records (to enable a process of following the money). The idea of retroactive reporting was something we added to the Interlaken manual, after we tested some of the ideas for different types of targeted financial sanctions in a group simulation exercise prior to completion of the text.

An Early (Unsuccessful) Effort to Influence Policy, 2002

Given that our work began with a concern about the unintended humanitarian consequences of comprehensive sanctions against Iraq, Sue Eckert and I decided to use our knowledge of simulation techniques and the drafting of the Interlaken manual to conduct a simulation exercise at the US Naval War College in Newport, Rhode Island, in 2002. The purpose of the exercise was to explore how the comprehensive sanctions against Iraq could be replaced with targeted sanctions and, ideally, create a new political consensus at the UN on the issue. We used a secure facility at the US Naval War College and invited a few senior UN Secretariat officials, as well as US and UK officials (who were comfortable sharing intelligence with one another), to simulate and develop concrete policy proposals. There was little in the Volcker Commission report on the operations of the UN Oil for Food Program (published years later) that I did not learn during our simulation, both how the program was corrupted and how it was evaded by Iraq. We were uniquely placed to convene this simulation exercise, it had the enthusiastic support of the UN Secretariat staff, and we financed it with a discretionary grant from the Carnegie Corporation.

I went to Washington, DC, in May 2002 to present the results of the simulation to policy practitioners in the State Department and at the National Security Council, accompanied by a former US ambassador who participated in our simulation. The general reaction we received at the State Department was, "We know all of this. Secretary Powell tried it and it failed." There appears to be, among some policy practitioners, a sense of both superiority to and intentional insularity from the academy. While this attitude is often mutual (as described in more detail below), some policy practitioners not only perceive the differences but seem to play on them to reduce the potential influence of scholars. The meetings at the National Security Council were more constructive, but we received the general impression that the policy had already moved beyond sanctions to a decision to use force and that our proposals were too little, too late.

Training Workshops at the Watson Institute, 2003 and 2004

Returning to a more customary academic role, we convened two training workshops for policy practitioners responsible for sanctions at the UN. We invited all 15 members of the UN Security Council, in addition to prospective Security Council members, major member state financial contributors, and UN Secretariat staff, to travel to the Watson Institute for a weekend workshop focused on the design of targeted sanctions. We began with presentations of the three international processes on targeted sanctions. Following Interlaken's focus on financial sanctions, the German government sponsored the Bonn-Berlin process on arms embargoes, aviation bans, and travel bans, while the Swedish government sponsored the Stockholm process on the implementation of targeted sanctions. At the workshops, the academic consultants and advisors to each of the three processes summarized the results and introduced their respective manuals. We then conducted a simulation exercise in which we produced a fictional case of a threat to international peace and security, indicated P5 consensus to act, divided up the participants into three working groups, and gave each group the task of designing a targeted sanctions UNSCR appropriate to the situation. Each group presented its draft resolution for comparative (and competitive) critique and commentary. In effect, it was like playing model UN with the real UN. Convening this kind of training exercise is something the academy is particularly well-placed to do.

One immediate impact was expressed by a Mexican diplomat who indicated that she had never realized there were so many options in the design of targeted financial sanctions. She described the routine process of marking up and commenting on a substantially completed UNSCR, typically drafted by a P5 member state. She found the simulation process "empowering." The longer-term impact is more difficult to gauge, although we did establish a strong relationship with UN Secretariat and UN Permanent Mission staff, some of whom used our simulation exercise to try out ideas they could never have put on the table or initiated on their own. This is an example of the potential synergy within a TPN. Scholars can create institutional occasions for moving an agenda forward that UN or member state officials could not initiate or undertake on their own.

The Watson Report, 2005 and 2006

Because Sue Eckert and I specialized in the design of targeted financial sanctions and because the UN's 1267 Al-Qaida/Taliban Sanctions Committee was arguably the most developed, extensive, and sophisticated targeted financial sanctions regime,[13] we received a commission, in 2005–6, from the governments of Switzerland, Sweden, and Germany—three of the so-called like-minded states concerned with procedural reforms at the UN Security Council level. They asked us to draft a comparative study of the adequacy of due-process considerations in the designation of individuals and corporate entities in all of the currently functioning UN sanctions committees, but with particular attention to the 1267 Committee. There was growing dissatisfaction with the violations of basic due-process procedures at the UN level for individuals designated by the 1267 Committee, reinforced by legal challenges underway both at the national level in all three countries and at the European level, at the European Court of Justice and the European Court of Human Rights.

We conducted a comprehensive analysis of the listing, procedural, and delisting practices of all UN sanctions committees operating at the time. We illustrated the variance in practice and procedure, teamed up with two prominent international legal scholars to identify criteria for evaluating due process—access, notification, fair hearing, and effective remedy—and drafted a series of policy recommendations. We presented a range of options and evaluated each according to these four due-process criteria. Many of the ideas we discussed in the report were not original to us—the idea of the creation of a focal point came from the French delegation, while that of an ombudsperson came from a "non-paper" produced by the Danes. What we provided was an organized, analytical framework for policy comparison, an independently and theoretically derived set of evaluation criteria, and an assessment of the degree to which different options met those criteria. We deliberately did not advocate a single option but laid out the range of choices from which member states could choose. Our report was titled *Strengthening Targeted Sanctions through Fair and Clear Procedures*, deliberately using the phrase employed in the 2005 World Summit Outcome document that called for "fair and clear procedures" of due process in sanctions that target individuals. The report subsequently became popularly known around the UN as the "Watson report."[14]

We presented our results at a meeting for UN diplomats and officials at the UN in New York in March 2006, hosted by the Swedish government. Our report was subsequently sponsored by the three governments that had funded it and was issued as an official UN document.[15] We were credited by a number of practitioners, both from member states and in the UN Secretariat, with playing a role in moving the debate along and having an influence in UNSCR 1730, passed in December 2006. That resolution created the focal point for receipt of applications for delisting from individuals who did not have the backing of a member state for their appeals. In a February 2009 cable later leaked by WikiLeaks, the US Embassy in London stated that the UK government was studying proposals in the Watson report as it prepared a draft UNSCR for an extension of the 1267 Committee mandate later that year.[16] It was gratifying to learn that our analytical work had become a standard reference for thinking about the reform of UN Security Council sanctions committee procedures.

Update of the Watson Report, 2009

At the precise moment the WikiLeaks cable was being sent, we were engaged in research interviews for an update of the Watson report. We thought that 2009 would be a propitious time for moving the agenda forward and creating a formal institutionalized review mechanism at the UN level. We acknowledged the significant procedural progress made by the Security Council since targeted sanctions were first introduced in the early 1990s, and particularly since the advent of the 1267 Committee in 1999. We analyzed the progress in terms of the four criteria identified in the original Watson report. Notification and access had been largely addressed, hence we made a strong recommendation for the creation of a review mechanism at the UN level to address the remaining issues of fair hearing and effective remedy. In effect, in 2009 we moved from scholarship into more of an advocacy role. We obtained a small grant from a semi-independent research organization in Switzerland and, with the advent of the Obama administration, used our improved networks of access to senior officials in Washington to make our case for further procedural reform at the UN level. We interviewed (in effect, convened a small seminar with) a group of US Treasury Department officials in the Office of Foreign Asset Control (OFAC) directly involved in many of the counterterrorism designations made in the immediate aftermath of the attacks of September 11, 2001, and tried to persuade them of the political need for due-process reforms at the UN.[17] My colleague went even further with an extended one-on-one meeting with the head of OFAC, using our research as a basis for arguing that Treasury should drop its resistance to UN-level reforms.

The UN Security Council passed resolution 1904 in December 2009, which created the position of an ombudsperson at the UN level to receive appeals, review cases, and assist designees with potential delistings. After the resolution's passage, a senior official at the US Mission to the UN referred to "our common efforts," wrote that much of our analysis and input had been incorporated into its approach, and even asked that we help convey to skeptics how far the United States had changed its position. In the months preceding the passage of the resolution, he said that he routinely plagiarized portions of our draft text in internal discussions with colleagues in Washington who were wary of making further procedural reforms at the UN level. We were also startled, not to mention slightly flattered, to hear a significant portion of the introduction of a draft version of our report read word for word (without acknowledgment) by a Belgian diplomat in October 2009 when introducing a European policy meeting in Brussels on the significance of the subject.

We were by no means the only scholars in the TPN working on the issue during the fall of 2009. A research team from Notre Dame University made a series of proposals for incremental procedural changes at the sanctions committee level but recommended against the creation of a review mechanism at the UN level as impractical because of P5 opposition. At the Brussels meeting, we publicly challenged their incrementalism as inadequate to addressing the core of the problem and maintained there was need for more significant reforms to address the issues of fair hearing and effective remedy. As indicated above, one of our proposals, for the creation of an office of ombudsperson, was adopted in UNSCR 1904 two months later.

International Targeted Sanctions Consortium, 2009–12

Following our brief stint with policy advocacy in 2009, we returned to a more conventional academic role within the transnational policy network. Targeted sanctions have been used by the UN for more than 20 years, and, for the foreseeable future, they are likely to be the *only* type of sanction imposed by the organization (even if the scope of targeting is occasionally broadened). They are used for a wide variety of purposes—to prevent conflict, enforce peace agreements, combat terrorism, support nonproliferation, and foster human rights and the restoration of democratically elected governments. Yet there has been no systematic, comprehensive study of their impacts or effectiveness. Hence, we formed an international consortium of researchers and policy practitioners engaged in the use of targeted sanctions to design a common framework for research and to conduct that research on all of the major UN targeted sanctions imposed over the past 20 years.

We created 15 different research teams, located in Europe, North America, Africa, and Asia, to engage in multidisciplinary research on the impacts and effectiveness of UN targeted sanctions. Many teams are composed of both scholars and former policy practitioners. We deliberately involved practitioners in the design of the research, to ensure that the research results would address their interests and concerns. Our goal has been to engage in a systematic comparative study of the most significant UN targeted sanctions regimes over the past 20 years (al-Qaida / Taliban, Angola, Côte d'Ivoire, Democratic Republic of the Congo, North Korea, Haiti, Iran, Liberia, Libya I and II, the former Republic of Yugoslavia, Sierra Leone, Somalia, and Sudan I and II). Our core unit of analysis, however, is not the national sanctions regimes but discrete episodes of targeted sanctions within them. This enables us to examine the effectiveness of different combinations of targeted sanctions applied to the same country over time and also increases our sample size. There is an average of three or four episodes within each country regime.

The project has five stages: (1) exploratory discussions/feasibility/needs assessment in 2008–9, (2) the development of a common research framework in 2009, (3) the conduct of research in 2010–11, (4) the analysis and dissemination of results in 2012 and 2013, and (5) ongoing support for capacity training. The final stage will probably involve a return to training workshops along the lines of those conducted at the Watson Institute in 2003 and 2004. Major financial support has come from the Ministry of Foreign Affairs of Switzerland, the Foreign and Commonwealth Office of the United Kingdom, and the Government of Canada.

The project is still very much underway at the time of this writing, so it is premature to assess its impact. In 2011 we convened a major conference with the heads of the research teams and an equal number of policy practitioners that was hosted by the Foreign and Commonwealth Office of the United Kingdom. Our intent was to compare and speak across the different cases rather than to present them in separate, sequential narratives. Although it has not been easy to secure government financing for the research project during the period of fiscal austerity in many parts of the world since 2008, we have deliberately sought governments' support to ensure their buy-in, participation, and use of the results of the research. There is also the pragmatic concern that some traditional scholarly outlets for research support tend to view our project as too close to policy and therefore not appropriate for their support. In 2009 and 2011, we conducted preliminary confidential briefings for foreign ministry officials from two of the countries funding us (United Kingdom, Canada) on topics of particular foreign policy interest to them. In 2013 we developed and released the first version of SanctionsApp, a multimedia interactive device designed to disseminate the results of our research and to facilitate greater discursive interaction on the UN Security Council. The app makes alternative draft text immediately available to policy practitioners in real time and also interactively generates appropriate analogies for situational comparison.

The Processes, the Players, and their Roles in TPNs

Moving from narrative to the broader analytical issues that motivate this volume: just what are the roles and forms of participation of individual scholars in a transnational policy network? As suggested above, TPNs consist of individuals from transgovernmental networks but go beyond government officials to include actors from the business sector, from international organizations, from international legal practice, and sometimes from academia. At first glance, the concept of a TPN appears very similar to the concept of an epistemic community. Peter Haas defined an epistemic community as a "network of professionals with recognized expertise and competence in a particular domain and an authoritative claim to policy-relevant knowledge within that domain or issue area."[18] This definition is similar to my conception of TPNs, and Haas even refers to "networks of knowledge-based experts" shortly before the description just quoted. It differs, however, in three key respects: relational, compositional, and hierarchical.

First, for Haas, the epistemic community exists separately from, and generally stands outside, the community of policy decision makers it sometimes successfully influences. Within a TPN, policy practitioners and scholars coexist, interrelating within the network in complex and varying ways, each influencing the other. Hierarchies are clearly present, depending on the issue domain (as illustrated below), and the participants are not necessarily equal in power or in the direction of influence.[19] Second, for Haas, members of an epistemic community share norms, causal beliefs, notions of validity, and a common policy enterprise.[20] Within TPNs, the individuals share a common expertise, a common technical language to communicate that expertise, broadly held normative concerns, but not necessarily agreement on specific policy alternatives. Third, there is an implicit hierarchy inherent in Haas's idea of an epistemic community, where members of the community have technical expertise that is of value to policy decision makers to whom "new ideas and information" are diffused.[21] State decision makers respond to new knowledge emanating from epistemic communities rather than participate in the creation of new knowledge themselves. Within a TPN, the learning is mutual, multifaceted, and issue-specific (policy practitioners have more experience with the details of implementation, while scholars are better equipped to analyze the effectiveness and design of the policy instruments).

Thinking about the different players and their respective roles in a TPN is one way to bring agency back into the heart of the norms literature, which, until recently, has tended to cede agency to norms at the expense of individual players.[22] Within the norms literature, the concept of a *policy entrepreneur* has been identified as a crucial actor in the development of international norms.[23] It is a useful construct, and as described in the narrative above, some key individuals from the UN Secretariat have played critically important entrepreneurial roles in the TPN concerned with targeted sanctions. The policy entrepreneur as concept is not sufficient on its own, however, and tends to focus on the actions of individuals, without examining the institutional environments from which they emerge and the networks within which they operate. That is why I prefer the concept of transnational policy networks operating with varying degrees of coherence and influence in different policy domains.

In addition to policy entrepreneurs there are also *brokers*, typically individuals who represent state players (but not necessarily official state policy). They can be channels to influence, to resources, and to convening functions at the UN (where states remain the preeminent actors). There are also *gatekeepers*, institutional or disciplinary conservatives who discourage radical changes or defend past practices that they helped develop or particular disciplinary or institutional conventions; *guardians* of expertise, a position acquired by virtue of their previous roles or past accumulated experience; and *legitimators*, often a role played by academics knowledgeable about the larger literature or about research methods used to analyze issues. When we scholars participate in TPNs (through consulting, task force participation, policy conferences, training workshops, commissioned research, or our own policy reports), it is not as neutral outsiders. We participate in ways that should be self-reflectively and critically examined. We lend our expertise and, by so doing, we are not innocents.

Given this brief characterization of different functional roles occasionally taken on by participants in TPNs, what do the different agents within such a network actually do? In general terms, they frame issues, they draw analogies, and they categorize.[24] But they do more than this. They also project their ideas, define problems, and articulate future threats and policy responses. They sometimes engage in rhetorical recomposition (as did the participants in the International Commission on Intervention and State Sovereignty in articulating the emergent norm of responsibility to protect).[25] Performance is constant and ongoing, and enactions and articulations take place in public and private meetings, in official statements, in reports, in lobbying efforts, and in any context that allows for argument and persuasion.

Beyond legitimation (to which I will return below), what can scholars contribute to TPNs? Drawing on the preceding narrative, in the first instance, they can conduct policy-oriented research that policy practitioners are interested in but do not have the time to conduct themselves. It is crucial, however, to engage practitioners in the design of the research. Too much policy research is a one-way street from the academy to the policymaker, in effect, with scholars second-guessing and trying to tell the practitioners what to do.[26]

Second, scholars can organize and conduct training workshops to disseminate the results of policy research, explore new concepts and ideas, and simulate alternative scenarios. In this context, academics can serve as agents for policy-practitioner principals who, on their own, could not initiate discussions of certain topics or suggest some policy proposals without attracting the attention or potential wrath of other colleagues within their institutions (or within the TPN). Scholars also have the advantage of being able to serve as the institutional memory or a historical register for a policy community experiencing rapid turnover in personnel. Individuals rarely go back and read through the files of their predecessors, and scholars can put a contemporary policy malaise in perspective and suggest how things actually once were worse (or better, as the case may be).

Third, scholars can participate in TPN processes (such as Interlaken, Bonn-Berlin, Stockholm) and make positive contributions, not only by posing critical questions, but also by serving as rapporteurs, co-chairing sessions, or engaging in third-track diplomacy with government officials.[27] Scholars are typically tasked with drafting manuals that come out of processes and disseminating the results of the processes in subsequent training workshops.

Fourth, academics can conduct briefings either for public audiences or for closed sessions with government officials. They can also convene meetings on their own to explore an issue, define a research agenda, or raise points too sensitive for government sponsorship. Scholars have to choose their sources of funding carefully. There are times when government support is essential, such as when you want to disseminate the results of research within the policy community, but also times when it should be avoided, to prevent excessive interference in the content of research.

Fifth, scholars can draft independent reports on cutting-edge, policy-relevant issues. They can integrate knowledge from different disciplines, provide documentation for policy debate, organize policy options, and legitimize ideas and proposals. Academics are able to perform a legitimation function because they possess the authority of expertise.[28] Because scholars are ultimately accountable to a larger community of peer scholars rather than to higher-ups in a hierarchical organization, they have the independence (if they choose to use it) both to legitimize and to criticize. Former US ambassador to the UN John Bolton was reported to have been "livid" over the publication of the Watson report, which he criticized for legitimating European ideas.[29] Scholars can also both suggest the need for policy reform and advocate for it.

On reflection, perhaps the greatest advantage the scholar has over the policy practitioner within the context of a TPN is the ability to convene meetings on controversial issues and draft reports. Even policy practitioners with far greater experience and expertise would be unlikely to undertake politically sensitive initiatives or activities of broad scope on their own. Practitioners are often less able to act independently, and while they might wish to see some issues raised, they could never do so from their institutional positions. Scholars thus can play the role of agents for some policy principals. Indeed, I believe we have a social responsibility to use the time we have and our analytical capabilities and techniques to contribute to constructive policy reform. We also have a responsibility to reflect consciously about what we are doing (and why). Because of our relative independence and because our accountability is primarily to our scholarly peers, we have a social responsibility to be critical, not in a destructive or dismissive sense, but in a constructive one. The challenge is determining when and how to speak truth to power. At what point do we go too far (in either direction)?

Normative Implications

Scholarly expertise in a given policy domain comes either from the publication of research on a topic or from iterative participation in policy debates and processes. Expertise comes from gradual learning about the policy process itself (particularly for someone like myself who has never been a policy practitioner) and is best defined operationally as clearly knowing what you do not know about a given subject. I only gradually developed "the authority of expertise" in this issue domain—defined as an ability to participate in technical conversations about the design of targeted financial sanctions, to provide external legitimacy, and to conduct research that no one inside the policy-practitioner community has the time or perhaps the inclination to undertake.

With expertise and policy engagement, however, comes responsibility. There are some important normative and ethical considerations of which scholars engaged in policy need to be aware, what Stanley Hoffmann once described as the "peculiar problems" of scholarly engagement in the policy process. He observed that "in their relations with the real world, the scholars are torn between irrelevance and absorption." He perceptively noted that the practice of international relations is often "an insider's game," and he is particularly insightful about the slippery slope of policy engagement.[30]

With our accumulated authority of expertise on targeted sanctions, we have been fortunate to have extraordinary access to policymakers interested in reforming current UN Security Council practices, a topic that several states, not only current members of the UN Security Council, have attempted to influence. Often eager to meet with us, policymakers are interested in giving us their particular policy position, but they also often ask us for our assessments (not necessarily out of politeness but to test out their arguments with each other). There are dangers of losing one's independence and critical perspective in these discussions, as well as dangers of self-censorship and temptations to value having access and influence over being "scholarly."

Given the iterative nature of the work, there is always a built-in constraint against saying anything too radical or critical. There are ways of being critical, but denunciating pronouncements in public meetings (the proverbial "speaking truth to power") are usually not advisable. This is a problem common to research dependent on elite access, one that journalists also face. As Hoffmann warned, there is often a trade-off between maintaining continued access and public criticism of a given set of policies.[31] It requires both learning patience and practicing diplomacy, two things that are not always learned, rewarded, or practiced in the academy.

Fortunately, and significantly, the privilege of academic tenure gives some of us the freedom to study and say what we think is important. Just as the institution of sovereignty entails both rights and responsibilities, so, too, does the institution of tenure in higher education. The challenge is figuring out how best to navigate the terrain between maintaining access and speaking critically and knowing how to recognize when principle matters more than continued access. Beyond this risk, the temptation to have one's policy work taken seriously and acted upon can lead to a form of self-censorship that can compromise the critical edge of scholarly inquiry.

We encountered some of these challenges in our research in the 2006 Watson report, upsetting some of the legal specialists in the governments that sponsored our research by not taking as uncompromising a line as they did on individual human rights and by stating things in our independent report that differed from the common position of the "like-minded states" group (of which, as noted earlier, all three of our sponsors were members). The lesson here is that states—and nongovernmental organizations, for that matter—need to recognize that this is one of the risks of commissioning scholarly based research. You can gain credibility from the authority of scholarly expertise, but you cannot control the outcomes of that research.

We have been fortunate to have had the access and influence that we have had, in part because of our constant innovation and strategic alliances with different members of the TPN in which we participate, but also in part because of where in the world we come from (Europe and North America). While policy engagement can be highly rewarding, one should not expect much in the way of respect for or recognition of this from one's scholarly colleagues. Not only is your work not likely to be counted in traditional academic measures of impact and output (and hence to be of limited value to your departmental peers), but it is also not likely to be read or cited by them. If you are going to engage in policy, it is probably best to lead a double life and have an abstract theoretical or methodological side to your publications and profile.[32] It can give you deeper insights into the processes in which you participate, and it sustains your credibility as a scholar—ultimately essential for maintaining the authority of expertise.

Despite the many institutionalized barriers against effective scholarly participation in the policy world, three recently published works by prominent scholars not typically known for their policy involvement have emphasized the need for scholars to become more engaged in the social world. Jörg Friedrichs and Friedrich Kratochwil call for greater pragmatism; Rudra Sil and Peter Katzenstein argue for analytical eclecticism; and David Lake challenges the dominance of "isms" in scholarly discourse and proposes a lexicon for transcending divisions.[33] These are important and timely contributions, yet it is striking that none of them offer any concrete ideas about how scholars might become more engaged in the policy world. Thus the need for this volume, with its detailed exploration of many different ways in which scholars and policy practitioners interact with one another in contemporary international affairs, from identifying problems to framing issues, developing policy options, and evaluating policy outcomes.

ACKNOWLEDGMENTS

I would like to thank Abraham Lowenthal for a lifetime of creating institutional spaces for the productive interaction of scholars and policy practitioners in international affairs, as well as the other participants in the conference organized in his honor at the University of Southern California (USC) in April 2011, who provided stimulating discussion and thought-provoking debate on the issues addressed in this chapter. I also thank Mariano Bertucci and Barbara Stallings for their detailed comments on an earlier version of this chapter.

NOTES

1. Reported on the website of the *Daily Telegraph* (London), *UK Studying Range of Options for 1267 Sanctions Review; under Logistical and Legal Pressure*, passed to the *Telegraph* by WikiLeaks on February 4, 2011, www.telegraph.co.uk/news/wikileaks-files/london-wikileaks /8305163/UK-STUDYING-RANGE-OF-OPTIONS-FOR-1267-SANCTIONS-REVIEW -UNDER-LOGISTICAL-AND-LEGAL-PRESSURE.html (accessed June 4, 2012).

2. Stephen Walt and Daniel Drezner are active users of blogging.

3. This is something both Joseph Nye and Arturo Valenzuela, among others, have notably done over the course of their careers.

4. I am grateful to Mariano Bertucci for suggesting three of the four elements of this typology, drawing on the background memorandum he prepared for the USC conference, "Scholar-Practitioner Relations in International Relations: A Quick Summary of the Salient Literature."

5. Stephen M. Walt, "The Relationship between Theory and Policy in International Relations," *Annual Review of Political Science* 8 (2005): 40.

6. Joseph Nye, "International Relations: The Relevance of Theory to Practice," in *The Oxford Handbook of International Relations*, ed. Christian Reus Smit and Duncan Snidal (Oxford: Oxford University Press, 2008), 657.

7. Ernest J. Wilson III, "Is There Really a Scholar-Practitioner Gap? An Institutional Analysis," *PS: Political Science and Politics* 40 (2007): 149.

8. Pierre Bourdieu, *The Logic of Practice* [*Le sens practique*] (Stanford, CA: Stanford University Press, 1990). A field is a structured social space with its own rules, roles, hierarchies, and range of legitimate views.

9. Anne Marie Slaughter, *A New World Order* (Princeton, NJ: Princeton University Press, 2005).

10. Thomas Weiss, David Cortright, George Lopez, and Larry Minear, *Political Gain or Civilian Pain? Humanitarian Impacts of Economic Sanctions* (Lanham, MD: Rowman and Littlefield, 1997).

11. Gary Hufbauer, Jeffrey Schott, and Kimberly Elliott, *Economic Sanctions Reconsidered: History and Current Policy*, 2nd ed. (Washington, DC: Institute for International Economics, 1985).

12. State Secretariat for Economic Affairs, Switzerland, *Targeted Sanctions*, www.seco.ad min.ch/themen/00513/00620/00639/00641/index.html?lang=en (accessed June 4, 2012).

13. The 1267 Committee was originally formed to put pressure on the Taliban regime in Afghanistan to turn over Osama bin Laden and others associated with the August 1998 bombings of US embassies in East Africa.

14. Watson Institute, Brown University, *Strengthening Targeted Sanctions through Fair and Clear Procedures*, white paper prepared by the Watson Institute Targeted Sanctions Project for the governments of Switzerland, Germany, and Sweden, presented at the United Nations, March 30, 2006.

15. UN Security Council and General Assembly document (A/60/887-S/2006/331), June 14, 2006.

16. *Telegraph* (London), *UK Studying Range of Options for 1267 Sanctions Review.*

17. Even though targeted financial sanctions are an important tool of diplomacy, the US State Department played a relatively marginal role in the policy, and State generally looked to Treasury to take the lead in the policy because of Treasury's technical and intelligence expertise.

18. Peter M. Haas, "Introduction: Epistemic Communities and International Policy Coordination," *International Organization* 46 (1992): 3.

19. Bourdieu, *Logic of Practice.*

20. Haas, "Epistemic Communities," 3.

21. Ibid., 4.

22. Bernd Bucher, "Processual-Relational Thinking and Figurational Sociology in Social Constructivism: The Rogueization of Liberal and Illiberal States" (PhD diss., University of St. Gallen, St. Gallen, Switzerland, 2011).

23. Martha Finnemore and Kathryn Sikkink, "International Norm Dynamics and Political Change," *International Organization* 52 (1998): 887–917.

24. Michael Barnett and Martha Finnemore, "The Politics, Power, and Pathologies of International Organizations," *International Organization* 53 (1999): 699–732.

25. International Commission on Intervention and State Sovereignty, *The Responsibility to Protect* (Ottawa: International Development Research Centre, 2001).

26. The one-way direction of policy advice is broadly characteristic of the EC's FP-6 and FP-7 programs designed to facilitate interinstitutional cooperation across Europe on policy-related contemporary issues.

27. In my experience, some governments send individuals to participate in meetings with a single issue or narrow agenda that can derail progress within working groups.

28. Rodney Hall and Thomas Biersteker, *The Emergence of Private Authority in Global Governance* (Cambridge: Cambridge University Press, 2002).

29. As indicated above, the French government had initially proposed the idea of a focal point, and the Danish government suggested the idea of an ombudsperson in a "non-paper."

30. Stanley Hoffmann, "An American Social Science: International Relations," in *International Theory: Critical Investigations*, ed. James Der Derian (London: Macmillan, 1995), 233, 235, 236.

31. Hoffmann, "American Social Science."

32. I did not even have a category for policy publications on my CV until after 2005.

33. Jörg Friedrichs and Friedrich Kratochwil, "On Acting and Knowing: How Pragmatism Can Advance International Relations Research and Methodology," *International Organization* 63 (2009): 701–31; Rudra Sil and Peter J. Katzenstein, "Analytic Eclecticism in the Study of World Politics: Reconfiguring Problems and Mechanisms across Research Traditions," *Perspectives on Politics* 8 (2010): 411–31; David A. Lake, "Why 'isms' Are Evil: Theory, Epistemology, and Academic Sects as Impediments to Understanding and Progress," *International Studies Quarterly* 55 (2011): 465–80.

CHAPTER NINE

Contributing to Policy through Evaluation
USAID and Democracy Promotion

MITCHELL A. SELIGSON

Policymakers often seem unaware of cutting-edge academic research, at least so it seems to many scholars whose hopes are all too often frustrated by the glacial pace at which research is incorporated into action. In fact, when the conditions are right, policy change can come about much more quickly than scholars expect. A key condition for scholarship to effectively inform policy is the presence *within* the bureaucracy of research-oriented, academically trained staffers. As this chapter shows, having scholarly allies on the inside has allowed important advances in evaluation research to move from the campus to the capital in a surprisingly short period of time.

Why Evaluate Democracy Programs When We Already Know That They Work?

A few years ago, at a conference on democracy promotion held in Washington, DC, I thought that I must have misunderstood the speaker when he said, "We know that democracy promotion works, so why throw away money on evaluations?" When I asked for clarification, the speaker repeated his words, arguing that the task before those who believed in democracy was to promote it, not to waste time, energy, and money asking "trivial academic" questions such as "Does democracy promotion actually work?" I wondered to myself on that occasion how many people in the audience, made up of an equal balance of practitioners and scholars, agreed with his point of view. If agreement in that audience was widespread, then efforts to *successfully* promote democracy were surely doomed, for if we have learned anything since 1990, when democracy promotion first became an important and explicit goal of the US government, it is that our understanding of the factors that promote democracy remains in its early stages. Before the fall of the Berlin Wall, democracy around the world had remained in a virtually steady-state condition, with gains often offset by losses. In the Latin American region, for instance, scholars had developed a theory of a "pendular" or "cyclical" pattern of democratic growth followed by reversal as the norm. Democracy had emerged in a number of countries in the 1940s and 1950s, only to be reversed by authoritarian regimes in the 1960s and 1970s, which then transitioned, once again, into democracies in the 1980s.[1] Little solid scholarship existed before 1990 on how to promote democracy.[2]

This chapter makes three points. First, if scholars are to have an impact on the foreign assistance bureaucracy they must have partners in that bureaucracy. Doing what scholars usually do—that is, publishing in leading journals and at university presses—is normally not going to be enough to have an impact. In the field of democracy promotion there has been an unusually close partnership between academia and democracy promoters, at least in the United States Agency for International Development (USAID). Second, scholarship can inform both the world of theory and the world of practice. Third, we have indeed learned something about democracy promotion and whether it works or not. A consensus is emerging about how to acquire new knowledge in the democracy promotion field, such that rigorous "gold standard" randomized research designs are now being implemented.

In this chapter I consider USAID, since it is *the* major agent of democracy promotion in the US government. The growth of USAID's spending on democracy programs has been spectacular. In 1990, when the major expenditures began, democracy and governance (DG) assistance amounted to $128 million (in constant 2000 US dollars). By 2005, this total had risen to $902 million. In current dollars, the increase from 1990 to 2005 was from $103 million to more than $1 billion. Since 1990, USAID has spent over $10 billion (in constant 2000 US dollars) in some 120 countries and territories.[3]

Do these democracy promotion efforts really work? Tax dollars are always scarce, so it is a fair question to ask whether the government has gotten its money's worth. The often large gap between scholars and the policy community is a key theme of this volume. In the area of democracy promotion, however, the nexus between the two is far more dynamic and productive than it may have been in other policy areas. A small group of policy experts who themselves had been members of the academic community prior to joining the government and whose academic backgrounds inclined them toward an evidence-based approach to the impact of democracy promotion were able to find a welcome audience in the broader policy community seeking to justify and legitimate the expenditure of taxpayer dollars.

Early Attempts at Evaluating Democracy Promotion

In the initial period of expansion of democracy promotion, USAID was operating pretty much in the dark. With little or no experience in promoting democracy, policymakers forged ahead as best they could when Soviet communism crumbled and opportunities for democratization appeared in dozens of countries around the world. In those early years, basic instincts and conventional wisdom led those engaged in the democratization process to posit a set of reasonable assumptions, one of which was that there could be no democracy without competitive elections but that elections themselves were no guarantee that democracy would be deep, resilient, and resistant to setbacks and breakdowns. A second assumption was that stable, inclusive democracies would rest on well-crafted institutions, a vibrant civil society, a free press, and the rule of law. In practice, some early notions of sequencing emerged, such that free and fair elections needed to be held first, and the rule of law ought to be established subsequent to that. For this reason, the attention (and funds) of many democracy promotion projects in the early years supported elections and reforms in the justice system.

As USAID expanded its programs and gained experience, initial evaluations of its democracy promotion programs began to roll in. Those evaluations, however, were based on the traditional system of evaluation that had long been in use in many program areas outside the field of health, which routinely had been subjected to rigorous evaluations. Post hoc evaluations were typically carried out by engaging a consulting firm to review project documents and interview program participants (town council members, legislators, judges, etc.) near the end of the life of the project. Many of these evaluations were quite revealing, but because they were done with little or no baseline data to compare findings against, it was (and remains) largely impossible to determine a program's impact. Indeed, as discussed below, a comprehensive review by the Social Science Research Council (SSRC) found that those post hoc evaluations were essentially useless as the basis of an impact evaluation.[4] If, for example, the goal of a USAID democracy promotion project was to increase confidence in the rule of law or to expand participation and trust in local government, the absence of baseline data made credible evaluations of impact virtually impossible. When hard data did exist at project start-up (such as ad hoc survey samples conducted by other agencies, local scholars, or the national government in the target country), all too often the baseline data did not map onto the program areas for USAID activities, so large leaps of faith had to be taken that the baseline data reflected the conditions on the ground. Even in those cases where baseline data did exist, only rarely was there also an end-of-project survey containing questions comparable to those of the baseline, thus permitting changes over time to be de-tected. Indeed, one of the more frustrating experiences for researchers was that even when such end-of-project surveys were planned for, the project funds often would run out before the end survey could be implemented.

Other evaluations were broader in scope than project-based studies. Academics with sterling credentials in area studies were hired by consulting companies to carry out regional assessments that allowed USAID to place its project activities into a broader context. In other instances, evaluations were cross-cutting, focused on a specific area of democracy promotion (e.g., rule of law), and asking academic experts to join with experienced project staffers to review projects from many world areas that dealt with the same theme in order to pick up on generalizable conclusions. Yet, at the end of the day, little hard, credible evidence emerged that could tell policymakers where to put their dollars to have the most effect.

Initial Steps toward Rigorous Impact Evaluations: The Emergence of a Scholar-Practitioner Partnership

As the first decade of democracy promotion drew to a close, a small group of US-AID senior staffers who themselves had served in academic posts prior to joining the agency began pressing for a more comprehensive look at the impact of democracy promotion. Leaders in this drive were Jerry Hyman and Margaret Sarles.[5] In 2006 they established the SORA (Strategic and Operational Research Agenda) initiative within the Democracy and Governance Office at USAID to facilitate research that would help the agency revise its activities by ending or revising ineffective programs, adding new programs, integrating better design and evaluation into programs, and engaging in dissemination and learning activities with a wider policy community. This is also a critical step toward firmly establishing the relatively new field of applied democratic development, which melds insights from the academic, policy, and practitioner worlds to improve foreign assistance policy. Eventually it should substantially improve USAID's ability to support countries' efforts.[6]

The first component of this effort was the establishment of a special committee by the SSRC, called the Democratization Technical Advisory Board, bringing together leaders in the democratization field from academia and the government. The scholars included an ideal mix of experts on democracy (Robert Bates, Dietrich Rueschemeyer, Brian Silver, and myself) and methodology (Thomas D. Cook), and the team was led by two scholars expert in both democracy and methodology (Kenneth Bollen and Pamela Paxton). The goal of the project was to review past evaluations of democracy programs and to develop a research design for a multiyear effort aimed at evaluating the impact of USAID's DG programs. The final product, completed in late 2003, provided a careful and well-thought-out design, highlighting the major obstacles USAID faced when attempting serious, systematic analysis of its DG programs: a lack of information on mission activities in the DG area, the influence of missions and embassy officials on USAID evaluations, and low incentives for undertaking reasonably rigorous data collection and evaluation.[7]

The report went on to make a series of thoughtful recommendations, the first of which was the most obvious to the panelists and on which there was no disagreement—namely, that USAID had to improve its information collection and storage systems. Bollen and Paxton encountered no end of frustration in attempting to cull information from reports, and in nearly every case in which they encountered a reference to hard data (e.g., a survey of the "beneficiary" population), all they could find were descriptive summary reports of the findings. The datasets themselves were nowhere to be found. This lacuna in itself deprived the research team of its ability to carry out systematic secondary analyses of DG programs. Second, Bollen and Paxton argued for the convening of a task force made up of academics and USAID staffers who would develop a set of guidelines for DG evaluations, with a focus on randomized experiments. On this latter point there was not full agreement, with some SSRC committee members expressing skepticism as to whether such rigor could be applied in the democracy area. Yet, the report did strongly recommend that USAID move away from post hoc evaluations and toward *impact evaluations*, the latter of which, as explained below, provide scientific controls to distinguish clearly between treated and untreated areas or subjects. The report noted, however, that such evaluations required considerably more resources than the standard post hoc evaluations, as well as considerably more autonomy for the evaluators than was traditionally the case. As the report states:

> Mission officials may also be influential once evaluation teams have arrived in the country. Mission officials may have their own agenda for the evaluation, naturally wanting to highlight certain areas for positive evaluation. Furthermore, political forces within the country may similarly impact the activities that can be evaluated by a research team. Either may shift the team away from the intended objectives of the evaluation. For example, in a recent study of South Africa, the evaluators were unable to study civil society due to pressure from the ANC [African National Congress].[8]

The report concluded that only through the use of rigorous methods would USAID ever be able to know with any degree of confidence and precision whether its programs were having an impact.

In operational terms, the SSRC report made the case that sufficient data were probably already available for USAID to carry out a "big picture" evaluation to determine whether its programs were having an impact worldwide. If USAID's expenditures were not making a difference on the whole, then serious rethinking of the decade-long effort would be needed. On the other hand, if the impact were measurable at the global level, then what would be needed next was to determine which programs were working better than others and under what circumstances. The USAID bureaucracy paid serious attention to the SSRC recommendations; in so doing, it subjected itself to the risk that studies being undertaken might find little or no positive impact or, possibly, find that the impact of DG programs was detrimental. It is hard to overstate the potential consequences of this risk. Each year, USAID makes a congressional presentation of its activities, and in the DG area, it has been difficult to "prove" impact. Of course, reports on the number of seminars held and journalists and mayors trained have been the standard, but evidence that democracy itself has been strengthened has not been available. Once USAID went down the path of rigorous evaluation of program impact, it risked the possibility of reporting no impact or negative impact, findings likely to be met with calls for funding cuts. As we shall see, their risk paid off handsomely.

One early outcome of the SORA process was that within the democracy promotion staff at USAID, a greater commitment emerged to the systematic gathering of survey-based data. Prior to the SORA process, ad hoc surveys of citizens' perceptions of democracy suffered from the dual problems of noncomparable questionnaires and noncomparable samples. Thus, it became a big stretch for missions to be able to compare how their country was doing, for example, on citizen support for the rule of law, on corruption, on victimization, on belief in democracy as a system of government, and so forth, based on those ad hoc surveys. Beginning in 2004, USAID Washington began to support the regional survey of the Latin American area that I direct, the Latin American Public Opinion Project (LAPOP). As a result, every two years the AmericasBarometer has been conducted, a broad-gauged survey focused on democratic governance and managed by a consortium of universities and think tanks throughout the Americas, including all USAID-presence countries in Latin America and the Caribbean, with other donors supporting surveys in other countries in the region.[9] In 2010 and again in 2012, for example, 26 countries in the Americas were included in the survey, involving over 40,000 interviews in each round. Since the United States and Canada are included, important "baseline" reference groups are available. Country-based studies have been written by collaborating partner institutions based in the Latin American and Caribbean region. For example, studies of Colombia are written by scholars at the Universidad de los

Andes, and studies of Peru are written and published by the Instituto de Estudios Peruanos.

Moreover, special samples are regularly drawn by LAPOP in project-specific areas (e.g., municipal government), facilitating comparisons of project areas and non-project areas.[10] These data also became important for the political culture components of the project discussed below. In effect, then, a cultural shift emerged within the DG bureaucracy toward relying on rigorously collected survey data to measure democratic development. But the effort did not stop there. Once again, academically oriented members of the USAID bureaucracy pushed hard to persuade individual missions to look to these surveys for guidance.

First Impact Evaluation Study: USAID "Moves the Needle"

Largely as a result of the SSRC study, in late 2004, USAID issued a request for applications (RFA) through the Association Liaison Office for University Cooperation in Development, an office of the American Council on Education and other academic associations that had joined together to promote higher education partnerships with the government. The RFA called for precisely the "big picture" study that was envisioned by the SSRC report. But it did so by requiring the winning proposal to incorporate two rather novel components in its design. First, from the outset, the design had to incorporate a panel of expert scholars who would be reviewing the research while it was in progress. Second, the results of the research as it was being carried out were to be presented both to USAID and to the external academic panel at various points along the way. This methodology was unusual. The scholarly community is used to doing research solipsistically, presenting findings at a conference or two and finally publishing the results in journals or as a book. Scholars are not used to working with an external group looking over their shoulders and are even less used to having to subject their work to the scrutiny of policymakers while the research products are in progress.

The research grant was awarded to a consortium led by Vanderbilt University that also included the University of Pittsburgh and University of Virginia; I was the principal investigator of the lead institution. The research team began with a considerable sense of skepticism that, given the myriad of potentially confounding factors influencing democratic development, it was even possible to single out and measure the impact of a USAID contribution. We knew, for example, that initial levels of economic development have a great deal to do with democratic growth and sustainability.[11] So, how much more could USAID be expected to contribute to that overall trend? Our skepticism was based in part on the limited amount of academic research that had been carried out up to that point. Abe Lowenthal was an early leader in promoting this skepticism in his *Exporting Democracy* volumes, which questioned the motivations behind efforts to "make the world safe for democracy," to quote the famous phrase of Woodrow Wilson in 1917 (a pioneering political scientist who, incidentally, became president of the United States and used that phrase to justify his request before Congress to declare war on Germany). We had read the works of Thomas Carothers, who had studied USAID's democracy promotion efforts and found that many of those efforts had not worked.[12] Beyond these qualitative assessments, the very limited systematic quantitative work that had been carried out showed that over the period 1975–2000, foreign assistance had had no impact on democracy—although that research was not focused on democracy assistance but rather on all foreign assistance, which of course includes many elements that were not in any way designed to have an impact on democracy.[13]

Our research team was skeptical, however, about concerns of a more basic nature than those raised by Lowenthal, Carothers, and others. We asked ourselves whether USAID records would contain sufficiently reliable and complete information to allow us to know just where and when it had spent its money to promote democracy. If this was not knowable, we could never measure the agency's impact. Fortunately, at the very time of the grant award, Andrew Green, a USAID Democracy Fellow, was completing his PhD dissertation; Green had been immersed in the USAID data archives for over a year, gathering precisely the kind of detailed, program-specific information that we needed to be able to determine the what, where, and when of USAID spending to promote democracy.[14]

What did we find? To the chagrin of those who had been unmitigatedly critical of USAID's DG programs, and disputing the "I told you so's" of those who had argued that evaluations were superfluous, we found that after controlling for all other factors that we could both think of and measure (economic growth, initial level of democracy, military assistance, population size, country's physical size, ethnic fractionalization, income inequality, state failure, etc.), DG assistance had a significant positive impact on democracy (as measured by Freedom House and Polity IV). We reported these results in several places, including an article in *World Politics*, thereby demonstrating that the findings passed muster with a very tough set of academic reviewers, as they had with the external review committee constituted at the outset of the research effort.[15] Moreover, we found that DG assistance was more important than growth of gross domestic product in increasing the level of democracy. The effect occurred over and above the normal pattern of democratic growth and occurred whether the USAID's DG assistance was calculated in raw or per capita terms, and the effect was cumulative, so that the initial impact of the assistance would increase in the following year.[16] The impact was large: "Ten million additional USAID dollars (measured in constant 1995 U.S. dollars, the equivalent of 11.8 million dollars in 2004) would produce—by itself—about a five-fold increase in the amount of democratic change that the average country would be expected to achieve, *ceteris paribus*, in any given year, based on the Freedom House measure of democracy."[17] This research was subsequently extended to cover the 1990–2004 period to take into account the "Iraq effect"—that is, the huge amount spent on that one country after the US invasion—yet the conclusions remained basically unchanged, finding even stronger long-term effects than had the original study.[18] The additional research found that the impact of USAID's DG assistance was larger in countries that were in greater need (i.e., countries that were poorer, were more socially divided, and had suffered from lower levels of human capital). Indeed, once countries became relatively well off, the impact tended to move toward zero. We also found that DG assistance was *less* effective in countries that received a large percentage of US military assistance, thus helping to explain the "Iraq effect." Finally, political culture was found to exert a positive force on the impact of DG assistance, such that in countries where the political culture was characterized by greater institutional trust, personal satisfaction, and social engagement, the impact of DG assistance was greater in the country's Freedom House score. Of the variables studied, interpersonal trust (i.e., social capital) stood out as key. The second study concluded: "We feel that the 14 years of data we have analyzed here provide a robust basis for drawing the conclusion that USAID DG assistance in the post–Cold War period has worked."[19]

These findings have become part of a new wave of rigorous empirical investigations into the impact of foreign aid. One study, for example, shows that foreign assistance can promote democratization in dictatorships that govern through broad distributional coalitions, a subject not covered by the Finkel et al. research. On the other hand, other studies remain skeptical of the positive impact of foreign assistance. What has changed is that the field of studying the impact of democracy promotion, which was heavily dominated by excellent case study scholarship, has now moved to focus on large-N, multination studies.

Further Study: What Works and What Does Not

While the macro-level study reported on above did find important positive impacts of USAID's DG assistance, it was not able to detect *which specific programs in which specific contexts* had worked well and which had failed. The Massachusetts Institute of Technology's Poverty Action Lab has led the way in such studies of programs to combat poverty. As Nora Lustig shows in chapter 6 of this volume, careful impact evaluations of the increasingly popular "conditional cash transfer programs" have already had a huge effect on this form of poverty assistance. But, what of measuring the impact of democracy promotion programs? It is in this area that the rise of impact evaluations based on randomized designs has become most important. The SSRC report had already signaled that a new approach, to replace the standard post hoc evaluation methodology, would be necessary to provide that kind of operational, on-the-ground advice to policymakers. To provide such guidance, a committee of the National Academy of Sciences was convened and, after nearly two years of research, field visits, consultations with experts and practitioners, and extensive deliberation, produced its report.[20] The committee took note of the findings of the Vanderbilt study reported on above, but also noted that there were many glaring failures of DG assistance, especially in Egypt and post-Soviet Russia; in the light of the events of 2011, however, one wonders whether the Egyptian case will ultimately be recorded as a failure. The 337-page report recommended that *impact evaluations* based on randomized designs should become the centerpiece of any evaluation effort, wherever feasible:

> As the committee uses the term, what distinguishes an impact evaluation is the effort to determine what would have happened in the absence of the project by using comparison or control groups, or random assignment of assistance across groups or individuals, to provide a reference against which to assess the observed outcomes for groups or individuals who received assistance. Randomized designs offer the most accuracy and credibility in determining program impacts and therefore should be the first choice, where feasible, for impact evaluation designs.[21]

The report also recommended investment in better indicators of democracy that would allow more fine-grained, sector-specific measurement than the type used by Freedom House or Polity. In addition, it strongly suggested that USAID rebuild its long-atrophied in-house evaluation capabilities.

Thus, the recommendation was clear: unless USAID could respond to the counterfactual assertion that any change found would have occurred in the absence of the program, it could not really demonstrate that a specific project had worked.

Having an Impact on Policy through Evaluation

The SSRC, Vanderbilt, and National Research Council reports were written by "a bunch of ivory tower academics" working outside bureaucracy, and thus they present an excellent case study of academic thinking penetrating the bureaucracy. The strong findings from the Vanderbilt study and their wide dissemination in semi-nars, journal articles, and book chapters were hard to ignore. Indeed, those in the bureaucracy who were looking for a persuasive "good news" story more substantive than the anecdotal evidence that had been used in the past were able to point with pride to the hard evidence based on a massive database. What impact, if any, did the lessons learned from these studies have on USAID's ways of formulating policy? Was the impact merely ephemeral, focused just on the "good news," with business returning to normal after the initial enthusiasm wore off? I present two pieces of evidence here that help demonstrate that the lessons were absorbed and produced a long-term shift in thinking at USAID.

First and perhaps most important, USAID's long-standing policies on evaluation have changed; these changes are clearly more than fleeting and have been codified into policy. In 2011, for the first time in memory, USAID issued a new evaluation policy.[22] The new policy closely reflects the lessons learned from the process that began with the USAID/SSRC effort in 2004 and culminated in the 2008 National Research Council report. The new policy, for the first time, requires that an impor-tant share of USAID projects move away from the traditional post hoc unsystematic evaluations that were so strongly critiqued by the SSRC study and instead be subject to the randomized controlled experiments at the center of the National Academy of Sciences study. The new evaluation policy states that evaluations should involve the gathering of baseline data, generally using surveys:

> When a project that will be subject to evaluation is initiated, baseline data, in-cluding variables that correspond to key outcomes and impacts, will be collected using high-quality methods and analyzed to establish a reference point. As a rule, baseline studies should collect sex-disaggregated data. To obtain baseline data, household or individual surveys are often valuable baseline data, and can be rep-licated toward the conclusion of implementations to assess changes.[23]

To be sure, the new evaluation policy does not require that impact evaluations be conducted for every project, but it encourages such evaluations using random as-signment and specifies that sufficient funds be set aside in a project to make such evaluations feasible. It also establishes that the evaluations should be done transpar-ently, by *external* evaluators, not by the implementing contractors, and that the quantitative data produced must be stored by USAID. In addition, it calls for the expansion of qualified evaluation specialists, both junior and senior, within USAID.

The second piece of evidence comes from the dramatic shift in the way USAID is evaluating its projects today compared with the period before the SSRC and Na-tional Academy of Sciences studies were completed. Serious efforts are already underway to carry out randomized impact evaluations. Under my direction, Vanderbilt University is now heading up a multiyear impact evaluation of efforts to prevent youth and gang violence at the neighborhood level in Central America, as part of the CARSI (Central America Regional Security Initiative) program. In that study, dozens of communities have been selected for "treatment," with matching communities as controls, and a series of baseline neighborhood, household, and leader surveys have been and are being conducted, along with systematic focus group and stakeholder qualitative interviews. In other cases, such as in the area of municipal development, USAID missions have commissioned baseline surveys of treatment and control municipalities to track impact. An inspection of recently issued RFAs reveals that project requirements for randomized controlled studies, carried out by experts entirely independent of those implementing the project, are rapidly becoming the new evaluation standard in USAID.

It is, of course, too soon to judge whether the new evaluation policy will become part of the culture of the way USAID "does democracy" or will be merely a passing fad, soon forgotten in the press of events and crises. Opportunities for democracy promotion in the Islamic world are opening. Hopefully, the lessons learned, as described above, will help USAID to evaluate what strategies are likely to work best in democracy promotion in that area of the world. At the same time, one hopes that the rush of events will not prevent appropriate steps being taken to gather the systematic data that will make determining impact feasible.

A critical element, if not *the* critical, element, in scholars' ability to affect the policy process is to have the support of scholars *within* the policy process. In the case study detailed here, USAID's evaluation policy shifted from a decades-long unscientific, post hoc process to a process in which major evaluations must adhere to a gold standard developed by the scholarly community. Certainly, not all evaluations will adhere to this standard, but in only a relatively short span of years, the exception has become the norm, thus promising more effective use of scarce foreign assistance dollars in the future.

NOTES

1. Mitchell A. Seligson, "Democratization in Latin America: The Current Cycle," in *Authoritarians and Democrats: The Politics of Regime Transition in Latin America*, ed. James M. Malloy and Mitchell A. Seligson (Pittsburgh: University of Pittsburgh Press, 1987).

2. One of the few "points of light" was Abraham F. Lowenthal, *Exporting Democracy: The United States and Latin America: Themes and Issues* (Baltimore: Johns Hopkins University Press, 1991).

3. Dinorah Azpuru et al., "Trends in Democracy Assistance: What Has the U.S. Been Doing?" *Journal of Democracy* 19 (2008): 150–59. The growth of USAID democracy programs relative to other areas of assistance is shown in table 9.1 and figure 9.1 (*see p. 168*). The distribution of DG assistance by program area is shown in table 9.2.

4. Kenneth Bollen, Pamela Paxton, and Rumi Morishima, *Research Design to Evaluate the Impact of USAID Democracy and Governance Programs* (Washington, DC: Social Science Research Council, 2003).

5. Margaret E. Sarles, "Evaluating the Impact and Effectiveness of USAID's Democracy and Governance Programs," in *Evaluating Democracy Support: Methods and Experiences*, ed. Peter Brunell (Stockholm: International Institute for Democracy and Electoral Assistance and Swedish International Development Cooperation Agency, 2007).

6. Drawn from "Special Request for Applications: Cross-National Research on USAID's Democracy and Governance Programs," an RFA issued by USAID, September 7, 2004.

7. Bollen, Paxton, and Morishima, *Research Design to Evaluate the Impact of USAID Democracy and Governance Programs*.

8. Ibid., 16.

9. All of these studies are available online, free of charge. A treasure trove of data has been accumulated over the years, all of which is freely available for online analysis at the University of Costa Rica partner website (www.LapopSurveys.org). A number of USAID missions set their DG targets based in part on the results of the AmericasBarometer surveys.

10. In such studies, covariates are introduced into the statistical models to control for project-area uniqueness (e.g., degree of urbanization, poverty).

11. Larry Diamond, "Economic Development and Democracy Reconsidered," in *Reexamining Democracy: Essays in Honor of Seymour Martin Lipset*, ed. Gary Marks and Larry Diamond (London: Sage, 1992); Seymour Martin Lipset, "Democracy and Working-Class Authoritarianism," *American Sociological Review* 24 (1959); 482–501; Adam Przeworski et al., *Democracy and Development: Political Institutions and Well-Being in the World, 1950–1990* (Cambridge: Cambridge University Press, 2000).

12. Thomas Carothers, *Aiding Democracy Abroad: The Learning Curve* (Washington, DC: Carnegie Endowment for International Peace, 1999), and *In the Name of Democracy: U.S. Policy toward Latin America in the Reagan Years* (Berkeley: University of California Press, 1991).

13. Stephen Knack, "Does Foreign Aid Promote Democracy?" *International Studies Quarterly* 48 (2004): 251–66.

14. In the end, the dataset that Green amassed covered 195 countries for the period 1990–2003, of which 30 cases were excluded from the analysis because they were advanced industrial democracies and therefore not eligible recipients of DG assistance. The final dataset therefore included all sovereign states considered eligible for foreign assistance. Because several countries in the USAID investment database would be excluded using the Small-Singer criteria, we considered to be part of the universe all territorial units that matched two criteria: (1) they were recognized (i.e., assigned a numeric code) by the United Nations Statistical Division; and (2) they were independent states—we excluded overseas territories (e.g., Martinique), islands in free association with a larger country (e.g., the Cook Islands, Puerto Rico), autonomous regions (e.g., the Aland Islands), or occupied territories (e.g., Tibet); when in doubt we

TABLE 9.1.
USAID democracy and governance (DG) assistance relative to other types of assistance, 1990–2005
(in millions of 2000 US dollars)

Year	DG assistance	Human rights	Agriculture and growth	Health	Environment	Education	Conflict manage-ment and mitigation	Humanitarian assistance
1990	128.08	0.00	5,699.53	813.86	543.12	403.16	0.00	33.20
1991	195.70	0.00	5,319.19	1,014.30	587.50	522.91	0.00	23.04
1992	259.82	0.00	4,374.49	1,013.01	535.48	392.73	0.00	43.99
1993	352.56	0.00	3,745.72	1,168.67	563.09	425.21	0.00	76.57
1994	414.37	0.00	4,087.54	1,175.38	620.00	393.51	0.00	67.41
1995	483.34	0.00	3,394.55	1,185.06	843.52	395.48	0.00	23.07
1996	418.10	0.00	3,102.82	992.43	620.97	309.75	0.00	25.74
1997	446.30	0.00	2,968.15	1,082.33	715.91	189.98	0.00	30.78
1998	555.92	0.00	3,134.42	1,187.96	441.32	209.46	0.00	37.32
1999	520.18	0.00	3,443.90	1,050.52	532.90	333.64	0.00	67.55
2000	539.59	0.00	3,406.16	1,097.22	621.89	294.32	0.00	45.80
2001	549.17	3.46	2,499.92	1,238.29	528.87	323.03	81.54	423.83
2002	753.62	8.36	3,466.27	1,406.00	462.70	395.31	94.61	381.16
2003	817.22	14.81	5,130.44	1,491.65	424.64	449.26	108.69	619.16
2004	1,134.44	15.42	4,429.15	1,846.23	488.24	606.12	145.09	580.89
2005	901.94	16.92	3,346.72	2,183.92	798.07	547.08	119.59	979.76
Total	8,470.36	58.96	6,1548.97	1,9946.83	9,328.20	6,190.96	549.52	3,459.27

Source: Azpuru et al., "Trends in Democracy Assistance."
Note: The third column (human rights) reflects only those programs dealing with human trafficking and assisting victims of torture and war. Other human rights activities (already in place by 1990) are covered under DG assistance.

Figure 9.1 General USAID (non-DG) assistance and democracy and governance (DG) assistance, 1990–2003 (millions of 1995 US dollars).

TABLE 9.2.
Distribution of US democracy and governance assistance by sector, 1990–2005 (in millions of 2000 US dollars)

Subsector	Total $ (millions)	Percentage of total
Elections	1,190.43	14.1
Rule of law	1,611.95	19.0
Governance	2,494.20	29.5
Civil society	3,173.78	37.5
Total	8,470.36	100.0

Source: Azpuru et al., "Trends in Democracy Assistance."

adopted the "date of independence" stated in the CIA's *World Factbook*. The Green dataset is incorporated into the online dataset available from Aníbal Pérez-Liñán at the University of Pittsburgh. See Steven E. Finkel, Aníbal Pérez-Liñán, and Mitchell A. Seligson, "Effects of U.S. Foreign Assistance on Democracy Building: Results of a Cross-National Quantitative Study" (paper presented at the Annual Meeting of the American Political Science Association, Philadelphia, 2006).

15. Steven E. Finkel, Aníbal Pérez-Liñán, and Mitchell A. Seligson, "The Effects of U.S. Foreign Assistance on Democracy Building, 1990–2003," *World Politics* 59 (2007): 404–40.

16. All of the statistical models controlled for omitted variable bias and endogeneity of USAID funding, with such controls actually increasing the strength of the original findings.

17. Finkel, Pérez-Liñán, and Seligson, "Effects of U.S. Foreign Assistance on Democracy Building, 1990–2003."

18. Steven E. Finkel et al., "Watering Not Transplanting: The Case for Democracy Assistance," *APSA-CP* 19, no. 2 (2008): 15–18.

19. Ibid.

20. National Research Council et al., *Improving Democracy Assistance: Building Knowledge through Evaluations and Research* (Washington, DC: National Academies Press, 2008).

21. Ibid., 5.

22. US Agency for International Development, *USAID Evaluation Policy* (Washington, DC: Bureau for Policy, Planning and Learning, 2011).

23. Ibid., 8.

CHAPTER TEN

Transforming Argentine Foreign Policy
Politicians, Scholars, and Diplomats

MARIANO E. BERTUCCI

International relations (IR) scholars helped transform Argentina's foreign policy toward the United States during the 1990s, and the "embedded intellectual capital" of scholar-practitioners (i.e., the ideas "created before they entered the maelstrom")[1] helped pave the way to a decade of historically unprecedented understanding and cooperation between the two countries. In democratic Argentina, it is mainly the president himself who makes foreign policy, but IR scholars had an important impact on policy in the 1990s.

For at least 100 years, ever since the first Pan American Conference was held in Washington, DC, in 1889, Argentine-US relations have been conflictive.[2] Argentina energetically rejected the Monroe Doctrine, systematically antagonized the United States in diplomatic forums such as the United Nations (UN) and the Organization of American States, remained neutral in World War I and until the very last moment in World War II, and at the outset of the Cold War, defined its foreign policy as the "Third Position," halfway between communism and capitalism.

Under President Carlos Menem (1989–99), however, Argentina developed a strong and unprecedented alliance with the United States. "Once Latin America's strongest voice against United States intervention in the Americas, now Argentina loyally accompanied the United States on numerous international military missions. Once inclined to shun the United States in favor of European trade partners, now Argentina closely followed U.S. recommended economic policies and pursued improved trade relations within the Americas."[3]

Changing US priorities brought about by the end of the Cold War, Argentina's democratization process, and Argentina's economic crisis, which by 1989 threatened the country's infant democracy, are often presented as salient structural factors accounting for the transformation of Argentina's foreign policy toward the United States. Other often-listed explanatory factors are the strong leadership of President Carlos Menem and his personal preference for having excellent relations with the

"Colossus of the North," along with the roles of Domingo Cavallo and Guido di Tella, Argentine ministers of foreign affairs during Menem's administration.[4]

Yet, the work of Argentine IR scholars was also important in shaping this dramatic transformation in policy. Almost all Latin American nations experienced the end of the Cold War, transitioned to democracy, and suffered economic crises toward the end of the 1980s, but only Argentina transformed its foreign policy toward the United States to achieve a "special relationship" with that country. Unless such collaboration were to threaten Argentina's economic interests and development, Menem's government decided to make cooperation with the United States a far-reaching priority.

By the mid 1980s, IR research on the economic costs suffered by Argentina due to its past confrontational foreign policy with the great powers had emerged from Argentine "ivory towers." This research helped scholars implement Argentina's alignment with the United States during the following decade. This became apparent in 1989 when Guido di Tella, an economist who graduated from the Massachusetts Institute of Technology, was appointed Argentina's ambassador to Washington and, particularly, when di Tella was appointed Argentina's minister of foreign affairs in 1991. That year, the work of scholars who became practitioners was crucial in aligning Argentina's voting profile with that of the United States at the UN. Although Argentina's voting profile had, historically, been similar to that of Brazil, Colombia, and Mexico, in 1990 only Cuba, Sudan, and Vietnam had a stronger anti-US vote than Argentina.[5] The work of scholar-practitioners, along with that of some Argentine career diplomats, was crucial in changing Argentina's anti-US stance at the UN, despite some resistance on the part of Argentina's foreign policy bureaucracy.[6]

From Autonomy to Alignment and Economic Development: The Transformation of Argentine Foreign Policy toward the United States

From 1889 to 1989, Argentina defined its international orientation and its relationship with the United States in terms of "autonomy." Unlike the governments of small countries in Central America and the Caribbean, Argentine leaders retained and exercised their right to choose when cooperation or discord with the United States was desirable.[7] Argentina rejected the Monroe Doctrine and, in particular, the Roosevelt Corollary, which self-proclaimed the United States as the hemispheric policeman with the right to intervene in cases of flagrant and systematic wrongdoing by Latin American nations. Argentina remained virtually neutral in both world wars because it was substantially profiting from the sale of supplies and agricultural products to the warring countries. Argentina also championed the so-called international Third Position in 1946 and joined the Non-Aligned Movement in 1973, seeking to assist other third world nations in thwarting the Cold War's great power bloc politics of hegemony and intervention. In 1982 Argentina invaded the disputed Falkland/Malvinas Islands, triggering a war against the United Kingdom in which the United States sided with the British. Like other Latin American countries such as Brazil and Chile, Argentina refused to sign the Non-Proliferation Treaty until the 1990s. Until 1994, Argentina also refused to ratify the Treaty of Tlatelolco, banning nuclear weapons in Latin America. Immediately after the advent of democracy in 1983 and until 1989, Argentina had good relations with the United States. Argentina's young and fragile democracy needed the support of the United States at the World Bank and the International Monetary Fund, while Reagan needed to show his support for Argentina as a means of demonstrating the democratic purpose of his administration's policy in El Salvador and Nicaragua.[8] However, Argentina's nascent democracy failed to declare the end of hostilities with the United Kingdom and to cancel a joint venture with Egypt, Iraq, and Libya for development of the Cóndor II project—an intermediate-range guided missile that, if ever fully operational, presented the possibility of bombing the Falkland/Malvinas Islands or Israel.

In the 1990s, however, virtually all attempts at "autonomy" were abandoned.[9] President Menem defined Argentina's national interest in terms of economic development and aligned the country's foreign policy with the international positions of the United States. Argentina abandoned the Non-Aligned Movement and adopted a clear pro-Western and pro-US voting profile at the UN. It also participated in two US-led military missions—the first Gulf war of 1990–91 and the 1995 invasion and occupation of Haiti—and was one of the staunchest supporters of the US-sponsored Free Trade Area of the Americas. Argentina also reestablished diplomatic relations with Britain, dismantled the Cóndor II project, and ratified the Treaty of Tlatelolco. As Minister di Tella put it, Argentina "aligned [its foreign policy] with the basic pillars of US foreign policy" as a means of paving the way to achieving the country's most salient interest—that is, economic development.[10]

Two Independent Policy Streams: Foreign Policymaking and IR Research in Argentina

Amid an acute economic crisis, Argentina's "special relationship" with the United States was originally decided on and implemented by President Carlos Menem and Domingo Cavallo (Argentina's minister of foreign affairs, 1989–91). Guido di Tella

(Argentina's minister of foreign affairs, 1991–99) also became an important player in the decision-making and implementation processes after 1991.

By the mid 1980s, a group of IR scholars working at the Instituto Di Tella (IDT) in Buenos Aires had concluded that in previous decades Argentina had suffered considerable economic losses due to its confrontational foreign policy toward the United States. Although an economist by training, Guido di Tella was strongly influenced by this IR research; this was apparent as soon as he became Menem's first Argentine ambassador in Washington, DC, in July 1989.

Economic Crisis and Foreign Policy: Deciding on Foreign Policy Transformation

Argentina's foreign policy of alignment with the international position of the United States was conceived as a crucial element in the country's strategy of establishing its economic recovery plan on a strong foothold. Menem had to inaugurate his government in July 1989 amid the collapse of the previous administration of Raúl Alfonsín and an economic crisis characterized by hyperinflation, capital flight, market dislocation, and riots and lootings. After a few failed attempts at stabilizing this situation, Menem embraced the policy of market reforms that promised to win the acquiescence of both domestic and foreign economic actors, even though these policies contradicted the main pillars of Menem's electoral campaign.

Menem's change of discourse and his decision not to follow his electoral mandate created a problem—showing that he was truly committed to the market reforms he was now endorsing and that such reforms weren't necessarily imposed by the country's grim economic situation and shaky governance apparatus. According to Juan Carlos Torre and others, it is in the light of this credibility issue that Argentina's efforts at forging a "special relationship" with the United States must be understood and that President Menem should be seen as the salient instigator of such relations (as when Menem alone decided on and, to an extent, directed Argentina's participation in the first Gulf war).[11] Menem, through many political gestures, tried to gain the confidence of potential investors and the business community, embracing policy statements that exalted the benefits of market-oriented economic policies, privatizations, liberalization, and the deregulation of trade. But this "ideological conversion was accompanied by two . . . political gestures" that were particularly significant: "a clear convergence with big business along with key cabinet appointments, and *bringing Argentine foreign policy into line with U.S. positions.*"[12]

Menem's first minister of foreign affairs, Domingo Cavallo, was an economist. When Cavallo took charge of the Ministry of Economy, his successor as minister of foreign affairs was Guido di Tella, also an economist. When Menem offered Cavallo the post of minister of foreign affairs (immediately after winning the presidential election in May 1989), Cavallo started thinking about how Argentina's foreign policy could serve the country's *economic* interests. And, according to Cavallo, "having good relations with the United States was crucial to overcome the situation the country was facing. For example, if we didn't have a good relationship it would be impossible to think about a solution to the problem of Argentina's foreign debt. [Menem and I] were certain about that."[13]

Thus, by his second year in government Menem was able to show that Argentina had reestablished full diplomatic relations with Britain after the Falklands/Malvinas war of 1982 and that he had already given the order to dismantle the Cóndor II missile project as requested by the United States. Menem could also show that Argentina was supportive of the new US-led world order, given Argentina's military participation in the first Gulf war and given that, at the domestic level, much of the deregulation, liberalization, and stabilization economic recipes that were being implemented followed closely much of the policy prescriptions suggested and endorsed by Washington.[14] Before the first anniversary of Menem's government, the US ambassador in Buenos Aires, Terence Todman, considered Argentine-US relations to be "good and improving."[15]

The IDT, FLACSO, and the Costs of Confrontation with the United States: Guido di Tella Goes IR

By the mid-1980s, an intense academic foreign policy debate emerged in Argentina. The Falklands/Malvinas war provided some dramatic arguments for the need to refocus the country's foreign policy. "The developmental costs of that unnecessary war . . . were enormous: the war jeopardized economic relations with the European Economic Community, alienated investors, and contributed to raising the country risk index to astronomical levels."[16] The foreign policy debate took place at the IDT and the Facultad Latinoamericana de Ciencias Sociales (FLACSO) in Buenos Aires, and it was animated by the idea of filling "the existing intellectual vacuum with an approach to interstate relations inspired basically by the need for development."[17]

Guido di Tella sponsored a number of IR research projects and meetings during the mid 1980s, at IDT and elsewhere. Carlos Escudé—a young Argentine IR scholar who had just returned to Buenos Aires after earning his PhD in political science at Yale University and whose doctoral dissertation was on the economic and political costs inflicted on Argentina, first by the United States and later by the United Kingdom, due to its neutrality during World War II—helped organized the meetings.[18]

The debates delved into the economic and political costs Argentina had suffered during and after World War II because, unlike Brazil, it did not align with the Allies until the very end of the conflagration.

In July 1986, for example, di Tella invited to Oxford some intellectual adversaries who were working on these ideas, such as Mario Rapoport and Carlos Escudé, as well as Joseph Tulchin (an American scholar specializing in Argentina), Stanley Hilton (an American historian specializing in Brazilian-US relations), and D. Cameron Watt (a British expert on US-UK relations). They debated triangular relations among Argentina, the United States, and Britain during the 1940s, a period that, according to Escudé, was the starting point of many mistakes in Argentina's foreign policy. Other meetings and debates helped Escudé refine many of the ideas he had already been working on: that Argentina missed many of the economic benefits that Brazil had harvested from aligning with the United States during War World II and, instead, had suffered from US economic sanctions. Specifically, Escudé showed that due to Argentina's neutrality, the country suffered an economic boycott and political destabilization by the United States and that, albeit limited, Brazil's alignment had translated into direct benefits such as installation of the Volta Redonda steel mill (which would become that country's industrialization base and is currently Latin America's largest steel producer), high coffee prices during the war, and easy access to Allied oil until the end of the conflict.[19]

Guido di Tella would be strongly influenced by such ideas as he summarized the conclusions of the Oxford meeting.[20] For instance, by the second half of the 1980s, di Tella was well aware of the historical trajectory of US-Argentine animosity and the economic benefits that Argentina reaped from its "special relationship," at the turn of the twentieth century, with the then hegemonic power, Great Britain. He was also aware of the extent to which Argentina's international and domestic policies had suffered from not having immediately adjusted to the changes in the international power structure between the United States and Britain after World War I. According to di Tella, failing to recognize this and to adjust the country's foreign policy to the international power transition taking place in the North Atlantic in the 1920s was *the* mistake on the part of Argentina's foreign policymakers. And di Tella also understood how "Brazil [received substantive US] help to develop her first steel mill during [World War II, while] Argentina's plans were being explicitly blocked," suggesting, on the part of Argentina, "a lack of appreciation of the real importance of an appropriate international alignment" with the United States.[21]

Thus, when di Tella was appointed Menem's first ambassador to the United States in 1989, he knew about the costs of unnecessary confrontations and the plausible economic benefits that Argentina could reap from an alignment, now, with the Colossus of the North, given the incipient post–Cold War context. And, on his arrival in Washington, di Tella immediately started paving the way for Menem's alignment policy. For instance, he argued that the Argentine government was "going to put an end to Argentine-US relations à la Caputo. For example, we are not going to irritate the United States with attitudes on distant issues for Argentina such as those in Central America and the Caribbean, and we will not advise the world on issues of war and peace."[22] Di Tella's embedded intellectual capital on Argentine international relations underpinned his staunch support of Argentina's alliance and alignment policy with the United States or, at least, of the idea that Argentina ought to cooperate with the United States on all issues save those that directly threatened the country's economic development interests. And to an extent, these were, by then, di Tella's own ideas—as Escudé recalls:

> Guido had already read all my books, we had talked about all these issues many times. And it happened that, before he appointed me, [di Tella] started making comments, to talk to the media about Argentine-US relations. And all of his interventions and comments appeared to be taken out of my books—he was using the exact same vocabulary. Indeed, there were people that would ask me—"Hey, you are with di Tella, right?!" "No, I am not with di Tella!" Until later on he appointed me as his adviser at the Ministry of Foreign Affairs.[23]

In sum, Menem and Cavallo recognized Argentina's credibility problem in relation to the great powers, and exploiting the opportunity opened by a national mood tinted by the deep economic crisis the country was facing, they redirected Argentina's foreign policy course toward the United States. At about the same time, and independently of such policy change, Argentine scholars concluded that Argentina's historical confrontational policy toward the United States had had considerable economic and political costs for the country—findings that offered policymakers an IR research–based rationale for further deepening Argentina's alignment with the Colossus of the North.

Transforming Argentina's Foreign Policy at the UN

Argentina's voting profile at the UN General Assembly offered a clear opportunity for Menem's government to implement its policy of greater alignment with the United States. In 1990, Argentina had a "strongly anti-US" voting profile at the UN. Argentine votes coincided with US votes as much as did those of Afghanistan and Yemen; only Cuba, Vietnam, and Sudan had a more anti-US voting profile than that of Argentina.[24] The goal was to change the votes to at least a "centrist" or "moderately pro-US" profile so as to generate more international credibility before developed nations and, ultimately, to present Argentina as the most reliable regional partner of the United States at the multilateral level.[25]

The major change in Argentina's UN voting profile came about in 1991 and was an outcome of the ideas and efforts of Minister of Foreign Affairs Guido di Tella and, in particular, of his closest adviser, IR scholar Carlos Escudé. According to Escudé, not only was it true that Argentine votes until 1990 were "too" anti-US—given what President Menem had decided, a few years before, Argentina's relations with that country should be—but also they were "too" anti-US for the previous Argentine government of Raúl Alfonsín and would have been "too" anti-US for any subsequent Argentine government. Thus, when the problem was identified by Escudé, di Tella decided to change Argentina's votes and put Escudé in charge of implementing such policy.[26]

Every year, Argentina's permanent mission in New York drafts the country's UN voting instructions. According to Escudé, the (very long) text is sent to Buenos Aires, where the director of international organizations of the Ministry of Foreign Affairs reviews it quickly, adjusts a few issues "of particular political relevance and sends it to the Minister, who sometimes signs it without reviewing it [and sends it back to New York]. That is, bureaucrats sometimes attempt to draft their own [voting] instructions, especially when a new government is attempting to change a time-honored foreign policy endorsed by the bureaucracy."[27] Thus, when di Tella was appointed minister of foreign affairs and decided to change Argentina's voting profile, the bureaucracy of the ministry did not pay attention to his orders. When, in September 1991, di Tella found out that only a few very minor votes had been changed, he put together an ad hoc commission to work on the matter. Constituted by Carlos Escudé and Rogelio Pfirter (later, Argentina's ambassador to London), the commission was mandated to discuss the issue with the members of Argentina's Permanent Mission in New York. However, as Escudé recalls, "[we] couldn't agree on anything—we argued for changing the votes, and [the bureaucrats] argued against and suggested that the specialized areas of the Ministry decide on each vote. And we knew that the specialized areas would say 'no,' that no changes were to be implemented. So we proposed to di Tella to *bypass* the specialized areas of the Ministry and to simply inform them of how we were going to vote with no further ado."[28]

What was needed to change Argentina's votes was an "outside intervention" of the implementation process, to use the language of Escudé. Votes at the UN needed to change rather immediately, given Argentina's international credibility problems and the foreign policy course established by President Menem two years before. Di Tella approved the "intervention" proposed by Escudé and Pfirter, who, from that moment on, drafted a memo specifying the new votes. A day later, and with the explicit approval of di Tella, Pfirter suggested to Escudé that the memo be transformed into actual voting instructions. Signed by di Tella, in September 1991 those instructions changed Argentina's votes from a "strongly anti-US" to a "centrist" profile.[29]

According to Escudé, there were two main reasons that, in 1991, Argentina's votes couldn't reach at least a "moderately pro-US" profile. First, Argentina's vote was tied to "(1) the Non-Aligned Movement, (2) Malvinas/decolonization, (3) the Latin American Bloc, and (4) Disarmament/anti–Non Proliferation Treaty and Tlatelolco. This way, Argentina's vote was more radicalized than that of Brazil because the latter's did not have any stakes in (1) and (2)."[30] Second, personal relationships with other third world ambassadors in New York were also relevant. Argentine foreign service officials would feel uncomfortable with their counterparts when trying to make sense of such a sudden and dramatic change in policy, as was already happening in the light of Argentina's sudden abandonment of the Non-Aligned Movement.[31]

In other words, changing Argentina's voting profile at the General Assembly was a policy that had to overcome a century-long history of conflictive relations with the United States. And, as such, it was a policy in need of a period of adaptation on the part of Argentina's diplomatic bureaucracy.[32] The new policy was designed and implemented by an Argentine IR scholar-practitioner who, due to his professional relationship with the politically appointed minister of foreign affairs and assistance from some diplomats, "intervened" in Argentina's foreign policy implementation process at the UN and bridged the so-called scholar-practitioner gap in international relations.

Lessons on the Role of IR Research in Transforming Argentina's Foreign Policy

The presence of IR scholar-practitioners in Argentina's foreign policy decision-making process is an important reason why Argentina aligned its foreign policy with that of the United States as no other Latin American country did, given roughly similar historical circumstances. The presence of a president (Carlos Menem) looking for new ways of strengthening the economy and a scholar and political broker (Guido di Tella) as minister of foreign affairs also helps explain this instance of academic access and influence. In democratic Argentina, however, this combination of factors facilitating scholar-practitioner interactions is somewhat exceptional. Argentina's 2001 political and economic crisis triggered another transformation in the country's foreign policy toward the United States—this time, from "alignment" to relations of "mutual convenience."[33] By 2003, Argentina's voting profile at the UN had, again, an anti-US character. Argentina's new president, Néstor Kirchner, was looking for new ways of jump-starting and strengthening the economy as much as Menem had done a decade before. However, IR scholars did not participate in any meaningful way in this new major change in foreign policy. In Argentina, direct academic access and influence in foreign policymaking mainly depend on whether the president and/or his politically appointed minister of foreign affairs decide to incorporate IR scholars in the government's highly centralized decision-making process.

Still, the Argentine experience suggests two ways in which IR scholars can contribute to foreign policy decision making and outcomes. First, IR scholars can conduct research that policymakers are interested in and cannot conduct themselves. It is crucial, however, to engage political brokers or (potential) allies in government in the design of such research, to identify strategic situations, to explore outcomes worth pursuing, to identify policy options for achieving them, and to develop relations of trust with (current or future) government officials. Doing so helps scholars influence policy because they develop a sense of empathy for the day-to-day challenges policymakers face, and practitioners acquire a better understanding of what could be gained from rigorous research.

Second, scholars can put contemporary foreign policy issues in historical perspective and help policymakers decide what specific policies are worth pursuing further or starting anew. Scholars can serve as the institutional memory of a policy-making process dominated by an actor, the president, who usually does not have the time (or interest) to go back and read through his predecessor's files (if available) to decide upon future policy courses. Independent reports on cutting-edge issues can help organize policy options and contribute to legitimizing ideas on alternative courses of action.

ACKNOWLEDGMENTS

I am very grateful to Carlos Escudé, Pat James, Chap Lawson, Abraham Lowenthal, and Roberto Russell for their comments and suggestions on earlier drafts of this chapter. Mistakes are mine alone.

NOTES

1. Joseph S. Nye, "International Relations: The Relevance of Theory to Practice," in *The Oxford Handbook of International Relations*, ed. Christian Reus-Smith and Duncan Snidal (New York: Oxford University Press), 656.

2. Joseph S. Tulchin, *Argentina and the United States: A Conflicted Relationship* (Boston: Twayne, 1990).

3. Deborah Norden and Roberto Russell, *The United States and Argentina: Changing Relations in a Changing World* (New York: Routledge, 2002), 1.

4. Norden and Russell, *United States and Argentina*; Luis Alberto Romero, *Breve historia contemporánea de la Argentina* (Buenos Aires: Fondo de Cultura Económica, 2001), 284; Juan Carlos Torre, "Critical Junctures and Economic Change," in *Argentina: The Challenges of Modernization*, ed. Joseph Tulchin and Allison Garland (Wilmington, DE: Scholarly Resources), 203–7; Jorge Castro, "La Argentina, Estados Unidos y Brasil: El Triangulo de la Década del '90," in *Política Exterior Argentina: 1989–1999: Historia de un éxito*, ed. Andrés Cisneros (Buenos Aires: GEL, 1998), 89; Andrés Cisneros, "Política Exterior Argentina 1989–1999: Historia de un éxito," in Cisneros, *Política Exterior Argentina*, 67, 74–75; Carlos Escudé, *El Realismo de los Estados Débiles: La política exterior del primer Gobierno Menem frete a la teoría de las relaciones internacionales* (Buenos Aires: GEL, 1995), 15–16; Joseph Tulchin, "Continuity and Change in Argentine Foreign Policy," in Tulchin and Garland, *Argentina*, 184–86.

5. Juan G. Tokatlián, "Política Exterior Argentina de Menem a De la Rúa: La Diplomacia del Ajuste," *Escenarios Alternativos* 4, no. 9 (Winter 2000); Francisco Corigliano, "Las 'relaciones carnales': los vínculos políticos con las grandes potencias 1989–2000," in *Historia General de las Relaciones Exteriores de la República Argentina*, ed. Carlos Escudé (Buenos Aires: GEL), 328.

6. With the end of the Cold War, Brazil, Colombia, Mexico, and other Latin American countries also tended to leave behind their anti-US voting profiles. However, no such change was as rapid and dramatic as that of Argentina. Tokatlián, "Política Exterior Argentina."

The "embedded intellectual capital" of scholar-practitioners is not the only mechanism through which scholarly outputs may influence policy. Two alternative mechanisms are captured by the "trickle-down" model and the role played in policymaking by think tanks and university-based research centers. The trickle-down model "assumes that new ideas emerge from academic 'ivory towers,' gradually filter down into the work of applied analysts (and especially people working in public policy think tanks), and finally reach the perceptions and actions of policy makers." Stephen Walt, "The Relationship between Theory and Policy in International Relations," *Annual Review of Political Science* 8 (June 2005): 40–41. For their part, think tanks and university-based research centers have come to offer relatively well-institutionalized transmission belts along which policy-relevant knowledge is effectively conveyed, which is particularly true in the United States. See Ernest J. Wilson III, "Is There Really a Scholar-Practitioner Gap? An Institutional Analysis," *PS: Political Science and Politics* 40 (Jan. 2007): 147–51. For a preliminary discussion of all three mechanisms in the Argentine context, see Roberto Russell, "The Scholar-Practitioner Interaction: The Case of Argentina," memorandum prepared for the International Workshop on Scholars and Practitioners, Center for International Studies, University of Southern California, 2011.

Thomas Biersteker (chap. 8, this volume) proposes a fourth mechanism of academic access to and influence on policymaking: the participation of scholars in "transnational policy networks," that is, a "group of individuals who share a common expertise, a common technical language to communicate that expertise, broadly shared normative concerns, but not necessarily agreement on specific policy alternatives" on a given issue.

7. Norden and Russell, *United States and Argentina*.

8. Mark Falcoff, "Comentarios," in *La Política Exterior Argentina en el Nuevo Orden Mundial*, ed. Roberto Russell (Buenos Aires: GEL, 1992), 205.

9. With the end of the Cold War, the notion of "autonomy" and its significance as an objective national interest disappeared from Latin American political and academic debates in general, not just in Argentina. However, not all Latin American countries replaced foreign policy "autonomy" with foreign policy "alignment" with the United States. Even by Latin American standards, Argentina's alignment with the United States was exceptional. Roberto Russell and Juan G. Tokatlián, "Beyond Orthodoxy: Asserting Latin America's New Strategic Options toward the United States," *Latin American Politics and Society* 53 (2011): 135.

10. Guido di Tella, "La política exterior argentina en los umbrales del siglo XXI" (keynote remarks at the Consejo Argentino para las Relaciones Internacionales, Capital Federal, Buenos Aires, Apr. 19, 1991). Such foreign policy transformation amounts to what Hermann defines as a "major" change in policy. A "major" change encompasses "program," "goal," or "international orientation" changes in policy, not "adjustment" changes. "Program and goal" modifications are changes in the ends and purposes of a given foreign policy. "Fundamental changes in a country's international orientation" are defined by changes in the global role and activities to be pursued by a given country. Minor "adjustments" in foreign policy are related to the level of effort or scope of recipients of a given policy—changes in foreign policy that tend to be of a quantitative nature. Charles Hermann, "Changing Course: When Governments Choose to Redirect Foreign Policy," *International Studies Quarterly* 34 (1990): 3–21. As Norden and Russell remind us, some disagreements remained in Argentine-US relations during the 1990s. Argentina's limited protection of intellectual property rights, US agricultural subsidies, and Argentina's unsuccessful efforts to gain access to the North American Free Trade Agreement were all issues that did not find a definitive solution during that decade. Politically, the United States continued to pressure Argentina to reduce corruption and to improve the administration of justice and human rights. On security affairs, Argentina was forced to concede its Cóndor II project. It had to come to terms with the need to relinquish its efforts to gain full membership in NATO, and it had to accept new US policies of arms sales to Latin America that appeared to favor countries with already larger military budgets. Norden and Russell, *United States and Argentina*, 73–74.

11. Mariano E. Bertucci, *Sobre el Origen de la Política de Convergencia Argentina Hacia los Estado Unidos Durante los '90: Política Exterior y Toma de Decisiones en la Argentina Menemista* (Buenos Aires: Universidad Torcuato Di Tella, 2006).

12. Torre, "Critical Junctures," 207. Other works emphasizing the role of an Argentine "special" relationship with the United States in the country's economic recovery strategy include Romero, *Breve historia contemporánea de la Argentina*; Castro, "La Argentina, Estados Unidos y Brasil"; Cisneros, "Política Exterior Argentina 1989–1999"; Escudé, *El Realismo de los Estados Débiles*; and Tulchin, "Continuity and Change in Argentine Foreign Policy."

13. Domingo Cavallo, *Pasión por Crear* (Buenos Aires: Grupo Editorial Planeta, 2001), 137–38. The need to have good relations with the United States and the Western world as a means of facilitating Argentina's way out of its foreign debt crisis (among other economic recovery goals) became clear to Menem and Cavallo back in 1988. In that year, Menem invited Cavallo to participate in a trip to Europe as part of his electoral campaign. As they met with several European leaders, it became obvious how important it would be for Argentina's

economy to normalize relations with Britain and the entire developed Western world. As they met with government and opposition leaders of different European countries, Menem and Cavallo kept on receiving the same message: "Solve your Malvinas conflict with Britain." "That way," Menem recalls, "a thorny issue moved up on my agenda. I understood how urgent it was for Argentina to overcome this situation, and I discussed it with Cavallo. We both understood that solving such issue was crucial for Argentina to gain access to the European Common Market." Menem returned to Buenos Aires having already decided to change Argentina's foreign policy to increased cooperative relations with all developed countries, including the United States. And, when elected president of Argentina, he offered Cavallo the Ministry of Foreign Affairs and made clear that there were four foreign policy priorities for Argentina: "first, deepening regional ties with both Brazil and Chile . . . Second, to develop a very close relation with the US, until we are considered their most important allies in South America . . . Third, to re-establish normal cooperative relations with Europe [and] Fourth, to develop a special relationship with the Middle East as a means of changing Argentina's anti-Israeli policy as embodied in the country's participation in the Non-Aligned Movement." All quotes are from Bertucci, *Sobre el Origen*.

14. See, for example, "Un amor platónico," *Página 12* (July 8, 1990): 23. According to Guido di Tella, then Argentina's ambassador in Washington, DC, Argentina's military participation in the first Gulf War "has been interpreted as a symbolic decision, showcasing the country's alignment with the Western world in general and the United States in particular, after fifty or seventy years of frictions between the two countries." "Las naves argentinas no entrarán al Golfo Pérsico," *Clarín*, September 22, 1990, 3. See also "Elogió Bush la determinación del Presidente," *La Nación*, September 21, 1990, 1, and "Beneplácito de los EE.UU. por la actitud argentina," *La Nación*, September 20, 1990, 1.

15. See "Un jefe militar de los EE.UU. con Romero," *Clarín*, May 15, 1990, 5.

16. Carlos Escudé, *Foreign Policy Theory in Menem's Argentina* (Gainesville, FL: University Press of Florida, 1997), 3.

17. Escudé, *Foreign Policy Theory*. See also Carlos Escudé's *Argentina: Paria Internacional?* (Buenos Aires: Sudamericana, 1984), *La Argentina vs. las Grandes Potencias: El Precio del Desafío* (Buenos Aires: Editorial de Belgrano, 1986), and "Política exterior argentina: Una sobredosis crónica de confrontaciones," in *La nueva democracia argentina (1983–1986)*, ed. Ernesto Garzón Valdés, Manfred Mols, and Arnold Spita (Buenos Aires: Editorial Sudamericana, 1988), 261–80; Roberto Russell, *La Política Exterior Argentina*; and the newsletter *America Latina/Internacional* (published by FLACSO, Buenos Aires), 8, no. 27 (Jan.–Mar. 1991) and no. 29 (July–Sept. 1991).

18. Guido di Tella and Carlos Escudé began their professional relationship in 1977. That year they were both at Oxford—di Tella as an associate fellow of St. Antony's College and Escudé as a graduate student. Di Tella was appointed as a sort of "mentor" or "academic adviser" to Escudé. On Escudé's return to Argentina he contacted di Tella, who invited him to join the IDT as an IR scholar. Dr. Carlos Escudé, Skype interview, November 4, 2011.

19. Carlos Escudé, *El Estado Parasitario. Argentina. Ciclos de Vaciamiento. Clase Política Delictiva y Colapso de la Política Exterior* (Buenos Aires: Lumiere, 2005), 101–7, 149.

20. The outcome of the meeting was the book Guido di Tella and D. Cameron Watt, eds., *Argentina between the Great Powers, 1939–46* (Pittsburgh, PA: University of Pittsburgh Press, 1990).

21. Guido di Tella, "Argentina between the Great Powers, 1939–46: A Revisionist Summing Up," in di Tella and Watt, *Argentina between the Great Powers*, 194–95.

22. See "Di Tella: 'Acá hubo una perestroika,' " *Página* 12 (July 2, 1989): 6. Dante Caputo was Argentina's minister of foreign affairs during the government of Raúl Alfonsín (1983–89).

23. Dr. Carlos Escudé, interview, Buenos Aires, December 19, 2006.

24. Tokatlián, "Política Exterior Argentina"; Corigliano, "Las 'relaciones carnales,' " 328.

25. According to Hagan, a "strongly anti-US" voting profile is one that opposes the United States in 59% of votes, agrees in less than 18%, and abstains in 24%. A "centrist" profile agrees with the United States in 33% of votes, abstains in 26%, and opposes the United States in 41%. A "moderately pro-US" profile agrees with the United States in 43% of votes, abstains in 24%, and opposes the United States in 33%. A "strongly pro-US" profile agrees with the United States in 54% of votes, abstains in 25%, and opposes the United States in 20% or less. Joe D. Hagan, "Domestic Political Regime Changes and Third World Voting Realignments in the United Nations, 1946–84," *International Organization* 43 (Summer 1989): 517.

During the 1990s there were three clearly differentiated periods regarding Argentine votes at the UN. A State Department report to the US Congress shows that the percentage coincidence of votes between Argentina and the United States was 13.3% in 1989 and 12.5% in 1990. In 1990, this percentage was similar to but less than that of Brazil (14.9%), Colombia (14.8%), and Mexico (15.2%). In the second period, from 1991 to 1995, the coincidence between Argentine and US voting was 41% in 1991, 44.4% in 1992, 53.8% in 1993, 67.9% in 1994, and 68.8% in 1995. In this period, Argentina's voting profile departed remarkably from that of other Latin American nations. Finally, from 1996 to 1999, Argentina's voting record moved toward that of its Latin American counterparts. Tokatlián, "Política Exterior Argentina." Still, Argentina's percentage voting coincidence with the United States remained higher than that of Brazil, Mexico, Chile, and Colombia and never fell below 44.4%—that is, unlike its Latin American counterparts, between 1992 and 1999 Argentina had at least a "moderately pro-US" vote at the UN.

26. Dr. Carlos Escudé, interview, Buenos Aires, December 19, 2006. See also Cisneros, "Política Exterior Argentina 1989–1999."

27. Quoted in Corigliano, "Las 'relaciones carnales,' " 217.

28. Dr. Carlos Escudé, interview, Buenos Aires, December 19, 2006.

29. A partial reproduction of the memo drafted by Escudé can be found in Corigliano, "Las 'relaciones carnales,' " 221–22.

30. Corigliano, "Las 'relaciones carnales,' " 219.

31. Dr. Carlos Escudé, Skype interview, November 5, 2011.

32. Cisneros, "Política Exterior Argentina 1989–1999."

33. Roberto Russell, "Política exterior y veinte años de democracia: Un primer balance," in *La historia reciente: Argentina en democracia*, ed. Marcos Novaro and Vicente Palermo (Buenos Aires: Edhasa, 2004), 257–69.

PART FIVE

PRAXIS AND THE ACADEMY:
PERSPECTIVES FROM POLICYMAKERS

CHAPTER ELEVEN

The Long Diplomacy
How a Changing World Creates New Opportunities for Partnership between Scholars and Practitioners

THOMAS A. SHANNON JR.

General John Abizaid famously described the fight against terrorism and extremism in the Middle East as "the long war." He said this struggle would be fought in different places at different times but always against a determined enemy intent on exploiting weak states, local conflict, social resentment, and fundamentalist religious beliefs to attack the strategic interests of the United States. In remarks at Harvard Kennedy School in 2006, he argued that this war was unavoidable: "We can walk away from this enemy, but they will not walk away from us."

The idea of a war that can morph from state-on-state conflict into civil war into insurgency and then back again is unsettling. It is a war without clear boundaries that features shadowy opponents, shifting alliances and coalitions, and few victories except securing our safety each and every day.

As we have fought this long war, the world around us has changed in fundamental ways. The reemergence of China and India as world powers, the insertion of their giant societies into the global economy, Russia's renewed claim to leadership in Eurasia, the rise of Brazil and regional powers such as Indonesia, Iran, Nigeria, Mexico, and South Africa, the economic and political turmoil facing Europe, and the vast migration of wealth from West to East—all have altered global power and decision making and created new challenges for the United States.

While the security concerns presented by radical groups such as Al-Qaida remain a priority and a paramount concern, it is evident that the well-being of the United States will depend not only on our success in the long war but also on how we engage with the new world that is being created around us. Although this engagement is just as unavoidable as our fight against terrorism, it will be of a different nature. Instead of a long war, it will be a long diplomacy.

A New World, a New Challenge

Our new world has several distinguishing characteristics. First, the states that are emerging alongside the United States as important world powers are still in the process of political, economic, and social development. Even those with large economies, such as China, India, and Brazil, have significant levels of poverty and face deeply ingrained social inequities. This means that these countries cast their engagement with the world in terms of obtaining or protecting the resources and energy necessary for national development, building the scientific and technological capacity to compete globally in manufacturing and services, constructing the infrastructure and logistical systems needed to build domestic markets and connect to regional and global economies, and securing access to the external markets necessary for economic growth, job creation, and international influence.

Second, the world is integrating regionally through economic markets. The emergence of regional stock exchanges and capital markets, efforts to connect and regulate financial flows, and the development of regional infrastructure to link markets highlight the growing dependency of emerging powers on neighbors and key economic partners for continued national development.

Third, the major emerging powers are largely committed to international law and organizations as fundamental mechanisms for ordering relationships between and among states. These powers want reforms in global political and economic organizations so as to reflect major changes in the world since their creation and give these powers a larger voice in international decision making. This desire to be recognized and included provides important ballast to international organizations charged with maintaining international peace and security.

Fourth, the United States is the only global player with the ability to project military power far beyond its borders. With a few exceptions, none of the emerging powers has the capacity, will, or popular support to impose military solutions on political and economic problems. Although the threat of state-on-state violence and conflict still exists in some regions, the major threats to national security for most states come from non-state actors, especially criminal and terrorist organizations.

Fifth, although states remain the most important building blocks of the international system, increasingly it is the relationships between societies and peoples that matter. In a regionally integrated and increasingly globalized world, societies are connecting rapidly. Whether through the private sector, civil society, universities and research institutions, churches and religious groups, or tourism, the desire of our societies to engage is increasingly driving the foreign policy agendas of governments. The emergence of this popular voice is redefining national interests and requiring foreign ministries, typically the most traditional of government institutions, to reshape national diplomacy.

Finally, the major challenges facing the world in the twenty-first century are increasingly global. Bilateral issues and disputes will still be important and will require, in some instances, international mediation, but they will be incidental. Our diplomacy, and that of the world, will be driven largely by issues such as energy and food security, management of arable land and fresh water, environmental stewardship and climate change, nonproliferation, and the fight against transnational crime and terrorism.

This new world of the twenty-first century is not without its dangers, some of them quite frightening, but it is a more hopeful world than that of the previous century. The powers that are emerging today to compete on the global stage, unlike the European powers of the early twentieth century, are not imperial nations intent on conquest and domination. They are not locked into antiquated dynastic alliances or finely wrought and brittle efforts to balance power. They will not be compelled to fight each other, or us. This means we have an opportunity to create an international environment in which conflict and struggle will be channeled through diplomacy, not warfare. There will still be differences, and the struggle for preeminence will still have ugly moments of high anxiety, but the threat of devastating global warfare will retreat.

When future historians evaluate and judge our generation, much of what we consider important will fade into insignificance. What will remain is the opportunity we had to build an international system that accommodated the desire of emerging powers for a larger voice in global affairs, our capacity to extend the benefits of economic well-being to all our citizens and to address the social aspirations of an emerging global middle class that wants a voice in determining national destiny, and the resources necessary to choose individual destinies. In short, a world defined by a balance of interests and not by a balance of power.

Looking at the Old, New World

As we contemplate what this long diplomacy might look like, it is worth examining our own hemisphere. Latin America has anticipated the events that are shaping the world in the twenty-first century. It is a region that has moved largely from authoritarian to democratic government, from closed to open economies, from exclusive to inclusive societies, from autarkic development to regional integration, and from isolation to globalization.

Latin America is the first developing region of the world to commit itself explicitly to democratic government through the Inter-American Democratic Charter, the first to link its social and economic development to democracy, and the first to build regional structures to promote and protect human rights.

While creating a broad base of shared political values, Latin America also constructed shared economic understandings and a commitment to market economies and free trade. In the process, it has built subregional integration and political dialogue through organizations such as the Common Market of the South, the Andean Community, the Union of South American Nations, and the Central American Integration System. All the while it has preserved larger hemispheric institutions, such as the Organization of American States and the Summit of the Americas process, that connect Latin America to the Caribbean and North America.

As Latin America moves into the twenty-first century, it is undergoing a second generation of change. Politically, it has consolidated democratic government and is now building democratic states and societies. This has opened up political institutions to new voices and actors, deepening the representativeness of many Latin American governments and challenging traditional elites and interests. In some countries, weak democratic institutions have not been able to contain the social energy unlocked by democratization, leading to populism and political polarization as groups struggle for control of the state. As troubling as this phenomenon can be, it does not define the democratization of the region but instead presents a challenge for the region to show it can address such incidents through the organizations and integration mechanisms it has created.

Economically, Latin America is building innovative integration mechanisms, such as the Pacific Alliance, and reaching into Asia and North America to find new and important economic partners. The globalization of Latin America is driven not only by the region's abundant commodities, especially food and energy, but also by growing middle classes that have created attractive markets for manufactured goods and services.

The profound changes unleashed in Latin America show clearly that democracy and markets can deliver economic development and address long-standing social inequities such as poverty and social exclusion. In effect, Latin America has used democracy and markets to launch peaceful social revolutions that are transforming many countries in important and long-lasting ways. Our ability to help promote the profound and dramatic change experienced in Latin America is an example of what the United States can accomplish by long diplomacy.

Understanding the New Roles of Scholars and Practitioners

Dean Acheson, in his book *Present at the Creation*, described the efforts of the Allies during World War II as being defined by three qualities: "ignorance of the situation, daring, and buoyant determination." As he looked beyond the destruction of that war and toward his efforts to build the structures of lasting peace and security, he wrote, "As we embark on this great journey that lies in front of us, one thing is certain, we only know the beginning—we do not know the end."

Today, with Acheson, we can say that we know only the beginning of our journey in this century. But, unlike Acheson, we cannot say that we are ignorant of the situation. The depth of our knowledge of the world and the resources we dedicate to study it in academia, business, and government are unprecedented in human history.

For the long diplomacy to work, and for the United States and its partners to build an enduring peace, we must link our study and our practice. We must find a way to connect the understanding that academia offers of the political, economic, and social transformations reshaping our world with the everyday work of diplomats carried out in hundreds of embassies and consulates around the globe. In this way, we will leaven and ground the study of the processes that define our world, while informing our response to them.

Given our information technology, this should not be hard. Today, we can connect scholar and practitioner instantaneously and in real time. We can share information, insight, and opinions and involve each in the work of the other.

The biggest obstacle to such collaboration, however, is not knowledge or technology. It is mentality. On the side of the scholar, it is a tendency toward ever narrower and more arcane study. It is a decline in the ability to analyze and synthesize information across disciplines and then to build a narrative that explains political, economic, and social phenomena. On the side of the practitioner, it is the arrogance of the moment and the belief that the urgent actions and decisions we take on a daily basis define the totality of our work. It is also the reluctance to acknowledge how broadly diplomacy has expanded. A profession that once required only knowledge of history and international law now requires familiarity with everything from nanotechnology to derivative financial products and public health.

But, as scholars and practitioners, we must overcome these narrow conceptions of ourselves and instead create a public intellectual setting where we can benefit mutually from our work. We need to create a setting where we can build a narrative and purpose to describe and inform our long diplomacy. In Acheson's words, we must understand that "detachment and objectivity seem to me less important than to tell a tale of large conceptions, great achievements, and some failures, the product of enormous will and effort."

What Comes Next?

Our efforts to better link scholars and practitioners should be both conceptual and contextual. In other words, we should identify a substantive agenda to which both can contribute and then create the proximity necessary for dialogue to lead to a diplomacy defined by better understanding and more efficacious action.

For substantive engagement, at least five tasks come to mind. First, build a thematic global agenda. The major issues of the twenty-first century will be global. Issues such as food security, energy security, climate change and environmental stewardship, nonproliferation, public health, and the fight against transnational crime and terrorism will define our challenges. To construct an effective and consistent diplomacy to face these challenges, we need a well-articulated global agenda. This will allow us to concentrate our personnel and resources where they will bring long-term success and avoid conflicts and confrontation that distract from this broader agenda. This will also allow us to evaluate the effectiveness of existing international organizations and propose changes that will make these organizations more meaningful and relevant to the challenges we face.

Second, recognize societies as the principal drivers of international relations and develop strategies to engage these new and amorphous players in foreign policy. Although governments will continue to be an important medium through which states express their interests, those interests will be defined by societies or peoples. As the world globalizes, as information and the ability to express opinions become more accessible, and as the capability to organize and express interests becomes more sophisticated, governments will find their agendas being set by their own people.

The old-world understanding of diplomacy as the pursuit of long-established, static interests is no longer valid. Our societies are reshaping national interests and looking for ways to compel governments to pursue these interests and to express the values that define our societies. This is happening with great earnestness in democracies, but even authoritarian regimes find their power challenged, confined, and directed by their societies. The tremendous internal pressures that are building in contemporary societies have opened an important opportunity for our diplomacy. We now have an expanded audience that extends far beyond government interlocutors and will require us to engage in nontraditional ways as we seek to build constituencies within and across states in support of our interests. This will also mean understanding how our own society relates to the world, whether it be through commerce and investment, education, religion, or tourism.

Third, proclaim "development as freedom" and focus on building the content of democracy. This phrase, first used by Nobel Prize–winning economist Amartya Sen, captures an important reality of the post–Cold War world. The "Rights of Man" in the twenty-first century will no longer be defined solely in political terms but also in the economic and social terms of development. Governments will be judged by how effectively they deliver the goods of development and combat poverty, inequality, and social exclusion.

The countries of the Americas, through the Inter-American Democratic Charter, made a radical commitment when they asserted that democracy is a right that all people should enjoy and all governments promote and that democracy is essential to the political, economic, and social development of all peoples. This commitment clearly challenges efforts in China and elsewhere to insist that only authoritarian governments can produce long-term development. To defend ourselves against this authoritarian alternative, however, our diplomacy needs to work with our partners to build the content of democracy. This means providing our citizens with the education, health care, and personal security necessary to become active members of our societies. To construct an effective model of democratic development, however, we will have to reach beyond our traditional development practices and partners. In effect, we have to capture the social innovation and success of development in countries such as Brazil and understand how we can best link to these efforts to enhance the ability of states and societies to define their own development agenda. With many of our traditional development partners in economic decline, we also have to identify those countries among the emerging powers that are prepared to work with us in support of democratic development.

Fourth, acknowledge that empowerment of individuals is the surest guarantor of democracy and our open society, and identify means and mechanisms to protect and strengthen the ability of individuals to be contributing members of our societies. Democratic development, as outlined above, creates an environment that promotes social inclusion and provides individuals with the tools and resources necessary to have a voice in determining national destiny. However, democratic development must go a step further and provide individuals with the opportunity to realize their individual destinies.

To achieve this, we must add two things to the combination of political rights and social and economic development: opportunity and respect. Opportunity is the clear recognition that people can use their political rights and the fruits of democratic development to aspire to and achieve a better life for themselves and their families. Respect is the lack of discrimination and prejudice in society and a commitment to ensure that prejudice in any of its guises—regarding gender, race, ethnicity, religion, or sexual orientation and identification—is not allowed to block the advancement of the individual. This is a complicated and challenging goal. It requires an ability to navigate around cultural barriers and traditional practices. Developing strategies to highlight the importance of social inclusion for economic advancement and for the long-term vitality of our open societies should be an area of special focus. In effect, it will change how we view the purpose of our diplomacy: our practice and our study must be relevant to the everyday lives of our citizens.

Finally, revive area studies. As the world flattens and as power disperses throughout the international system, the importance of regional relations and integration grows. At one level, regional relations have always been the building blocks of diplomacy. In academia and many foreign ministries, however, regionalism has fallen into the chasm between globalism and bilateralism. We have lost a clear understanding of how regional contexts shape the behavior of states. In the dynamic world of today, with national interests in many countries being redefined by new and emerging domestic political voices, regional relationships are being reimagined and remade with important consequences for our interests.

The impact of this phenomenon on our diplomacy is significant, if not always well understood. During the Cold War there was a natural ordering mechanism that required countries to line up in one of three camps: ours, theirs, or nobody's. Whatever the choice, it was always done in relation to our struggle with the Soviet Union. Today, this ordering mechanism no longer exists. While strong magnetic forces still operate within the international system, most countries respond to neighbors and near neighbors before responding to distant powers. For the United States, this means that our influence is challenged by emerging regional powers and that every day we must prove our relevance to our historic partners. In the twenty-first century, geography will trump ideology. However, shared interests will permeate all regional constructs, and we can build off our long-standing globalism to maintain influence in regions that are integrating and building new models of economic cooperation and political dialogue.

As we create the substantive agenda of our long diplomacy, we must also create the space for practitioners and scholars to meet and address the agenda. Some of this has already been done, and there is no need to alter some of the most successful aspects of this engagement. The presence of diplomats in universities through diplomat-in-residence programs and the presence of scholars in the Department of State and other US government institutions through scholar-in-residence programs are useful exchanges. These build common understandings and common experiences that facilitate communication and cooperation.

Also, the think tanks that work on foreign policy issues can provide a useful meeting point for practitioners and scholars and can assert some discipline over dialogue by directing it to specific purposes. Universities remain the best place, however, to construct the engagement between scholars and diplomats that lies at the heart of our long diplomacy. Universities have convoking authority, they bring intellectual prestige and standing to such gatherings, and they have the resources to maintain such engagement over time. They are not driven by crises, overwhelmed by the urgent, or subject to the political winds that often blow in our government's foreign policy community. By providing for the constancy and consistency of engagement, universities can ensure a high-quality and meaningful product that will be important for the success of our diplomacy. In effect, universities will be helping to midwife a new kind of public intellectual. On both sides of the divide between scholars and practitioners, engagement will produce men and women comfortable with the exacting demands of public life and the accountability that defines government service, while embracing the rigor, expertise, quiet reflection, and curiosity that exemplify academic life.

Much of the work that needs to be done between practitioners and scholars will be piecemeal and driven by specific events or needs. However, we cannot expect a larger agenda or product to emerge only from incidental engagement. Instead, we need a gathering, ideally convened by the US secretary of state, to bring together presidents of leading universities, respected academics, and influential opinion makers to set an agenda for cooperation and create the mechanisms necessary to promote collaboration around points similar to those listed above. The initial work agenda does not have to be comprehensive, but it must be specific, relevant, and of immediate interest to those who will work on the agenda items. In this fashion, success and cooperation will build confidence and purpose and will lead to an organic growth of the work agenda.

The Task That Lies before Us

Surveying the international landscape in the aftermath of World War II, Secretary of State Dean Acheson said that the task that lay before the United States was as big as Genesis: "to create a world out of chaos." Today, our task is the reverse: to prevent an ordered world from collapsing into chaos. This task, like that facing Acheson, requires us not to be distracted from "the effort to affect the world around us."

It also requires us to remember that American diplomacy has never been about sustaining a status quo or maintaining a balance of power. It has been about responding to the great changes that modernity has unleashed in the world and finding a means to shape and affect those changes in ways that benefit our interests and are consonant with our values.

It is clear that the twenty-first century will require a new and different kind of diplomacy: a diplomacy that understands the profound forces at work in the world, that recognizes how these forces shape the behavior of states, and that can marshal the resources, people, and energy necessary to meet challenges of unprecedented complexity. Diplomats alone cannot meet this challenge. But diplomats and scholars, working together to blend practice and knowledge, action and reflection, experience and wisdom, can meet this challenge. Together, the two can lay out a course for a long diplomacy respectful of our past, worthy of our present, and ever mindful of our posterity.

CHAPTER TWELVE

How Scholars Can Contribute to Policymaking
Lessons from Mexico

RAFAEL FERNÁNDEZ DE CASTRO

At schools of public policy and political science, it is common to hear two major assertions about decision-making processes in government: first, that time is too scarce for decision makers to reflect on different public policy alternatives; and second, that government decisions are not necessarily rational—that is, they are based on personal, political, and bureaucratic considerations and interests. During almost two decades of academic life, I came to believe in the validity of these two assertions; during my three years in a Mexican presidential administration, I realized that they must always be kept in mind.

This chapter advances two arguments. The first is that a public official has much to gain by consulting academic experts whenever a decision must be made in a policy area that marks uncharted territory. This entails adopting some practices used in academic circles, such as the free deliberation and discussion of ideas—free, that is, of a hierarchy where the leader is "always right." The second is that coming up with a good idea is not enough for that idea to surface as the right course of action. It is also necessary to advocate, explain, and persuade others to adopt good ideas during the decision-making process.

To illustrate these arguments, I analyze three such processes in which I participated—two of these as foreign policy advisor to Felipe Calderón, the president of Mexico (2006–12). The first process was Mexico's proposal to Brazil to negotiate a free trade agreement, presented in August 2009 during Calderón's visit to President Luiz Inácio Lula da Silva. The second was the North American Export Initiative (NAEXI), proposed during Calderón's state visit to Washington, DC, in May 2010. The third case I discuss—which preceded the other two chronologically—is the proposal for an agreement on immigration that President Vicente Fox presented to President George W. Bush during a February 2001 meeting at Fox's ranch in San Cristóbal, Guanajuato.

An Agreement to Transform Binational Relations and Advance Latin American Integration: Free Trade between Mexico and Brazil

Felipe Calderón entered the presidency wanting to transform and improve Mexico's relationship with Latin America. As he indicated during his first international tour, "Mexico is essentially Latin American; its heart, culture, people, and history are here. Like all countries, we are a country with multiple contexts and challenges, and in spite of the fact that geographically we belong to the North American region, we know that our essence, our substance, our history, our past and our future are in Latin America."[1] Latin America was the region he traveled to the most, and presidents Álvaro Colom of Guatemala (2008–12) and Álvaro Uribe of Colombia (2002–10) were the heads of state he visited most frequently. Without a doubt, the most important stop in Calderón's Latin American pilgrimage was Brazil, a country that would gain recognition as the region's emerging economic star halfway through Calderón's six-year presidential term. Furthermore, Brazil's global leadership was projected as part of a new, greatly influential group of emerging countries—the BRIC countries—consisting of Brazil, Russia, India and China.[2]

When President "Lula" da Silva visited Calderón at the beginning of the latter's administration in 2007, he extended an open invitation to Calderón to visit Brazil. It was not until the beginning of 2009 that the two countries' Ministries of Foreign Affairs (Tlatelolco and Itamaraty) and Offices of the Presidency (Los Pinos and Planalto) arranged a visit for August of that year.

In June 2009, we at the Mexican Ministry of Foreign Affairs and the Office of the Presidency initiated preparations to ensure that the visit to Brazil would be a success. We saw the visit as an opportunity to improve relations between the two leaders, whose personal relationship had been rocky.[3] The stage was set for Mexico to attempt a new initiative, aimed to leave behind decades of distant relations with Brazil.[4]

I reached agreement with Salvador Beltrán del Río, undersecretary for Latin America in Mexico's Ministry of Foreign Affairs, to convene a group of experts—made up of scholars, consultants, social leaders, businessmen, legislators, and public officials—to gather ideas and proposals that could strengthen the agenda for the Brazil visit. We intended the meeting to entail academic reflection and "brainstorming." A large group of people (32) arrived at Los Pinos, including not only those whom we had initially invited but also others who asked to attend. The explanation for the eager response is very simple: experts in Mexico are interested in improving relations with such an important country as Brazil.

To manage the discussion, we divided the attendees into four subgroups: financial matters, trade, and investment; energy and the environment; science and technology; and regional and global dialogue. We agreed on a process during the first meeting: each of the subgroups would meet separately to prepare a list of recommendations, which they would then present in a plenary session at the final meeting. The most noteworthy recommendations, adopted for the Brazil Visit Agenda, were those from the subgroup on financial matters, trade, and investment and from the science and technology subgroup.

Trade experts like Jaime Zabludovsky, former Mexican negotiator for the North American Free Trade Agreement (NAFTA) and the Free Trade Agreement between the European Union and Mexico, promoted the idea of negotiating a free trade agreement with Brazil. Their reasoning was the following: The foundering of Brazil's international trade policy—because of the failure to achieve a free trade agreement with the European Union and suspension of the World Trade Organization Doha Round—created a unique opportunity for Mexico. Brazilian exporters, especially those in the state of São Paulo, demanded open markets for their products and were eager for Mexico to become a platform, not only for access to the 110 million Mexican consumers, but also as a link to the United States and Canada, with over 330 million potential consumers. An experienced commercial negotiator from the Mexican private sector, Rafael Urquiza, seconded Zabludovsky's proposal.

The science and technology subgroup, under the leadership of researchers José Antonio de la Peña, director of the Mathematical Research Center, and Xavier Soberón, general director of the National Genomic Medicine Institute, proposed concrete scientific agreements that were indeed signed during the visit. Four science and technology agreements were signed; all those proposals came from our group of experts. The agreements include "Memorandum of Understanding on Matters Regarding Energy Cooperation"; "Memorandum of Understanding on Scientific, Technological, Academic and Innovation Cooperation"; and "Protocols of Intent between the National Council of Science and Technology (CONACYT) and the Ministry of Science and Technology (MCT) for creating the Mexican-Brazilian Virtual Nanotechnology Center (CMBNano), and the Brazilian-Mexican Virtual Biotechnology Center (CBMBio)."

The Mexico-Brazil free trade proposal ended up being the main event of the visit. The idea of proposing to Brazil the negotiation of a free trade treaty encountered various obstacles, however. The public official in charge of the matter, Gerardo Ruíz Mateos, who was the Mexican secretary of economy and consequently the head of trade negotiations, was opposed to it. Further, it was widely known that leaders in agriculture business, the National Agriculture Council, and the Senate would all eventually oppose the treaty. Brazil, an agribusiness powerhouse, represented too much of a threat to Mexican agricultural interests.

What was it, then, that allowed the adoption of the group of experts' recommendation on a free trade agreement with Brazil? There were two explanations. In the first place, President Calderón was genuinely interested in achieving a breakthrough in relations with Brazil. He also was convinced that free trade is the best engine for growth: "In a word, my friends, we must remember that if we want our people to prosper, they will have to prosper through the best instrument in history, which is the free market."[5] The second explanation is related to the wide access I had as Calderón's foreign policy advisor. I was able to argue the benefits of the agreement with those who were opposed to the proposal, such as the secretary of economy.

If President Calderón had any doubts at all regarding the free trade proposal, they vanished in São Paulo during the first visit to Brazil. There, a large group of the city's businessmen resolutely expressed to the Mexican leader their interest in having a wider and more open framework for their economic relations with Mexico.

Lula da Silva did not just accept Calderón's proposal; he went further and proposed elements that would surpass the free trade agreements of previous decades, such as cooperation between the development banks of the two countries. Throughout 2010, we worked on preparing the negotiation. Mexico even replaced its ambassador in Brazil with a very experienced trade negotiator, Alejandro de la Peña. But, despite the good intentions of both President Lula and President Calderón to forge trade and economic agreements between Brazil and Mexico, this did not materialize. Near the end of his second term, an overwhelmed President Lula lacked the time and political will to foster enough consensus in both government and private circles to negotiate and approve the agreement. On his side, President Calderón lacked the leadership to charm the private sector, which was becoming obsessed with the brutal drug war haunting Mexico.

A State Visit by President Felipe Calderón to Washington, DC, May 2010

President Calderón's presidency coincided with the last two years of the George W. Bush administration, 2007 and 2008. Calderón made the political decision not to request a state visit to Washington while Bush was in office. Once Barack Obama arrived at the White House in January 2009, Mexican diplomats requested a state visit, which was granted and scheduled for May 2010. Calderón would be the second leader, after India's Manmohan Singh, to be welcomed with red-carpet treatment at the White House and to give a speech to a joint session of Congress.[6]

To support the visit to Washington, the Office of the Presidency (where I worked) and the secretary of economy decided again to gather a group of experts to help us put together new ideas on how to move beyond the current economic integration arrangement with the United States and to increase North America's regional competitiveness. During the deliberations with specialists and scholars, including Jaime Serra Puche, a former secretary of commerce, Luis de la Calle, a former trade negotiator, and Gustavo Vega, a professor at El Colegio de México, we reached the conclusion that a new regional integration scheme was needed that could go beyond NAFTA.

During the two brainstorming work sessions, a new proposal emerged: the North American Export Initiative. This initiative took advantage of President Obama's proposal (in his February 2010 State of the Union Address) to double US exports in five years, which came to be known as the National Export Initiative. The reasoning behind NAEXI was that Obama would need a new trade alliance with his country's neighbors, Mexico and Canada, to achieve his export goals. The Mexican proposal comprised four main elements: (1) identifying the most competitive North American production sectors in order to strengthen integration around them, (2) improving border efficiency, (3) doubling efforts on renewable energy, and (4) reconciling existing regulatory frameworks.

Calderón did not propose NAEXI to Obama, however. The proposal remained pigeonholed in the offices of the undersecretary for trade negotiations and of President Calderón's international affairs advisor—that is, my office.

Why did President Calderón choose not to endorse NAEXI and propose it to Obama? There were three reasons. First, Calderón wanted to emphasize security and drug trafficking, not economic issues. In his speech before both houses of Congress, his most important message was the need to improve bilateral cooperation on drug trafficking and organized crime. He even urged Congress to reapprove the assault weapons ban.[7] Second, Mexico had not reached domestic consensus on the proposal; the presidential cabinet, the Ministry of Foreign Affairs, and even the secretary of economy were not sure about it. Third, a proposal to the United States, the country that absorbs almost 80% of Mexico's foreign trade, requires greater consensus than a proposal to Brazil. There is so much at stake in Mexico's relationship with the United States that any novel policy proposal is much more difficult to adopt and implement than with any other country.

The exercise was not in vain, however. Three of the four NAEXI elements— border efficiency, strengthening cooperation on clean energy, and regulatory homogenization—formed part of the agreements announced during the visit and appeared as such in the joint statement, as Calderón and Obama established a select committee for promoting a twenty-first-century border and created the High-Level Regulatory Cooperation Commission.

A Comprehensive Immigration Agreement to Take Advantage of the Honeymoon between Vicente Fox and George W. Bush

With the arrival of Vicente Fox to the Mexican presidency in 2000, years before my work as foreign policy advisor to Mexico's president, I witnessed—from an academic vantage point—an important episode in which the ideas of the academic world were adopted by decision makers: a proposal on an immigration agreement between Mexico and the United States.

In September 2000, when Vicente Fox was still president-elect, former ambassador Andrés Rozental was paying close attention to news in the United States. A retired diplomat with much experience in Mexican-US relations, Rozental was also the half-brother of Mexico's soon to be appointed minister of foreign affairs, Jorge G. Castañeda. Rozental became aware of the new pro-immigration attitude of the powerful US labor union, the AFL-CIO, and saw that this might create an unprecedented possibility for cooperation in the area of immigration.

Rozental asked two scholars for help—Demetrios Papademetriou, then director of the Carnegie Endowment for International Peace Immigration Program in Washington, and myself, as head of the Department for International Studies at Instituto Tecnológico Autónomo de México (ITAM). The Carnegie Endowment and ITAM convened a binational panel of immigration experts to analyze how Mexico and the pro-immigration communities of the United States could take advantage of a double window of opportunity: the AFL-CIO's change in attitude toward migrant workers and the simultaneous launch of the Fox and Bush presidencies. (Due to the two countries' electoral calendars, the beginning of the presidential terms in Mexico and the United States coincides every 12 years.)

The binational panel invited an array of experts and scholars from both countries, including Rodolfo Tuirán, a demographer, and Remedios Gómez, an internationalist, both at El Colegio de México, and Frank Sharry, a pro-immigration activist in Washington, among others. The panel of experts met twice and concluded that it would be beneficial to negotiate a comprehensive bilateral agreement covering four main elements: establishing programs for guest workers, regularizing undocumented workers in the United States, undertaking joint responsibility for the economic development of those regions in Mexico with the highest migration rates, and establishing joint management of the border.

In February 2001, during the first meeting between Fox and Bush at Fox's ranch in San Cristóbal, Guanajuato, the Mexican leader followed the binational panel's recommendation and suggested that Mexico and the United States negotiate a comprehensive immigration agreement. The response of Bush, who had barely had time to settle in the White House (he had been in office for less than a month), was to create a commission, presided over by the US secretary of state and attorney general and their Mexican counterparts, the minister of foreign affairs and minister of the interior.[8]

Why did Vicente Fox agree to present the proposal to Bush during their first meeting? The simple answer is that his new minister of foreign affairs, Jorge Castañeda, a writer and scholar, had convinced him to do so. But Castañeda was able to convince Fox largely because of the document produced by a binational group of scholars, with ideas that clearly explained the benefits of negotiating an immigration agreement. Furthermore, Castañeda himself had taken part in the last meeting of experts and had helped formulate the recommendations. No less important, he had invited a group of the panel members to a meeting with Fox to discuss the agenda items for Bush's visit to San Cristóbal.[9]

As it turned out, negotiation of an immigration agreement never got off the ground, in part because of the impact of the terrorist attacks of September 11, 2001. But the central binational panel proposals—regularization of undocumented workers, programs for guest workers, and joint border management—were picked up by subsequent immigration reform packages considered by the US Congress in 2005, 2007, and 2008, and they were at the heart of the comprehensive immigration reform considered by Congress in 2013.

Lessons Learned

What lessons can we draw from the three cases discussed here? First, the academic process of free discussion without hierarchical protocol is appropriate for generating new ideas for government decisions. In my three-year experience at Los Pinos, I learned that discussions among public officials tend to be limited and that hierarchy is a serious impediment. A subordinate does not often criticize the ideas of the leader, even in private, and much less in public.

Second, decision makers have a lot to gain by reaching out to scholars and experts for help in generating new ideas and proposals. This is because, in government, there is no time for long deliberations, and government procedures inhibit the free exchange of ideas.

Third, ideas generated by experts and scholars are most likely to be taken into consideration by the decision makers when there are special circumstances and/or a concrete need to generate a new agenda. In two of the three cases analyzed here—the Free Trade Agreement with Brazil and NAEXI—the proposals were developed in preparation for presidential meetings. The immigration proposal was prepared in response to a window of opportunity due to the AFL-CIO's change of position regarding immigration and the simultaneous launch of the Fox and Bush presidencies. Also, the Bush visit presented an opportunity to elevate the issue to the highest level.

A fourth lesson is that academic ideas do not flow freely to decision makers' desks. One needs to make sure they get there. There are two ways to do this. The first technique, though common, is passive and far from foolproof: the scholar presents an idea in a book or article, which may be read by a public official who, in turn, may decide to apply it. The second and much more direct and probably more effective way is to have an ally or *broker* in government who can help in gaining access to high levels of power. In the Free Trade Agreement with Brazil and NAEXI cases, as the president's foreign policy advisor, I was able to create the link with the groups of scholars and experts. In the case of the immigration agreement, it was Andrés Rozental who acted as broker due to his proximity and influence with Minister of Foreign Affairs Castañeda.

Fifth, it is not sufficient for the idea simply to reach a decision maker's desk. Even if the president is truly interested, the idea may still not be adopted as a policy decision. In those cases where an idea was converted into actual policy despite the opposition of cabinet members and other public officials close to the president—such as free trade with Brazil and the immigration agreement with the United States—a clear and detailed reasoning about the costs and benefits of the proposal, developed by scholars and experts and brokered by a persistent foreign policy advisor, was fundamental to its adoption and implementation.

Academics who publish and teach on different aspects of foreign policymaking can gain a valuable perspective from working in government and having to merge analysis and theory with practice. Scholars who take government jobs and positions will naturally become more attuned to the harsh realities that politicians necessarily face when attempting to adapt and transform academic ideas into policy programs. Scholars who do not have these experiences are more likely to remain inside "the bubble" of academia and run the risk of oversimplifying the processes that policies must endure to be adopted. Also, a lack of such experience might, for example, cause scholars to use facile catch-all explanations, such as "government inefficiency," that can lead to unwarranted criticism of policymakers, needlessly creating antagonisms due to perceived academic "arrogance." I am a firm believer in sound critical analysis, but I also strongly believe that government experience helps create a finer-grained understanding of public policy processes.

Those academics who directly experience the process of policymaking can produce strategies that aim at refreshing the system while, at the same time, enhancing their understanding of the very real constraints inherent in governing. During my three-year tenure in the office of the Mexican president, I did my best to implement academic practices—enhancing group processes and nonhierarchical debates—to enlighten the foreign policy decisions of the state under President Calderón. In return, I gained an understanding of the life of the policymaker, an experience that I believe will enhance my policy analysis and my ability to shape academic theory and ideas in ways that will increase their attractiveness to those who must make policy decisions—and thus lead to real change.

NOTES

1. President Felipe Calderón's remarks during a meeting with Daniel Ortega Saavedra, President of the Republic of Nicaragua, Managua, Nicaragua, January 10, 2007, http:// calderon.presidencia.gob.mx/2007/01/el-presidente-calderon-durante-la-reunion-que -sostuvo-con-el-senor-comandante-daniel-ortega-saavedra-presidente-electo-de-la -republica-de-nicaragua (accessed Dec. 19, 2012).

2. The BRICs are a group of countries considered the most important emerging economies in the world because of their natural and energy resources, the scale of their gross domestic product, and their sustained growth and volume of exports. Some experts estimate that by 2050, these countries could become the main world economies. Gabriel Mario Santos Villarreal, *Grupo BRIC: Brasil, Rusia, India y China*, April 2010, www.diputados.gob.mx /cedia/sia/spe/SPE-ISS-09-10.pdf (accessed Dec. 19, 2012).

3. In January 2007, just a few weeks into his presidency, Calderón met with Lula da Silva at a conference organized by the World Economic Forum in Davos, Switzerland. Calderón's harsh criticism of Hugo Chávez for meddling in Central American political processes caused some discomfort for the Brazilian president.

4. Cecilia Soto, "Mexico y Brazil: ¿podemos cooperar?" in *En la Frontera del Imperio*, ed. Rafael Fernández de Castro (Mexico City: Editorial Planeta, 2003), 29.

5. President Felipe Calderón's remarks to the Mexico–United States Chamber of Commerce, December 7, 2007, http://calderon.presidencia.gob.mx/2007/12/el-presidente-calderon-en-la -comida-con-los-miembros-de-la-camara-de-comercio-mexico-estados-unidos (accessed Dec. 19, 2012).

6. In a state visit such as Calderón's there is a more extensive protocol, and meetings take place with all the branches of government: executive, legislative, and judicial.

7. "Obama Administration Should Heed Mexico's Call to Crack Down on Guns" (editorial), *Washington Post*, May 21, 2010, www.washingtonpost.com/wp-dyn/content/article /2010/05/20/AR2010052004943.html (accessed Dec. 19, 2012).

8. Joint Statement, read in Spanish by the Mexican minister of foreign affairs, Jorge G.

Castañeda, and in English by the US secretary of state, Colin Powell, at a press conference given by the leaders of both nations, Guanajuato, Mexico, February 16, 2001, http://fox .presidencia.gob.mx/actividades/?contenido=549 (accessed Dec. 19, 2012).

9. A few days before the two presidents met at San Cristóbal, Minister of Foreign Affairs Jorge Castañeda invited four Mexican panel members to converse with President Fox. In Castañeda's own words, he invited us to "convince Fox to ask Bush for an immigration agreement."

PART SIX

UNDERSTANDING, RESPECTING, AND GAINING FROM DIFFERENCES

CHAPTER THIRTEEN

Scholars and Policymakers
Canadian and Asia Pacific Experiences

PAUL EVANS

> The intellectual lives in a world that is both separate from and potentially intertwined with that of the politician. The two worlds are separate because they are oriented toward different ultimate values: The intellectual seeks truth; the politician, power . . . In his search for the truth, the ideal type of intellectual is oblivious to power; in his pursuit of power, the politician at best will use truth as a means to his end. —*Hans Morgenthau, "Truth and Power"*

Policymaking around the world involves irrationality, unpredictability, conflict, competing interests, and politics in the many forms that are described in other chapters of this volume. In making policy soup, rational decision making rarely applies.

Most scholars and policymakers around the world have some comprehension of the academic-policy nexus in the United States. Many see it as a model, or at least the most developed form, of what needs to exist in a well-functioning state. For reasons of geographic proximity, history, common civilizational foundations, and US dominance, the experience of the United States is either the focus or the inferred reference point in most discussions of scholar-practitioner relations. American policy soup may not be the universal dish, but we understand its ingredients, preparations, and academic sous-chefs better than any other's.

Hans Morgenthau's conception of the values of intellectual work and its connection to the world of policy—the interactions of truth and power—is rooted in a long tradition of Western thinking.[1] My aim here is to take issue with two of the premises built into his view. The first is that the worlds of one form of intellectual, the international relations academic, and of the policymaker are more separate than intertwined. The second is that the separation should be treasured. Rather than the intersection of two binary domains, there is a spectrum of interactions in most countries and across their borders that blur the lines of separation. In many settings, especially in Asia, the concept of the scholar having a truth and vocation separate from the person in power is neither an ideal nor a reality.

I am a policy-engaged Canadian social scientist who has spent a career inside universities and think tanks in a country that is hugely influenced by the norms and institutions of US academic practice and where most of us share with our colleagues south of the border similar assumptions about the calling of the professor. My area of specialization is Asia, much of my expertise generated as a participant, chronicler, and occasional leader in about 150 policy-related meetings and exchanges with Asian counterparts on regional security matters over the past 25 years.

Domestic contexts differ dramatically, not just across the Pacific but within the Western hemisphere. Even in Canada and the United States, two democratic countries living side by side in generally harmonious ways, academic interactions with the makers of public policy play out in different ways. This also holds in Asia—including in countries that have strong alliance and educational links with the United States—where the values and structures of academic-policy connections differ substantially.

At the same time, international interactions can have a major influence on these domestic contexts and, on occasion, can open spaces for policy impact. All politics may be local, but ideas, communication, and information operate across national boundaries. As Thomas Biersteker captures with his concept of transnational policy networks (chapter 8), the flowering of trans-Pacific and intra-Asian dialogue processes in the past quarter-century illustrates how differing domestic systems approach and adapt to international work focused on specific policy problems.

A Canadian Tale

Universities, policy schools, and think tanks are far fewer in number in Canada than in the United States, even on a per capita basis, and generally are more separated from the corridors of government policymaking. Almost all universities receive substantial public funding, and governments and parties at all levels are populated by their graduates. But very few Canadian academics rotate in and out of government positions. As in Argentina—and unlike in Chile—academics and former academics are almost never appointed to ambassadorial positions. A few enter elected public life, and a few of these have risen to ministerial status, usually under Liberal governments.

The professionalization of political science and the academic study of international relations in the United States described by Chappell Lawson (chapter 1) have partially taken hold in Canada, where the same journals, methodological debates, and standards for tenure and promotion hold. There are a few international relations scholars who are dedicated to theoretical quality and methodological rigor above all else. And there are some of a critical disposition, the kind of "committed" or "organic" intellectual described by Roberto Russell drawing on Antonio Gramsci, who see their policy role as standing outside government policy and critiquing it, speaking truth to power with a demurely sharp Canadian accent.[2] But most have an eye on contemporary policy problems and devote considerable attention to communicating their views and shaping their research to engage policy and policymaking circles. Government and academy may be separate structures, but unlike in Blanca Heredia's account of Mexico (chapter 5), the level of "reciprocal institutional insularity" is low.

At my own institution, the University of British Columbia, we have developed a four-tiered typology to discern the different ways that university-based research can connect to the policy world.

1. *Traditional scholarship.* For many if not most academics, their calling does not lead them to target their research at communities outside the university world. Whether searching for the perfect theory, the great generalization, or simply the fact-based truth, the game of prescription and influence is some combination of distraction, irrelevance, and even perversion. Academic work may have policy implications, but it is not the scholar's job to directly define or advance it and certainly not to directly engage those who make it. As Lawson notes (chapter 1), this "may produce policy-relevant research, but it does so only incidentally." Curiously, the incidental approach sometimes has the biggest policy impact. I did an informal survey in 2002 of 25 individuals in and outside government who were active, senior, and long-term participants in Asia Pacific dialogue processes. When asked what kind of knowledge they thought was most important to shaping decisions, the overwhelming majority pointed to history. When asked what book or idea was most influential in their own sense of the Asia Pacific policy world, most pointed to an individual they became aware of during their own education, almost all of whom were dead, and few of whom had an overriding interest in policy.

2. *Policy-relevant research.* This includes research that is conducted primarily for consumption by other scholars but is consciously constructed to be cognizant of the kinds of issues that policymakers confront. This can be done with greater or lesser sophistication and greater or lesser knowledge of the world of policy choices, but coming up with something of possible relevance to the policy community is an avowed goal.

3. *Policy-related research.* This includes projects that are conceived and conceptualized not just with policymakers in mind but with them as partners in the design,

involved in the definition of the topic, the choice of methodology, and the nature (if not the content) of the findings. In Robert Cox's terms, the studies are almost always of a problem-solving rather than critical disposition.[3] Examples include Nora Lustig's account of the history of the Progresa/Oportunidades program in Mexico (chapter 6), Jane Jaquette's discussion on the field of women in development in the United States in the 1970s and 1980s (chapter 3), and the whole enterprise of "track-two dialogues"—policy-related exchanges that involve government officials in their private capacities interacting with policy experts, including scholars, journalists, and occasional business and nongovernmental organization (NGO) leaders—that I will turn to shortly.

4. *Advocacy-based research.* This involves not just doing research and producing policy recommendations but systematically attempting to influence their implementation in collaboration with—or, as necessary, in opposition to—groups and individuals inside government. This goes beyond advising officials and politicians and extends into working with the like-minded in government circles at home and elsewhere to establish the conditions for policy implementation in a desired direction. In Canada, two of the best examples are the enormous effort by climate change scientists to influence public opinion and government policy on greenhouse gas emissions and the earlier efforts by groups of scholars involved in the international campaign to ban the use of antipersonnel landmines.

Each of these orientations has its own risks and rewards. Most Canadian scholars do not see themselves as engaging policy issues in their professional capacity, though they certainly have views as citizens. The field of international relations is somewhat different, and the attraction to policy-relevant, policy-related, and advocacy-based research is relatively strong and growing. Those wishing to engage policy matters directly have conjoined an increasingly intense relationship with many of the agencies and departments of the federal government since the 1980s. While few go directly into positions in the bureaucracy or party politics (and even fewer return to the university if they do), Liberal and Progressive Conservative governments and the public service have gradually expanded their academic connections in various ways, including assigning a scholar to serve in a select number of embassies (China in particular), providing grants for chairs, undertaking increasingly frequent policy consultations, and extending support for academic-driven networks.

A domain of concerted effort involving scholars and officials has been the creation of bilateral and multilateral institutions across the Pacific twinned with the transnational associational revolution in Eastern Asia that accompanied the region's spectacular economic growth and integration. The track-two processes that preceded and connected to formal government activities proliferated between the late

1980s and 2000. They ranged from ad hoc meetings to multiyear series and institutionalized dialogue mechanisms with membership committees, working groups, and long-term agendas—among them, the Pacific Economic Cooperation Council, the Council for Security Cooperation in the Asia Pacific, and the Northeast Asia Cooperation Dialogue that has run parallel to successive government initiatives to manage the North Korean nuclear problem. Scores of other channels were created, including a 10-year series "Managing Potential Conflicts in the South China Sea," cohosted by Indonesia and Canada, nonclaimant states in the conflict. Others include the multiple meetings organized by the Japan Center for International Exchange on topics including Asia Pacific community building and issues in Japan's regional and global roles. Institutes in the member countries of the Association of Southeast Asian Nations (ASEAN) have been the anchors of many of the processes, including sponsorship for 25 years of the Asia Pacific Roundtable in Kuala Lumpur. There are now more than 300 track-two meetings per year that concentrate on Asia or the Asia Pacific region and some aspect of economic or security issues.[4]

Under successive Liberal and Progressive Conservative governments in Ottawa, starting in the late 1980s, Canada participated in track-two multilateralism Asia Pacific style and took the lead in several initiatives, including the North Pacific Cooperative Security Dialogue, a precursor to the Six Party Talks on the North Korean nuclear issue. Participation in these processes changed the face of Canadian diplomacy and academic institutions. Academics were thrust into directly policy-related discussions and needed a kind of information and support they had never had before on a collective basis. Government officials needed ideas and contacts to understand how Asians and other participants were using track-two events to shape regional outcomes. Without revolving doors in and out of government, institutional innovations were necessary. Some of these included new mechanisms for commissioning and funding academic research, new ways to bring academics into short-term policy positions, new organizations like the Canadian Consortium on Asia Pacific Security, and creation of the Canadian member committees of the Pacific Economic Cooperation Council and the Council for Security Cooperation in the Asia Pacific that government agencies both supported financially and joined. Examples were the collaborative work initiated on proposals for a Free Trade Agreement for the Asia Pacific and, in the security field, extensive activity involving officials, academics, and NGOs in support of the human security agenda's focus on the Responsibility to Protect.[5]

This produced a cohort of senior academics across the country connected to each other, connected to the Canadian government, and connected to counterparts around the region. Several dozen younger scholars were brought into these networks, with considerable impact on their career paths and topic areas. And ideas about Asia and its new institutions radiated out to a generation of undergraduate and graduate students across the country.

In some policy areas, in some periods, under some administrations, academic work can make a difference, as Jane Jaquette notes (chapter 3), if political will and bureaucratic incentives coincide. There are "magic moments" of the kinds described by Blanca Heredia when accessible research, academics, and transnational policy networks come together (chapter 5). Foreign service establishments rarely welcome scholarly work that challenges what Amaury de Souza in his analysis of Brazilian policymaking calls "prevailing mental maps and paradigms," but they do welcome scholarly input that fits within them.[6]

If policy windows can open, they also can close. The election of Stephen Harper's minority Conservative government in January 2006 produced a new chapter. The Harper government rejected the traditional foreign policy orientation of the middle power and multilateralism, turned to what it saw as more efficient coalitions of the willing, centralized decision making on foreign policy to a small group in which the prime minister played the dominant role, and generally distrusted and ignored academic and other expert opinion, including from within the civil service.

Effective involvement in track-two processes requires the blessing and at least tacit support of the political leadership, bureaucratic involvement and resources, and an expert community able to participate and occasionally lead. The Harper government withdrew this political blessing, curtailed funding, and constricted channels of access and coordination. Diplomats and ministers were under explicit instructions not to use foreign policy phrases that Canada had actively advocated under past governments, among them "cooperative security," "human security," and the "responsibility to protect."

After the Conservatives' six years in power, and now possessing a parliamentary majority, there are signs in Ottawa of policy shifts and increased comfort with broader ventilation of policy options. Perhaps the most important lesson from the Canadian case is that government preferences and style can be decisive in structuring the scholar-practitioner interface, at least in the short run. The fusion of executive and legislative power within Westminster systems combined with a dominant role of state financing for independent policy networks means that patterns and traditions developed over several decades can be dramatically altered in short order. Contrary to Amaury de Souza's argument, the assault on a consensus does not necessarily produce creative debate.

Asia Comparisons

In an Asian continent that includes Japan, South Korea, and Singapore as well as Laos and North Korea, the differences in academic structures, ethos, and objectives, not to mention regime types, languages, cultures, economic systems, and policy-making processes, are overwhelming. Although context is king, there are at least three areas where some broad generalizations hold.

First, the conception of the scholar as fundamentally separated from the state, much less in opposition to it, does not prevail. In most countries in Asia, scholars are considered public officials, albeit with a focus on education, not direct policy work. This becomes very clear in track-two economic and security processes where almost all of the Asian participants perceive their purpose as supporting government processes rather than standing outside them or creating civil society connections that are valuable in their own right. Enlightened policymakers in many Asian countries see the virtues of calling on outside advice and providing some measure of independence for their experts. But in general, policymakers don't doubt that those intellectuals should be serving the state. Nor, for that matter, do the experts themselves. To serve the government is not just a matter of personal ambition but a natural inclination performed with little anxiety about autonomy or a separate intellectual's calling. Although this ideal of the scholar-official is built on historical traditions and ethics deeply ingrained in Asian states, it is functionally similar to views of the roles and identity of many think tanks worldwide.

Asian participants in track-two processes operate in complicated political contexts. They worry about access to power but rarely share the ambivalence of North American and Australian colleagues about autonomy from it. The concept of critical theory advanced by Robert Cox and framed by Arlene Tickner as informing policy on the behest of forces outside the state is alive and well in track-three (that is, civil society–based) networks but rarely penetrates processes closer to government.

Second, the democratic-authoritarian divide does not tell us a great deal about how much weight think tanks and universities have in influencing government policy. Arlene Tickner's generalization that "the more open the political culture of a given society is to public debate, the greater the potential interaction between the state and academia" does not apply easily.[7] With the possible exception of North Korea and Myanmar, every government in Asia has developed mechanisms for commissioning studies and research, interacting with select researchers and academics, and, in many cases, recruiting them into government positions. As demonstrated in the case of Conservative Canada, political leaders have the capacity to shape the flow and content of the information they ingest. China is a perplexing case of an authoritarian system with multiple channels for engaging academic and think tank work at the highest levels of policymaking. It may be a stretch, but academic expertise in universities and research institutes may at this moment have more impact on national policymaking in China and Singapore than in Canada.

Third, Arlene Tickner's idea of "venues of effective exchange" deserves more study in individual Asian countries, especially concerning new structures in universities, policy schools, and research institutes that are receiving enormous injections of financial and human resources. These also are important at the international level as the track-two processes demonstrate. They have had a significant impact in Canada and also have helped shape regional discourse and domestic structures for recruitment, exchange, and control.

Thomas Biersteker's analysis of the transnational policy networks around sanctions (chapter 8) parallels Asia Pacific processes in several respects. Though the processes he discusses are both more targeted and more exclusive, their Asia Pacific cousins are populated by a similar set of individuals playing roles as policy entrepreneurs, brokers, gatekeepers, guardians of institutional memory, and, occasionally, educators of the public. They are also a venue for vetting, preparing, and socializing scholars who will be recruited into top government positions. In Korea, for example, most of the ministers of foreign affairs and trade in the past 20 years have had extensive experience and exposure in track-two projects. Occasionally these activities involve the application of sophisticated research, simulations, and scenario-building exercises to specific policy problems related to issues in free trade negotiations and simulated humanitarian emergencies and military clashes. And they are very largely conducted in English, often delivered by nonnative speakers.

Track-two processes have made officials more aware of the resources and talent base in universities, have demanded regular contact, and have increased scholars' policy knowledge about the political forces and personalities that constrain and compel choice. Role reversals are not uncommon, with senior officials giving a better conceptual analysis of an issue than any academic, and scholars defining a policy problem more clearly than the officials. Ambassadors can be more analytical than scholars, and, occasionally, scholars can be more diplomatic than ambassadors.

The number of international relations scholars capable of participating in track-two processes, especially the multilateral ones that are almost always conducted in English, is relatively low in most Asian countries. But the numbers swell as the track-two agenda shifts to nontraditional security issues in which topics like environment, demography, water, migration, and infectious disease center the agenda. Scholars who participate in these processes are a favored few or, more precisely, a carefully screened few, usually outnumbered on the nongovernmental side by individuals from think tanks. The act of partnership bestows a certain responsibility of confidentiality, discretion, and circumspection—precisely the obligations that academic traditionalists in the West feel may hamper the workings of the independent mind. The risks for the policymaker are occasionally significant. For the academic, as Biersteker notes, there are real challenges within the university where jealousy, professional standards, and suspicions about too cozy a relationship with those in power can have negative professional consequences. How to convince tenure and promotion committees that a report adopted by the ASEAN Regional Forum is equal in the generation of knowledge to a peer-reviewed article in a first-class disciplinary journal?

Policy Impact and the Scholar-Practitioner Divide

Whatever the opportunities and dilemmas presented to individuals, what do the track-two processes tell us about policy impact? Whether the Asia Pacific region is more prosperous, more peaceful, and more cohesive because of the dialogues is difficult to assess. These processes have been just one factor in a very complicated equation. They signal a willingness to engage in multilateral dialogue and reflect complex interactions among political and diplomatic elites that, in turn, are a product of more deeply integrated economies and vastly expanded transnational interactions.

Track-two dialogues have affected the policy processes in many countries, in part by breaking down institutional insularity. The Canadian example is instructive, both in what occurred in the two decades before 2006 and in the subsequent Conservative reversal in which boundaries were reestablished.

They have certainly changed the regional discourse. Terms like "open regionalism," "multilateralism," "cooperative security," and "human security" have entered, if not transformed, policy discussions in academic and government circles in many parts of the region.[8]

They have helped promote and legitimate new international institutions, among them the Asia Pacific Economic Conference forum, the ASEAN Regional Forum, and the East Asia Summit process. They have been able not only to plant some ambitious projects—like Asia Pacific community and the creation of regional institutions—but also to water and nourish them for lengthy periods. The experience in Asia might well be relevant to Robert Pastor's efforts to advocate the "North American idea" (chapter 2).

Track-two dialogues have been able to insert some sophisticated research and analysis into regional discussion, including the international legal dimensions of territorial disputes in the South China Sea and elsewhere. At the same time, they demonstrate that university professors are just one category of knowledge producers. Think tanks, government agencies, consultants, journalists, social media, and the blogosphere are increasingly key providers. Academic monopolies over knowledge and analysis, if they ever existed, are long gone.

What does this mean for scholars engaged with policy issues? Their role should not be discounted. What happens in classrooms, laboratories, and libraries matters. Their specific policy impact, like that of others, depends upon a combination of personal connections, opportunity, chance, and institutional constructions that emerge from those in authority trying to deal with complex policy problems that demand cross-national cooperation.

Yet, to a new generation of international relations scholars in North America and Asia with a bent for problem solving, the gap between the world of the university and the halls of power is far less substantial than it was when Morgenthau and his generation defined the practice of scholarship after World War II. Contrary to his observation that scholars and practitioners are engaged in different enterprises with different values and different roles, the two worlds, for better or worse, have never been more intertwined and are likely to become more so in future, the Conservative experience in Canada notwithstanding.

It may be a symptom of a globalized world, but rare now is the international relations scholar in Asia or the West who feels in possession of the truth. And rarer still is the one unwilling to share academic wisdom with those in positions of authority in government or society.

NOTES

1. Hans Morgenthau, "Truth and Power," in *Truth and Power, Essays of a Decade, 1960–1970* (New York: Praeger, 1970).

2. Roberto Russell, "The Scholar-Practitioner Interaction: The Case of Argentina," memorandum prepared for the International Workshop on Scholars and Practitioners, Center for International Studies, University of Southern California (USC), 2011.

3. Robert Cox, "Social Forces, States and World Orders: Beyond International Relations Theory," *Millennium: Journal of International Affairs* 10 (Summer 1981): 165–66.

4. For an inventory and analysis, see the *Dialogue and Research Monitor*, now produced by the Japan Center for International Exchange and available online at www.jcie.or.jp/drm. The best attempt to assess the early impact of these efforts is Brian Job, "Track 2 Diplomacy: Ideational Contribution to the Evolving Asian Security Order," in *Asian Security Order: Instrumental and Normative Features*, ed. Muthia Alagappa (Stanford: Stanford University Press, 2003).

5. For a review and analysis, see Peter Jones, *Canada and Track Two Diplomacy*, Canadian International Council, December 2008, www.canadianinternationalcouncil.org. On Asia Pa-

cific in particular, see Paul Evans, "Canada and Asia Pacific's Track-Two Diplomacy," *International Journal*, Autumn 2009, 1027–38.

6. Amaury de Souza, "Crafting Brazil's Foreign Policy: Scholars, Practitioners and the Policy Process," memorandum prepared for the International Workshop on Scholars and Practitioners, Center for International Studies, USC, 2011.

7. Arlene Tickner, "Scholar-Practitioner Interaction: Comparative Latin American Experiences," memorandum prepared for the International Workshop on Scholars and Practitioners, Center for International Studies, USC, 2011.

8. For a history of the origins, usage, and evolving meanings of several key terms in regional security discourse, see David Capie and Paul Evans, *The Asia-Pacific Security Lexicon*, 2nd ed. (Singapore: Institute of Southeast Asian Studies, 2007).

CHAPTER FOURTEEN

On the Scholar-Practitioner Interface
Separation and Synergy

LAURENCE WHITEHEAD

In theory there is no difference between theory and practice. In practice there is.

—*Yogi Berra*

As a large and sophisticated leading modern democracy, the United States has often been on the frontline of scholar-practitioner linkages to shape public policy, and it has been energetic in promoting its influence and example. Focusing on scholar-practitioner relations in the late and post–Cold War era, this volume encompasses a range of political contexts and policy domains.[1] The chapters illustrate the variability in scholar-practitioner relations and provide rich insights about the crossover between the two domains. Not a few of these insights are drawn from the personal histories of the contributors. There is, however, an underlying unity: these scholar-practitioner linkages have to do with "globalization," arising from a period of economic and political liberalization and policy convergence, during which Washington-supported approaches to modern democratic governance, including expert-influenced policymaking and public accountability, have become much more widely accepted across the Western hemisphere and internationally. Thus, one of this book's merits is that it addresses a timeless and universal issue, but also the highly specific and distinctive form this issue has taken under recent conditions of liberalization and globalization. Another of its great strengths is that while all the contributors address the same set of broad questions, they also offer first-hand testimony of the dynamics in the United States and, to a lesser extent, Argentina, Canada, Mexico, Asia, and some international organizations.

This chapter contextualizes the American and international experiences highlighted in this volume by reflecting on the historical development of the scholar-practitioner relationship and on the desirability of "narrowing the gap" between the two domains. It starts from the broadest and most all-encompassing standpoint, adopting a "wide-angle" approach to the scholar-practitioner interface, to lay bare the sources of underlying conflict that have tended to be masked by the US pragmatist and can-do traditions.

In the second section I reflect on the scholar-practitioner matrix in the United States today, with reference to the other contributions to this volume, considering the conditions for, and limits of, a constructive synergy between academia and the policy world. Such synergy matters: modern governments try to ground policy choices on evidence and research. They justify their decisions by reference to reasoned arguments that can unite their officials and provide them with a sense of direction. Reasoned justifications are also needed to elicit support and compliance from citizens and to stabilize policy implementation over time. Modern democratic governments may be held accountable for their decisions. Their policymakers, who must operate under the constraints of media scrutiny, institutional checks and balances, and even the possibility of judicial review, are even more under pressure to act on the basis of evidence and diligent inquiry.

The chapter then considers proposals to "narrow the gap" between the two domains. It accepts the logic of such proposals, at least in the context of contemporary Washington-influenced international relations, but highlights the needs for limits to synergies. In the major areas of policymaking that are well represented in this volume, applied scholarship stands to gain in precision, relevance, and utility if it has access to the information available to decision makers and is fully informed of both their capabilities and their constraints. Such access can serve as a valuable corrective to the academic temptation to concentrate on less productive lines of scholarly inquiry. Policymakers can also benefit from independent and objective evidence-based advice. But, at the same time, scholarly detachment also requires a clear understanding of the limits to such synergies (both thematic and contextual). The chapter concludes with reflections on three possible models of scholar-practitioner relations and the challenges posed by each.

The Scholar-Practitioner Divide over Time

> I recover some hope that one time or other this writing of mine may fall into the hands of a sovereign, who will consider it himself . . . and by the exercise of entire Sovereignty . . . convert the Truth of Speculation into the Utility of Practice.
> —*Thomas Hobbes,* Leviathan

To reach durable and broadly applicable conclusions about how to achieve a good balance and relation between scholarship and policymaking, it is essential to harvest the lessons of the past and adapt them to current realities. For a full appreciation of the tensions between scholarship and policymaking, it makes sense to situate the recent American tradition in a more universal and long-term setting. The liberal optimism that characterizes much current thinking about scholar-practitioner relations is not necessarily a permanent given. As Robert K. Merton wrote half a century ago, "the honeymoon of intellectuals and policymakers is often nasty, brutish, and short."[2] More recently, Lisa Anderson has argued that the relationship "contains far more tension and ambiguity even than we ordinarily acknowledge. The dual aspiration to understand and to change the world of which early modern social science was born marked it with a profound ambivalence about power and policy. The story of the development of the social sciences is a story of repeated oscillations between the embrace of active, indeed assertive, participation in policymaking, and retreat into the ostensibly neutral posture of scientific objectivity." The growth of "American political and economic power in the world, and concomitant increasing U.S. influence in shaping social science and public policy research seemed to permit a complacency about the sources and purposes of social science insight," but a less unipolar twenty-first century is likely to challenge any such complacency.[3]

At the most abstract level, any kind of political initiative involves communication and the organization of collective activity. All political practitioners need certain types of skills and knowledge: how to issue clear instructions and check whether they are understood and correctly implemented; how to obtain and distribute the resources needed for organized political life; how to assess dangers and anticipate adverse reactions; and how to explain and justify decisions to those whose compliance is required. Successful political practice requires a repertoire of lessons learned and techniques of leadership mastered. Political leaders and activists are more likely to flourish if they have access to appropriate sources of training and accumulated experience. On a broad definition this means counselors, transmitters of traditional wisdom, bearers of useful forms of expertise, and possibly even original thinkers. Successful political practitioners are likely to seek out and make use of the knowledge of these various types of advisors—in a word, these teachers and scholars.

The rulers of states need to keep track of many complex aspects of these entities. Administration requires records and hierarchical procedures; consistency over time and space gives rise to legal expertise; taxation means numeracy; enforcement implies military training and skills; diplomacy involves trying to understand and bargain with neighboring political actors beyond the ruler's direct control; and internal peace requires consent by the governed, which in turn implies some means of instructing subjects about what is expected of them and what they can expect in return. So, durable states promote various useful forms of knowledge transmission, including literacy, law, accountancy, diplomacy, religion, and civics. Scholarship does not derive solely from the requirements of a stable political system, of course, but as states and empires grew and consolidated, useful forms of knowledge acquisition were often encouraged and even flaunted as evidence of good government. Over generations, successful political practitioners promoted scholarship (at least some varieties, and within prudential limits).

There has always been a tension between knowledge and power. In addition to large areas of symbiosis between scholars and democratic political leaders there is considerable scope for mutual incomprehension and even outright conflict. Traditional rulers were often all too clear that scholarship could be subversive, even if it originated from within state-sheltered institutions. And once knowledge systems had attained a certain stability and social density, subversive scholarship could also be nurtured outside the reach of public officials. Hence, the long history of Western social thought records the checkered experiences of so many political thinkers who had at some point in their careers served as tutors to princes or had otherwise attempted to translate their doctrines into practice by advising the powerful.[4] Here is how Machiavelli saw the question:

> Those who give advice to a republic and those who give advice to a prince find themselves amidst these difficulties: that is, if they do not recommend without reservation the policies that they believe to be useful, either to the city or to the prince, they fail in their duties; and if they give such advice they place their lives and their position at risk . . . Since men judge things by their results, all the evil that comes about is blamed upon the one who gave the advice, and if things turn out well, he is commended for it; but the reward is far from counterbalancing the blame . . . After considering how to avoid either this infamy or this danger, I see no other path to follow than that of choosing moderate undertakings and never seizing upon any of them as your own, and that of speaking your mind without passion and, without passion, defending it with modesty; so that if the city or the prince follows this advice, they follow it willingly, without it appearing that they are pulled along by your insistence.[5]

For several millennia, prior to the advent of modern constitutional regimes with guaranteed rights to free expression, free speech, and freedom of conscience, the activity of "speaking truth to power" was a perilous undertaking, one that required the utmost prudence, since the speaker was exposing himself without defense to the reactions of the power holder. By the time of the American and French Revolutions, scholarship was moving toward a fundamentally more modern position. Both the ethical and the technical aspects of scholarly input into politics had to be transformed. New fields of scholarship were required (statistics, demography, economics, constitution writing, education for citizenship, journalism under conditions of press freedom, and even political science), and new educational institutions to train the rising generations of public servants and policymakers. The changes involved much more than increased specialization, in that modern government would have to be founded on quite different principles.

Although *raison d'état* played a crucial role in the development of many modern scholarly disciplines and practices, it would be very one-sided to picture all this as simply the product of political will and direction. Of ever growing importance have been the scholarly demands arising from the emergence of participatory politics, liberal institutions, rights cast in universalistic terms, and, eventually, what we now refer to as democratic societies. The thinkers and researchers who pursued this agenda created a fundamentally different and more freewheeling approach to inquiry, including inquiry into matters that were profoundly unsettling to established political authorities. Although they produced an unending expansion of "useful" knowledge, its effects may be unsettling and even politically explosive. Darwinism provides one spectacular illustration of this from the nineteenth century, with nuclear physics occupying a similar role in the twentieth. Contemporary climate change science may be the twenty-first-century equivalent. Even though the scientific methods employed are as objective and dispassionate as possible, such scholarship shakes preexisting assumptions, threatens powerful established interests, and generates ethical as well as practical consequences.

The following general points emerge from a historical survey. First, across a very wide range of experiences there has been coevolution between scholarship and organized politics. Each has been shaped by and benefited from the support of the other. Second, the interactions between them have typically been far from harmonious. Scholarship can be costly and unhelpful to those in power, as well as threatening and destabilizing. Third, specialized knowledge systems may aim to avoid direct political entanglement, but some types of scholarship seem so useful to government that policymakers can hardly afford to leave them alone, let alone allow them to be put at the service of political rivals. Fourth, at the more general level, the unfettered pursuit of knowledge involves forms of questioning that are inherently at variance with smooth administration by an established power structure. So even the most liberal of policymakers may try to "tame" scholarship and muffle its unwelcome aspects.

At a very early stage, the United States adopted an approach to scholarship that highlighted its social usefulness and reduced its potential for confrontation with the policy world. For example, in 1818, when drawing up a report to the governor of Virginia on a plan to create the state university, Thomas Jefferson highlighted "the incalculable advantage of training up able counselors to administer the affairs of our country in all its departments, legislative, executive, and judiciary, and to bear their proper share in the councils of our national government, nothing more than education advancing the prosperity, the power, and the happiness of a nation."[6]

There was a long way to go before this characteristically pragmatic American approach to learning and scholarship came to full fruition, but the distinctiveness of this statement of intentions and expectations merits emphasis. Unlike in Europe, history and/or philosophy played only a limited role in shaping social science in the United States, where there was little reason to defer to history, and social research was free to emulate that most modern of intellectual pursuits, natural science.[7] In the leading universities of Europe before 1914, matters were far less straightforward. The conflicts between producers of knowledge and bearers of power overshadowed the commonalities in most of the world's main centers of learning for much of the nineteenth century.[8] In twentieth-century Europe these clashes became so extreme that many of its great universities were ruined, and many of the most creative researchers fled across the Atlantic to the more sheltering academic environment of North America.

After 1945, US academia not only flourished as never before but also grew even closer to the holders of political office.[9] It certainly multiplied its avenues of access and cross-fertilization with federal policymakers. The US model also became the template by which older university and knowledge systems were increasingly assessed and, not infrequently, restructured. Even so, it would be a mistake to conclude that a US-inspired natural harmony between scholars and practitioners is on the way to becoming the global norm. In much of Europe the older traditions of collusion, friction, and distrust remain in place. The new stratum of Eurocrats working out of Brussels, for instance, is still struggling, with doubtful success, to establish a sufficiently flourishing scholarly support base.

In Asia or in much of Latin America, the scholar-practitioner matrix is generally more incestuous, conflictive, and ragged than in the contemporary United States. The state is more likely to intrude directly into academic life, the policy challenges in a developmental state impose more immediate demands on social science advisors, and the background liberal assumptions that both shelter and empower US scholarship are either more tenuous or simply absent. There is still deep disagreement, even in Chile, over whether the "Chicago Boys" were the bearers of the best scholarly understanding of how to conduct good public policy there or bearers of an externally validated intellectual agenda ("neoliberalism") that served to legitimize a particular set of questionable priorities and interests. In Mexico, scholars and practitioners have coevolved throughout the post-revolutionary period, but their interactions have often been both incestuous and fraught. The role of Spanish and

South American intellectual exiles and the recent in-flood of influences from north of the border merit close examination in this case. In Argentina and Venezuela, the story is more about scholarly outflows. In Brazil, and notably with regard to the Itamaraty and inter-American relations, the scholarly community is becoming more autonomous, self-reliant, and, arguably, more nationalist.

In short, Latin America's scholar-practitioner matrixes are complex and diverse. Even within contemporary US academia, the *convivencia* between knowledge and power is not always as straightforward or stable as is sometimes imagined, as there are deep clashes between faith and reason, patriotism and cosmopolitanism. Indeed, scholars and practitioners in various settings are challenging benevolent assumptions about globalization. Various Latin American governments and scholars have reacted against "Washington Consensus" and international financial institution prescriptions and attempted to craft alternative approaches. In some countries, local scholarly expertise has been mobilized to support "counterhegemonic" projects. So contemporary policymaking can still leave scope for considerable disagreement over the appropriate role for various types of scholarship and expertise in the shaping of policy outcomes.

Some of the chapters in this volume may tacitly assume that policymakers operating in a reasonably free society can always be held to account. But many Latin American and Asian scholars are less confident that advising policymakers counts as serving the public good, and in numerous European regimes that are classified as democracies, the contrary presumption remains widespread. Even in the United States, such basic consensus about the public good has not always been a given. Even the most modern, sophisticated, and rational of democracies make choices that express underlying values and identity commitments, which trump instrumental rationality. Even the best-researched alternatives are subject to such a margin of uncertainty that political discretion must be deployed. And even the best-educated democracies have prior commitments or policy blind spots, so that inconvenient evidence is denied a proper hearing. So the scope for practitioners to take scholarship into account is not unrestricted. There is a "discursive" logic to official policy justifications that needs to be taken into account. Scholarship that is readily encompassed by the prevailing official discourse is better received than that which could prove too unsettling. These issues arise in today's inter-American domain as well (with regard to Cuba, drugs, and immigration, for example, where nonacademic considerations often crowd out proposals derived from academic research). This is a core theme in the history of scholar-practitioner interactions, and although modern democratic governance may have masked it, it has not disappeared.

The modern state and modern academia are vastly more specialized, knowledge-dependent, and impersonal, but these predemocratic antecedents still have some resonance. Modern policy advisors should recall Machiavelli's points about modesty and the avoidance of passion. His warning that results can always prove unexpected and that blame for bad outcomes can cost far more than the rewards for success remains extremely pertinent. In fact, the rationale for broad-based and credible protective bridging institutions is precisely to guard against the disincentives to truthful speaking that Machiavelli identified. Although the balance of rewards and protections has been shifted strongly in favor of scholarly candor since his time, it would be an error to suppose that modern academia is securely protected against retaliation from disgruntled public authorities. To the extent that recent experiences in North America have been reassuring, the long-run history should serve as a corrective to overconfidence. In any case, in many parts of the world at the beginning of the twenty-first century, older traditions of practitioner abuse and scholarly self-censorship are alive and well.

The relationship between knowledge and power has always been close but troubled. Scholars are almost invariably convinced that the world would be a better place if their insights and discoveries were more fully appreciated and applied by those in positions of command. Policymakers have many reasons to doubt that conviction and tend to be on their guard against aspects of scholarship that might undermine their authority or threaten their control. But they must be effective, so they are disposed to use and support aspects of learning that can be put to practical use. The resulting matrix of interactions, mutual dependencies, and multidimensional exchanges has grown more complex and reciprocally constraining as modern and democratic forms of government have developed and as expertise has invaded an ever wider array of policy issues. Nowhere else and at no other time has a nation's political class been so intimately intertwined with a highly professionalized academic infrastructure as in the United States.

The US Scholar-Practitioner Matrix Today

Three features differentiate the United States from counterpart twentieth- and twenty-first-century democracies in Europe, Latin America, and further afield: the centrality of the law school as a source of training and recruitment into the political career structure; the scale, specialization, and autonomy of the national political science community; and the intensity of the two-way traffic between universities, research centers, and think tanks, on the one hand, and public officials and elected officeholders, on the other. It may be that in this respect, the United States has paved the way for others, but it is important to distinguish what refers specifically to this well-established and still distinctly American current and what has more unrestricted applicability across time and space.

Historically, the great majority of thinkers who tried to guide political practitioners in earlier periods and on other continents do not meet the strict tests currently in force in the United States to qualify as university-licensed (peer-reviewed, tenure-tracked) contemporary scholars. Equally, not all American scholars can be counted as "thinkers." Many prefer to think of themselves as technicians or specialists. In fact, in contemporary US society, *scholars* is an umbrella term, including a diverse array of students, analysts, advocates, and technicians. Some examples of the contrasting occupations encompassed are public intellectuals, diplomatic historians, think tank policy advocates, econometricians, legal theorists, and area studies experts. Likewise, *policymakers* is an umbrella term, which can cover senators, ambassadors, governors, agency heads, international civil servants, congressional aides, and perhaps clerks to high court justices. Many-stranded linkages connect US academics and policymakers, but these connections resemble a thicket rather than a tidy principal-agent relationship.

The area of scholarship in question also makes a difference. Some of the material in this volume concerns US foreign policy, and a fair case can be made that if a democracy faces potentially dangerous rivals and enemies, there is a patriotic and a scholarly justification for trying to enhance its international understanding and effectiveness. In other academic areas, the license to advise may extend further. A law scholar might be justified in counseling a despotic regime if the purpose is to improve the likelihood that it will pursue its objectives through legitimate channels, rather than illegally. Health experts should not decline to offer medical policy advice because government authorities are unsavory. Economists have a particularly strong track record of giving policy guidance to all comers, acting on the assumption that this can help to correct errors and maximize social benefits, almost regardless of the political or historical context.

For other social sciences, the possible misuse of scholarly inputs by policymakers may be more complicated. For example, anthropologists who take great care to win the trust and confidence of the communities they study are rightly sensitive about any suggestion that they may be passing privileged knowledge to public authorities, the goals and intentions of which may not be accepted by their original informants. Such issues can also arise in sociology, political science, and area studies, especially for scholars engaged in bottom-up or ethnographic research. There is a strong contrast between macro and micro styles of scholarship: the former is more disposed to thinking like public policymakers, the latter to identifying with the often bewildered recipients of state initiatives they do not understand. There is also a contrast between "normative" and "realist" or "empiricist" scholars, who aim to focus on how the existing world really works.

Many of the most successful members of these highly differentiated occupational categories are individuals who are engaged in lifelong one-track careers. Most contemporary scholars seek advancement and recognition within their relatively narrow disciplines. They remain within professional silos that are often quite rigorously sealed off from adjacent career tracks, each with its own boundaries, markers, codes, and disciplines.[10] The costs of transgressing professional boundary lines can be high, as can be the rewards of sheltering within a familiar and well-understood community of professional peers. Of course, some scholars are driven by their intellectual curiosity and their talent to reach out beyond their comfort zones. But this is exceptional, only for the very bold or talented.

The same applies to practitioners. Political careers are typically punctuated by breakpoints, but those who achieve electoral office have passed a selection barrier that makes it much more likely that they will run again; likewise for those who achieve other forms of public recognition, such as ambassadors or public opinion leaders. There may be more scope for lateral advance among practitioners, but most build their reputations by concentrating on activities and networks where they are already established.

In contrast to scholars, for whom the key question is "why," the central question practitioners need to address is "how." Too much deliberation over the theoretical justification for or controversial foundations of policy choices can impede prompt action.[11] Conversely, scholars have a professional bias in favor of thoroughly researched argumentation. They tend to be averse to what they regard as too little reflection before acting. But as this volume shows, this dichotomy is too stark. In modern bureaucratic practice, "how" and "why" are typically fused together. Different types of scholarship may be enlisted at different stages in the policy process.[12]

All this raises a key question: why should scholars be allowed to act as if they had the authority to influence top-level policymaking? What are their credentials, what do they bring to the table, and what are the risks both to scholarship and to legitimate political processes? A researcher who has specialized in, say, techniques to eradicate malaria may not find it hard to explain why that knowledge should be sought after by health policy practitioners charged with that task. But the matter is not so straightforward for a scholar whose expertise bears on, say, targeted sanctions,[13] or on establishing more balanced and durable integration of the three member states of the North American Free Trade Agreement (NAFTA). This type of academic may require additional credentials, such as those earned by Robert Pastor through his public service,[14] and can expect to undergo more elaborate screening before gaining the right to advise democratic legislators and executives. The codes governing such policy access tend to be subtle and contextually specific. Only a select minority can hope to penetrate this maze, and most lack both the means and the inclination, not least because of the reputational risks.

In the US system, high-level crossovers (in both directions) are a crucial part of the game. Both Tom Biersteker and Bob Pastor provide striking illustrations of how this may affect macro-policy outcomes. At an even higher level, the careers of Zbigniew Brzezinski, Henry Kissinger, and Condoleezza Rice all show that scholar-practitioners can combine the two roles into a single package. These top-ranking executives derived a substantial part of their authority from their standing in the academic community, and all three used their scholarly networks to reinforce their effectiveness as policymakers. To take one example, the Kissinger Commission needed to demonstrate that its recommendations on Central America were based on expert knowledge, not just on partisan ideological preferences. Among others, Carlos Díaz Alejandro provided the commission with a scholarly and liberal gravitas that would otherwise have eluded the Reagan administration.[15]

Overall, in contrast to many other nations and to the long history of fraught scholar-practitioner interactions (especially in Europe), the United States has often generated effective public policy innovations at least in part because of the excellence of its educational and research infrastructure and the responsiveness of its policymakers to well-founded expert advice. This "can-do" style of policymaking has attracted admirers and currently inspires imitators in many other countries, not least among various recently democratized republics in the Americas. Although even Washington has experienced deviations and countercurrents, this does not nullify the positive side of this record.

Notwithstanding its failings, the US formula compares well with most alternatives, including much that takes place in the rest of the Western hemisphere. But this US matrix is not static or unchallengeable. It can be weakened or deformed, for example, if academic institutions suffer roll-back or in other respects lose their way, or if policymaking becomes so polarized and money-driven that expert advice no longer gets a fair hearing. There has always been a seesaw rhythm to the management of such risks, and contemporary Washington seems at least as prone to missteps as in most periods of the past.

Narrowing the Gap or Constructive Interaction?

Looking to the future from the perspective of a next generation of young social scientists who wish to do well in academia but also to support constructive and effective policymaking, what priorities should they pursue? Many of the chapters in this volume make a good case for narrowing the gap between scholar and practitioner networks, and in some key areas it does seem clear that there is a serious gap to be narrowed. In political science and international relations, for example, the professional disconnect between public policy and schools of government seems to have intensified. Silo-like academic boundary building can deprive applied scholars of indispensable insights into the subject matter of their inquiries, can reduce the likelihood of well-informed and evidence-based policymaking, and can deprive the research community of resources and recognition that would help it navigate through hard times.

Good applied scholarship requires much effort on two fronts at once: (1) to address the practical issues in a way that demonstrates the value added of objectivity and scholarly detachment and (2) to engage with best practice in each discipline, to steer work toward relevant topics and issues. Some aspects of policymaking, such as the evaluation of outcomes, lend themselves more readily to this type of approach, while others, such as macro-strategic choices, are inherently more problematic from a professional scholarly perspective. So, while narrowing the gap is a worthwhile goal, students of public policy and international relations would do well to consider the conditions under which it can be fruitfully pursued. They also need to understand the prerequisites for constructive engagement with policymaking, including the importance of keeping the two spheres separate, as well as the benefits of pursuing synergies between them.

If policymaking can be improved through more research and better analysis, and if scholars are in any case generating relevant knowledge, albeit confined to academia, then it looks unproblematic to advocate a narrowing of the gap between these unnecessarily separate activities. From that standpoint, the key question is to explain what prevents the two sides from connecting better and to identify remedial measures. But constructive engagement assumes certain background conditions if it is to generate policy pragmatism and consensus. Looking beyond the positive cases recorded in this volume, it is evident that such conditions cannot always be taken for granted. So there is also a need for explicit analysis of their conditions of existence, even in the United States and for inter-American affairs.

Lisa Anderson highlights how possibly transient conditions favored the American "mutual expectation among scholars and practitioners that, if each would only recognize the merits, the culture, and the demands of the other's domain, science and policy would both be better for it." In particular, such attitudes reflected "a historically and culturally specific commitment to a sort of traditional American liberalism, one that was simultaneously skeptical of and reliant upon the state, unselfconscious in its embrace of equality and the reality of privilege, and supremely confident of the susceptibility of social problems to human intervention." Anderson further asserts that "in creating the illusion that truth and power are separable domains, social scientists claimed the pursuit of truth as their own and relegated the exercise of power to 'practitioners' . . . thanks to the conceit that these sciences were in essence apolitical, this illusion also contributed to the enormous influence that American versions of social science would have in the rest of the world." She singles out peer review as one of the key ingredients of this approach, adding, however, that although it guaranteed academic freedom and discouraged personal or political bias, "it also fostered a self-referential focus on the estimates of professional colleagues at the expense of attention to society at large and it reinforced already calcified disciplinary boundaries."[16]

But these are background conditions that cannot be counted on to persist indefinitely and do not necessarily travel well beyond their places of origin. They do not have exact counterparts in Caracas, Beijing, or Buenos Aires—and a doubt could be raised even for Miami. In such contexts, the protection of academic autonomy, independent thinking, and democracy may have to take priority over narrowing the gap with the locally empowered policymakers. Indeed, in much of the contemporary world, including many formally democratic countries, policymaking needs to become much more evidence-based and rationally accountable, less rhetorical and more results oriented.

Scholarship would also need restructuring, including inducements to work on "relevant" topics, to network with the best internationally available epistemic communities, and to make use of rapidly advancing information technologies. In a context in which the resources of states are far outstripped by private corporate interests, the relationship between academia and corporate interests may require as much attention as the classic question of state power. These desiderata could be as essential as the more traditional concerns about reinforcing academic autonomy and protecting universities from political encroachment. Some of those changes, indeed, could imply a widening rather than a narrowing of the gap between the two camps.

In fact, there are multiple gaps to be considered in a more globalized world. Some of them are too wide, others possibly too narrow. These issues concern not just scholar-practitioner matrixes in single countries. Across the Americas there are international epistemic communities of academics and policymakers to consider. The "Chicago Boys" provide one particularly high-profile example of a dense network of interconnections. Beyond the realm of neoliberal economics, one could add democracy promoters, human rights practitioners, health advisors, deforestation analysts, climate change monitors, and many more. Closer collaboration and better policy access may be beneficial for most of these region-wide networks, but each context needs to be evaluated on its own terms. In the field of international relations scholarship and practice, for example, while some parts of the network are becoming more self-confident and capable of independent innovation, others tend to be more other-directed and reliant on North American leadership; the contrast between Brazil and Mexico is a case in point.

Depending on the country involved and the area of scholarship in question, proposals to widen some gaps might be as worthy of consideration as efforts to narrow them. For example, Latin American policymakers addressing the disastrous consequences for their societies of the prevailing orthodoxies concerning the war on drugs may be well advised to build up their own communities of analytical and policymaking expertise, in order to achieve more independence from currently dominant centers of authority. Financial deregulation or arms trafficking are other domains where too much academic legitimacy has been conferred on doubtful or failed approaches, so both truth and power might be served by an increased degree of scholarly pluralism and even institutional delinking.

Reverting to the United States, there are some major and controversial policy areas where similar considerations apply. Bad decisions in the counternarcotics domain not only arise from lack of expertise or scholarly counsel; good scholarship may even serve to reinforce and cover for erroneous policies. Expertise can be misappropriated, and the scholars who allow their work to be used for such purposes can be regarded as complicit in the bad decisions they have helped to generate; this, in turn, can damage the morale and academic integrity of the disciplines from which they hail. Such risks are unevenly distributed across issue areas and types of scholarship. Even where the risks are greatest, there is usually more to gain than to lose from well-crafted dialogue between the two sides. But in such cases—which include much of the higher levels of policy advice, beyond the reach of purely technical considerations—instead of focusing on how to narrow the gap it would be better to explore the prerequisites for constructive interactions that also attend to the proper separation between the two domains.

The most basic prerequisite is that the two sides should share a common framework of understanding and joint purpose. It is easier to take that condition for granted in the United States or Canada than in, say, Argentina or Mexico.[17] Even within the United States, however, it is more of a given in some periods (during the Cold War or immediately after 9/11) and some policy domains (Homeland Security, perhaps) than in others (health care or taxation). Perhaps the most striking current example of a potentially severe divide between scholars and leading practitioners in Washington could concern the science of climate change.

Where such disconnects threaten to be most disruptive, serious work may be needed to reinforce bridging institutions that are broad-based and respected by technical experts and capable of restoring trust and cooperation on both sides, to preserve high-quality dialogue between competing scholarly viewpoints, and to lengthen the time frames over which rival claims are assessed. In some instances, that may require these institutions to protect unpopular scholars from punitive censure.[18] A related procedural issue concerns pluralism and time horizons. Dissenting scholars may need some institutional security and enough time to establish whether the evidence favors their "Team B" alternative arguments. Multilingual and even multicultural collaborative arrangements could both enrich research and scholarship in various domains and add to the repertoire of available policy options.

The other basic prerequisite is harder to engineer. Policymakers need to be reasonably receptive to fresh scholarly inputs, and academic advisors to be attuned to the temporal, institutional, and other practical constraints limiting feasible choice sets. In contemporary Washington, these mutually reinforcing dispositions are promoted via a dense network of think tanks, consultancy arrangements, and congressional hearings, and by the permeability of career tracks enabling a significant stratum of qualified individuals to go back and forth across the academic-practitioner divide as "in-and-outers."[19]

Various chapters in this volume draw attention to the tensions and limitations of this system, but by comparative standards, the United States stands out for its flexibility and fluidity. To a greater extent than elsewhere, it has established most of the prerequisites for productive exchange between scholars and practitioners. Maintaining and reinforcing this system requires continuous attention to its foundations. Modern policy advisors would do well to recall Machiavelli's points about modesty and the avoidance of passion. His sense that results can always prove unexpected and that blame for bad outcomes can far outweigh rewards for a success remain extremely pertinent. In fact, the main rationale for the broad-based and credible protective bridging institutions advocated here is precisely to guard against the disincentives to truthful speaking that Machiavelli identified. Think tanks may proliferate, evidence-based policymaking may increasingly be made the norm in regulatory agencies, and multiple forms of expertise can claim the authority to counteract uninformed policymaking. But, although the balance of rewards and protections has been shifted strongly in favor of scholarly candor since Machiavelli's day, it would be an error to suppose that modern academia is securely protected against all retaliation from disgruntled political (or commercial) power centers. At any rate, it is evident that in many parts of the world at the beginning of the twenty-first century, older traditions of practitioner abuse and scholarly self-censorship demonstrably live on.

Classic procedural protections such as peer review and academic autonomy remain as indispensable as ever, but their benefits do not arise from an unquestioning defense of past legacies. In a much more connected world information system, with many more international and horizontal linkages and a massified and commodified system of scholarship and research, a great deal of institutional innovation will be required to keep the scholar-practitioner matrix functional and balanced. Open-source research raises far-reaching issues about intellectual property rights and the funding of academic work. In fact, the entire model of research organization, career patterns, and individualistic ownership of scholarly outputs that underpinned the liberal universities of the past century is coming under intense pressure from rapid technical change, which is also likely to prove disruptive to existing patterns of public policymaking. No doubt new forms of interaction and partnership between scholars and practitioners can be constructed in this greatly changed context, but it seems unlikely that inherited arrangements can simply persist through inertia. For technical as well as political reasons, big adjustments are to be expected.

In summary, an unduly instrumental approach to the pursuit of knowledge has often involved a high cost to scholarship. So the endorsement of narrowing the gap carries two reservations. First, there may well be scope to enhance dialogue and exchange across the boundary dividing academia from government, but not at the price of obliterating their separate identities and institutional logics. Although narrowing the gap may often be desirable, there are also points at which defending separation and the preservation of distinctive rationales is yet more critical, even from the standpoint of achieving productive synergies. For reasons of democratic accountability and integrity and to achieve synergy, it is also essential to preserve the integrity of the scholarly realm. From the other side of the divide, of course, an effective government cannot operate like a debating society. Second, the gap in question is not just between scholars and practitioners within the United States; it is of at least equal interest to build better bridges between scholars across the Americas and between scholars and practitioners in the Latin American republics.

Conclusions: Three Contrasting Standpoints

At least in the market democracies of the Western hemisphere and Europe, a deeply entrenched and strongly institutionalized sphere of scholarship and professionalized academic research operates with a high degree of autonomy from political practice. The judiciary, the media, civil society, and the private sector all offer some shelter to this independent realm of knowledge, expertise, and pluralism. Also, on the other side of the divide, most policymakers accept—at least in principle—that the complex and multifaceted decisions they have to take require public justifications that need to include some respect for the findings of the research community and the rules of evidence practiced by academia. Even so, there are still tensions in all democracies, old as well as new. For example, even if research shows that light regulation of immigration flows is good for both economic growth and social stability, many democratic politicians nevertheless judge it impolitic to be seen acting accordingly.

Likewise, even if academics can show that a fierce "war on drugs" produces more social evils than a policy based on public health principles, including a substantial degree of legalization and health regulation, political leaders who fear losing the next election may resist that finding. Given such divergences, some scholars may bend over as far as they can to conduct research within the limits of the "politically practical," and many practitioners may try to strike electorally popular stances, while, at best, quietly doing what they can to take into account research evidence.

In summary, the contemporary Western hemisphere context is a favored, and indeed sheltered, environment compared with the broad flow of scholar-practitioner relations across time and space. But even so it contains tensions, and even the potential for a return to more serious difficulties, if not well managed. To close the University of Southern California conference that gave rise to this book, Abe Lowenthal convened a panel on the theme "Can scholars contribute to improving policy? When? And how? Or, why not?" In my brief 10 minutes I offered the following three (overlapping) responses to these very broad questions.

The first can be called the approach of the busy practitioner, who might say: "There is no reason why scholars should not be able to help me improve my policies, provided they supply me with clear, definite, and operational ideas and proposals. In return I will need to make sure they are fully informed about the factors we are considering and the alternatives already under review. So they have to accept the same confidentiality conditions as we do, and they need to be focused and timely. They also need to observe the same disciplines as the rest of us when their proposals are overruled or set aside, and they need to stick with the policy process until its conclusion, not opt out halfway through. If they can't accept these terms, their contributions are unlikely to be heard."

The second is the approach of the mainstream scholar, who would contend that "to contribute effectively I require precise ground rules. You need to understand the nature of my discipline, and the methodology it employs. Within those parameters I can deliver relevant research and even policy recommendations. But there may well be aspects of your problem that fall outside the scope of my expertise, and you may need to turn to a different type of advisor for these parts of the task. The way you frame the issue is also important for me. My scholarship relies on a tightly structured and specifically defined terminology. Within my framework I can comfortably advise you, but I do not wish to become associated with language, concepts, and methods that are not well respected by my peers. If you require that of me, then I would prefer to return to my core research agenda."

The third is the approach of the critical scholar, who can sometimes contribute to improve policymaking. This scholar might argue thus: "Before I can begin making recommendations of any kind, I need to understand who I am really dealing with (the contours of the relevant 'power structure'), and I may also try to deconstruct the 'legitimizing discourse' that underpins the policy. Having determined whether there are hidden assumptions that need to be uncovered, I will be equipped to decide the terms on which I might be willing to advise you. My advice would most likely be different from that of the mainstream scholar or the technician and might well raise some hackles within your agency. However, it could improve your policies by challenging the 'groupthink' and institutional biases that would otherwise distort your decision making. Scholarship inherently involves challenges as well as improvement, and good critical scholarship may do more to improve your operations than any amount of unreflective research input."

These three fundamentally different approaches need not be mutually exclusive. In practice, the real challenge is to select the best approach for each task. There are relatively technical issues where an objective and scholarly assessment of the evidence may generate a "best practice" finding that would command widespread academic support. There are more hotly contested issues where, nevertheless, part of the art of good policymaking involves taking into account the relevant evidence-based research, while also going beyond academic conventional wisdom where necessary, to provide political leadership. At a third level—often involving the highest decision-making authorities and the most challenging and intractable policy issues—the input from scholarly research may still add some value, notably by cautioning against rash and inadequately examined initiatives; but discretionary political choices are required, and practitioners will act largely according to their criteria—to which academic input may seem irrelevant.

NOTES

1. The broad array of policy domains covered in this volume includes border cooperation, targeted financial sanctions, democracy promotion, gender issues, the war on drugs, citizen security, and antipoverty programs, among other issues.

2. Robert K. Merton, *Social Theory and Social Structure* (Glencoe, IL: Free Press, 1957), 222.

3. Lisa Anderson, *Pursuing Truth, Exercising Power: Social Science and Public Policy in the Twenty-First Century* (New York: Columbia University Press, 2005), 3, 39.

4. Plato's attempt to advise the Tyrant of Syracuse; Aristotle's brief role as tutor to Alexander the Great; Seneca's disastrous experience as instructor to Nero; Hobbes's effort to educate the future King Charles II—all could be cited to illustrate the temptations and pitfalls of scholarly involvement in high politics in the era of unrestricted personal power.

5. Niccolo Machiavelli, *Discourses on Livy* (Oxford: Oxford University Press, 1997), book 3, chap. 35, 338–39. The quotes are slightly reorganized.

6. "Report of the Commissioners for the University of Virginia," in *The Portable Thomas Jefferson*, ed. Merrill D. Peterson (New York: Viking Press, 1975), 337.

7. Anderson, *Pursuing Truth*, 14. Anderson also underscores the distinctively unfettered and liberal stance of the American research university "outside the state, supporting the regime" (72). She highlights the ambivalence about "understanding" and "changing" the world as a "distinctly American element of the story of the rise of the social sciences."

8. Max Weber characterized the German case thus: "The examination diploma or the title of professor . . . bestows absolutely no political qualification on its holder . . . Where were they when the grave errors of the old regime were being committed? They collaborated in and applauded almost all the mistakes of German policy before the war and the lack of judgement nourished by irresponsible demagogy during the war . . . [That] section of society was blind, and always will remain blind, following its instincts rather than sober reflection; this is how university men, in the mass, will always behave in Germany." Max Weber, *Parliament and Government in Germany*, originally published in Munich in 1918. This translation is from *Weber Political Writings*, ed. Peter Lassman and Ronald Spiers (Cambridge: Cambridge University Press, 2003), 267.

9. According to Anderson, any "residual reluctance to collaborate with government" on the part of US scholars "was entirely extinguished by the outbreak of World War II." Anderson, *Pursuing Truth*, 27.

10. Chappell Lawson (chap. 1, this volume) is particularly eloquent on this point.

11. Alexis de Tocqueville was dismissively ironic about "men of letters who have written history without being involved in public business" and politicians "who have always been concerned with generating events, never with describing them." Alexis de Tocqueville, *Souvenirs* (Paris: Calmann Levy, 1893), 83. To take a more recent example of a common practitioner complaint against unworldly scholars, in 2001, David Featherman, former president of the US Social Science Research Council, stated that it was "perhaps ironic that academics in disciplines such as economics, political science, and sociology—in their quest for professional integrity and scientific objectivity—may have unintentionally undermined these disciplines' long term relevance to policy and thereby conceded the main battlefield to the private, often partisan, think tanks." David L. Featherman and Maris A. Vinovskis, eds., *Social Science and Policymaking: A Search for Relevance in the Twentieth Century* (Ann Arbor: University of Michigan, 2001), 2.

12. Thus, in this volume, Bertucci and Lowenthal distinguish between policy articulation, formation, implementation, and evaluation (chap. 15); Biersteker underscores the scope for "policy entrepreneurs" to intervene at the first stage (chap. 8); Lustig shows how scholars can contribute to effective implementation (chap. 6); and Seligson highlights the scope for input over evaluation (chap. 9). It is also useful to differentiate between short- and longer-term policy approaches, which may require more analytical groundwork.

13. As Biersteker notes (chap. 8), on this topic a policy-relevant scholar is "not innocent."

14. Bob Pastor has devoted his career to criss-crossing the scholar-practitioner divide and to reflecting as an academic and insider on the complex dynamics, including uncertainty, contingency, happenstance, and the frequent ironies involved. More than most, he has drawn attention to the "macro" issues, in particular the long-run North America–wide challenges that follow from NAFTA. His contribution on the Carter administration (chap. 2) is unusually wide ranging, focusing on the stock of ideas provided to that administration by the Linowitz and Murphy commissions. This is only part of a long history of US-based academic-linked initiatives aimed at guiding incoming presidential administrations through the intricacies of inter-American relations. A more institutionalized forum is the Inter-American Dialogue, a scholar-practitioner interface that Abe Lowenthal helped to establish in the early 1980s.

15. Díaz Alejandro could take that risk at least in part because of Kissinger's standing as an intellectual. But scholars who get too close to the highest reaches of political power leave themselves exceptionally vulnerable to discredit and the misuse of the ideas. An example of the dangers of injecting academic insights into presidential-level decision making is the 1959 lecture "The Political Uses of Madness," given by Daniel Ellsberg to Henry Kissinger's Harvard seminar. According to Seymour M. Hersh, Ellsberg's main example was "Hitler's conscious use of his reputation as a madman to win victories without firing a shot in the Rhineland, Austria, and Munich before World War Two." Ellsberg "didn't even imagine that an American president could consider such a strategy" but speculated that it might work with the nuclear threat. Hersh claims that Nixon embraced just such a theory to extricate his administration from the morass of the Vietnam War and that Kissinger may have been responsible for "Nixon's adoption of the phrase 'the madman theory.'" If so, a provocative seminar contribution resulted in practitioner consequences far removed from what the scholar intended or foresaw. Whether or not one accepts this account, the Ellsberg story cautions that "narrowing the gap" may be a worthwhile pursuit but not an unqualified desideratum. Seymour M. Hersh, *The Price of Power: Kissinger in the Nixon White House* (New York: Simon and Schuster, 1983), 53.

16. Anderson, *Pursuing Truth*, 2, 6, 3, 33. Anderson provides an illuminating overview of the ebb and flow of American attitudes and practices on this subject across the twentieth century and helps to clarify the tensions concealed by a liberal worldview that disguises underlying conflicts. She also draws attention to the rapid pace of change in the post–Cold War world and the many ways in which marketization and globalization are transforming the context of scholar-practitioner interactions.

17. For a survey of the Latin American experience, see Laurence Whitehead, "The Politics of Expertise," in *Latin America: A New Interpretation* (New York: Palgrave Macmillan, 2010).

18. The integrity of public statistical information and of national audit offices can provide a litmus test here.

19. Joseph S. Nye, "The Costs and Benefits of 'In and Outers,'" in "Forum: Risks and Opportunities of Crossing the Academy/Policy Divide," ed. Ann Tickner and Andrei Tsygankov, *International Studies Review* 10 (2008): 156–60.

CHAPTER FIFTEEN

Scholars, Policymakers, and International Affairs
Toward More Fruitful Connections

MARIANO E. BERTUCCI AND ABRAHAM F. LOWENTHAL

A widely noted gap exists between scholars and policymakers who work on international affairs in the United States; this is also true, to varying degrees, in Europe, Canada, and Latin America.[1] This gap has in most respects widened in recent years, largely as a result of trends in academic work that have emphasized subjects of limited interest beyond the disciplines and have often seemed to privilege research techniques over substantive content.[2] The changing agenda, processes, and pace of international policymaking have further contributed to this disconnect.

This book argues that the possibilities and potentially mutual benefits of overcoming the scholarship-policymaking divide are widely underestimated.[3] We focus first on analyzing the reasons for the observed gap, then on exploring what can be gained on both sides by bridging it, and finally on suggesting practical ways to foster more effective interactions among scholars and policymakers, without losing sight of their different roles and imperatives.

Understanding the Scholar-Policymaker Disconnect

Most social scientists in North American, many European, and some prestigious Latin American research universities—particularly those in political science, including comparative politics and international relations—have interests, methods, and modes of operation that contrast sharply with those of policymakers in governments, international institutions, and nongovernmental organizations (NGOs). Such scholars tend to limit their inquiries to questions that can be answered on the basis of readily accessible, already available, and reliable data. They seek primarily to understand and to explain, not to make things happen; indeed, they are taught to avoid advocacy. They focus on social structures, historical legacies, and socioeconomic circumstances as determinants of policies and outcomes, thus emphasizing factors that policymakers cannot easily affect.

Most aspire to methodological rigor—with replicable research designs, testable hypotheses, and robust empirical findings—and seek to ensure the quality and reputation of their work by subjecting it to anonymous peer review. They achieve career advancement through appointment, tenure, and promotion decisions that rely mostly on publication venues within their discipline, citation counts, and confidential evaluation by outstanding scholars from other institutions. Scholars value theory—the more general, abstract, original, and parsimonious the better.

Scholars often take considerable time to design and conduct their research and then communicate their findings; years can elapse between initiating a project and publishing its results. Targeting their publications to fellow specialists, they employ methodologies, terms, and specialized jargon that are intelligible to these colleagues but not necessarily to broadly educated professionals outside their discipline. They write for colleagues who can devote adequate time to reading long articles and books, because doing so is at the heart of their profession. Work is honed through exposure to the review processes of and publication in peer-reviewed academic journals and books as well as exposure to academic conferences and meetings of professional associations, all among a narrow range of participants. Young scholars concentrate on having their writing recognized by a handful of more established peers. Graduate students attach themselves to professorial mentors, who understandably train them to become professors like themselves. Incentives and role models are scant for multidisciplinary exploration, broad integration of perspectives from different subfields, and experience outside the academy. Although these tendencies are not prevalent in most of Latin America and some other regions where scholars and policymakers move back and forth and relate to each other easily, the tendency in prestigious elite universities in Latin America and elsewhere is increasingly to emulate the US model.[4]

Practitioners in the policy world, by contrast, achieve professional recognition and promotion by demonstrating political and administrative skills in the political arena or within a bureaucracy. They have their own jargon, much of it expressed in acronyms. Whereas scholars achieve professional advancement by presenting original ideas and findings for which they claim intellectual property rights, there can be no plagiarism in governments or other action organizations. Policymakers must integrate ideas and information from multiple sources, usually without attribution; in fact, having one's formulations adopted by others is a sign of success. Their cachet depends less on original ideas than on their effectiveness in framing issues and operating within established frameworks to solve problems.

In their (mostly infrequent) interaction with scholars, policy officials seek practical assistance in strictly limited time. When they do so, they want clearly presented and concise information and analysis about issues and places they think are important. They look to scholars for accurate descriptions and informed diagnosis of problematic situations; for specific country or area expertise; for identification of important trends, their causes, and likely evolution; for insights about the psychological traits and political qualities of relevant foreign decision makers; for clear lessons from retrospective analysis of previous situations; and, when possible, for pertinent prescriptions.

Their main aim is usually to decide what to do (or to recommend) in order to increase the chances of a favorable outcome—or to reduce the likelihood of adverse developments—with regard to a specific problem at hand. They are less interested in structural conditions they cannot affect and more concerned with policy levers on which they can exercise agency. Sometimes officials seek to attain support for, legitimize, or find new ways of articulating policy courses they (or their superiors) have already decided upon. Chronically pressed for time, they often seek immediate answers, even when providing these is impossible. They want the answers to be presented in accessible language that will resonate with higher-level officials. These officials—political leaders and their principal advisors—typically have broad knowledge and, often, sound judgment, but they often lack relevant specialized expertise.[5]

The prevailing cultures of these two realms differ. Most scholars primarily toil on their own, striving for individual recognition, though collaborative and even interdisciplinary work is beginning to gain more favor. For policymakers, however, success almost always depends on managing interpersonal relations: maneuvering within a hierarchy; mastering the art of timing; building political support; negotiating, writing, and speaking clearly; engaging and persuading decision makers; and deflecting opponents.[6] Scholars are often put off by their perception that many policymakers value glibness more than profound analysis. Practitioners are often disdainful of what they regard as obsessive academic concern with methods and of scholars' reluctance to make unqualified assertions or to hazard predictions.

The distance between the worlds of scholarship and policy has widened in recent years, as fashions in the social sciences—and especially in political science, comparative politics, and international relations—have moved toward specialized subfields, formal modeling, refined statistical techniques, experimental research, and ever more precise answers to ever less policy-relevant questions, and as quasi-academic think tanks, unconnected to universities, have occupied much of the space for policy-oriented and policy-relevant research. Policymakers, for their part, have often become less open to academic perspectives as they respond to a 24/7 news cycle, instant worldwide flows of information, and the democratization of what used to be more closed and deliberative decision making.

Respecting Differences, but Seeking Synergies

A clear separation between the academic and policy worlds can be salutary in some respects. Institutions of higher learning have long faced external attempts to curb intellectual freedom in order to prevent challenges to the established order. Such practices as peer review of publications, career-long tenure, and the granting of tenure and promotion only after careful evaluative procedures have developed in part to protect the quality and independence of research and instruction. The academic world strives to provide circumstances conducive to sustained reflection and disciplined analysis, free of pressures to reach premature or foreordained conclusions. It is useful to have an autonomous profession of those who can "speak truth to power" from a protected domain.

Expanding the influence of scholars on public policies, moreover, is not always desirable or effective. The racist immigration regime adopted by the United States from 1924 through the mid-1960s, for example, was largely based on the leading academic theories of the era.[7] So were some of the policies employed by the United States in Vietnam, such as using the calibrated escalation and de-escalation of bombing to secure desired behavior from the Vietcong. The socially regressive structural adjustment policies in the 1980s also came from the academic world, as did the extensive work by governments and international institutions on economic and political development that was largely based on modernization theory, the financial deregulation policies that contributed to the Great Recession beginning in 2008, and the austerity policies being pursued today in much of Europe (and, to a lesser extent, in the United States).[8] Having academic ideas influence government policymakers is no guarantee that the resulting policies will be sound or that they will work well in practice.

There is the danger, too, that scholars entering the policy arena may be seduced by access to power and its trappings and may therefore lose the critical distance necessary to offer sound advice based on rigorous research and analysis; they may also, over time, diminish their capacity to conduct such research.[9] There is also a danger that oversimplified and distorted versions of scholarly research can become insinuated into policy discourse in ways that result in poor scholarship shaping inadequate policies.

Efforts to bridge the gap between scholars and policymakers are ultimately worth undertaking only if better policies or improved academic research and teaching, or preferably all three, are likely to result. The risks both to academia and to policy of uncritical or low-quality engagement must be taken into account.[10] Yet we believe that connecting the work of good scholars interested in illuminating policy issues with the needs of open-minded policymakers looking for ideas and analysis can lead to productive synergies and that these are worth promoting.

The Case for Building Bridges

Stephen Krasner reports that his several years in Washington reinforced his "conviction that the gap between academia and the policy world is unbridgeable" and that "no one is going to build a bridge between the two worlds."[11] We disagree. As the chapters in this volume show, bridges and intersections between scholars and policymakers *can* be constructed, and they can sometimes lead to sounder policies and also contribute to enhanced research and teaching.[12] We believe there are ways to increase the likelihood that such connections can be fashioned more often and made more effective, with better prospects of achieving positive results. The difficulties of spanning the academic-policy divide are often exaggerated and are too often stipulated as dogma, generating self-fulfilling prophecies of failure that unnecessarily discourage both scholars and policymakers from making the effort.[13] We urge a concerted return to bridge building from both banks of the chasm.

How Scholars Can Contribute to Better Policymaking

Scholars can contribute to improved policymaking in many ways:

- Scholars can provide data and analysis on trends, sometimes not previously noted or taken into account by policymakers, which may alter the agenda or the environment for problem solving. They can recognize and frame new policy challenges and develop categories and vocabulary to analyze and respond to them, as they did with the introduction of nuclear weapons, the growth of asymmetric conflict, and the breakdown of authoritarian regimes. Analysis of the economic, social, and political implications of demographic trends further illustrates this point, as do analyses of levels and patterns of violence, conflicts over resources, and many other studies.
- Scholars can describe and analyze the history, social and economic structures, politics, institutions, and decision-making patterns of foreign countries and international entities and the likely impact of all of these on how current policy issues are perceived and options are decided upon.[14] They can provide other important context-setting elements, including comparative biographical analysis of individuals and cohorts, studies of interest groups and bureaucratic politics, and even linguistic skills useful for interpreting important nuances.[15]

- Because their perspectives and time horizons are so different from those of policy officials, scholars are well positioned to undertake structured, focused comparisons of how policies affect outcomes in different issue areas, or how they affect the same issue as it is presented in different countries or regions. Such studies may help policymakers reconceive a specific conundrum by understanding it as part of a broader genre or may lead them to refashion instruments to take into account differences in context.[16]

- Scholars can develop conditional generalizations about causal relationships among specified variables, presenting the kind of "mid-range theories" that are most likely to offer policymakers what Alexander George called "diagnostic value" and "useful knowledge."[17] Examples of important academic contributions of this type in recent years include work on such diverse issues as deterrence, disarmament, coercive diplomacy, conflict resolution, economic sanctions, democratic peace, fragile states, election monitoring, civil-military relations, ethnic conflict, identity, community, and transitional justice.[18]

- As Biersteker points out (chapter 8), scholars can provide institutional memory, making policymakers aware of relevant prior experiences occurring before their watch and what can be learned from these. More generally, they can draw lessons from previous experiences by undertaking and assembling disciplined case studies and comparisons.[19] They can also pose questions for analysis and structured discussions that allow representatives of governments and other interested parties to engage issues they cannot comfortably address on their own initiative.

- As discussed by Lustig (chapter 6) and Seligson (chapter 9), scholars can offer detailed cost-effectiveness analyses as well as systematic and comparative evaluation of the observable effects of prior and ongoing policies. A good example, beyond the conditional cash transfers program discussed by Lustig, is the work on development policy carried out at the Abdul Latif Jameel Poverty Action Lab, based at the Massachusetts Institute of Technology. Scholars there, mostly economists, assess the effectiveness of development policies throughout Latin America, Africa, South Asia, and Europe, using randomized controlled tests.[20] Similar work has been done in political science as well, on, for example, improved schooling in Africa, the enforcement of wages and working conditions and health and safety standards in the United States, and the diffusion of labor standards across global supply chains.[21]

- As discussed in this volume by Lawson, Pastor, Jaquette, Lustig, Heredia, Evans, and others, scholars can develop and promote new concepts that reframe problems and open up opportunities to act. Scholars have been at the forefront of introducing such policy-driving notions as "human development" indicators, "human security," "women and development," "collaborative border management," "fragile states," and the "responsibility to protect," and of reconceptualizing state sovereignty as contingent rather than absolute.[22]

· Scholars can challenge mindsets and conceptual frameworks by identifying simplistic concepts, questionable premises, implicit assumptions, dubious analogies, and faulty reasoning, and by revealing their flaws.[23] They can demonstrate these points retrospectively by highlighting alternative policies that might have been recommended on the basis of scholarly analysis, and they can develop strategies and even specific proposals to deal with future contingencies.[24] Scholars can aid policymakers in thinking through such issues by helping to design and engage with them in simulation exercises, forecasting, and the construction of scenarios.

Scholars, in sum, can and do contribute data, concepts, diagnosis, legitimation, evaluation, critiques, strategizing, policy design, and sometimes actor-specific prescription. They have a lot to offer, in different ways, to those who make and execute policy. This value should be recognized. Such work should be reinforced and expanded, not belittled.

How Scholars and Academia Can Gain from Policy Engagement

By the same token, there are many good reasons, ranging from the broadly altruistic to the narrowly self-interested, that academic institutions should encourage efforts by motivated scholars to engage in the policymaking process. First, scholars have civic and professional responsibilities as citizens with special expertise. Professional analysts of comparative politics and international relations can offer insights for policymaking and for broader public understanding on important issues that affect the whole community. We strongly reaffirm that responsibility, as part of the university's mission, in the context of today's underinformed and often polemical public discussion of policy issues.[25]

Second, a greater focus on understanding, assessing, and influencing policy—how and why choices are made and their consequences—can improve the quality of political science by linking it more closely to substance.[26] Separating the study of international relations and comparative politics from the actors, interests, competition for power, and concrete stakes that define and shape those relations tends to deprive the discipline of much of its meaning and significance. Theories are crafted and must be understood in the context of the particular social, economic, and political environments to which they respond.[27] As Terry Karl points out, "to separate theory and practice (and disparage the latter) while insisting on the 'science' of politics to the exclusion of its passions is to set aside the hard questions of public life that do not lend themselves to parsimony, and to define away the problems that do not already have a pre-existing data set."[28]

Beyond civic duty, the broad public interest in soundly based policies, and the health and relevance of social science, scholars and their institutions can gain from participation in the policy process in several concrete ways:

- Participation in policymaking can broaden the disciplinary-specific perspectives within which most scholars work, helping them incorporate previously neglected factors into their analysis.[29] On returning to their academic work, scholars with policymaking experience should better understand how policies are actually made and implemented and how ideas, constructs, and procedures shape judgments and decisions, enabling these scholars to refine and add appropriate complexity to their analytical models.[30] They may also engage more systematically with research methods that can illuminate the realities and constraints of policymaking, such as interviews, survey research, and "causal process-tracing." And they can and should teach these methods, of great value to policy-oriented social scientists.[31]

- As pointed out by Lustig, Pastor, Jaquette, and Fernández de Castro, scholars who participate for a time in policymaking are also likely to observe significant factors they had not previously identified or to which they had not assigned much importance and to which, on their return to academia, they can devote more systematic consideration.[32] A stint in government can even present an opportunity to undertake ethnographic participant observation, at least in informal ways, leading to improved theoretical understanding of cognitive processes, decision making, and policy design and implementation in governments, international organizations, and other relevant bureaucracies.[33] This enhanced knowledge should contribute to better research and teaching.

As Bruce Jentleson observes, experience working in the policy environment enables academics to "genuinely reality-test our theories, if not under methodologically strict control conditions, at least as plausibility probes. We can do a type of field work empirical data gathering that is less systematic than opportunistic, but gives unique and potentially rich insights."[34] Lawson, Biersteker, Pastor, and Fernández de Castro make similar points. Participating directly, for a time, in policy processes should not weaken academic acuity but rather reinforce and sharpen it.[35]

- Experience with policymaking can also help scholars improve the quality of their teaching and its relevance to the needs of their students. Scholars with relevant experience can teach students how policies are shaped in practice, often at variance with formal rules, institutions, and standard operating procedures. That teaching will be particularly useful for students who will work outside academia—the great majority of undergraduates and an increasing number of graduate students. The degree to which many professors ignore the likelihood that their graduate students will go on to work not as professors but in nonacademic positions is often irresponsible. One of the advantages of having scholars with experience in the policy world is that this may help them imagine the kinds of responsibilities for which many of their students should be preparing. Professors can also usefully draw on their policy experience to develop case studies, problem-solving and negotiation exercises, simulations, scenarios, and policy task forces, all of which students find extraordinarily useful, not only for building theory but as preparation for a variety of careers.[36]

- Scholars with experience in policymaking environments often develop an improved interest in and capacity for the art of clear, precise, concise, and persuasive written and oral exposition, skills that their students will find useful no matter what profession they enter. And it is not only the students who benefit when teachers emphasize and teach these skills; professors themselves can enhance their intellectual discipline and teaching.[37] They also can improve their own expository skills, thus enabling them to expand the audiences for their writing and lecturing, prepare more compelling and persuasive research and funding proposals, write more effective memoranda in their universities and in other professional contexts, and strengthen program-building competence.

- Scholars with policy experience can gain access to and help develop transnational and multisectoral networks in governments, international institutions, NGOs, business, and the media that may affect policy but also may facilitate future research, expand possibilities for research support, and multiply their ability to help place students in internships and employment opportunities. Such networks may also turn out to be especially valuable should the scholar eventually return to a policymaking role, as often demonstrated in the careers of various scholar-statesmen and "technopols."[38]

- Finally, greater involvement by social scientists in the conceptualization, formulation, implementation, and assessment of policy should enhance public awareness of the societal value of academic research. Thoughtful social scientists and university administrators understand that the prevailing tendency in several disciplines toward ever more definitive answers to what often seem like trivial questions runs the risk of undercutting the support needed for future research and teaching.[39] Scholars who shed light on problems that are widely understood to be important, and who help to confront these, showcase a university's broader value. Senior university administrators, on an ad hoc basis, sometimes accord to policy-oriented faculty the recognition that is frequently denied to them by those departmental peers for whom engagement with policy and the public is somehow marginal or even suspect; such recognition should become the rule, not the exception.

Enhancing the Participation and Influence of Scholars in Policymaking

We turn now to a practical discussion—drawing upon the chapters in this volume, other material presented at the USC workshop, the general literature, and our own experiences and observations—of how to enhance the participation and influence of scholars in the policymaking process.[40] An important first step toward tackling this question is to understand that "scholars" and "policymakers" comprise broad categories that obscure important differences within each realm. These differences are highly relevant in considering how to bridge the gap between those who should be better connected. Scholars in the social sciences do different kinds of work. Some focus at a high level of abstraction on developing, testing, debating, and sometimes modeling academic theories, often consciously choosing to favor rigor over policy relevance. Others concentrate on applying theoretical concepts to test their empirical value. Some try to use theoretical concepts to illuminate "real-world" problems and, on occasion, to clarify specific policy issues and choices. This last role may involve providing concepts, information, and analysis that can explain particular events and/or can be operationally useful for policymakers. These aims, in turn, may require "translating" abstract concepts and empirical findings into accessible prose.

Individual scholars can play any of these roles at different times. All these roles can have a degree of policy relevance, and all can contribute to the development of better theories.[41] It is when scholars undertake the last kind of work—explaining particular events and tendencies or illuminating policy choices and their likely results—that they are most likely to provide perceived value to policy officials. Scholars who want to affect policy should think through what particular approach best fits their own interests, aims, and skills at a specific juncture, and on what issues and in which circumstances and venues they are most likely to have the kind of influence they seek.

Policy officials, too, play a variety of roles. Only rarely, and mostly close to the top of policymaking hierarchies, do they explicitly determine the aims of policy and then choose among alternative approaches in the kind of deliberative process most easily imagined and related to by scholars. Mostly, they make incremental adjustments to standard operating procedures, drawn from a relatively fixed set of policy instruments, to deal with slightly changed conditions within an established framework.[42] Scholars are usually better prepared to challenge frameworks and to evaluate the results of policies than to fine-tune their quotidian application.

The advice of scholars is more likely to be taken into account on slow-moving, medium- and long-term matters than in times of crisis that demand immediate action. It is also more likely to be considered in development agencies, in democracy promotion programs, and in various domestic and economic agencies than in entrenched security, financial, and diplomatic bureaucracies, especially those with elaborate clearance procedures.[43] The work of scholars is more likely to be influential when there is a high degree of expert consensus, as distinct from those issues on which almost everyone's opinions may appear to have equal weight, such as how to reduce crime and violence in Central America.[44] And it is more likely to be called upon when transformational changes are occurring internationally that require new concepts and definitions or when new policy issues burst into view and fresh conceptual models and prescriptions, as well as new tools for assessment, are evidently required.

Scholars (and other outsiders) are least likely to have an immediate impact on highly politicized issues—drug policy, citizen security, and US relations with Cuba, for example—where policy stances are frozen and largely impervious to cost-benefit analysis and other evidence. It is precisely on such issues, however, that scholars can often make important contributions as public intellectuals by helping to prepare the terrain for future reconsideration of policy frameworks, when political circumstances permit.[45] Scholars of comparative politics and international relations can provide well-reasoned analysis and persuasive assessment of prior policies and their failures, can offer constructive proposals for new policy proposals and instruments that take into account political and bureaucratic realities, and can help reframe public debate.

The chances that scholars will be able to contribute effectively within governments and international institutions may well be greatest in the policy planning offices that are charged with formulating and articulating broad approaches and drafting statements and speeches by high officials and in staff positions on the US president's National Security Council or comparable posts in other countries.[46] The prospects for directly affecting policy are also relatively favorable in program planning and evaluation offices, such as those described by Seligson (chapter 9) in the US Agency for International Development; in bureaus of intelligence and analysis, such as the State Department's office of Intelligence and Research and the CIA's National Intelligence Council; or on the personal staffs of senior officials who are high enough in the policymaking establishment to have the confidence to raise critical questions and propose alternative approaches.

The advice of scholars is most likely to have an impact when it is invited from inside the policymaking realm by a policy entrepreneur or broker, often someone with his or her own academic training and networks. Identifying and building relationships with such brokers is one of the most effective ways for scholars to enhance the chances that their research and ideas may have an impact.

Building better connections between scholars and policymakers, in short, is not about bridging undifferentiated communities on one side with similarly undifferentiated actors on the other. Rather it is about exploring how to identify and link the most likely prospects in each camp, how to focus on the issues for which new ideas are most needed, and how to spot or create windows of opportunity for academic input.

Such windows sometimes depend on political leadership. As Jaquette, Heredia, Evans, and Bertucci show, Carter's administration was more open to academic expertise than Reagan's; Mexico's PRI (Institutional Revolutionary Party) was more accessible to technocrats than was the PAN (National Action Party); the Liberals in Canada were more comfortable with academic input than is the current Harper government; and Carlos Menem's minister of foreign affairs, Guido di Tella, sought scholarly advice to implement Argentina's foreign policy alignment with the United States. Policy windows may be opened in many other ways, however: by individual policy entrepreneurs and bridge figures, by dramatic events that shake up established ways of thinking, or by special action-forcing deadlines, such as the advent of a new administration or scheduled presidential summits, as Pastor and Fernández de Castro point out. Scholars who want to participate in the policy process should understand that windows of opportunity are more often opened than encountered. To anticipate potential openings, they need to think empathetically about what motivates policymakers and how decisions are made. Analyses of when and how policy windows can be developed are good questions for social scientists to address.[47]

This volume clearly demonstrates that scholars can and sometimes do find ways to bridge the scholar-policymaker gap and that they can derive significant personal and professional satisfaction from doing so. Young scholars who want to combine academic careers with "making a difference" beyond their disciplines and beyond the campus should find strong encouragement here.

As the chapters by Casas-Zamora, Heredia, Jaquette, and Lustig poignantly illustrate, a prime requisite for scholars who want to participate in the policymaking process is to have data, concepts, and analysis that are useful to those with policy responsibility. Scholars who want to affect policy should ask themselves what specific policy issues they want to engage and why. They should identify, preferably in consultation with relevant practitioners, what questions need to be answered with regard to these issues. They should consider how best to address these questions, drawing on their substantive expertise and preferred methods of inquiry, and how to generate findings that they (and/or others) can convey to policymakers in accessible terms.

Scholars who aim to cross the academic-policy divide should commit themselves to all phases of this sequence. They should choose research questions that interest them, at least in part, because of their policy relevance, in addition to but independent of what they contribute to theory building in the discipline. They should conduct their research in an analytically rigorous fashion, by no means abandoning their academic and intellectual standards. They should decide, and then reconsider at various stages of their career, whether they are most likely to be engaged comfortably by entering the policymaking sphere directly for a time, or whether they prefer to participate in policy-relevant activities one or two steps removed. They can do this in university departments, in university-based research centers or institutes, or in think tanks or other intermediary institutions, including commissions and study groups, intergovernmental and international organizations, foundations, NGOs, transnational networks, and consulting firms. There are many different institutional niches where significant policy-related and policy-relevant research can be conducted and from which its results can be channeled, often effectively, into policymaking processes. For individual scholars, different vantage points will work best at different stages.

Wherever they sit, scholars with an interest in affecting policies should certainly invest in learning how to communicate their plausibly policy-relevant results in ways that can connect with the concerns and the vocabulary of policymakers. All scholars, even those who stoutly resist policy involvement, should certainly be able and encouraged to crisply explain their research questions and why these are important, to state their findings concisely, and to explain what practical difference, if any, their findings might make. Improving their skills at communicating and articulating these points will help scholars connect with policymakers and opinion shapers, if they wish, as well as in many other ways.[48]

Scholars who choose to connect with the policy world will have to learn new skills to increase the likelihood that they will have an impact: presenting oral briefings, preparing extremely brief policy memoranda, meeting strict and immediate deadlines, and learning how to ensure that a meeting achieves its desired outcome.[49] They will encounter predictable tensions that they must manage—between rigor and relevance, access and autonomy, certainty and timeliness, individual recognition and effectiveness in influencing policies. They will also have to confront the normative implications of their research. Learning how to identify, sort out, and deal with all these tensions is part of the bridging challenge for scholars, whose vocation, after all, is to continue learning.

Finding good mentors is perhaps the best way to prepare for this. Having skillful and dedicated mentors facilitates effectiveness in the policy world, as in many other spheres, and there is often an element of serendipity in connecting with such mentors. Serendipity happens most often to those who are prepared for it, however. Mentorship arises more often from protégés' actively seeking mentors than from established figures' seeking protégés.

Connections are more likely to be made and to produce benefits, no doubt, if they are fashioned from both sides. Government officials, senior officers of international organizations, and others in policymaking roles can readily increase the prospects for fruitful interactions with scholars. They can send signals—by convening small meetings or consulting individual scholars, for example—that they are actively interested in the perspectives of academic specialists. These specialists are often well informed about the countries with which the policymakers are dealing and/or with the substantive agenda or issue domain, and they usually have had more time than policymakers to analyze recent trends and their implications.

Sending ambassadors or other policymakers to campuses to give "outreach" speeches does not usually advance meaningful scholar-policymaker dialogue. But organizing the participation of officials in reasonably frank, off-the-record discussion with selected academic experts can be substantively fruitful and can open channels and build relationships for further and more concerted interaction. Officials who reach out to scholars and other qualified outsiders to solicit feedback on policy issues and on draft policy statements can attract valuable interlocutors, whose ideas and advice may help them do their jobs. Similarly, scholars who test their own ideas and drafts with relevant policymakers, after building the necessary personal relationships, can obtain valuable information and perspectives from officials with unique sources of information and insight. Not all gifted analysts of international relations work in the academic world, nor do all insights on diplomacy come from professional diplomats. Cross-fertilization can produce added value.

Policymakers can also take the initiative of identifying what puzzles or surprises them with regard to the issues they are handling, and why, and they can try to specify what information and comparative experience they might find most helpful in resolving these conundrums in order to deal with the issues they must manage. Professional diplomats are often superb at recording, reporting, and analyzing what is said to them, but are sometimes less creative at identifying the questions they should be asking and the conversations they should initiate. Academic interlocutors can be effective partners with policymakers in framing more useful inquiries. Indeed, concerted efforts by scholars and policymakers to formulate researchable questions collaboratively could pay rich dividends for both.[50]

Experienced policymakers should take fuller advantage of diplomat-in-residence programs, "professor of the practice" university appointments, on-campus workshops, and participation in transnational policy networks to exchange ideas with scholars, seeking ways to supplement each other's insights. Working together, academic and policy entrepreneurs should be especially attentive to opportunities to map new or particularly challenging policy issues and to develop alternative ways to confront them. Involving policymakers in the design of policy-relevant research projects can be a particularly effective way of simultaneously improving the quality of research and the connections necessary to obtain data and convey the results of the research to policymakers, as Biersteker suggests.

Toward More Fruitful Connections: Suggestions for Action

We conclude by highlighting some suggestions, keyed to particular actors, to foster more fruitful connections between scholars and policymakers on international affairs. Some of our proposals are no doubt easier said than done, which does not mean they should not be tried. Even useful ideas must be considered, of course, in the light of available resources, competing imperatives, and opportunity costs, but one way to be sure that ideas will not be influential is never to offer them.

US universities are widely appreciated for their capacity to foster innovation. In truth, however, many university departments in political science and international relations today exhibit a rather conservative deference to what have become the dominant trends in the discipline. Scholars who aspire not only to expand academic knowledge but to make a difference on policy questions are routinely advised by their professors and peers to focus exclusively on writing books and articles for university presses and the top-ranked peer-reviewed academic journals, as only these publications will count for earning tenure and for subsequent merit reviews and promotion.

As Stephen Walt points out, the norms in academic departments that discourage scholars from striving for policy relevance are not divinely ordained; they are collectively determined by members of the discipline, and they can be and are being challenged.[51] Like Walt and Michael Desch, we believe that policy relevance should be elevated as a criterion of evaluation, together with rigor, empirical validity, and creativity.[52] Senior university administrators—deans, provosts, presidents—should push back against the tendency of many academic departments to devalue policy-relevant work. Without diluting the standards for rigorous social science research, they should encourage scholars not only to publish the results of their research in learned journals but also to address policy audiences and, where appropriate, the broader public. Publication in such journals as *Foreign Affairs*, *Foreign Policy*, *Journal of Democracy*, the *Washington Quarterly*, the *American Interest*, the *Wilson Quarterly*, *The American Prospect*, and *Perspectives on Politics*, or in equivalent journals in other countries—as well as participation in policy-focused study groups and commissions, track-two activities, and the media—should be included in annual faculty reports and taken into account in tenure and promotion reviews. Scholars who engage in policy-relevant activities might be invited to provide information about this, together with suggested methods for assessing their work beyond academia.

These activities should also be highlighted by departments in their reports to senior university officers and to funding sources and prospects. Such publications and activities are often scholars' most visible and influential work, even for academic colleagues outside their particular disciplinary subfield. They should be evaluated and valued as such for their contributions to research, teaching, public policy, and citizen understanding. The fact that people outside an academic discipline read and gain from a scholar's work should be recognized, not ignored or derided.

To more consistently recognize policy-relevant publications based on rigorous research, university authorities should award prizes at academic convocations, highlighting such work while also showcasing the university's social relevance. Scholars and donors who want to send similar signals might cooperate in establishing awards in political science and international studies associations to recognize academic contributions to international policymaking. University authorities should encourage departments to provide tangible support for scholars who want to spend a period of leave in government, international organizations, or other policy-making environments and provide ways for them to draw on such experience in their subsequent teaching and research. An important concrete step would be to stop the "tenure clock" for a period of immersion in active policy work. Particularly in schools of public policy and international affairs, but also more generally, faculty with policy experience should be encouraged to bring active policymakers and recently retired senior officials to campuses for structured exchanges with faculty and students and for consultation on research projects.

Scholars with policy interests should invest limited but focused energy in building networks: with other scholars working on shared issues; with personnel from governments, international organizations, and NGOs who have related interests; and with journalists and bloggers who cover these topics. By framing useful questions for consideration, they can put themselves at the center of such networks—reinforcing their own contributions, visibility, and influence, as well as the other professional benefits they derive. Junior scholars and graduate students can contribute to and gain from such networks; they can make themselves indispensable by preparing and circulating bibliographical reviews and rapporteurial summaries of seminars on significant issues. Senior scholars should actively look for opportunities to introduce younger colleagues and graduate students to the meeting spaces for scholar-policymaker interaction and to internships and mentoring opportunities.

University-based institutes or centers for international affairs and for area studies can play distinct and important roles in connecting academic expertise with the policy process. An institute or center, separate from a disciplinary department, makes most sense when it plays a catalytic role in causing things to happen that would not otherwise occur—such as interdisciplinary research, collaborative research, and research intended to be useful beyond academia to the policy community. Topics particularly appropriate for research in university-based institutes rather than in Washington think tanks are those dealing with medium- and long-term tendencies, those requiring a rethinking of concepts, frameworks, and assumptions, and those likely to benefit greatly from an exchange of ideas and perspectives across disciplinary or scholar-practitioner divides. University-based centers should tackle such questions, especially those with policy implications, rather than concentrate primarily on replicating or supporting the work of disciplinary departments.[53]

Think tanks—independent institutions that conduct or draw on research to analyze policy issues and frame recommendations—are vital bridges between the academic and policy worlds, especially in the United States but increasingly in other countries of the Americas, Europe, Asia, the Middle East, and Africa.[54] Scholars can help think tanks tease out the policy implications of academic research by designing and carrying out projects that reframe problems, evaluate the consequences of policies, or compare the likely impact of alternative policy options.

Think tanks, in turn, can help scholars learn how to draw more effectively on their research to fashion brief and engaging statements of policy-relevant conclusions and implications, thus helping them "translate" academic and technical language into more user-friendly terms.[55] They can mentor scholars on how to write for policymakers, as well as for policy journals, op-eds, and specialized blogs. Think tanks can also develop and draw on comparative advantages to deliver substantive content to concentric circles of prospective audiences: executive decision makers in governments and international organizations and their staffs, legislators and their staffs, relevant civil society organizations, corporations and other interest groups, the media, and others in the attentive public who help shape the political contexts and constraints that frame policy debates.

Think tanks could do even more to build bridges between scholars and policymakers. They can ask those who make policy to pose questions for which academic research could be helpful to them and then identify or commission scholars to take up these questions, thus serving as brokers. Think tanks can also exercise a "periscope" function, consulting with scholars of international relations and comparative politics as well as policymakers to identify and explore emerging issues on the horizon for which academic analysis might be helpful. They can commission and conduct studies on these and make sure that the resulting analyses and recommendations are made available to policymakers when the issue reaches their in-boxes. The Peterson Institute for International Economics, directed from 1977 until 2013 by C. Fred Bergsten, provides a model for doing this successfully, featuring annual retreats to identify issues not yet on the front burner on which research should be initiated.

Further, think tanks can train future bridge builders by involving graduate students and young scholars in policy-relevant projects, teaching the skills and attitudes necessary to build professional competence and relevant networks in both worlds, and helping them connect to and develop such networks.[56] The International Affairs Fellowships (IAF) offered by the Council on Foreign Relations provide a good model for doing so, by arranging for scholars to devote up to a year to working in a policymaking environment, but in recent years it has become more difficult to attract academic applicants who meet the program's age limit (no more than 35 years).[57] University encouragement for young scholars to seek such exceptional opportunities —not only the IAF program but posts offered by the World Bank and other agencies —by stopping the tenure clock in such cases could make a crucial difference.[58]

Such private foundations as Ford, Rockefeller, Hewlett, and MacArthur, the Carnegie Corporation of New York, and the Rockefeller Brothers Fund used to be the most important funding sources for strengthening academic work on comparative politics, area studies, and international relations, and for supporting policy-relevant work in university centers and at think tanks. This support declined drastically in recent years, however, as academic work became much less connected to pressing international issues and as foundations turned to other priorities.

With a turbulent world in flux and many old paradigms no longer apt, the time is ripe for thoughtfully crafted foundation investments in policy-relevant research on key international trends and issues and in fostering more fruitful connections between the next generation of scholars working on emerging international questions and those with policymaking responsibilities. Important positive steps in this direction are the Bridging the Gap program jointly established in 2007 by American University, Duke University, and the University of California, Berkeley, mainly supported by the Carnegie Corporation of New York; the Teaching and Research in International Policy project at the College of William and Mary; the Carnegie Policy Relevance Project at the University of Notre Dame; and the Tobin Project, supported by the Carnegie Corporation and by the John D. and Catherine T. MacArthur Foundation.[59] More such initiatives are needed, particularly to ensure that young internationalists get enough meaningful experience abroad and that adequate mentoring with role models is provided for graduate students and young scholars interested in policy-relevant research, as well as to ensure the application of rigorous social science to important policy issues, evaluations, and assessments.

Policy journals such as *Foreign Affairs* and *Foreign Policy* should become more proactive in seeking contributions from scholars on the policy implications of their work and in eliciting academic critiques of the essays they publish or consider for publication. It might be worthwhile to include a section, a couple of times a year, highlighting academic work in progress that has implications for international policy, thus offering a window into potentially relevant research that otherwise would long remain invisible to the foreign policy community. Peer-reviewed academic journals, too, could usefully include, as one of their criteria for evaluating submitted manuscripts, whether the analysis provides any value relevant to policy, as *International Security* does; surely it should count for something when a scholarly article provides worth beyond the academy. Such university-based, student-managed journals as *Harvard International Review*, the *Brown Journal of World Affairs*, *The Fletcher Forum of World Affairs*, the *SAIS Review of International Affairs*, and *Columbia Journal of International Affairs* could play more active roles in stimulating and publishing scholar-practitioner dialogue and exchange on well-posed questions.

Government offices, international and intergovernmental institutions, and NGOs all play important roles in conducting and commissioning policy-relevant research and in connecting with scholars and their work. The World Bank, the Inter-American Development Bank, the United Nations Development Program and other UN programs, the International Development Research Centre in Canada, and the Department for International Development in the United Kingdom are all good examples. So are the US National Intelligence Council, the US State

Department's Office of Intelligence and Research, the National Endowment for Democracy and its International Forum for Democratic Studies, the International Institute for Democracy and Electoral Assistance, and various other national and international agencies that have important relevant assets and felt needs for policy-relevant academic research. Often, however, these organizations work with limited numbers of favored consultants, losing the advantages of casting a wider net. We recommend more frequent use and wider distribution of requests for proposals on well-posed questions, as well as more frequent and structured interaction by such agencies with scholars who share their concerns, developing research agendas in a more interactive way. The role of Brown University's Watson Institute in developing and extending the transnational policy network on targeted financial sanctions illustrates how much could be gained by more active cultivation of links between universities and action agencies, as does MIT's Energy Initiative, which engages social scientists, natural scientists, engineers, planners, and business school faculty; there are other good examples.

Our final advice is offered to graduate students and young scholars who want to have successful academic careers as social scientists in universities but also hope to have meaningful opportunities to help improve the quality of public and international policies. Our conviction that combining these roles may not be as difficult as contemporary academic lore suggests was one of the motivations for preparing this volume.

The conventional wisdom, even among those senior scholars who have themselves successfully combined academic and policy roles, is that junior scholars should postpone any attempt to do so until after they have been awarded tenure.[60] That advice may be wise in some cases and contexts, given procedures in many academic departments.

We are inclined, however, to offer different counsel. Young scholars with strong training and disciplinary prowess as social scientists who are passionate about applying their skills to important issues beyond the discipline should not be forced to repress their passion in order to be accepted into the academic guild, nor should they be forced to live a double life, hiding their policy-relevant interests. They should, of course, hone their scholarly methods and apply them rigorously to a dissertation, a book, and peer-reviewed publications. But we think that such scholars are well advised to begin early to develop skills that will serve them well both inside and beyond the academic world. They should be encouraged to test the relevance of their work to policy issues, learn to interact with policymakers, communicate with those who respect academic methods but also want to confront problems that require attention, and develop policy-relevant networks.

Cultivating and reinforcing, early in one's career, the habits of mind, modes of conduct, and styles of communication and self-presentation that facilitate linking with the policy process and the broader community may eventually turn out to be as important to a scholar's own sense of accomplishment, and to his or her professional visibility and stature, as an extra academic publication or two. We would urge young scholars to consider writing a policy journal article or two early in their careers, soon after their first academic publications and perhaps drawing on them; to participate in policy task forces and conferences on issues close to their expertise; to learn how to conduct interviews with leaders in governments, business, international institutions, and civil society organizations; and to translate their research findings into policy-friendly prose. They should also use university committee assignments, as well as opportunities outside the university, to learn how consensus is formed and how decisions are implemented (or not). They should seek out and work with mentors who have had experience in the policy arena, just as they seek out academic mentors. Above all, they should develop the skills for clear and direct communication, written and oral. Both academia itself and the broader community will share the fruits of these early investments.

The time is at hand for concerted efforts to enhance the likelihood that some academic work in comparative politics and international relations will be useful for understanding and confronting policy conundrums: from mitigating the effects of climate change to constructing democratic governance; from strengthening international norms on human trafficking or labor standards to bolstering conflict-resolution processes and building durable peace. Pursuing this aim is not counter to assuring the use of sound and rigorous methods. On the contrary, dealing with such meaningful questions can help political scientists and other scholars to improve their research methods and products and to think harder about what difference their work might make, to whom, and how and why.

ACKNOWLEDGMENTS

We gratefully acknowledge helpful comments on earlier drafts of this chapter by Thomas Biersteker, Paul Evans, Rafael Fernández de Castro, Claudia Fuentes-Julio, Kevin Gallagher, Eric Hamilton, Blanca Heredia, Jane Jaquette, Bruce Jentleson, Chappell Lawson, Richard Locke, Michael Lowenthal, James McGuire, Richard Snyder, Pamela Starr, Laurence Whitehead, and Ernest Wilson.

NOTES

1. This gap has not always existed in the United States in political science, and the relationship between academia and policymaking seems less distant today in some parts of Latin America and Asia. In its first several decades as a discipline, political science in the United States was dominated by scholars who participated actively in public affairs. Woodrow Wilson, Charles Merriam, James Bryce, and Harold Lasswell are examples, as were such pioneers in the study of politics as Aristotle, Machiavelli, and Hobbes, who brought their studies to bear on the polity by advising rulers. Even in recent decades, political science—and, specifically, work in comparative politics and international relations in the United States—has featured prominent roles in international policymaking by such scholars as Zbigniew Brzezinski, McGeorge Bundy, Michael Doyle, Francis Fukuyama, Samuel Huntington, Henry Kissinger, Stephen Krasner, Joseph Nye, Condoleezza Rice, John Ruggie, Anne Marie Slaughter, Stephen Stedman, and others. During the course of the twentieth century, and especially since the 1960s, tensions about power and policy and their relation to academic inquiry produced increasing distance between the spheres of social science analysis and public policymaking. This separation is perceptively discussed by Lisa Anderson in *Pursuing Truth, Exercising Power: Social Science and Public Policy in the Twenty-first Century* (New York: Columbia University Press, 2003).

Combined careers in academia, politics, and policy are not uncommon in contemporary Latin America, where such holders of social science PhDs as Fernando Henrique Cardoso, Ricardo Lagos, Sebastian Piñera, Rafael Correa, Carlos Salinas, Ernesto Zedillo, and Felipe Calderón have served as presidents in the past three decades, and where almost every finance minister in recent years has had an international PhD in economics. The foreign ministries of a number of Latin American countries, especially Chile, have incorporated numerous scholars into their senior ranks. See, for example, Jorge I. Domínguez, ed., *Technopols: Freeing Politics and Markets in Latin America in the 1990s* (University Park: Penn State University Press, 1997); Juan Gabriel Valdés, *Pinochet's Economists: The Chicago School in Chile* (New York: Cambridge University Press, 1995); and Jorge Heine, "Scholars, Practitioners and Inter-American Relations: Chile's Experience," memorandum prepared for the International Workshop on Scholars and Practitioners, Center for International Studies, University of Southern California (USC), 2011.

2. Lisa Anderson quotes David Featherman, former president of the Social Science Research Council, as observing that "it is perhaps ironic that academics in disciplines such as economics, political science and sociology—in their quest for professional integrity and scientific objectivity—may have unintentionally undermined these disciplines' long term relevance to policy and thereby conceded the main battlefield to the private, often partisan, think tanks." David L. Featherman and Morris A. Vinovskis, eds., *Social Science and Policymaking: The Search for Relevance in the Twentieth Century* (Ann Arbor: University of Michigan Press, 2001), 2, as quoted in Anderson, *Pursuing Truth,* 47. See also Joseph Lepgold and Miroslav Nincic, *Beyond the Ivory Tower: International Relations Theory and the Issue of Policy Relevance* (New York: Columbia University Press, 2001), and Stephen M. Walt, "Rigor or Rigor Mortis? Rational Choice and Security Studies," *International Security* 23 (1999): 5–48.

A mordant discussion of the growing irrelevance of international relations theory to policy is provided by James Kurth, who argues that "rational choice" theory and "postmodern theory" have taken over the academic study of international relations but are utterly without "interest and relevance to anyone outside of themselves." James Kurth, "Inside the Cave: The Banality of IR Studies," *National Interest* 53 (Fall 1998): 29–40. A more balanced, nuanced, and constructive discussion of the gaps between international relations theory building, policy analysis, and policymaking is Philip Zelikow, "Foreign Policy Engineering: From Theory to Practice and Back Again," *International Security* 18 (Spring 1994): 143–71.

A different but not unrelated point is that much of the academic work on international relations today has shifted away from rigorous theorizing to simplistic hypothesis testing, with the result that the research is less useful both for building the discipline and for policy debates. For a provocative argument on this point, see John J. Mearsheimer and Stephen M. Walt, "Leaving Theory Behind: Why Simplistic Hypothesis Testing Is Bad for International Relations," *European Journal of International Relations* 19 (2013): 427–57.

3. Indeed, we agree on the whole with Roland Paris that scholarly ideas often do percolate into policy discourse, thus shaping the ways in which key actors define and respond to policy problems; and therefore that "the much lamented gap between the work of scholars and practitioners may be less pronounced, and understandably more complex, than is often assumed." Roland Paris, "Ordering the World: Academic Research and Policymaking on Fragile States," *International Studies Review* 13 (2100): 58–71, esp. 67.

4. This appears to be true at ITAM (Instituto Tecnológico Autónomo de México) and CIDE (Centro de Investigación y Docencia Económicas) in Mexico, the Los Andes University in Bogotá, the University of Chile in Santiago, and Di Tella University in Buenos Aires, among other places. Rafael Fernández de Castro emphasizes this point in a personal communication, and it corresponds with our observations.

5. Alexander George discusses the importance of judgment in policymaking, distinguishing key roles that policymakers must often exercise: evaluating tradeoffs, assessing multiple and sometimes contradictory risks, determining the relative importance of short-term and longer-run considerations, deciding whether to optimize or to satisfice, dealing with value complexities, and determining appropriate timing. Competence in the social sciences does not necessarily equip scholars with comparative advantages in considering such issues. See Alexander L. George, *Bridging the Gap: Theory and Practice in Foreign Affairs* (Washington, DC: United States Institute of Peace, 1993), 22–28. See also Stanley Renshon and Deborah Welch Larson, eds., *Good Judgment in Foreign Policy: Theory and Application* (Lanham, MD: Rowman and Littlefield, 2003).

6. These points are emphasized in this volume by Lawson, Pastor, Jaquette, Biersteker, and Fernández de Castro, and they are often mentioned in the literature. See, for example, works by Lisa Anderson, Michael Desch, Alexander George, Emily Goldman, Bruce Jentleson, Joseph Lepgold and Miroslav Nincic, Thomas Mahnken, David Newsom, Joseph Nye, Stephen Walt, Ernest Wilson, and Philip Zelikow cited in the bibliography of this volume; two edited forums, J. Ann Tickner and Andrei Tsygankov, eds., "Risks and Opportunities of Crossing the Academy/Policy Divide," *International Studies Review* 10 (2008): 155–77, and Thomas G. Weiss and Anoular Kittikhoun, eds., "Theory vs. Practice: A Symposium," *International Studies Review*: 13 (2011): 1–23; a symposium, "The Relevance of Comparative

Politics for Public Life," *APSA-CP* 14, no. 2 (Summer 2003); and a cluster of autobiographical reflections by leading political scientists on bridging the policy-academy divide published in the *Cambridge Review of International Affairs* 22 (2009): 111–28.

7. Roberto Suro, "Scholars, Practitioners and Inter-American Relations: Immigration," memorandum prepared for the International Workshop on Scholars and Practitioners, Center for International Studies, USC, 2011.

8. See, for example, John Williamson and Pedro Pablo Kuczynski, eds., *After the Washington Consensus: Restoring Growth and Reform in Latin America* (Washington, DC: Peterson Institute for International Economics, 2003); Michael E. Latham, *Modernization as Ideology: American Social Science and "Nation Building" in the Kennedy Era* (Chapel Hill: University of North Carolina Press, 2000); Robert Packenham, *Liberal America in the Third World* (Princeton, NJ: Princeton University Press, 1973); Mark Blyth, *Austerity: The History of a Dangerous Idea* (New York: Oxford University Press, 2013); and Jeffry Frieden and Menzie Chinn, *Lost Decades: The Making of America's Debt Crisis and the Long Recovery* (New York: W. W. Norton, 2011).

9. These dangers are highlighted in Christopher Hill, "Academic International Relations: The Siren Song of Policy Relevance," in *Two Worlds of International Relations: Academics, Practitioners, and the Trade in Ideas*, ed. Christopher Hill and Pamela Beschoff (New York: Routledge, 1994). See also Robert Keohane, "Beware the Bad Fairy: Cautionary Note for the Academic in the Policy Realm," *Cambridge Review of International Affairs* 22, no. 1 (2009), 124–28; Janice Gross Stein, "Evolutionary Hubris, False Certainty, and Structural Skepticism: The Academic-Policy Divide," *Cambridge Review of International Affairs* 22, no. 1 (2009), 120–24; Amitav Acharya, "Engagement or Entrapment? Scholarship and Policymaking on Asian Regionalism," *International Studies Review* 13 (Mar. 2011): 12–17; and Stanley Hoffmann, "An American Social Science: International Relations," *Daedalus* 106 (Summer 1977): 41–60.

10. For thoughtful introductions to these issues, see Laurence Whitehead, chap. 14, this volume, and Andrew Hurrell, "The Theory and Practice of Global Governance: The Worst of All Possible Worlds?" *International Studies Review* 13 (Mar. 2011): 144–54.

11. Stephen Krasner, "Government and Academia: A Chasm Not a Gap," memorandum presented at the USC workshop, a revised version of "Government and Academia: Never the Twain Shall Meet, Well Almost Never," *Cambridge Review of International Affairs* 22 (2009): 111–16. Similar comments, expressed less provocatively, have been made by many scholars. See, for example, Daniel W. Drezner, "Gartzke on Policy, Political Science, and Zombies," *Foreignpolicy.com*, February 27, 2011, http://drezner.foreignpolicy.com/posts/2011/02/27/gartzke _on_policy_political_science_and_zombies (accessed Feb. 17, 2014), and Hurrell, "Theory and Practice of Global Governance."

12. All the chapters in this book, in different ways and to different degrees, illustrate this point. In addition to the references cited in n. 6 above, see also writings by Richard Betts, Kenneth Lieberthal, Robert Putnam, Ezra Vogel, and Philip Zelikow listed in the bibliography.

13. The academic lore is replete with statements discouraging work on policy. A classic formulation is Hedley Bull's dictum: "The prostitution of inquiry to practical ends is the foremost obstacle to the development of the science of politics." Hedley Bull, "What Is the Commonwealth?" *World Politics* 11 (July 1959): 587. Statements from the other end of the spectrum can be equally dismissive. Governor Chris Christie of New Jersey said, for example,

"College professors basically spout out ideas that nobody ever does anything about." Quoted in Maureen Dowd, "Less Bully, More Pulpit," *New York Times*, August 28, 2013, A-23.

14. For example, Robert Jervis, *Why Intelligence Fails: Lessons from the Iranian Revolution and the Iraq War* (Ithaca, NY: Cornell University Press, 2011); Richard Solomon, *Chinese Negotiating Behavior: Pursuing Interests through "Old Friends"* (New York: United States Institute of Peace, 1999); and Alexander L. George, "The 'Operational Code': A Neglected Approach to the Study of Political Leaders and Decision-Making," *International Studies Quarterly* 13 (June 1969): 190–204.

15. This has been the case, for example, on issues ranging from US-China security relations and the interpretation of bureaucratic changes in China's government to the negotiation of North Korea's nuclear program. See Kenneth Lieberthal, "Initiatives to Bridge the Gap," *Asia Policy* 1 (Jan. 2006): 8–10.

16. At one point during the Carter administration, for example, different National Security Council staff members working on Iran and Nicaragua were dealing at the same time with similar issues, arising from the need to disentangle the United States from long-term intimate relations with failing autocrats, but without realizing how many comparable issues, also faced in previous situations, they were dealing with. Robert Pastor, *Condemned to Repetition: The United States and Nicaragua* (Princeton, NJ: Princeton University Press, 1987); Gary Sick, *All Fall Down: America's Tragic Encounter with Iran* (New York: Random House, 1986); Martin Staniland, *Falling Friends: The United States and Regime Change Abroad* (Boulder, CO: Westview Press, 1991).

17. See Alexander George and Andrew Bennett, "Case Studies and Policy-Relevant Theory," in *Case Studies and Theory Development in the Social Sciences*, ed. Alexander George and Andrew Bennett (Cambridge, MA: MIT Press, 2005), 263–85; Charles E. Lindblom and David K. Cohen, *Usable Knowledge: Social Science and Social Problem Solving* (New Haven, CT: Yale University Press, 1979); and Bruce Jentleson, "In Pursuit of Praxis: Applying International Relations Theory to Foreign Policymaking," in *Being Useful: Policy Relevance and International Relations Theory*, ed. Miroslav Nincic and Joseph Lepgold (Ann Arbor: University of Michigan Press, 2000),129–49.

18. See, for example, Kathryn Sikkink, *The Justice Cascade: How Human Rights Prosecutions Are Changing World Politics* (New York: W. W. Norton, 2011); David Forsythe, "Forum: Transitional Justice: The Quest for Theory to Inform Policy," *International Studies Review* 13 (2011): 554–78; Bruce W. Jentleson, "Economic Sanctions and Post-War Conflicts: Challenges for Theory and Policy," in *International Conflict Resolution after the Cold War*, ed. Paul C. Stern and Daniel Druckman (Washington, DC: National Academy Press, 2000); Robert A. Pape, "Why Economic Sanctions Do Not Work," *International Security* 22 (Fall 1997): 90–136; Daniel Drezner, *The Sanctions Paradox: Economic Statecraft and International Relations* (New York: Cambridge University Press, 1999); Alexander L. George and Richard Smoke, *Deterrence in American Foreign Policy: Theory and Practice* (New York: Columbia University Press, 1974); William Zartman, *Negotiation and Conflict Management—Essays on Theory and Practice* (Oxford: Routledge, 2008); Stephen J. Stedman, Donald Rothschild, and Elizabeth Cousens, *Ending Civil Wars: The Implementation of Peace Agreements* (Boulder, CO: Lynne Rienner, 2002); Stephen Stedman, Thomas Ohlson, and Robert Davies, *New Is Not Yet Born: Conflict Resolution in Southern Africa* (Washington, DC: Brookings Institution Press,

1994); Robert Axelrod, *The Evolution of Cooperation* (New York: Basic Books, 2006); Dale R. Herspring, *Civil-Military Relations and Shared Responsibility: A Four Nation Study* (Baltimore: Johns Hopkins University Press, 2018); Judith G. Kelley, *Monitoring Democracy: When International Election Observation Works, and Why It Often Fails* (Princeton, NJ: Princeton University Press, 2012); and Robert Keohane, *After Hegemony: Cooperation and Discord on the World Political Economy* (Princeton, NJ: Princeton University Press, 1984).

19. Several such studies are presented by Richard E. Neustadt and Ernest R. May in *Thinking in Time: The Uses of History for Decision-Makers* (New York: Free Press, 1986). Lowenthal's edited volume *Exporting Democracy: The United States and Latin America* (Baltimore: Johns Hopkins University Press, 1993) provides further examples of such work.

20. See Abhijit Banerjee and Esther Duflo, *Poor Economics: A Radical Rethinking of the Way to Fight Global Poverty* (New York: Public Affairs, 2012).

21. See, for instance, James Habyarimana, Macartan Humphreys, Daniel Posner, and Jeremy Weinstein, *Coethnicity: Diversity and the Dilemmas of Collective Action* (New York: Russell Sage Foundation, 2010); David Weil, *The Fissured Workplace: Why Work Became So Bad for So Many and What Can Be Done to Improve It* (Cambridge, MA: Harvard University Press, 2013); and Richard M. Locke, *The Promise and Limits of Private Power: Promoting Labor Standards in a Global Economy* (New York: Cambridge University Press, 2013).

22. See, for example, Jennifer Ramos, *Changing Norms through Actions: The Evolution of Sovereignty* (New York: Oxford University Press, 2013), and Anoular Kittikhoum, "The Myth of Scholarly Irrelevance for the United Nations," *International Policy Review* 13 (2011): 18–23.

23. See Ernest R. May, *Lessons of the Past: The Use and Misuse of History in American Foreign Policy* (New York: Oxford University Press, 1973), 52–86, analyzing the role of dubious analogies in shaping Truman's decisions regarding Korea in 1950. Cf. Graham Allison, *Essence of Decision: Explaining the Cuban Missile Crisis* (Boston: Little, Brown, 1971), which introduced new ways of thinking about foreign policy decisions, both to academia and to the policy world. A good example of challenging a simplistic concept is Robert S Litwak's discussion of the "rogue state" rubric in *Rogue States and US Foreign Policy: Containment after the Cold War* (Washington, DC: Woodrow Wilson Center Press, distributed by Johns Hopkins University Press, 2000).

24. Alexander George illustrates this way of contributing in his study "The Inadequate Knowledge Base of US Policy toward Iraq, 1988–91," in his *Bridging the Gap*, 33–103. Scholars contributed to formulating new strategies in the recasting of US policy toward China from containment to engagement, as Stephen Krasner emphasizes in "Conclusion: Garbage Cans and Policy Streams: How Academic Research Might Affect Foreign Policy," in *Power, the State, and Sovereignty: Essays on International Relations*, ed. Stephen Krasner (New York: Routledge, 2009), 254–74. Two studies that illustrate how conceptual models are turned into actual foreign policy strategies are Stephen R. Rock, *Appeasement in International Politics* (Lexington: University Press of Kentucky, 2000), and Bruce Jentleson, ed., *Opportunities Missed, Opportunities Seized* (Lanham, MD: Rowman and Littlefield, 2000).

25. For a thoughtful and eloquent articulation of the civic responsibility of scholars, see Robert D. Putnam's Presidential Address to the Annual Meeting of the American Political Science Association in 2002, "The Public Role of Political Science," *Perspectives on Politics* 1 (June 2003): 249–56. Putnam calls for a more problem-driven political science. Robert Keo-

hane also discusses the scholar's responsibility to address policy problems in "Beware the Bad Fairy."

26. Jacob Hacker is compelling on this point. "A focus on policy forces us to grapple with substance, the significant things that government actually does in real societies . . . [This] serves as a useful corrective to the tendencies of much contemporary political science to veer into discussions of matters deemed trivial by most of the world outside the academy. We need to bring policy back in, not just to better understand what government does, but also to better understand why." Jacob S. Hacker, "Healing the Rift between Political Science and Practical Politics," *The Forum* 8 (2010): 1–7, published by Berkeley Electronic Press.

27. See Thomas J. Biersteker, "Interrelationships between Theory and Practice in International Security Studies," *Security Dialogue* 4, no. 6 (2010), 1–8.

28. Terry Karl, "Not on Your Vita," *APSA-CP* 14 (Summer 2003): 18.

29. See, for example, the testimony by Lawrence Summers in his foreword to Joseph Aldy and Robert Stavins, *Architectures for Agreement: Addressing Global Climate Change in a Post-Kyoto World* (Cambridge: Cambridge University Press, 2007).

30. See Robert Jervis, "Complexity and the Analysis of Political and Social Life," *Political Science Quarterly* 12 (Winter 1997–98): 569–93.

31. Bradley C. Parks and Alena Stern discuss this tendency in "In-and-Outers and Moonlighters: An Evaluation of the Impact of Policy-Making Exposure on IR Scholarship," *International Studies Perspectives* 15 (2014): 73–93.

32. This point is emphasized by Joseph Nye, who attributes his work on nuclear ethics and, later, on the limited utility of unilateralism in US foreign policy to stimulation of his interest in these topics by experience in government. Daniel Drezner makes a similar point in discussing the impact of government experience on his work analyzing the role of great powers in creating and policing international regulatory regimes. See Joseph S. Nye's "The Costs and Benefits of In and Outers," in "Forum: Risks and Opportunities of Crossing the Academy/Policy Divide," ed. J. Ann Tickner and Andrei Tsygankov, *International Studies Review* 10 (2008): 156–60; *Nuclear Ethics* (New York: Free Press, 1988); *The Paradox of American Power: Why the World's Only Superpower Can't Go It Alone* (New York: Oxford University Press, 2003); and "Bridging the Gap between Theory and Policy," *Political Psychology* 29 (2008): 593–603. See also Daniel Drezner, *All Politics Is Global: Explaining International Regulatory Regimes* (Princeton, NJ: Princeton University Press, 2007).

33. See, for example, Iver B. Neumann's study of the Norwegian foreign ministry, *At Home with the Diplomats: Inside a European Foreign Ministry* (Ithaca, NY: Cornell University Press, 2012).

34. Jentleson, "In Pursuit of Praxis," 145–46.

35. According to a recent study, scholars who work on policy issues within governments or international organizations are more likely than those whose policy exposure has been limited to part-time consulting to publish in top policy journals such as *Foreign Affairs* and *Foreign Policy*, presumably because of value gained from their special experience and observation. See Parks and Stern, "In-and-Outers and Moonlighters."

36. The Policy Task Force exercise pioneered at Princeton's Woodrow Wilson School of Public and International Affairs has long been a model and usually relies on faculty guidance by teachers with policy experience. In Lowenthal's experience at USC, students ranked policy task forces among the best courses they had taken because of the skills they developed.

37. Ezra Vogel recounts that when he began working in the National Intelligence Council, he was at first put off by the requirement to adhere to one-page limits for policy briefs, but he soon learned that this constraint forced intellectual discipline, impelling him to think harder about what his most important points were and why. On returning to Harvard, he taught students these skills and discipline. Ezra F. Vogel, "Some Reflections on Policy and Academics," *Asian Policy* 1 (Jan. 2006): 34. A recent book examines the causes and consequences of "bad writing" in the social sciences: Michael Billig, *Learn to Write Badly: How to Succeed in the Social Sciences* (New York: Cambridge University Press, 2013).

38. Heraldo Muñoz, an outstanding scholar-practitioner with a PhD in international relations from the University of Denver, provides examples of the utility in practice of networks forged in academia in his keynote remarks to the USC workshop. Heraldo Muñoz, "Scholars and Practitioners: Reflections from Both Worlds," remarks prepared for delivery at Workshop on Scholars and Practitioners, USC, April 25, 2011.

39. Lisa Anderson discusses this danger in *Pursuing Truth*.

40. This section draws in part on cogent arguments advanced in Joseph Lepgold, "Policy Relevance and Theoretical Development in International Relations: What Have We Learned?" in Nincic and Lepgold, *Being Useful*, 363–80.

41. See the discussion of the tensions and tradeoffs between analytical rigor and contemporary policy relevance, emphasizing the usefulness of methodological pluralism, in Laurence Whitehead, "Twenty-First Century Democratizations: Experience versus Scholarship," in *Democratization: The State of the Art*, ed. Dirk Berg-Schlosser (Opladen, Germany: Barbara Budrich, 2004), 111–32.

42. This point is made in Ernest J. Wilson, "How Social Science Can Help Policymakers: The Relevance of Theory," in Nincic and Lepgold, *Being Useful*, 109–28. For an early appreciation of this distinction, see Abraham F. Lowenthal et al., *The Conduct of Routine Relations: The United States and Latin America*, appendix 1, "The Report of the Commission on the Organization of the Government for the Conduct of Foreign Policy" (Washington, DC: US Government Printing Office, 1975).

43. This point is suggested by Andreas, Pastor, Jaquette, Seligson, and Casas-Zamora in their chapters.

44. See Casas-Zamora, chap. 7, this volume. Jorge Heine shows, by contrast, how a consensus among Chile's experts on international relations that the US government would not link the free trade issue with Chile's opposition to the US position on Iraq at the United Nations convinced Chilean decision makers that it was safe to reject US pressure to fall in line with Washington at the UN Security Council. Heine, "Scholars, Practitioners and Inter-American Relations."

45. Scholars are often able to influence the framing and assessment of policies on intractable issues through think tank reports, essays in policy journals, op-eds, and interviews and in specially convened commissions and study groups. They are able to marshal arguments and gather support until political circumstances bring their ideas to the fore. The experiences of Lowenthal and Pastor in the Linowitz Commission on US–Latin American Relations and of Lowenthal and Michael Shifter in the Inter-American Dialogue provide multiple examples. See Pastor, chap. 2, this volume, and Michael Shifter, "Scholars, Practitioners and Inter-American Relations: The Inter-American Dialogue," and Cynthia Arnson, "Scholars, Practitioners, and Inter-American Relations: The Wilson Center's Latin American Program,"

memoranda prepared for the International Workshop on Scholars and Practitioners, Center for International Studies, USC, 2011. Cf. Chappell Lawson's discussion in chapter 1 of the impact of the Pacific Council / COMEXI joint task force on the border management policies of the Obama and Calderón administrations.

46. The chapters by Lawson, Pastor, and Fernández de Castro illustrate this point. In his memorandum for the USC workshop, Richard E. Feinberg provides good examples of how academic ideas can be drawn on by well-positioned staff within government to shape high-level articulations of policy frameworks. Richard Feinberg, "Scholar-Practitioner Relations: A View from the White House," memorandum prepared for the International Workshop on Scholars and Practitioners, Center for International Studies, USC, 2011. Bruce Jentleson provides other examples in "In Pursuit of Praxis."

47. See, for example, John W. Kingdon, *Agendas, Alternatives, and Public Policies*, 2nd ed. (London: Pearson, 2010), and Leslie Pal, *Beyond Policy Analysis: Public Issue Management in Turbulent Times*, 3rd ed. (Toronto: Nelson Education, 2006).

48. Harvard's Graduate School of Arts and Sciences has been investing in an experimental program, open on a competitive basis to advanced graduate students from all disciplines, that trains students in how to communicate the gist and significance of their work to people outside their discipline. Graduate student participants report that this process clarifies their own thinking about and appreciation of the broader significance of what they are doing, and university administrators suggest that such presentations make it easier to attract financial support for specialized research.

49. Richard N. Haass provides lucid pointers on how to be successful within government policymaking processes in *The Bureaucratic Entrepreneur: How to be Effective in Any Unruly Organization* (Washington DC: Brookings Institution Press, 1999).

50. As Philip Zelikow notes, Adam Yarmolinsky long ago pointed out that much of the problem in scholar-policymaker dialogue stems from the inability of officials to formulate the kind of questions that academics can usefully answer. Adam Yarmolinsky, "How Good Was the Answer? How Good Was the Question?" in *Controversies and Decisions: The Social Sciences and Public Policy*, ed. Charles Frankel (New York: Russell Sage Foundation, 1976), 259–72, as quoted in Zelikow, "Foreign Policy Engineering," 149.

51. Stephen M. Walt, "The Relationship between Theory and Policy in International Relations," *Annual Review of Political Science* 8 (2005): 23–48.

52. See Peter Campbell and Michael C. Desch, "Rank Irrelevance: How Academia Lost Its Way," *Foreign Affairs*, September 15, 2013, and Paul C. Avey and Michael C. Desch, "What Do Policymakers Want from Us? Results of a Survey of Current and Former Senior National Security Decision-Makers," *International Studies Quarterly* 58 (Dec. 2014). Cf. Daniel W. Drezner, "What's Rank in Political Science?" *Foreignpolicy.com*, September 23, 2013, www .foreignpolicy.com/posts/2013/09/23/what_should_matter_in_political_science (accessed Feb. 17, 2014).

53. For a thoughtful and informative discussion of the challenges and opportunities faced by "progressive community-engaged research centers" (PCERCS) within US universities, see Jeffrey O. Sacha, Jared P. Sanchez, Ange-Marie Hancock, and Manuel Pastor, *A Foot in Both Worlds: Institutionalizing Progressive Community-Engaged Research Centers within Universities,*

Los Angeles Program for Environmental and Regional Equity (PERE) (Los Angeles: University of Southern California, December 2013).

54. See, for example, James McGann, *2010 Global Go-To Think Tanks Report*, Think Tanks and Civil Societies Program (Philadelphia: University of Pennsylvania, International Relations Program, 2010), and Diana Stone and Andrew Denham, eds., *Think Tank Traditions: Policy Analysis across Nations* (Manchester, UK: Manchester University Press, 2004).

55. At several Canadian universities—including the University of Toronto and its Munk School of Global Affairs; the University of British Columbia, especially its Institute of Asian Research; the Balsillie School of International Affairs at the University of Waterloo; and the Wilfred Laurier University, in partnership with the Centre for International Governance Innovation—innovative work is being done on "knowledge translation" or "knowledge mobilization" to bring academic work to bear on policy questions. Paul Evans, personal communication.

56. Lowenthal recalls that, when he was writing his dissertation as a research fellow at the Brookings Institution in 1968, the late Kermit Gordon, then president of Brookings, offered him funding to identify promising professionals interested in Latin America and under age 40, from the US government and Latin American embassies, international institutions, NGOs, think tanks, universities, law firms, and the media, to meet monthly for dinner discussions. Identifying and recruiting these young professionals and organizing the dinners jump-started Lowenthal's network.

57. See the data cited in Walt, "Relationship between Theory and Policy," 39.

58. We also urge that the age requirement for the IAF program be eased somewhat to accommodate those interested junior scholars who are strongly advised not to interrupt their academic trajectory before they achieve tenure.

59. See School of International Service, American University, *Bridging the Gap*, www.american.edu/sis/btg.

60. This advice is provided by, among many others, Joseph S. Nye in his "Relevance of Theory to Practice," in *Oxford Handbook of International Relations*, ed. Christian Reus-Smit and Duncan Snidal (New York: Oxford University Press, 2008), 658.

Acharya, Amitav. "Engagement or Entrapment? Scholarship and Policymaking on Asian Regionalism." *International Studies Review* 13 (March 2011): 12–17.

Acheson, Dean. *Present at the Creation: My Years in the State Department.* New York: W. W. Norton, 1987.

Adato, Michelle, and John Hoddinott. *Conditional Cash Transfers in Latin America.* Washington, DC: IFPRI, 2010.

Adler, Patricia A. *Wheeling and Dealing: An Ethnography of an Upper-Level Drug Dealing and Smuggling Community.* New York: Columbia University Press, 1987.

Alderman, Harold. "The Effects of Income and Food Price Changes on the Acquisition of Food by Low-Income Households." International Food Policy Research Institute, draft. Washington, DC: IFPRI, 1984.

Alderman, Harold, and Joachim von Braun. *The Effects of the Egyptian Food Ration and Subsidy System on Income Distribution and Consumption.* Research report 45. Washington, DC: IFPRI, 1984.

Aldy, Joseph, and Robert Stavins. *Architectures for Agreement: Addressing Global Climate Change in a Post-Kyoto World.* Cambridge: Cambridge University Press, 2007.

Allison, Graham T. *Essence of Decision: Explaining the Cuban Missile Crisis.* Boston: Little, Brown, 1971.

Alvarez, Sonia. "Advocating Feminism: The Latin American Feminist NGO 'Boom.'" *International Feminist Journal of Politics* 1 (1999): 181–209.

Anderson, Lisa. *Pursuing Truth, Exercising Power: Social Science and Public Policy in the Twenty-First Century.* New York: Columbia University Press, 2003.

Andreas, Peter. *Border Games: Policing the U.S.-Mexico Divide.* Ithaca, NY: Cornell University Press, 2000.

———. "Scholars, Practitioners, and Drug Policy in U.S.–Latin American Relations." Memorandum prepared for the International Workshop on Scholars and Practitioners. Center for International Studies, University of Southern California, 2011.

Andreas, Peter, Eva Bertram, Morris Blachman, and Kenneth Sharpe. *Drug War Politics: The Price of Denial.* Berkeley: University of California Press, 1996.

Andreas, Peter, and Kelly M. Greenhill. *Sex, Drugs, and Body Counts: The Politics of Numbers in Global Crime and Conflict.* Ithaca, NY: Cornell University Press, 2010.

Andreas, Peter, and Ethan Nadelmann. *Policing the Globe: Criminalization and Crime Control in International Relations.* New York: Oxford University Press, 2006.

Arnson, Cynthia. "Scholars, Practitioners, and Inter-American Relations: The Wilson Center's Latin American Program." Memorandum prepared for the International Workshop on Scholars and Practitioners. Center for International Studies, University of Southern California, 2011.

Axelrod, Robert. *The Evolution of Cooperation.* New York: Basic Books, 2006.

Azpuru, Dinorah, Steve Finkel, Aníbal Pérez Liñán, and Mitchell A. Seligson. "Trends in Democracy Assistance: What Has the U.S. Been Doing?" *Journal of Democracy* 19 (2008): 150–59.

Babb, Sarah. *Managing Mexico: Economists from Nationalism to Neoliberalism.* Princeton, NJ: Princeton University Press, 2004.

Bagley, Bruce, and William O. Walker, eds. *Drug Trafficking in the Americas.* Miami: University of Miami North-South Center, 1994.

Bailey, John, and Jorge Chabat, eds. *Transnational Crime and Public Security: Challenges to Mexico and the United States.* La Jolla, CA: Center for U.S.-Mexican Studies, 2002.

Bakker, Isabella, ed. *The Strategic Silence: Gender and Economic Policy.* London: Zed Books, 1994.

Banerjee, Abhijit, and Esther Duflo. *Poor Economics: A Radical Rethinking of the Way to Fight Global Poverty.* New York: Public Affairs, 2012.

Barham, Tania. "Providing a Healthier Start to Life: The Impact of Conditional Cash Transfers on Infant Mortality." PhD dissertation / working paper. Department of Agriculture and Resource Economics, University of California, Berkeley, 2005.

Barnett, Michael, and Martha Finnemore. "The Politics, Power, and Pathologies of International Organizations." *International Organization* 53 (1999): 699–732.

Basu, Amrita. *Women's Movements in a Global Era.* Boulder, CO: Westview Press, 2010.

Bateman, Milford. *Confronting Microfinance: Undermining Sustainable Development.* Boulder, CO: Kumarian Press, 2011.

Bautista, Sergio, et al. "Impacto de Oportunidades en la Morbilidad y el Estado de Salud de la Población Beneficiaria y en la Utilización de Servicios de Salud: Resultados de Corto Plazo en Zonas Urbanas y de Mediano Plazo en Zonas Rurales." In *Evaluación externa de impacto del programa Oportunidades.* Book 2, *Salud.* Edited by Bernardo Hernández and Mauricio Hernández. Mexico City: CIESAS/INSP, 2004.

Behrman, Jere R. "Health and Nutrition." In *Handbook on Economic Development.* Volume 1. Edited by Hollis B. Chenery and T. N. Srinivasan. Amsterdam: North Holland Publishing, 1988.

———. *Policy-Oriented Research Impact Assessment (Poria) Case Study on the International Food Policy Research Institute (IFPRI) and the Mexican Progresa Anti-Poverty and Human Resource Investment Conditional Cash Transfer Program.* Impact Assessment Discussion Paper No. 27. Washington, DC: IFPRI, December 2007.

Behrman, Jere R., and Anil B. Deolalikar. "Will Developing Country Nutrition Improve with Income? A Case Study for Rural South India." *Journal of Political Economy* 95 (June 1987): 108–38.

Behrman, Jere R., and John Hoddinott. "Program Evaluation with Unobserved Heterogeneity and Selective Implementation: The Mexican *Progresa* Impact on Child Nutrition." *Oxford Bulletin of Economics and Statistics* 67 (2005): 547–69.

Behrman, Jere R., Piyali Sengupta, and Petra Todd. "Progressing through PROGRESA: An Impact Assessment of a School Subsidy Experiment in Mexico." *Economic Development and Cultural Change* 54 (2000): 237–76.

Behrman Jere R., and Emmanuel Skoufias. "Mitigating Myths about Policy Effectiveness: Evaluation of Mexico's Antipoverty Program." *Annals of the American Academy of Political and Social Science* 606 (2006): 244–75.

Beneria, Lourdes. *Gender, Development, and Globalization: Economics as if People Mattered.* New York: Routledge, 2003.

Bertucci, Mariano E. "Scholar-Practitioner Relations in International Relations: A Quick Summary of the Salient Literature." Memorandum prepared for the International Workshop on Scholars and Practitioners. Center for International Studies, University of Southern California, 2011.

————. *Sobre el Origen de la Política de Convergencia Argentina Hacia los Estado Unidos Durante los '90: Política Exterior y Toma de Decisiones en la Argentina Menemista*. Buenos Aires: Universidad Torcuato Di Tella, 2006.

Besley, Timothy, and Ravi Kanbur. "Food Subsidies and Poverty Alleviation." *The Economic Journal* 98 (1998): 701–19.

————. *Principles of Targeting*. Working Paper Series 385. Washington, DC: World Bank, 1990.

Betts, Richard, "Should Strategic Studies Survive?" *World Politics* 50 (1997): 7–33.

Biersteker, Thomas J. "Interrelationships between Theory and Practice in International Security Studies." *Security Dialogue* 4 (2010): 1–8.

————. "The Role and Influence of Academic Research on Financial Sanctions." Memorandum prepared for the International Workshop on Scholars and Practitioners. Center for International Studies, University of Southern California, 2011.

Billig, Michael. *Learn to Write Badly: How to Succeed in the Social Sciences*. New York: Cambridge University Press, 2013.

Blair, Patricia. *Women's Issues in U.S. AID Administration: Implementation of the Percy Amendment*. Washington, DC: Equity Policy Center, 1983.

Blumberg, Lesser. *Gender, Family, and Economy: The Triple Overlap*. Thousand Oaks, CA: Sage, 1990.

Blyth, Mark, *Austerity: The History of a Dangerous Idea*. New York: Oxford University Press, 2013.

Bollen, Kenneth, Pamela Paxton, and Rumi Morishima. *Research Design to Evaluate the Impact of USAID Democracy and Governance Programs*. Washington, DC: Social Science Research Council, 2003.

Boserup, Ester. *Woman's Role in Economic Development*. London: Allen and Unwin, 1970.

Boswell, Christina. *The Political Uses of Expert Knowledge: Immigration Policy and Social Research*. Cambridge: Cambridge University Press, 2009.

Bourdieu, Pierre. *The Logic of Practice (Le sens practique)*. Stanford, CA: Stanford University Press, 1990.

Browner, Carole H., and Carolyn F. Sargent, eds. *Reproduction, Globalization, and the State*. Durham, NC: Duke University Press, 2011.

Bucher, Bernd. "Processual-Relational Thinking and Figurational Sociology in Social Constructivism: The Rogueization of Liberal and Illiberal States." PhD dissertation. University of St. Gallen, St. Gallen, Switzerland, 2011.

Bull, Hedley. "What Is the Commonwealth?" *World Politics* 11(July 1959): 577–87.

Byman, Daniel, and Kenneth M. Pollack. "Let Us Now Praise Great Men: Bringing the Statesman Back In." *International Security* 25 (Spring 2001): 107–46.

Caldés, Natalia, David Coady, and John A. Maluccio. "The Cost of Poverty Alleviation Transfer Programs: A Comparative Analysis of Three Programs in Latin America." *World Development* 34 (2006): 818–37.

Cameron, Maxwell. "A Democracy Traffic Light for the Americas?" Memorandum prepared for the International Workshop on Scholars and Practitioners. Center for International Studies, University of Southern California, 2011.

Capie, David, and Paul Evans. *The Asia-Pacific Security Lexicon*. 2nd edition. Singapore: Institute of Southeast Asian Studies, 2007.

Carothers, Thomas. *Aiding Democracy Abroad: The Learning Curve*. Washington, DC: Carnegie Endowment for International Peace, 1999.

———. *In the Name of Democracy: U.S. Policy toward Latin America in the Reagan Years*. Berkeley: University of California Press, 1991.

Carrillo, Laura, and Juan Pablo Guerrero. *Los Salarios de los Altos Funcionarios en México desde una Perspectiva Comparativa*. Documento de Trabajo 124. Programa de Presupuesto y Gasto Público. Mexico City: CIDE-FORD, 2003.

Casas-Zamora, Kevin. *Guatemala: Between a Rock and a Hard Place*. Washington, DC: Brookings Institution Press, September 16, 2011.

———. *La Polis Amenazada: (In)Seguridad Ciudadana y Democracia en América Latina y el Caribe*. Washington, DC: Brookings Institution Press, 2012.

———. "Missing Scholars and Hard-Nosed Cops: The Weak Research behind Citizen Security Policies in Latin America." Memorandum prepared for the International Workshop on Scholars and Practitioners. Center for International Studies, University of Southern California, 2011.

———. *The Travails of Development and Democratic Governance in Central America*. Brookings Institution, Foreign Policy Paper No. 28. Washington, DC: Brookings Institution Press, June 2011.

Castro, Jorge. "La Argentina, Estados Unidos y Brasil: El Triangulo de la Década del '90." In *Política Exterior Argentina: 1989–1999. Historia de un éxito*. Edited by Andrés Cisneros. Buenos Aires: GEL, 1998.

Cavallo, Domingo. *Pasión por Crear*. Buenos Aires: Grupo Editorial Planeta, 2001.

Chant, Sylvia. "Dangerous Equations: How Female-Headed Households Became the Poorest of the Poor: Causes, Consequences, and Cautions." In *Feminisms in Development: Contradictions, Contestations, and Challenges*. Edited by Andrea Cornwall, Elizabeth Harrison, and Ann Whitehead. London and New York: Zed Books, 2007.

Cisneros, Andrés. "Política Exterior Argentina 1989–1999. Historia de un éxito." In *Política Exterior Argentina: 1989–1999. Historia de un éxito*. Edited by Andrés Cisneros. Buenos Aires: GEL, 1998.

Coady, David. "Interview Related to IFPRI Evaluation of the PROGRESA/*Oportunidades* Program," Interview by Jere Behrman in appendixes of Jere R. Behrman, *Policy-Oriented Research Impact Assessment (Poria) Case Study on the International Food Policy Research Institute (IFPRI) and the Mexican Progresa Anti-Poverty and Human Resource Investment Conditional Cash Transfer Program*. Impact Assessment Discussion Paper No. 27. Washington, DC: IFPRI, 2007.

———. "The Welfare Returns to Finer Targeting: The Case of Progresa in Mexico." *International Tax and Public Finance* 13 (2006): 217–39.

Coady, David, and Rebecca Harris. "Evaluating Transfer Payments within a General Equilibrium Framework." *The Economic Journal* 114 (2004): 778–99.

Cohen, Michael D., James G. March, and Johan P. Olsen. "A Garbage Can Model of Orga-nizational Choice." *Administrative Science Quarterly* 17 (1972): 1–25.

Cohn, Carol. *Women and Wars*. London: Polity, 2012.

Commission on U.S.–Latin American Relations. *The Americas in a Changing World*. New York: Center for Inter-American Relations, October 1974.

———. *The United States and Latin America: Next Steps*. New York: Center for Inter-American Relations, December 1976.

Corigliano, Francisco. "Las 'relaciones carnales': los vínculos políticos con las grandes poten-cias 1989–2000." In *Historia General de las Relaciones Exteriores de la República Argentina*. Obra dirigida por Carlos Escudé. Buenos Aires: GEL, 1999.

Courtwright, David T. *Forces of Habit: Drugs and the Making of the Modern World*. Cam-bridge, MA: Harvard University Press, 2001.

Cox, Robert. "Social Forces, States and World Orders: Beyond International Relations The-ory." *Millennium: Journal of International Affairs* 10 (Summer 1981): 165–66.

Dahlkemper, Lesley. "What Does Scientifically Based Research Mean for Schools." *SEDL Letter* 15, no. 1 (December 2003). www.sedl.org/pubs/sedl-letter/v15n01/2.html. Accessed January 12, 2012.

Deere, Carmen D., and Magdalena León. *Empowering Women: Land and Property Rights in Latin America*. Pittsburgh: University of Pittsburgh Press, 2001.

Desch, Michael C. "Professor Smith Goes to Washington." *Notre Dame Magazine*, Spring 2009.

Desmond Arias, Enrique. *Drugs and Democracy in Rio de Janeiro: Trafficking, Social Networks, and Public Security*. Chapel Hill: University of North Carolina Press, 2006.

de Soto, Hernando. *El Otro Sendero: La Revolución Informal*. Lima: Instituto Libertad y Democracia, 1990.

de Souza, Amaury. "Crafting Brazil's Foreign Policy: Scholars, Practitioners and the Policy Process." Memorandum prepared for the International Workshop on Scholars and Prac-titioners. Center for International Studies, University of Southern California, 2011.

Diamond, Larry. "Economic Development and Democracy Reconsidered." In *Reexamining Democracy: Essays in Honor of Seymour Martin Lipset*. Edited by Gary Marks and Larry Diamond. London: Sage, 1992.

Díaz, Juan José, and Sudhanshu Handa. "An Assessment of Propensity Score Matching as a Nonexperimental Impact Estimator." *Journal of Human Resources* 41 (2006): 319–45.

di Tella, Guido, and D. Cameron Watt, eds. *Argentina between the Great Powers, 1939–46*. Pittsburgh: University of Pittsburgh Press, 1990.

Domínguez, Jorge I., ed. *Technopols: Freeing Politics and Markets in Latin America in the 1990s*. University Park: Penn State University Press, 1997.

Drezner, Daniel. *All Politics Is Global: Explaining International Regulatory Regimes*. Princeton, NJ: Princeton University Press, 2007.

———. "Gartzke on Policy, Political Science, and Zombies." *Foreignpolicy.com*, February 27, 2011. http://drezner.foreignpolicy.com/posts/2011/02/27/gartzke_on_policy_political _science_and_zombies. Accessed February 20, 2011.

———. *The Sanctions Paradox: Economic Statecraft and International Relations*. New York: Cambridge University Press, 1999.

Elson, Diane. "The Male Bias in Macro-economics: The Case of Structural Adjustment." In *The Male Bias in the Development Process*. Edited by Diane Elson. Manchester, UK: Manchester University Press, 1995.

Escudé, Carlos. *Argentina: Paria Internacional?* Buenos Aires: Editorial Sudamericana, 1984.

———. *El Estado Parasitario. Argentina. Ciclos de Vaciamiento. Clase Política Delictiva y Colapso de la Política Exterior*. Buenos Aires: Lumiere, 2005.

———. *El Realismo de los Estados Débiles: La política exterior del primer Gobierno Menem frete a la teoría de las relaciones internacionales*. Buenos Aires: GEL, 1995.

———. *Foreign Policy Theory in Menem's Argentina*. Gainesville: University Press of Florida, 1997.

———. *La Argentina vs. las Grandes Potencias: El Precio del Desafío*. Buenos Aires: Editorial de Belgrano, 1986.

———. "Política exterior argentina: Una sobredosis crónica de confrontaciones." In *La nueva democracia argentina (1983–1986)*. Edited by Ernesto Garzón Valdés, Manfred Mols, and Arnold Spita. Buenos Aires: Editorial Sudamericana, 1988.

Esquivel, Gerardo, Nora Lustig, and John Scott. "Mexico: A Decade of Falling Inequality: Market Forces of State Action?" In *Declining Inequality in Latin America: A Decade of Change?* Edited by Luis F. López-Calva and Nora Lustig. Washington, DC: Brookings Institution Press; New York: United Nations Development Program, 2010.

Evans, Paul. "Background Memo for the Conference on Scholars and Practitioners: Theory, Policy and Inter-American Relations." Memorandum prepared for the International Workshop on Scholars and Practitioners. Center for International Studies, University of Southern California, 2011.

———. "Canada and Asia Pacific's Track-Two Diplomacy." *International Journal* 64, no. 4 (Autumn 2009): 1027–38.

Evans, Peter. *Embedded Autonomy: States and Industrial Transformation*. Princeton, NJ: Princeton University Press, 1995.

Falcoff, Mark. "Comentarios." In *La Política Exterior Argentina en el Nuevo Orden Mundial*. Edited by Roberto Russell. Buenos Aires: GEL, 1992.

Farer, Tom, with the assistance of Claudia Fuentes Julio. "Scholars and the Policy Process." Memorandum prepared for the International Workshop on Scholars and Practitioners. Center for International Studies, University of Southern California, 2011.

Farmer, R. "How to Influence Government with Your Research: Tips from Practicing Political Scientists in Government." *PS: Political Science and Politics* 43, no. 4 (October 2010): 717–19.

Featherman, David L., and Maris A. Vinovskis, eds. *Social Science and Policymaking: A Search for Relevance in the Twentieth Century*. Ann Arbor: University of Michigan Press, 2001.

Feinberg, Richard. "Scholar-Practitioner Relations: A View from the White House." Memorandum prepared for the International Workshop on Scholars and Practitioners. Center for International Studies, University of Southern California, 2011.

Felbab-Brown, Vanda. *Shooting Up: Counterinsurgency and the War on Drugs*. Washington, DC: Brookings Institution Press, 2010.

Fernández de Castro, Rafael. "Ideas académicas y especialistas en la diplomacia mexicana: NAFTA, acuerdo migratorio, libre comercio con Brasil y NAEXI." Memorandum prepared for the International Workshop on Scholars and Practitioners. Center for International Studies, University of Southern California, 2011.

Finkel, Steven E., Aníbal Pérez-Liñán, and Mitchell A. Seligson. "Effects of U.S. Foreign Assistance on Democracy Building: Results of a Cross-National Quantitative Study." Paper presented at the Annual Meeting of the American Political Science Association. Philadelphia, 2006.

———. "The Effects of U.S. Foreign Assistance on Democracy Building, 1990–2003." *World Politics* 59 (2007): 404–39.

Finkel, Steven E., Aníbal Pérez-Liñán, Mitchell A. Seligson, and C. Neal Tate. *Deepening Our Understanding of the Effects of US Foreign Assistance on Democracy Building: Final Report.* Washington, DC: USAID, 2008.

———. "Watering Not Transplanting: The Case for Democracy Assistance." *APSA-CP* 19, no. 2 (2008): 15–18.

Finnemore, Martha, and Kathryn Sikkink. "International Norm Dynamics and Political Change." *International Organization* 52 (1998): 887–917.

Fiszbein, Ariel, and Norbert Schady with Francisco H. G. Ferreira, Margaret Grosh, Nial Kelleher, Pedro Olinto, and Emmanuel Skoufias. *Conditional Cash Transfers: Reducing Present and Future Poverty.* World Bank Policy Research Report. Washington, DC: World Bank, 2009.

Forsythe, David. "Forum: Transnational Justice: The Quest for Theory to Inform Policy." *International Studies Review* 13 (2011): 554–78.

Fraser, Arvonne. "Seizing Opportunities: USAID, WID and CEDAW." In *Developing Power: How Women Transformed International Development.* Edited by Arvonne Fraser and Irene Tinker. New York: Feminist Press, 2004.

Fraser, Arvonne, and Irene Tinker, eds. *Developing Power: How Women Transformed International Development.* New York: Feminist Press, 2004.

Frieden, Jeffry, and Menzie Chinn. *Lost Decades: The Making of America's Debt Crisis and the Long Recovery.* New York: W. W. Norton, 2011.

Friedrichs, Jörg, and Friedrich Kratochwil. "On Acting and Knowing: How Pragmatism Can Advance International Relations Research and Methodology." *International Organization* 63 (2009): 701–31.

Friman, H. Richard, ed. *Crime and the Global Political Economy.* Boulder, CO: Lynne Rienner, 2009.

George, Alexander L. *Bridging the Gap: Theory and Practice in Foreign Policy.* Washington, DC: United States Institute of Peace Press, 1993.

———. "The 'Operational Code': A Neglected Approach to the Study of Political Leaders and Decision-Making." *International Studies Quarterly* 13 (June 1969): 190–204.

George, Alexander L., and Andrew Bennett. "Case Studies and Policy-Relevant Theory." In *Case Studies and Theory Development in the Social Sciences.* Edited by Alexander George and Andrew Bennett. Cambridge, MA: MIT Press, 2005.

———. *Case Studies and Theory Development in the Social Sciences.* Cambridge: MIT Press, 2005.

George, Alexander L., and Richard Smoke. *Deterrence in American Foreign Policy: Theory and Practice.* New York: Columbia University Press, 1974.

Gertler, Paul. "Do Conditional Cash Transfers Improve Child Health? Evidence from PRO-GRESA's Controlled Randomized Experiment." *American Economic Review: Papers and Proceedings* 94 (2004): 336–41.

Goetz, Anne Marie, ed. *Getting Institutions Right for Women in Development.* London: Zed Books, 1997.

Goldman, Emily O. "Closing the Gap: Networking the Policy and Academic Communities." *Asia Policy* 1 (January 2006): 16–24.

Gómez de León, José, and Susan Parker. "The Impact of Anti-poverty Programs on Female Labor Force Participation and Women's Status: The Case of Progresa in Mexico." Paper prepared for the 1999 IUSSP Conference on Women in the Labor Market. Mexico City, 1999.

———. *The Impact of Anti-poverty Programs on Labor Force Participation: The Case of Progresa in Mexico.* Mexico City: PROGRESA, 1999.

Greenspun, Samantha. "Assessing Mexico's Anti-poverty Program 'Oportunidades': Combining and Comparing *Objective* and *Interview-based Indicators.*" MA thesis. Tulane University, New Orleans, 2011.

Gross Stein, Janice, "Evolutionary Hubris, False Certainty, and Structural Skepticism: The Academic-Policy Divide." *Cambridge Review of International Affairs* 22 (2009): 120–24.

Haas, Peter M. "Introduction: Epistemic Communities and International Policy Coordination." *International Organization* 46 (1992): 1–35.

Haass, Richard N. *The Bureaucratic Entrepreneur: How to Be Effective in Any Unruly Organization.* Washington, DC: Brookings Institution Press, 1999.

Habyarimana, James, Macartan Humphreys, Daniel Posner, and Jeremy Weinstein. *Coethnicity: Diversity and the Dilemmas of Collective Action.* New York: Russell Sage Foundation, 2010.

Hacker, Jacob S. "Healing the Rift between Political Science and Practical Politics." *The Forum* 8 (2010): 1–7. Published by Berkeley Electronic Press.

Haddad, Lawrence. "Interview Related to IFPRI Evaluation of the PROGRESA/*Oportunidades* program." Interview by Jere Behrman in appendixes of Jere R. Behrman, *Policy-Oriented Research Impact Assessment (Poria) Case Study on the International Food Policy Research Institute (IFPRI) and the Mexican Progresa Anti-Poverty and Human Resource Investment Conditional Cash Transfer Program.* Impact Assessment Discussion Paper No. 27. Washington, DC: IFPRI, December 2007.

Haddad, Lawrence, John Hoddinott, and Harold Alderman, eds. *Intrahousehold Resource Allocation in Developing Countries: Models, Methods, and Policy.* Baltimore: Johns Hopkins University Press, 1997.

Haddad, Lawrence, and Ravi Kanbur. *Are Better-off Households More Unequal or Less Unequal?* Working Paper Series 373. Washington, DC: World Bank, March 1990.

———. *How Serious Is the Neglect of Intrahousehold Inequality?* Working Paper 296. Washington, DC: World Bank 1998.

Haddad, Lawrence, and Thomas Reardon. "Gender Bias in the Allocation of Resources within Households in Burkina Faso: A Disaggregated Outlay Equivalent Analysis." *Journal of Development Studies* 29 (1993): 260–76.

Hagan, Joe D. "Domestic Political Regime Changes and Third World Voting Realignments in the United Nations, 1946–84." *International Organization* 43 (1989): 505–41.

Hall, Rodney, and Thomas Biersteker. *The Emergence of Private Authority in Global Governance.* Cambridge: Cambridge University Press, 2002.

Hawkesworth, Mary E. *Political Worlds of Women: Activism, Advocacy, and Governance in the Twenty-First Century.* Boulder, CO: Westview Press, 2012.

Heckman, James, Hidehiko Ichimura, and Petra E. Todd. "Matching as an Econometric Evaluation Estimator: Evidence from Evaluating a Job Training Programme." *Review of Economic Studies* 64 (1997): 605–54.

Heckman, James, and Petra E. Todd. *Assessing the Performance of Alternative Estimators of Program Impacts: A Study of Adult Men and Women in JTPA.* Technical Report. Chicago: University of Chicago Press, 1996.

Heine, Jorge. "Scholars, Practitioners and Inter-American Relations: Chile's Experience." Memorandum prepared for the International Workshop on Scholars and Practitioners. Center for International Studies, University of Southern California, 2011.

Henshall Momsen, Janet. *Gender and Development.* London: Routledge, 2004.

Heredia, Blanca. "Speaking Truth to Power in Mexico: Gaps, Bridges, and Trampolines." Memorandum prepared for the International Workshop on Scholars and Practitioners. Center for International Studies, University of Southern California, 2011.

Hermann, Charles. "Changing Course: When Governments Choose to Redirect Foreign Policy." *International Studies Quarterly* 34 (1990): 3–21.

Hernández, Bernardo, et al. "Evaluación del Impacto de Oportunidades en la Mortalidad Materna e Infantil." In *Evaluación Externa del Impacto del Programa Oportunidades.* Volume 2. Edited by Bernardo Hernández Prado and Mauricio Hernández Ávila. Cuernacava, Mexico: Instituto Nacional de Salud Pública, 2003.

Hersh, Seymour M. *The Price of Power: Kissinger in the Nixon White House.* New York: Simon and Schuster, 1983.

Herspring, Dale R. *Civil-Military Relations and Shared Responsibility: A Four Nation Study.* Baltimore: Johns Hopkins University Press, 2013.

Hill, Christopher. "Academic International Relations: The Siren Song of Policy Relevance." In *Two Worlds of International Relations: Academics, Practitioners, and the Trade in Ideas.* Edited by Christopher Hill and Pamela Beschoff. New York: Routledge, 1994.

Hill, Christopher, and Pamela Beshoff, eds. *Two Worlds of International Relations: Academics, Practitioners, and the Trade in Ideas.* New York: Routledge, 1994.

Hirschman, Albert. "Morality and the Social Sciences: A Durable Tension." In *Essays in Trespassing: Economics to Politics and Beyond.* Edited by Albert Hirschman. Cambridge: Cambridge University Press, 1981.

Hoffmann, Stanley. "An American Social Science: International Relations." In *International Theory: Critical Investigations.* Edited by James Der Derian. London: Macmillan, 1995.

Hufbauer, Gary, Jeffrey Schott, and Kimberly Elliott. *Economic Sanctions Reconsidered: History and Current Policy.* 2nd edition. Washington, DC: Institute for International Economics, 1985.

Hurrell, Andrew. "The Theory and Practice of Global Governance: The Worst of All Possible Worlds?" *International Studies Review* 13 (March 2011): 144–54.

Instituto Ciudadano de Estudios sobre la Inseguridad (ICESI). *Séptima Encuesta Nacional sobre Inseguridad.* Mexico City: ICESI, 2010. www.icesi.org.mx/estadisticas/estadisticas_encuestasNacionales_ensi7.asp.

Instituto Nacional de Estadística y Censos de Costa Rica (INEC) and Programa de Naciones Unidas para el Desarrollo (PNUD). *Resultados módulo sobre victimización: Encuesta de Hogares de Propósitos Múltiples.* San José, Costa Rica: INEC-PNUD, 2008. www.pnud .or.cr/images/stories/Mdulo_Victimizacin_PNUD_INEC.pdf.

International Food Policy Research Institute (IFPRI). *Report 1986.* Washington, DC: IFPRI, 1986.

Jain, Devaki. *Women, Development, and the UN: A Sixty-Year Quest for Equality and Justice.* Bloomington: Indiana University Press, 2005.

Jaquette, Jane S. "Academics and the Institutionalization of Women in (Gender and) Development." Memorandum prepared for the International Workshop on Scholars and Practitioners. Center for International Studies, University of Southern California, 2011.

————. "The Family as a Development Issue." In *Women at the Center: Development Issues and Practices for the 1990s.* Edited by Gay Young, Vidyamali Samarasinghe, and Ken Kusterer. West Hartford, CT: Kumarian Press, 1993.

————. "Gender and Justice in Economic Development." In *Persistent Inequalities.* Edited by Irene Tinker. New York: Oxford University Press, 1990.

Jaquette, Jane S., and Kathleen Staudt. "Women as 'At-Risk Reproducers': Women and US Population Policy." In *Women, Biology, and Public Policy.* Edited by Virginia Sapiro. Beverly Hills, CA: Sage, 1985.

————. "Women, Gender and Development." In *Women and Gender Equity in Development Theory and Practice.* Edited by Jane S. Jaquette and Gale Summerfield. Durham, NC: Duke University Press, 2006.

Jaquette, Jane S., and Sharon L. Wolchik. "Introduction." In *Women and Democracy in Latin America and Central and Eastern Europe.* Edited by Jane S. Jaquette and Sharon L. Wolchik. Baltimore: Johns Hopkins University Press, 1998.

Jentleson, Bruce W. "Economic Sanctions and Post-War Conflicts: Challenges for Theory and Policy." In *International Conflict Resolution after the Cold War.* Edited by Paul C. Stern and Daniel Druckman. Washington, DC: National Academy Press, 2000.

————. "In Pursuit of Praxis: Applying International Relations Theory to Foreign Policymaking." In *Being Useful: Policy Relevance and International Relations Theory.* Edited by Miroslav Nincic and Joseph Lepgold. Ann Arbor: University of Michigan Press, 2000.

————. "The Need for Praxis: Bringing Policy Relevance Back In." *International Security* 26 (Spring 2002): 169–83.

————, ed. *Opportunities Missed, Opportunities Seized.* Lanham, MD: Rowman and Littlefield, 2000.

Jervis, Robert. "Complexity and the Analysis of Political and Social Life." *Political Science Quarterly* 12 (Winter 1997–98): 569–93.

————. *Why Intelligence Fails: Lessons from the Iranian Revolution and the Iraq War.* Ithaca, NY: Cornell University Press, 2011.

Job, Brian. "Track 2 Diplomacy: Ideational Contribution to the Evolving Asian Security Order." In *Asian Security Order: Instrumental and Normative Features.* Edited by Muthia Alagappa. Stanford, CA: Stanford University Press, 2003.

Kabeer, Naila. *Reversed Realities: Hierarchies in Development Thought.* London: Verso, 1994.

Kagan, Robert A. *A Twilight Struggle: American Power and Nicaragua, 1977–1990.* New York: Free Press, 1996.

Karl, Terry L. "Not On Your Vita: The Relevance of Comparative Politics for Public Life." *American Political Science Association–CP Newsletter* 14 (Summer 2003): 14–19.

Kehoe, Timothy J., and Jaime Serra-Puche. "A General Equilibrium Analysis of Price Controls and Subsidies on Food in Mexico." *Journal of Development Economics* 21 (April 1986): 65–87.

Kelley, Judith G. *Monitoring Democracy: When International Election Observation Works, and Why It Often Fails.* Princeton, NJ: Princeton University Press, 2012.

Kelling, George L., and Catherine M. Coles. *Fixing Broken Windows: Restoring Order and Reducing Crime in Our Communities.* New York: Free Press, 1998.

Keohane, Robert. *After Hegemony: Cooperation and Discord on the World Political Economy.* Princeton, NJ: Princeton University Press, 1984.

———. "Beware the Bad Fairy: Cautionary Note for the Academic in the Policy Realm." *Cambridge Review of International Affairs* 22, no. 1 (2009): 124–28.

Kingdon, John W. *Agendas, Alternatives, and Public Policy.* 2nd edition. Boston: Addison-Wesley Educational, 1995.

Kittikhoum, Anoular. "The Myth of Scholarly Irrelevance for the United Nations." *International Policy Review* 13 (2011): 18–23.

Kleiman, Mark. "Surgical Strikes in the Drug Wars." *Foreign Affairs* 90 (September/October 2011): 89–101.

Knack, Stephen. "Does Foreign Aid Promote Democracy?" *International Studies Quarterly* 48 (2004): 251–66.

Kotchegura, Alexander. *Civil Service Reform in Post-Communist Countries.* Leiden: Leiden University Press, 2008.

Krasner, Stephen D. "Conclusion: Garbage Cans and Policy Streams: How Academic Research Might Affect Foreign Policy." In *Power, The State, and Sovereignty: Essays on International Relations.* Edited by Stephen D. Krasner. New York: Routledge, 2009.

———. "Government and Academia: A Chasm Not a Gap." Memorandum prepared for the International Workshop on Scholars and Practitioners. Center for International Studies, University of Southern California, 2011.

———. "Government and Academia: Never the Twain Shall Meet, Well Almost Never." *Cambridge Review of International Affairs* 22 (2009): 111–16.

Krug, Etienne G., Linda L. Dahlberg, James A. Mercy, Anthony B. Zwi, and Rafael Lozano. *World Report on Violence and Health.* Geneva: World Health Organization, October 3, 2002. www.who.int/violence_injury_prevention/violence/world_report/en.

Kuhn, Thomas. *The Structure of Scientific Revolutions.* Chicago: University of Chicago Press, 1962.

Kurth, James, "Inside the Cave: The Banality of IR Studies." *The National Interest* 53 (Fall 1998): 29–40.

Lakatos, Imre. *The Methodology of Scientific Research Programmes.* Cambridge: Cambridge University Press, 1978.

Lake, Anthony. *Somoza Falling: The Nicaraguan Dilemma.* Boston: Houghton Mifflin, 1989.

Lake, David A. "Why 'isms' Are Evil: Theory, Epistemology, and Academic Sects as Impediments to Understanding and Progress." *International Studies Quarterly* 55 (2011): 465–80.

Lassman, Peter, and Ronald Spiers, eds. *Weber Political Writings.* Cambridge: Cambridge University Press, 2003.

Latham, Michael E. *Modernization as Ideology: American Social Science and "Nation Building" in the Kennedy Era*. Chapel Hill: University of North Carolina Press, 2000.

Latinobarómetro Corporation. *2008 Report*. Santiago, Chile: Latinobarómetro, 2008. www.asep-sa.org/latinobarometro/LATBD_Latinobarometro_Report_2008.pdf.

————. *2010 Report*. Santiago de Chile: Latinobarómetro, 2010. www.asep-sa.org/latino barometro/LATBD_Latinobarometro_Report_2010.pdf.

Lawson, Chappell. "Quasi-Academics and the Policy World: New Bridges in Scholar-Practitioner Interactions?" Memorandum prepared for the International Workshop on Scholars and Practitioners. Center for International Studies, University of Southern California, 2011.

Lepgold, Joseph. "Policy Relevance and Theoretical Development in International Relations: What Have We Learned?" In *Being Useful: Policy Relevance and International Relations Theory*. Edited by Joseph Lepgold and Miroslav Nincic. Ann Arbor: University of Michigan Press, 2000.

Lepgold, Joseph, and Miroslav Nincic, eds. *Being Useful: Policy Relevance and International Relations Theory*. Ann Arbor: University of Michigan Press, 2000.

————. *Beyond the Ivory Tower: International Relations Theory and the Issue of Policy Relevance*. New York: Columbia University Press, 2001.

Levy, Santiago. "Interview Related to IFPRI Evaluation of the PROGRESA/*Oportunidades* Program." Interview by Jere Behrman in appendixes of Jere R. Behrman, *Policy-Oriented Research Impact Assessment (Poria) Case Study on the International Food Policy Research Institute (IFPRI) and the Mexican Progresa Anti-Poverty and Human Resource Investment Conditional Cash Transfer Program*. Impact Assessment Discussion Paper No. 27. Washington, DC: IFPRI, 2007.

————. "La pobreza en Mexico." In *La pobreza en México: Causas y políticas para combatirla*. Edited by F. Vélez. Mexico City: ITAM and FCE, 1994.

————. *Poverty Alleviation in Mexico*. Policy Research and External Affairs Working Paper 679. Washington, DC: World Bank, 1991.

————. *Progress against Poverty: Sustaining Mexico's Progresa-Oportunidades Program*. Washington, DC: Brookings Institution Press, 2006.

Lieberthal, Kenneth. "Initiatives to Bridge the Gap." *Asia Policy* 1 (January 2006): 7–15.

Lindblom, Charles E., and David K. Cohen. *Usable Knowledge: Social Science and Social Problem Solving*. New Haven, CT: Yale University Press, 1979.

Lipset, Seymour Martin. "The Social Requisites of Democracy Revisited." *American Sociological Review* 59 (1994): 1–22.

————. "Some Social Requisites of Democracy: Economic Development and Political Legitimacy." *American Political Science Review* 53 (1959): 65–105.

Lipton, Michael. *Demography and Poverty*. Staff Discussion Paper 623. Washington, DC: World Bank, 1983.

————. *Poverty, Undernutrition, and Hunger*. Staff Discussion Paper 597. Washington, DC: World Bank, 1983.

————. "A Problem in Poverty Measurement." *Mathematical Social Sciences* 10 (1985): 91–97.

————. "Who Are the Poor? What Do They Do? What Should We Do?" Unpublished manuscript. Michigan State University, East Lansing, 1988.

Litwak, Robert S. *Rogue States and US Foreign Policy: Containment after the Cold War.* Washington, DC: Woodrow Wilson Center Press, 2000. Distributed by Johns Hopkins University Press.

Locke, Richard M. *The Promise and Limits of Private Power: Promoting Labor Standards in a Global Economy.* Cambridge: Cambridge University Press, 2013.

Londoño, Juan Luis, Alejandro Gaviria, and Rodrigo Guerrero, eds. *Asalto al Desarrollo: Violencia en América Latina.* Washington, DC: Inter-American Development Bank, 2000.

Lowenthal, Abraham F. *The Dominican Intervention.* Cambridge, MA: Harvard University Press, 1972.

———, ed. *Exporting Democracy: The United States and Latin America: Case Studies.* Baltimore: Johns Hopkins University Press, 1991.

———. "Foreign Aid as a Political Instrument: The Case of the Dominican Republic." *Public Policy* 14 (1965): 141–60.

Lowenthal, Abraham F., et al. *The Conduct of Routine Relations: The United States and Latin America.* Appendix 1, "The Report of the Commission on the Organization of the Government for the Conduct of Foreign Policy." Washington, DC: US Government Printing Office, 1975.

Lustig, Nora. *Food Subsidy Programs in Mexico.* Working Paper No. 3. Washington, DC: IFPRI, January 1986.

———. "Interview Related to IFPRI Evaluation of the PROGRESA/*Oportunidades* program." Interview by Jere Behrman in appendixes of Jere R. Behrman, *Policy-Oriented Research Impact Assessment (Poria) Case Study on the International Food Policy Research Institute (IFPRI) and the Mexican Progresa Anti-Poverty and Human Resource Investment Conditional Cash Transfer Program.* Impact Assessment Discussion Paper No. 27. Washington DC: IFPRI, December 2007.

———. "Investing in Health for Economic Development: The Case of Mexico." In *Advancing Development: Core Themes in Global Economics.* Edited by George Mavrotas and Anthony Shorrocks. New York: Palgrave Macmillan in association with United Nations University–World Institute for Development Economics Research, 2007.

———. "Solidarity as a Strategy of Poverty Alleviation." In *Transforming State Society Relations in Mexico: The National Solidarity Strategy.* Edited by Wayne Cornelius, Ann L. Craig, and Jonathan Fox. San Diego: Center for U.S.-Mexican Studies, University of San Diego, 1994.

Machiavelli, Niccolo. *Discourses on Livy.* Oxford: Oxford University Press, 1997.

Magaloni, Ana Laura. *The Juicio Ejecutivo Mercantil in the Federal District Courts of Mexico: A Study of Uses and Users and Their Implications for Judicial Reform.* World Bank Report 22635. Washington, DC: World Bank, 2002.

Magaloni, Ana Laura, and Marcelo Bergman. *Encuesta de la población en reclusión.* Programa de Estudios de Seguridad Pública y Estado de Derecho, División de Estudios Jurídicos, CIDE. Mexico City: CIDE, 2002.

Magaloni, Ana Laura, and Layda Negrete. *El Poder Judicial y su política de decidir sin resolver.* DEJ Working Paper 1. División de Estudios Jurídicos, CIDE. Mexico City: CIDE, 2001.

Mahnken, Thomas G. "Bridging the Gap between the Worlds of Ideas and Action." *Orbis* 54, no. 1 (2010): 4–13.

May, Ernest R. *Lessons of the Past: The Use and Misuse of History in American Foreign Policy.* New York: Oxford University Press, 1973.

McCoun, Robert, and Peter Reuter. *Drug War Heresies: Learning from Other Vices, Times, and Places.* Cambridge: Cambridge University Press, 2001.

McGann, James. *2010 Global Go To Think Tanks Index Report.* Think Tanks and Civil Societies Program. Philadelphia: University of Pennsylvania, International Relations Program, 2010.

McGinnis, John O. "A Politics of Knowledge." *National Affairs* 10 (Winter 2012): 58–74.

Mead, Lawrence M. "Scholasticism in Political Science." *Perspectives on Politics* 8 (June 2010): 453–64.

Mearsheimer, John J., and Stephen M. Walt, "Leaving Theory Behind: Why Simplistic Hypothesis Testing Is Bad for International Relations." *European Journal of International Relations* 19 (2013): 427–57.

Méndez, José Luis. "Implementing Developed Countries Administrative Reforms in Developing Countries: The Case of Mexico." In *Comparative Administrative Change and Reform: Lessons Learned.* Edited by Jon Pierre and Patricia Ingraham. Montreal: McGill-Queen's University Press, 2010.

Merton, Robert K. *Social Theory and Social Structure.* Glencoe, IL: Free Press, 1957.

Meyer, Lorenzo, and Manuel Camacho. "La ciencia política en México." In *Ciencias Sociales en México, Desarrollo y Perspectivas.* Edited by Lorenzo Meyer and Manuel Camacho. Mexico City: El Colegio de México, 1979.

Molyneux, Maxine. "Mobilization without Emancipation? Women's Issues, the State, and Revolution in Nicaragua." *Feminist Studies* 11 (1985): 127–54.

Molyneux, Maxine, and Shahra Rahzavi, eds. *Gender, Justice, Development, and Rights.* Oxford: Oxford University Press, 2003.

Morgenthau, Hans. "Truth and Power." In *Truth and Power: Essays of a Decade, 1960–1970.* New York: Praeger, 1970.

Muhlhausen, David B. *Evaluating Federal Social Programs: Finding out What Works and What Does Not.* Heritage Foundation, Backgrounder No. 2578, July 18, 2011. http://thf_media .s3.amazonaws.com/2011/pdf/bg2578.pdf. Accessed January 12, 2012.

Muñoz, Heraldo. "Scholars and Practitioners: Reflections from Both Worlds." Remarks prepared for delivery at University of Southern California, April 25, 2011.

———. "What Can Policymakers Do to Draw More Effectively on Academic Concepts and Research?" Memorandum prepared for the International Workshop on Scholars and Practitioners. Center for International Studies, University of Southern California, 2011.

Nadelmann, Ethan. *Cops across Borders: The Internationalization of U.S. Criminal Law Enforcement.* University Park: Penn State University Press, 1993.

———. "Global Prohibition Regimes: The Evolution of Norms in International Society." *International Organization* 44 (Autumn 1990): 479–526.

———. "U.S. Drug Policy: A Bad Export." *Foreign Policy* (Spring 1988): 83–108.

National Research Council, Jack A. Goldstone, Larry Garber, John Gerring, Clark C. Gibson, Mitchell A. Seligson, and Jeremy Weinstein. *Improving Democracy Assistance: Building Knowledge through Evaluations and Research.* Washington, DC: National Academies Press, 2008.

Neumann, Iver B. *At Home with the Diplomats: Inside a European Foreign Ministry.* Ithaca, NY: Cornell University Press, 2012.

Neustadt, Richard E., and Ernest R. May. *Thinking in Time: The Uses of History for Decision-Makers.* New York: Free Press, 1986.

Newman, J., Laura Rawlings, and Paul Gertler. "Using Randomized Control Designs in Evaluating Social Sector Programs in Developing Countries." *World Bank Research Observer* 9 (1994): 181–201.

Newsom, David. "Foreign Policy and Academia." *Foreign Policy* 101 (Winter 1995–96): 52–67.

Norden, Deborah, and Roberto Russell. *The United States and Argentina: Changing Relations in a Changing World.* New York: Routledge, 2002.

Nussbaum, Martha. *Women and Human Development: The Capabilities Approach.* Cambridge: Cambridge University Press, 2000.

Nye, Joseph S. "Bridging the Gap between Theory and Policy." *Political Psychology* 29 (2008): 593–603.

———. "The Costs and Benefits of 'In and Outers.'" In "Forum: Risks and Opportunities of Crossing the Academy/Policy Divide," edited by Anne J. Tickner and Andrei Tsygankov. *International Studies Review* 10 (2008): 156–60.

———. "International Relations: The Relevance of Theory to Practice." In *The Oxford Handbook of International Relations.* Edited by Christian Reus-Smit and Duncan Snidal. Oxford: Oxford University Press, 2008.

———. *Nuclear Ethics.* New York: Free Press, 1988.

———. *The Paradox of American Power: Why the World's Only Superpower Can't Go It Alone.* New York: Oxford University Press, 2003.

Olson, Lynn, and Debra Viadero. "Law Mandates Scientific Base for Research." *Education Week* 21, no. 20 (January 30, 2002): 1, 14, 15. www.edweek.org/ew/ew_printstory .cfm?slug=20whatworks.h21. Accessed January 12, 2012.

Orozco, Manuel. "International Workers Remittances and the Role of Scholars and Policy Practitioners in Inter-American Relations." Memorandum prepared for the International Workshop on Scholars and Practitioners. Center for International Studies, University of Southern California, 2011.

Ottaway, Marina, and Thomas Carothers. *Funding Virtue: Civil Society Aid and Democracy Promotion.* Washington, DC: Carnegie Endowment for International Peace, 2000.

Packenham, Robert. *Liberal America in the Third World.* Princeton, NJ: Princeton University Press, 1973.

Pal, Leslie. *Beyond Policy Analysis: Public Issue Management in Turbulent Times.* 3rd ed. Toronto: Nelson Education, 2006.

Pape, Robert A. "Why Economic Sanctions Do Not Work." *International Security* 22 (Fall 1997): 90–136.

Pardo, Maria del Carmen. "La propuesta de modernización administrativa en México: Entre la tradición y el cambio." *Foro Internacional* 200 (2010): 393–421.

Paris, Roland, "Ordering the World: Academic Research and Policymaking on Fragile States." *International Studies Review* 13 (2010): 58–71.

Parker, Susan. "Evaluación del Impacto de Oportunidades sobre la Inscripción, Reprobación, y Abandono Escolar." In *Evaluación Externa del Impacto del Programa Oportunidades.*

Edited by Bernardo Hernández Prado and Mauricio Hernández Ávila. Mexico City: Instituto Nacional de Salud Pública, 2003.

———. "Interview Related to IFPRI Evaluation of the PROGRESA/*Oportunidades* Program." Interview by Jere Behrman in appendixes of Jere R. Behrman, *Policy-Oriented Research Impact Assessment (Poria) Case Study on the International Food Policy Research Institute (IFPRI) and the Mexican Progresa Anti-Poverty and Human Resource Investment Conditional Cash Transfer Program.* Impact Assessment Discussion Paper No. 27. Washington, DC: IFPRI, 2007.

Parker, Susan W., Luis Rubalcalva, and Graciela Teruel. "Evaluating Conditional Schooling–Health Transfer Programs." In *The Handbook of Development Economics.* Volume 4. Edited by T. Paul Schultz and John Strauss. Amsterdam: North-Holland/Elsevier, 2007.

Parks, Bradley C., and Alena Stern. "In-and-Outers and Moonlighters: An Evaluation of the Impact of Policy-Making Exposure on IR Scholarship." *International Studies Perspectives* 15, no. 1 (2014): 73–93.

Pastor, Robert A. "Congress' Impact on Latin America: Is There a Madness in the Method?" and "U.S. Sugar Politics and Latin America: Asymmetries in Input and Impact." In *The Conduct of Routine Economic Relations: U.S. Foreign Policy-Making to Latin America.* Volume 3. Part 1. Edited by Abraham F. Lowenthal. Commission on the Organization of the Government for the Conduct of Foreign Policy. Washington, DC: US Government Printing Office, 1975.

———. "Coping with Congress' Foreign Policy." *Foreign Service Journal* 52 (December 1975): 83–104.

———. "Mediating Elections." *Journal of Democracy* 9 (January 1998): 154–63.

———. *The North American Idea: A Vision of a Continental Future.* New York: Oxford University Press, 2011.

———. *Not Condemned to Repetition: The United States and Nicaragua.* 2nd and revised edition. Boulder, CO: Westview Press, 2002.

———. "On the Congressional Effort to Influence U.S. Relations with Latin America: Congressional Foreign Policy at Its Best." *Inter-American Economic Affairs* 29 (1975): 85–94.

———. "The United States and Central America: Interlocking Debates." In *Double-Edged Diplomacy: International Bargaining and Domestic Politics.* Edited by Peter Evans, Harold K. Jacobson, and Robert D. Putnam. Berkeley: University of California Press, 1993.

Peterson, Merrill D., ed. *The Portable Thomas Jefferson.* New York: Viking Press, 1975.

Pinstrup-Andersen, Per. "Food Prices and the Poor in Developing Countries." *European Review of Agricultural Economics* 12 (1985): 69–85.

Pinstrup-Andersen, Per, and Elizabeth Caicedo. "The Potential Impact of Changes in Income Distribution on Food Demand and Human Nutrition." *American Journal of Agricultural Economics* 60 (August 1978): 402–15.

Porter, Marilyn, and Ellen Judd, eds. *Feminists Doing Development: A Practical Critique.* London: Zed Press, 1999.

Programa de Naciones Unidas para el Desarrollo (PNUD). *Venciendo el Temor: (In)seguridad Ciudadana y Desarrollo Humano en Costa Rica—Informe Nacional de Desarrollo Humano 2005.* San José, Costa Rica: PNUD–Costa Rica, 2006.

Przeworski, Adam, Michael E. Alvarez, Jose Antonio Cheibub, and Fernando Limongi.

Democracy and Development: Political Institutions and Well-being in the World, 1950–1990. Cambridge: Cambridge University Press, 2000.

Przeworski, Adam, and Henry Teune. *The Logic of Comparative Social Inquiry.* New York: Wiley-Interscience, 1970.

Putnam, Robert D. "APSA Presidential Address: The Public Role of Political Science." *Perspectives on Politics* 1 (June 2003): 249–55.

Quisumbing, Agnes. "Intergenerational Transfers in Philippine Rice Villages: Gender Differences in Traditional Inheritance Customs." *Journal of Development Economics* 43 (1994): 167–95.

Rai, Shirin. *The Gender Politics of Development: Essays in Hope and Despair.* London: Zed Books, 2008.

Ramos, Jennifer. *Changing Norms through Actions: The Evolution of Sovereignty.* New York: Oxford University Press, 2013.

Renshon, Stanley, and Deborah Welch Larson, eds. *Good Judgment in Foreign Policy: Theory and Application.* Lanham, MD: Rowman and Littlefield, 2003.

Reuter, Peter. "The Mismeasurement of Illegal Drug Markets: The Implications of Its Irrelevance." In *Exploring the Underground Economy.* Edited by Susan Pozo. Kalamazoo, MI: Upjohn Institute, 1996.

Reutlinger, Shlomo, and Harold Alderman. "The Prevalence of Calorie-Deficient Diets in Developing Countries." *World Development* 8 (1980): 399–411.

Rivera, J. A., D. Sotres-Alvarez, J. P. Habicht, T. Shamah, and S. Villalpando. "Impact of the Mexican Program for Education, Health, and Nutrition (Progresa) on Rates of Growth and Anemia in Infants and Young Children." *JAMA* 291 (2004): 2563–70.

Rock, Stephen R. *Appeasement in International Politics.* Lexington: University Press of Kentucky, 2000.

Romero, Luis Alberto. *Breve historia contemporánea de la Argentina.* Buenos Aires: Fondo de Cultura Económica, 2001.

Roness, Paul G., and Sætren Harald, eds. *Change and Continuity in Public Sector Organizations: Essays in Honour of Per Lægreid.* Bergen, Norway: Fagbokforlaget, 2009.

Russell, Roberto. "Política exterior y veinte años de democracia: Un primer balance." In *La historia reciente: Argentina en democracia.* Edited by Marcos Novaro and Vicente Palermo. Buenos Aires: Edhasa, 2004.

———. "The Scholar-Practitioner Interaction: The Case of Argentina." Memorandum prepared for the International Workshop on Scholars and Practitioners. Center for International Studies, University of Southern California, 2011.

Russell, Roberto, and Juan G. Tokatlián. "Beyond Orthodoxy: Asserting Latin America's New Strategic Options toward the United States." *Latin American Politics and Society* 53 (2011): 127–46.

Sacha, Jeffrey O., Jared P. Sanchez, Ange-Marie Hancock, and Manuel Pastor. *A Foot in Both Worlds: Institutionalizing Progressive Community-Engaged Research Centers within Universities.* Los Angeles Program for Environmental and Regional Equity (PERE). Los Angeles: University of Southern California, December 2013.

Sachs, Carolyn. *The Invisible Farmers: Women in Agricultural Production.* Lanham, MD: Rowman and Littlefield, 1983.

Sarles, Margaret E. "Evaluating the Impact and Effectiveness of USAID's Democracy and Governance Programs." In *Evaluating Democracy Support: Methods and Experiences.* Edited by Peter Brunell. Stockholm: International Institute for Democracy and Electoral Assistance and Swedish International Development Cooperation Agency, 2007.

Schultz, T. Paul. *The Impact of Progresa on School Enrollments: Final Report.* Washington, DC: IFPRI, 2000.

———. "Interview Related to IFPRI Evaluation of the PROGRESA/*Oportunidades* program." Interview by Jere Behrman in appendixes of Jere R. Behrman, *Policy-Oriented Research Impact Assessment (Poria) Case Study on the International Food Policy Research Institute (IFPRI) and the Mexican Progresa Anti-Poverty and Human Resource Investment Conditional Cash Transfer Program.* Impact Assessment Discussion Paper No. 27. Washington, DC: IFPRI, 2007.

———. "Testing the Neoclassical Model of Family Labor Supply and Fertility." *Journal of Human Resources* 25 (1990): 599–633.

Scobie, Grant. *Food Subsidies in Egypt: Their Impact on Foreign Exchange and Trade.* Research Report 40. Washington, DC: IFPRI, 1983.

Scott, John. *Distribución de la ayuda alimentaria en México: La revolución de los noventa.* Documento de Trabajo 240. División de Economía, CIDE. Mexico City: CIDE, 2002.

———. *Eficiencia redistributiva de los programas contra la pobreza en México.* Documento de Trabajo 330. División de Economía, CIDE (Trabajo de Investigación comisionado por SEDESOL). Mexico City: CIDE, 2004.

———. *La Otra Cara de la Reforma Fiscal: La Equidad del Gasto Público.* Brochure. Programa de Presupuesto y Gasto Público, CIDE-FORD. Mexico City: CIDE-FORD, 2001.

———. *Who Benefits from Social Spending in Mexico?* Documento de Trabajo 208. Programa de Presupuesto y Gasto Público, CIDE-FORD. Mexico City: CIDE-FORD, 2010.

Seligson, Mitchell A. "Democracy Promotion: How the Bureaucracy Can Find out If It Works." Memorandum prepared for the International Workshop on Scholars and Practitioners. Center for International Studies, University of Southern California, 2011.

———. "Democratization in Latin America: The Current Cycle." In *Authoritarians and Democrats: The Politics of Regime Transition in Latin America.* Edited by James M. Malloy and Mitchell A. Seligson. Pittsburgh: University of Pittsburgh Press, 1987.

Sen, Amartya. "Gender and Cooperative Conflicts." In *Persistent Inequalities: Women and World Development.* Edited by Irene Tinker. New York: Oxford University Press, 1990.

Shannon, Thomas. "Theory vs. Policy: Scholars and Practitioners in United States–Latin American Relations." Remarks prepared for Roundtable at the Annual Meeting of the International Studies Association. New Orleans, 2010.

Sherman, Laurence W., Denise C. Gottfrenson, Doris L. MacKenzie, John Eck, Peter Reuter, and Shawn D. Bushway. *Preventing Crime: What Works, What Doesn't, What's Promising.* Washington, DC: US Department of Justice, 1998.

Shifter, Michael. "Scholars, Practitioners and Inter-American Relations: The Inter-American Dialogue." Memorandum prepared for the International Workshop on Scholars and Practitioners. Center for International Studies, University of Southern California, 2011.

Sick, Gary. *All Fall Down: America's Tragic Encounter with Iran.* New York: Random House, 1986.

Sikkink, Kathryn. "Do Human Rights Prosecutions Make a Difference? Scholar-Practitioner

Relations on Transnational Justice in Latin America." Memorandum prepared for the International Workshop on Scholars and Practitioners. Center for International Studies, University of Southern California, 2011.

————. *The Justice Cascade: How Human Rights Prosecutions Are Changing World Politics.* New York: W. W. Norton, 2011.

Sil, Rudra, and Peter J. Katzenstein. "Analytic Eclecticism in the Study of World Politics: Reconfiguring Problems and Mechanisms across Research Traditions." *Perspectives on Politics* 8 (2010): 411–31.

Slaughter, Anne Marie. *A New World Order.* Princeton, NJ: Princeton University Press, 2005.

Smith, Peter H., ed. *Drug Policy in the Americas.* Boulder, CO: Westview Press, 1992.

Solomon, Richard. *Chinese Negotiating Behavior: Pursuing Interests through "Old Friends."* New York: United States Institute of Peace, 1999.

Soto, Cecilia. "Mexico y Brazil: ¿podemos cooperar?" In *En la Frontera del Imperio.* Edited by Rafael Fernández de Castro. Mexico City: Editorial Planeta, 2003.

Sparr, Pamela. *Mortgaging Women's Lives: Feminist Critiques of Structural Adjustment.* London: Zed Press, 1994.

Staniland, Martin. *Falling Friends: The United States and Regime Change Abroad.* Boulder, CO: Westview Press, 1991.

Staudt, Kathleen. "Gender Politics in Bureaucracy: Theoretical Issues in Comparative Perspective." In *Women, International Development, and Politics: The Bureaucratic Mire.* 2nd edition Edited by Kathleen Staudt. Philadelphia: Temple University Press, 1997.

————. *Policy, Politics, and Gender: Women Gaining Ground.* West Hartford, CT: Kumarian Press, 1998.

————. *Women, Foreign Assistance, and Advocacy Administration.* New York: Praeger, 1985.

Stedman, Stephen J., Thomas Ohlson, and Robert Davies. *New Is Not Yet Born: Conflict Resolution in Southern Africa.* Washington, DC: Brookings Institution Press, 1994.

Stedman, Stephen J., Donald Rothschild, and Elizabeth Cousens. *Ending Civil Wars: The Implementation of Peace Agreements.* Boulder, CO: Lynne Rienner, 2002.

Stone, Diana, and Andrew Denham, eds. *Think Tank Traditions: Policy Analysis across Nations.* Manchester, UK: Manchester University Press, 2004.

Streeten, Paul. *Hunger.* Discussion Paper 4. Boston: Boston University, Institute for Economic Development, 1989.

————. *Poverty: Concepts and Measurement.* Discussion Paper 6. Boston: Boston University, Institute for Economic Development, 1989.

Suro, Roberto. "Scholars, Practitioners and Inter-American Relations: Immigration." Memorandum prepared for the International Workshop on Scholars and Practitioners. Center for International Studies, University of Southern California, 2011.

Tama, Jordan. *Commissions and National Security Reform: How Commissions Can Drive Change during Crises.* New York: Cambridge University Press, 2011.

Tenorio, Mauricio. "Stereophonic Scientific Modernism: Social Science between Mexico and the United States." *Journal of American History* 85 (1999): 1156–87.

Thacher, David. "Order Maintenance Reconsidered: Moving beyond Strong Causal Reasoning." *Journal of Criminal Law and Criminology* 94 (2004): 381–414.

Thoumi, Francisco E. "The Numbers Game: Lets All Guess the Size of the Illegal Drug Industry!" *Journal of Drug Issues* 35, no. 1 (2005).

Tickner, Ann J., and Andrei Tsygankov, eds. "Risks and Opportunities of Crossing the Academy/Policy Divide." *International Studies Review* 10 (2008), 155–77.

Tickner, Arlene. "Scholar-Practitioner Interaction: Comparative Latin American Experiences." Memorandum prepared for the International Workshop on Scholars and Practitioners. Center for International Studies, University of Southern California, 2011.

Tiessen, Rebecca. *Everywhere/Nowhere: Gender Mainstreaming in Development Agencies.* Bloomfield, CT: Kumarian Press, 2011.

Timmer, C. Peter, and Harold Alderman. "Estimating Consumption Parameters for Food Policy Analysis." *American Journal of Agricultural Economics* 61 (December 1979): 982–94.

Tinker, Irene. "Challenging Wisdom, Changing Policies: The Women in Development Movement." In *Developing Power: How Women Transformed International Development.* Edited by Arvonne S. Fraser and Irene Tinker. New York: Feminist Press, 2004.

———. *Street Foods: Urban Food and Employment in Developing Countries.* New York: Oxford University Press, 1997.

Tinker, Irene, and Gale Summerfield, eds. *Women's Rights to House and Land: China, Laos, Vietnam.* Boulder, CO: Lynne Rienner, 1999.

Tocqueville, Alexis de. *Souvenirs.* Paris: Calmann Levy, 1893.

Tokatlián, Juan G. "Política Exterior Argentina de Menem a De la Rúa: La Diplomacia del Ajuste." *Escenarios Alternativos* 4, no. 9 (Winter 2000).

Torre, Juan Carlos. "Critical Junctures and Economic Change." In *Argentina: The Challenges of Modernization.* Edited by Joseph Tulchin and Allison Garland. Wilmington, DE: SR Books.

Troy, Tevi. "Devaluing the Think Tank." *National Affairs,* 10 (Winter 2012): 75–90.

Tulchin, Joseph S. *Argentina and the United States: A Conflicted Relationship.* Boston: Twayne, 1990.

United States Agency for International Development. *USAID Evaluation Policy.* Washington, DC: Bureau for Policy, Planning and Learning, 2011.

United States Senate Committee on Governmental Affairs and United States House of Representatives Committee on Government Reform. *United States Government Policy and Supporting Positions (Plum Book), 2008.* www.gpoaccess.gov/plumbook/2008/2008_plum_book.pdf. Accessed January 12, 2012.

Valdés, Juan Gabriel, *Pinochet's Economists: The Chicago School in Chile.* Cambridge: Cambridge University Press, 1995.

Valenti, Giovanna. "Tendencias de la institucionalización y la profesionalización de las ciencias sociales en México." In *Desarrollo y organización de las ciencias sociales en México.* Edited by Francisco Javier Paoli. Mexico City: Porrúa, 1990.

van Dijk, Jan, Robert Manchin, John van Kesteren, Sami Nevala, and Gergely Hideg. *The Burden of Crime in the EU—Research Report: A Comparative Analysis of the European Survey of Crime and Safety (EU ICS) 2005.* Brussels: UNICRI, Gallup, Europe-Max, Planck Institute, CEPS, Geox, 2005.

Villalobos, Joaquín. "De los zetas al cartel de la Havana." Memorandum prepared for the International Workshop on Scholars and Practitioners. Center for International Studies, University of Southern California, 2011.

Vogel, Ezra F. "Some Reflections on Policy and Academics." *Asia Policy* 1 (2006): 31–34.

von Braun, Joachim, and Hartwig de Haen. *The Effects of Food Price and Subsidy Policies on Egyptian Agriculture.* Washington, DC: IFPRI, 1983.

Walt, Stephen M. "The Relationship between Theory and Policy in International Relations." *Annual Review of Political Science* 8 (June 2005): 23–48.

———. "Rigor or Rigor Mortis? Rational Choice and Security Studies." *International Security* 23 (1999): 5–48.

Waylen, Georgina. *Engendering Transitions: Women's Mobilization, Institutions, and Gender Outcomes.* Oxford: Oxford University Press, 2007.

Weil, David. *The Fissured Workplace: Why Work Became So Bad for So Many and What Can Be Done to Improve It.* Cambridge, MA: Harvard University Press, 2013.

Weiss, Thomas, David Cortright, George Lopez, and Larry Minear. *Political Gain or Civilian Pain? Humanitarian Impacts of Economic Sanctions.* Lanham, MD: Rowman and Littlefield, 1997.

Weiss, Thomas G., and Anoulak Kittikhoun, eds. "Theory vs. Practice: A Symposium," *International Studies Review* 13 (2011): 1–23.

Whitehead, Laurence. *Latin America: A New Interpretation.* New York: Palgrave Macmillan, 2010.

———. "Twenty-First Century Democratizations: Experience versus Scholarship." In *Democratization: The State of the Art.* Edited. by Dirk Berg-Schlosser. Leverkusen, Germany: Barbara Budrich, 2004.

Williamson, John, and Pedro Pablo Kuczynski, eds. *After the Washington Consensus: Restoring Growth and Reform in Latin America.* Washington, DC: Peterson Institute for International Economics, 2003.

Wilson, Ernest J., III. "How Social Science Can Help Policymakers: The Relevance of Theory." In *Being Useful: Policy Relevance and International Relations Theory.* Edited by Miroslav Nincic and Joseph Lepgold. Ann Arbor: University of Michigan Press, 2000.

———. "Is There Really a Scholar-Practitioner Gap? An Institutional Analysis." *PS: Political Science and Politics* 40 (January 2007): 147–51.

Winslow, Anne, ed. *Women, Politics, and the United Nations.* New York: Praeger, 1995.

Yarmolinsky, Adam. "How Good Was the Answer? How Good Was the Question?" In *Controversies and Decisions: The Social Sciences and Public Policy.* Edited by Charles Frankel. New York: Russell Sage Foundation, 1976.

Zartman, William. *Negotiation and Conflict Management: Essays on Theory and Practice.* Oxford: Routledge, 2008.

Zelikow, Philip. "Foreign Policy Engineering: From Theory to Practice and Back Again." *International Security* 18 (Spring 1994): 143–71.

PETER ANDREAS, Professor of Political Science and Associate Director of the Watson Institute for International Studies, Brown University

MARIANO E. BERTUCCI, Post-Doctoral Fellow at the Center for Inter-American Policy and Research, Tulane University

THOMAS J. BIERSTEKER, Gasteyger Chair in International Security and Director of the Programme for the Study of International Governance, the Graduate Institute of International and Development Studies, Geneva; former Director of the Watson Institute for International Studies, Brown University

KEVIN CASAS-ZAMORA, Secretary for Political Affairs, Organization of American States; nonresident Senior Fellow, Brookings Institution; former Vice President and Minister of National Planning and Economic Policy of Costa Rica

PAUL EVANS, Professor of Asian and trans-Pacific international relations, University of British Columbia; former Co-CEO of the Asia Pacific Foundation of Canada

RAFAEL FERNÁNDEZ DE CASTRO, Chair, Department of International Studies, Instituto Tecnológico Autónomo de México (ITAM); foreign policy advisor to the president of Mexico (2008–11); founding editor of *Foreign Affairs Latinoamérica*

BLANCA HEREDIA, Professor, Centro de Investigación y Docencia Económicas (CIDE), and Director General Sociometrix; Comisionada para el Desarrollo Político, Secretaría de Goberanción (2009–10); Head of the OECD Latin America Centre (2007–8); Provost, CIDE (1996–2004)

JANE S. JAQUETTE, Bertha Harton Orr Professor in the Liberal Arts and Professor of Politics Emerita, Occidental College; policy analyst in the Office of Women in Development of the United States Agency for International Development (1979–80); President, Latin American Studies Association (1995–97)

CHAPPELL LAWSON, Associate Professor of Political Science, Massachusetts Institute of Technology; Executive Director of Policy and Planning and Senior Advisor to the Commissioner of US Customs and Border Protection (2009–11); Director of Inter-American Affairs, National Security Council, The White House (1998)

ABRAHAM F. LOWENTHAL, Professor Emeritus, University of Southern California; President Emeritus, Pacific Council on International Policy; nonresident Senior Fellow, Brookings Institution; Adjunct Professor, Brown University; founding Director of the Inter-American Dialogue and of the Wilson Center's Latin American Program

NORA LUSTIG, Samuel Z. Stone Professor of Latin American Economics, Tulane

University; nonresident Fellow, Center for Global Development and the Inter-American Dialogue; former Senior Advisor and Chief, Poverty and Inequality Unit, the Inter-American Development Bank; Co-director of the World Bank's World Development Report 2000 *Attacking Poverty*

ROBERT A. PASTOR (1947–2013), Professor, School of International Service, and former Vice-President for International Programs, American University; Latin American Director of the National Security Council (1977–81); Director of the Latin American Program of the Carter Center

MITCHELL A. SELIGSON, Centennial Professor of Political Science and Professor of Sociology (by courtesy),Vanderbilt University; Founder and Director of the Latin American Public Opinion Project (LAPOP)

THOMAS A. SHANNON JR., Counselor, US Department of State; former US Ambassador to Brazil and former Assistant Secretary of State for Western Hemisphere Affairs

LAURENCE WHITEHEAD, Senior Research Fellow in Politics, Nuffield College, University of Oxford; President du Conseil Scientifique, Institut des Ameriques, Paris; Editor of *Oxford Studies in Democratization*, Oxford University Press